A SUMMARY OF

CHRISTIAN

HISTORY

A SUMMARY OF
CHRISTIAN HISTORY

Robert A. Baker
Revised by John M. Landers

BROADMAN
& HOLMAN
PUBLISHERS

Nashville, Tennessee

ISBN: 0-8054-2754-6

Dewey Decimal Classification: 270
Subject Heading: CHURCH HISTORY
Library of Congress Catalog Number: 93-11779
Printed in the United States of America

Unless otherwise stated, all quotations are from the *Holy Bible, New International Version,* copyright © 1973, 1978, 1984 by International Bible Society.

Library of Congress Cataloging-in-Publication Data

Baker, Robert Andrew.
    A summary of Christian history / Robert A. Baker, John M. Landers.
—Rev. ed.
        p.   cm.
    Includes bibliographical references and index.
    ISBN 0-8054-2754-6
    (ISBN 0-8054-1064-3 hard-cover edition, out of print)
    1. Church history.   I. Landers, John M., 1941–   .   II. Title.
BR146.B2   1994
270—dc20   93-11779
                                                                            CIP

04 05 06 10 9 8 7 6 5 4

Contents

Maps

Documents

Preface

This text began as an attempt to present an overview of Christian history for beginning students. Dr. Robert A. Baker believed that beginners often lost themselves in the maze of historical facts presented in massive textbooks. The success of his book for more than three decades indicates that it has filled a need.

Baker claimed neither originality nor comprehensiveness for his text. He painted the broad picture. With this before them, students were challenged to fill in details by reading from the more comprehensive histories and source documents listed in the bibliographies. In this edition, the General Bibliography contains only books that cover the whole sweep of Christian history. The bibliographies at the end of each of the six sections are devoted to more specialized studies.

Since 1959 many changes have come about in the Christian world. Baker's original book has needed revision for several years, but many teachers still use it. Unfortunately Dr. Baker was unable to revise the text himself because of declining health. Before his death, however, he authorized the present revision. Every effort has been made to maintain the vision of the original publication. Only the bibliographies and the final chapters have been radically revised.

Those who studied with Dr. Baker remember how he brought the past to life by reading aloud from original sources. This Revised Edition has included historical documents in each chapter. Some were chosen because Baker used them. Others were selected to add a feminine perspective. I thank particularly my wife Sharon and daughter Ginny for their help in selecting the documents and preparing this revision for publication.

I. Period of Christian Beginnings (4 B.C. to A.D. 100)

Introduction to the Period

Jesus was born between 6 and 4 B.C. (Dates have been calculated according to Christ's birth since the sixth century. Unfortunately, those who set up the system made a mistake of several years in their calculations). The Roman Empire ruled the Mediterranean world at the time of Jesus' birth. Roman armies had overrun Palestine about sixty years before. Most of that time Herod the Great (37-4 B.C.) ruled Palestine. After Herod's death, Rome divided Palestine among his three sons: Philip ruled the northern area east of Jordan; Herod Antipas ruled Galilee and Perea; and Archelaus received the larger central section of Palestine (Judea, Idumea, and Samaria). Philip and Herod Antipas were in office during Jesus' ministry and are mentioned in the New Testament, but the Roman emperor removed Archelaus in A.D. 6. After his death, Rome appointed governors or procurators who ruled this part of Palestine. Pontius Pilate (A.D. 26-36) was the procurator during Jesus' ministry.

Christianity spread rapidly and maintained pure doctrine during the first century, and it was relatively unaffected by the destruction of Palestine in about A.D. 70

Points of Special Interest

Notice that God prepared for revelation in Christ, not only in Judaism but also among other peoples. Students should also notice the New Testament pattern of a functioning church, its local character, its officers, its organization, and its autonomy. Later developments turned away from this original simplicity.

1

The Beginnings of
Historical Christianity

Any thoughtful person will probably be curious about the description of the apostle Paul in Acts 21:37-40. Paul had stirred up his customary riot this time in the Temple at Jerusalem. Roman soldiers on patrol had saved him from severe injury at the hands of the Jewish mob. As Paul endeavored to speak to the people from the stairs of the prison castle, four aspects of his life appeared in quick succession.

- Paul spoke the Greek language and was a citizen of a city noted for Greek culture.

- Paul was a Roman citizen (Acts 21:39; 22:25-29).

- Paul was a Jew and spoke Hebrew fluently.

- Paul was a Christian, bearing testimony of the Master to his people.

Understanding Paul requires understanding the ethnic, linguistic, and religious diversity of his background. Customs, parties, traditions, and allusions constantly appear in the New Testament, but are meaningless unless explained in historical terms.

Greek Influence on Christianity

Greek elements in the world in which Christianity came may be traced to the conquests of Alexander the Great (356-323 B.C.). This Macedonian soldier scattered Greek culture in Palestine and most of the known world. After Alexander's death, his generals and their successors ruled Palestine for over 150 years. Greek philosophy, Greek language, and Greek spirit contributed to the Christian movement.

1. *Greek philosophy* was scattered everywhere and helped prepare for the coming of Christ. Atheistic and skeptical philosophy turned many from superstition and intensified their hunger for the true God. Other varieties of Greek philosophy helped prepare for the coming of Christ by glorifying the human spirit and valuing spiritual and moral truth.

2. The *Greek language* became the common tongue throughout the Mediterranean world. This common language brought a sense of unity to the various nations in the Roman Empire. Palestinian Jews learned to speak Greek in order to carry on trade in the markets. When some of them became Christian missionaries, they preached widely without needing to learn another language. Christians found Greek fully adequate as the language of the New Testament.

3. The *Greek spirit* also contributed to the Christian movement. This spirit included daring initiative, sweeping vision, and intense love for truth.

Roman Influence on Christianity

Greek rule in Palestine ended when Jewish patriots under Judas Maccabeus established independence (about 167 B.C.). A century later, Roman soldiers took possession of Palestine (63 B.C.). The New Testament reveals evidence of Roman rule—Roman guards, Roman jailers, Roman castles, Roman governors, Roman centurions. The Pharisees asked Jesus if a Jew should serve under Roman rule. Publicans, like Matthew, were unpopular because they collected taxes for Rome.

Roman rule helped and hindered Christianity. The strong centralized government provided a measure of peace and protection. Rome did not allow violence within her empire lest an uproar should serve as a cloak for political revolt. It was possible for Christian missionaries to move among the many people of the Mediterranean world with little political friction. Local officials protected Roman citizens like Paul from unjust treatment. A network of Roman highways and seaways made travel safer and more convenient. Two hundred years later the language of the Romans would be adopted as the principal medium for religious expression.

Yet the Roman government became the greatest enemy of Christianity before the end of the first century. The imperial government hardly valued the individual, preferring religious devotion in the service of the state. Roman armies accepted the gods of every nation they conquered, requiring only that the subjugated nation accept Roman gods, including the Roman emperor. The government persecuted Christians who refused to worship the Roman emperor.

Jewish Influence on Christianity

The history of the Hebrews as related in the Old Testament is well known. God chose a family of faith, which under divine care, developed into a nation. Several factors combined to bring political division about 975 B.C. The Northern kingdom was carried into Assyrian captivity about 722 B.C. The Southern Kingdom stood until about 587 B.C., when it fell to the Babylonians. After about seventy years, the Persian Empire permitted a remnant of the Southern Kingdom to return to Palestine. These Jews remained subject to the Persians until about 334 B.C., when Alexander the Great conquered them. The Greek period (334-167 B.C.), the century of Jewish independence (167-63 B.C.), and the beginning of Roman rule (63 B.C.) make up the history of the Jewish people to the New Testament era.

During this long history the Jewish people were, to some extent unconsciously, making preparation for the coming of Christ. They carefully preserved the revelation that God had given them. Through adversity and captivity two great truths were burned into their souls: (1) there is only one God, and (2) the relationship of God to humans is personal, not national. Before the Babylonian Exile the Jews had often fallen in idolatry and polytheism, but after their return to Palestine they became zealous monotheists. Before the Exile the Jews had sometimes conceived of God in national terms, but in captivity their isolation from every material reminder of a national deity brought them to understand that the individual must commune with God. This lesson was worth the suffering of Babylonian captivity.

Although some, like Jonah, were reluctant witnesses, the ancient world became familiar with Jewish beliefs and practices. A movement known as the Dispersion began early in the Greek period. Many Jews from Palestine relocated voluntarily to almost every part of the Mediterranean world. Wherever they went the Jews made numerous proselytes to their religion, establishing synagogues for teaching God's revelation, witnessing to the sovereignty of one God, and looking to the heavens for the Messiah. This Dispersion prepared the world for Christ's coming.

During the Babylonian captivity, when no temple was available in exile, the *synagogue* developed as a place of teaching and worship.

After the Jews returned from exile *Scribes* appeared in the synagogues. At first their chief duty was copying Scriptures. Soon they became experts in what the Scriptures said, and their duties included scriptural interpretation and instruction.

The *Essenes* arose about 150 B.C., perhaps influenced by Persian religious ideas. In the days of Jesus they numbered about four thousand. They were characterized by rigorous orthodoxy, celibacy, communal ownership, and the elimination of animal sacrifices in worship.

The *Pharisees* took distinct form during the Maccabean struggle (beginning about 167 B.C.), but they reflected a separatist attitude that may date back to the Samaritans in the days of Ezra and Nehemiah (about 500 B.C.). The New Testament pictures the Pharisees as narrow, bigoted, and to some extent hypocritical. They were numerous and respected in the days of Jesus, rallying to traditional supernaturalism and ceremonial exactness.

The *Sadducees* probably arose during the second century before Christ. They were friendly to Roman and Greek culture, and represented religious and political liberalism. Their rationalism led them to deny the resurrection and divine providence, to refuse all tradition, and to emphasize the freedom of the human will.

The *Samaritans* arose through the intermarriage of Jews left in Palestine after the beginning of the Babylonian captivity with Gentiles who had been brought into the land.

The *Herodians* were Jewish political patriots who supported Herod's family against Rome.

The *Zealots* were Jewish nationalists, probably heirs of the Maccabean tradition of fervent zeal to throw off the yoke of foreigners.

The Life of Jesus (4 B.C.-A.D.30)

This was the world in which Jesus was born. Almost all that is known of His earthly life may be found in the Synoptic Gospels (Matthew, Mark, and Luke) and in John. John's Gospel describes Jesus' eternal nature and preincarnate existence; Matthew and Luke record His genealogy. Matthew probably gives the genealogy of Joseph while Luke deals with the genealogy of Mary. Matthew and Luke recount the birth and childhood of Jesus and John the Baptist, His forerunner.

All of the Gospels speak of John's ministry and look at the life of Christ from different points of view.

The birth of Jesus Christ occurred about 4 B.C. He began His public ministry about A.D. 27 and was crucified about A.D. 30. The Lord's ministry may be divided into seven sections.

1. *Early Judean Ministry.* Jesus' early Judean ministry, described principally in John's Gospel, includes the calling of the first disciples and the first cleansing of the Temple.

2. *Great Gallilean Ministry.* The great Gallilean ministry covers the principal period of Christ's work and lasted about a year and a half. During this time the Lord was rejected at Nazareth, moved to Capernaum, chose the twelve apostles, set forth the Sermon on the Mount, and toured Galilee three times.

3. *Withdrawals.* Jesus' several withdrawals from the press of the crowds gave opportunity for special instruction to the disciples, for securing the great confession at Caesarea Philippi, and for the transfiguration experience.

4. *Later Judean Ministry.* Luke and John related that Jesus spent about three months in Judea later in His ministry. During these days Jesus and His disciples attended the Feasts of Tabernacles and of Dedication in Jerusalem.

5. *Perean Ministry.* All four Gospels tell of Jesus' brief Perean ministry. During this brief time, Jesus worked His last miracles, taught through parables, and foretold His resurrection.

6. *Last Week.* John's Gospel treats in great detail Jesus' last week in Jerusalem. The final week began with the triumphal entry and closed with the crucifixion.

7. *Postresurrection Ministry.* The postresurrection ministry of Jesus for about forty days before His ascension marks the close of the Gospel accounts.

Both the method and content of Jesus' teachings were remarkable. He used parables, questions, discourses, and debates to teach the people. God's person and purpose were revealed in Christ's life and teachings. Love was the dominant theme of Christ's life. Because God loves humankind, Christ died on the cross for their sins. By personal trust in Christ, each individual can receive a birth from above and assurance of eternal life. The conquering power of the cross and the ultimate triumph of the kingdom of God were central to Christ's teachings. He established His church, a local autonomous body where two or three gathering together in prayer could find His presence and power.

After the death and ascension of Christ, the disciples whom He had chosen and instructed set out on the seemingly impossible task contained in the Great Commission. Despite efforts of many other religions to attract persons, Christianity began growing like a mustard seed. From a human standpoint, there are several possible reasons for this tremendous development.

- Paganism could not answer the call of hungry hearts.

- The great welter of religions of every description clamoring for devotees could not compete with God's revelation in Christ.

- Christians became missionaries; the sacred fire leaped from friend to friend.

- Christians had a burning conviction that Christ alone could save the lost world about them. They believed that there was no time to be lost since the return of Christ was imminent.

The First-Century Church

The seventy years of Christian growth from Christ's death to the death of the last apostle may be divided into three periods.

Period of Local Witnessing (A.D. 30-45)

The first twelve chapters of Acts describe the history of the Christian movement during the first fifteen years after Christ's death and resurrection. The Holy Spirit was given in accordance with the promise of Christ, providing power for witnessing in a hostile world, bringing the presence of Christ to the people for fellowship and strength, and giving leadership from Christ in the initiation of important movements. At Pentecost persons from every part of the world were saved, and they went back to their own cities to establish Christian churches. Persecution, want, and internal bickering were only temporary hurdles (see Acts 3-6).

The martyrdom of Stephen marked a turning point in two respects: (1) it began the persecution that drove Christians from Jerusalem into all Judea and Samaria in their witness, and (2) it moved Saul the persecutor toward personal conversion to Christ. The local witness grew because of the preaching of Peter to a Gentile (for which he was required to give explanation to the church at Jerusalem), the founding of the Gentile church at Antioch, and the martyrdom of James, son of Zebedee. The conversion of Saul, his preparation for service, and his ministry at Antioch provide the background for the second stage of Christian development.

Period of Missionary Expansion (A.D. 45-68)

Under the leadership of the Holy Spirit a new direction of witnessing was begun with the inauguration of the missionary journeys of Paul and Barnabas. Paul made at least three great missionary journeys between the years 45 and 58, when he was seized in the Temple at Jerusalem. During these thirteen years he wrote two letters to the church at Thessalonica, at least two to the Corinthians, one to the Galatians, and one to the Romans. After his imprisonment in Rome about A.D. 61 he wrote the letters known as Philemon, Colossians, Ephesians, and Philippians. He probably was released for four or five years, but the extent of his travel during this time is not known. He wrote two letters known as 1 Timothy and Titus in this interim. Tradition suggests that he may have gone as far west as Spain or even Britain on one journey. He was imprisoned again about A.D. 67 at Rome. Just before his death at the hands of Nero he wrote 2 Timothy.

Tradition may be correct in speaking of extensive missionary activity by other apostles, but such accounts are too meager to be of much value. Paul's missionary activity accounts for the rise of practically all of the important Christian centers of the first century. Churches were established through his efforts in some of the strongest cities of the empire.

Between the first and second missionary journeys, Paul and Silas attended a conference at Jerusalem (about A.D. 50). James presided at the meeting and the question of whether persons must become Jews first in order to become Christians was discussed. After some people, including the apostle Peter, had spoken, James announced his decision that any Gentile could find salvation by simple faith in Christ without going through Judaism.

During this period, which closes with the death of the apostle Paul at Rome in A.D. 68, nine other New Testament books were written— James, Mark, Matthew, Luke, Acts, 1 Peter, Jude, 2 Peter, and Hebrews, perhaps in that order.

Period of Westward Growth (A.D. 68-100)

After Peter's death the center of Christian strength moved toward the western section of the Mediterranean area. Although the material for this period is scarce, it is easy to find reasons to substantiate the tradition of the westward move. The Jewish War broke out in Palestine about A.D. 66; a Roman army under Titus completely destroyed Jerusalem in A.D. 70. This catastrophe marked the end of Herod's Temple and the sacrifices of the Jews; at the same time it uprooted the Christian church in Jerusalem and scattered the people abroad. In what direction should Christianity move? Tradition reports that the apostle John went to Ephesus about the time Jerusalem was destroyed. This is plausible, since the most logical move would be toward the church centers in the West established by the apostle Paul. Scattered references in later literature hint that Christians may have gone to every part of the western Mediterranean. The tradition of Christianity in Britain is very early; perhaps one of the soldiers chained to the apostle Paul was won by him to Christ and then transferred to the British garrison, there to witness and organize a Christian church. Possibly a similar situation sent the good news to central Europe, North Africa, and elsewhere to the fringes of the Roman Empire.

Conservative scholars assign five books by the apostle John to this period. Written by a "son of thunder," these books contain warnings against diluting Christianity and minimizing either the humanity or the deity of Christ. The advocates of such heretical views cannot be identified, but their presence is significant in view of the rise of these same doctrinal aberrations in the next century. Apparently John was exiled from Ephesus to the Isle of Patmos during the course of a severe persecution under the Roman Emperor Domitian (81-96). The Book of Revelation, written in the last decade of the apostolic period, defied the Roman Empire's attempt to force Christians to worship the emperor.

❑ ❑ ❑ ❑ ❑

The literature that became the New Testament canon had not as yet been brought together in one book. The various churches used the Old Testament, together with such Christian writings as they might possess. The evidence shows that at the close of the century the Christian movement was pure in doctrine and growing in numbers. Although there were efforts on every hand to dilute the nature of

Christianity, apostolic leadership helped to maintain strong internal unity.

(Document 1)

Paul Addresses the Pastors of Ephesus

Paul called the pastors of the Ephesian church "elders" or "presbyters," but he also called them "overseers" or "bishops." Their function was to "shepherd" or "pastor." The distinction between local presbyters and territorial bishops developed after the New Testament period.

From Miletus, Paul sent to Ephesus for the elders of the church. . . . Keep watch over yourselves and all the flock of which the Holy Spirit has made you overseers. Be shepherds of the church of God, which he bought with his own blood (Acts 20:17, 28).

The functioning New Testament church showed no signs of developing into an ecclesiastical hierarchy or spiritual despotism; it was a local, autonomous body with two offices and two ordinances. The two offices were pastor (sometimes called bishop, presbyter or elder, minister, or shepherd) and deacon. These leaders usually worked to earn a living and were not supported by the church. No artificial distinction was made between clergy and laity. Pastors had no more authority in offering salvation through Christ than did other members of their body. Their distinguishing marks were the gifts of leadership given them through the Spirit and their willingness to be used of God. Each church was completely independent of external control. There is no indication anywhere in the literature of this period that the apostle Peter ever served as pastor in Rome; nor is there any basis for believing that the church at Rome was founded by any apostle. Doubtless it was organized by persons converted at Pentecost.

The two ordinances were baptism and the Lord's Supper. These were symbolical memorials. Salvation or spiritual gifts did not come through either one. The transference of spiritual regeneration and spiritual merit to these ordinances is a development that came through later corruptions. Worship was simple, consisting of hymn singing, praying, Scripture reading, and exhortations.

Bibliography

Blomberg, Craig. *The Historical Reliability of the Gospels.* Downers
Grove, Ill.: Inter Varsity Press, 1987.

Cate, Robert L. *A History of the New Testament and Its Times.* Nashville: Broadman Press, 1991.

Ferguson, Everett. *Backgrounds of Early Christianity.* Grand Rapids:
Eerdmans, 1987.

II. Period of Pagan Domination (A.D. 100-325)

Introduction to the Period

The period from A.D. 100 to 325 was perilous for Christianity. Two dangers confronted it: (1) hostility and violence from the pagan government and (2) corruption and division within.

From the outside the principal danger came from the Roman Empire. After the close of the apostolic era (A.D. 100), Roman emperors viewed Christianity as an illegal religion; it was death to bear the name *Christian*. On two occasions during that period, determined efforts were made to exterminate Christianity throughout the world. Relief came when Constantine espoused the Christian cause—perhaps from political motives—and fought his way to the place of sole emperor in 323. This period closed with the first world council of Christians at Nicaea in 325, when Christianity began to develop in a new direction.

Within Christianity the danger of corruption and division grew out of its close relationship with Jewish and pagan movements. Christianity was influenced internally by its environment. Sometimes the reaction from fighting heresy was as harmful as the corruption.

This period is discussed in three chapters—one describing the struggle against outward forces, one describing the struggle against internal corruptions, and one summarizing the condition of Christianity in 325.

Points of Special Interest

Several matters are of interest in the study of this period.

(1) The sort of response the Christians made when they were persecuted—no military action like that of the Jews, no general compromise of principle to the pagan state, but the development of an effective literature to enlighten the persecutors, and the display of Christian fortitude and constant testimony. (2) The gradual infiltration of error, as displayed in the writings of the second century. (3) No specific date of change can be named, but the Christian vocabulary began to take on new meanings and to grow rapidly, changing radically from the New Testament pattern. (4) The influence of the various parties in the pagan environment of Christianity produced many innovations.

2

Pagan Opposition
to Christianity

The principal opponents of Christ in the New Testament were Jews. During the next several centuries the Romans were the most formidable foes of Christ's followers. Writings of Paul do not speak unfavorably of the Roman government, but this does not mean Rome was friendly to Christianity. Rome probably did not recognized that Christianity would develop into a movement separate from Judaism. The Jewish War of 66-70 accentuated the difference between the two, for the Christians refused to join in the Jewish insurrection. Christians were never in doubt about the fact that their worship of Christ was completely incompatible with the demands of the Roman government that all faithful citizens worship the Roman emperor.

The death of Paul was occasioned more by the caprice of the Emperor Nero than any policy of persecuting Christians. Nero (54-68) had set fire to Rome. In order to shift blame from himself, he accused Christians of burning the city and brutally slaughtered them. The second pagan persecution, under Domitian (81-96), was not a universal movement against Christianity, but was directed against anyone who would not worship the emperor; this included Christians. The last book of the New Testament, written in the closing decade of the first century, names the Roman Empire with its emperor worship as the opponent of God.

After the first century, opposition to Christianity took three general forms: popular antagonism, intellectual assaults, and physical persecution.

Popular Antagonism

Despite its remarkable growth, Christianity was not a popular movement in the second century. Its character, different from anything known by the people of the Roman Empire, made it an object of suspicion and hate. During the second century many floods, earthquakes, and other natural catastrophes occurred. Immediately the populace cursed the Christians. Many believed the old gods were displeased and were punishing them because of this new religion. Either willfully or ignorantly, the pagans twisted the vocabulary of the Christians to involve atheism (no idols), cannibalism (eating the Lord's body and drinking His blood), immorality (growing out of a sensual conception of the word "love"), and magic and sorcery (in the Lord's Supper and baptism).

The large gulf between the ethical ideas of the Christians and those of the pagans constantly exposed Christianity to the ire of the people. Christians refused to attend immoral and brutal shows and contests, refused to murder their young children by abandoning them in lonely places, and refused to live by standards that glorified lust and material possessions.

The exclusiveness of Christianity caused it to become an offense economically. Christians refused to recognize any other gods. In so doing they struck at several well-established types of business in the communities where they lived. Those who manufactured pagan idols or raised animals for pagan sacrifices found Christianity was hurting their business. Like Demetrius the silversmith (Acts 19:24), they vehemently opposed the movement that touched them at such a sensitive point.

Intellectual Assaults

The intellectual assaults on Christianity represent one of its severest struggles and greatest victories. Pagan writers, skilled in logical argumentation and trained in the best scholarship of the revived classical era, leveled against Christianity every criticism that modern unbelievers have used. With ridicule and sarcasm they attacked Christian beliefs about the person of Christ and His miracles and resurrection, the truth and authority of the Christian Scriptures, grace, regeneration, heaven and hell, and life after death. The principal names in the attack were Celsus and Porphyro, Greek philosophers of the second and third centuries.

These literary attacks were disguised blessings to Christianity. They stirred up Christians to produce literary monuments to second-century Christianity. Christians had already produced some literature (edificatory writings of the second century will be discussed in the next chapter). The external attacks upon Christianity called for a group of writings known as apologies; the internal struggle for purity resulted in writings known as polemics; both the external and internal struggles helped to bring forth systematic expositions of Christian beliefs. In this chapter the apologetical writings will be discussed.

The Apologists. The group of trained writers in the second and third centuries who endeavored to justify the doctrines of Christianity against the attacks of the pagan philosophers were called "apologists." In general, the apologists defended Christianity from charges of atheism, licentiousness, and cannibalism. They linked Christianity with the prophetic Scriptures of the Old Testament to show that the movement was no innovation, but was quite ancient and respectable.

The principal apologist of the second century was Justin, a Samaritan philosopher converted to Christianity in his maturity. He retained his philosopher's garb and traveled as an evangelist who preached to the educated class. His great *Apology,* prepared about 150, was addressed to Emperor Antoninus Pius and his adopted son Marcus Aurelius. In the first section of the *Apology,* Justin argued that Christians should not be condemned without a hearing. They are not atheists, but worshipers of the true God. They are not dangerous to the political safety of the Roman Empire, but with a wonderful ethic constitute its strength. Their doctrine of the resurrection is both reasonable and glorious. In the second section Justin asserted that Christianity alone has full truth; that Jesus Christ the Son of God actually became incarnate; and that paganism consists of fables invented by demons. The final section of the *Apology* describes the religious practices of Christianity. Justin was slain as a martyr about 165.

In his imaginary *Dialogue with Trypho the Jew,* Justin defended Christianity against Jewish attacks, especially attacks upon the person and work of Christ.

Other prominent apologists of the second century were Quadratus of Athens, who addressed Emperor Hadrian; Aristides, who addressed the same emperor; Athenagoras, of Athens, who addressed Emperor Marcus Aurelius and the emperor's son Commodus; Melito, of Sardis, and Apollinaris, of Hierapolis, who addressed Marcus Aurelius.

(Document 2)
Justin Martyr: Early Christian Worship

Justin Martyr defended Christians against many of the false charges made against them. In the following passage from his Apology, *Martyr describes Christian worship services in about* A.D. 150.

We afterwards continually remind each other of these things. And the wealthy among us help the needy; and we always keep together; and for all things wherewith we are supplied, we bless the Maker of all through His Son Jesus Christ, and through the Holy Ghost. And on the day called Sunday, all who live in cities or in the country gather together in one place, and the memoirs of the apostles or the writings of the prophets are read, as long as time permits; then, when the reader has ceased, the president verbally instructs, and exhorts to the imitation of these good things. Then we all rise together and pray, and as we before said, when our prayer is ended, bread and wine and water are brought, and the president in like manner offers prayers and thanksgivings, according to his ability, and the people assent, saying Amen; and there is a distribution to each, and a participation of that over which thanks have been given, and to those who are absent a portion is sent by the deacons. And they who are well to do, and willing, give what each thinks fit; and what is collected is deposited with the president, who succors the orphans and widows, and those who, through sickness or any other cause, are in want, and those who are in bonds, and the strangers sojourning among us, and in a word takes care of all who are in need. But Sunday is the day on which we all hold our common assembly, because it is the first day on which God, having wrought a change in the darkness and matter, made the world; and Jesus Christ our Savior on the same day rose from the dead. For He was crucified on the day before that of Saturn [Saturday]; and on the day after that of Saturn, which is the day of the Sun [Sunday], having appeared to His apostles and disciples, He taught them these things, which we have submitted to you also for your consideration.

Although not generally considered apologists, Tertullian (about 160-220) prepared apologies against paganism and Judaism on behalf of Christianity, and Origen (184-254) wrote an apologetical work *Against Celsus,* probably the ablest production of early Christianity against paganism.

Other results of intellectual assaults. There were other results from the intellectual assaults against Christianity. Christianity became intellectually respectable in a world in which that was important. These assaults, together with internal controversies described in the next chapter, helped show the necessity for an authoritatively recognized canon or collection of inspired writings. For generations the churches had been testing the writings that now comprise the New Testament. Through the leadership of the Holy Spirit and in the crucible of Christian experience, they had already indicated their conviction that these writings were inspired of God. It was many decades before the external ecclesiastical machinery placed its official stamp of approval on these collected books, but it seemed that this action constituted simply a formality.

Physical Persecution

Jesus warned His disciples the world would treat them as it had treated Him. If tradition can be trusted, most of the disciples experienced martyrdom. Unnumbered thousands of Christians were slain at the hands of the imperial soldiers during the second and third centuries. The popular hatred of Christianity can be understood in the light of religious, social, and economic tensions. The intellectual assaults on Christianity are understandable, since pagan philosophers attacked any system that differed from their own. Why would the government of Rome engage in the destruction of its own citizens simply because they were Christians?

The answer is found in the Roman conception of religion. As suggested in the first chapter, Romans practiced religion mainly for political reasons. The religious department was a branch of government. Through it attempts were made to appease known and unknown gods and to foretell the future. Christian ideas of morality and personal immortality had no counterpart in the Roman view of religion. Gods were numerous, and the Roman state claimed deity in the person of the emperor. Conquered nations were required to worship Roman gods, including the emperor. At the same time Rome "legalized" any local gods in these nations so long as the local worship did not interfere with loyalty to the Roman state.

Jews were exempted from this government rule because of their spirited refusal to worship any god but Jehovah and because of respect for their great antiquity. When Christianity separated itself from Judaism and refused to worship Roman deities, it was officially entitled an "illegal religion." The laws of the Roman Empire demanded prosecution, even though the action seemed to the Christians to be persecution. When the Christians, fearing violence, met secretly for worship, they were accused of the worst crime a Roman could imagine——plotting to overthrow the government.

Before the close of the apostolic period the Roman government had moved against the Christians. Nero began persecution in 67-68; Paul was among his victims. The persecution by Domitian in the last decade of the first century did not constitute a general policy against Christianity, but it was an attempt to make them conform to the ancient laws. After the close of the apostolic period two types of physical persecution may be identified: local and universal.

Local and intermittent persecution. The period from 96 to 180 was one of outward prosperity in the Roman Empire. The five "good" emperors (Nerva, Trajan, Hadrian, Antoninus Pius, and Marcus Aurelius) were comparatively diligent in government and successful in meeting contemporary problems in and out of the empire. During the reign of Emperor Trajan (98-117), the imperial pattern for the persecution of Christianity was developed. In 112, Pliny, the Roman governor in the Asia Minor province of Bithynia-Pontus, wrote Trajan a description of how he was handling the superstition known as Christianity. By using torture he had learned that the movement was rather harmless, involving mainly the worship of Jesus Christ as God and a resolution to live nobly. Pliny's method had been to demand that Christians deny Christ and leave the sect. If they refused after three requests, they were executed because of their "obstinacy." If they agreed, they were released without further punishment. Trajan's reply commended Pliny's conduct, suggesting no effort be made to search out the Christians but that if responsible men brought charges, the death penalty should be pronounced on those who refused to deny the Christian faith. This comparatively lenient pattern was followed in the empire for over a century.

The kind of persecution that could have been leveled against Christianity may be glimpsed in the imperial persecution of the Jews. By specific law the Jews were forbidden to practice their religion, including such vital features as the observance of the Sabbath and circumcision. As a direct blow at the Jews, the site of Jerusalem was to be made a Roman city with pagan temples. Enraged beyond reason, Jews proclaimed a messiah about 132 in the person of Bar Cochba (Son of the Star). Making the destroyed city of Jerusalem their rallying point, they attempted to throw off the Roman yoke. It took the Romans three years to crush the movement. During this time about half a million Jews were slaughtered.

Universal attempt at extermination. Political conditions played a large part in the two efforts by the Roman government to destroy

Christianity. The severest persecutions ever directed against Christians grew out of attempts to restore the ancient glory of the Roman Empire. The "golden age" of the empire was under Augustus (31 B.C.—A.D. 14). Various relatives succeeded him in the office, but could not match his accomplishments, and this method of securing an emperor was discontinued with the death of Nero in 68. Vespasian, a strong military commander, seized the throne in 69; his two sons ruled after him until 96. The Roman senator, Nerva, was elected by his fellow senators. Nerva introduced a new method of imperial succession, not by blood or election, but by personal selection. Each of the five emperors following Nerva selected his own successor. Following the death of Commodus in 192, the Roman armies named his successor and continued to name the emperors for about a century.

Although not all of the reasons for the striking decline of the Roman Empire after the death of Marcus Aurelius (161-80) are clear, one very important contributing factor was the weakness of imperial leadership. Almost all of the "barracks emperors" secured the throne by violence and were the victims of violence. Internal decay and external aggressors combined to tear away the foundations of the empire.

Christianity entered this picture because it was conceived as an innovation that in some way had contributed to the general decline of the glory of Rome. Religious pagans attributed all of their ills—natural calamities, heavy taxation, invading barbarians—to the anger of the pagan gods because Christianity was allowed to continue. Some political thinkers, influenced by these attitudes, wondered if the extermination of Christianity would help restore the glory of Rome that had existed before the Christian movement began. These ideas were discussed widely in 248, when the Roman Empire celebrated the one-thousandth anniversary of the founding of Rome. The new emperor, Decius (249-51), decided to restore the empire's ancient glory and, among other things, determined to destroy Christianity and restore the worship of the spirit of the Roman state. In 250 an edict was prepared requiring every Christian to deny the faith or be subject to extreme penalties, including death. His successor Valerian (253-60) continued this persecution. Many Christians were slain, many were tortured, and many compromised. The continued decline of the empire, despite the effort to exterminate Christianity, contributed to the cessation of active persecution after the death of Valerian.

A similar persecuting effort was made under Emperor Diocletian (284-305). Hoping to stop the evident decay of the Roman state and

(Document 3)
Pliny to Trajan: The Sect of Christians

Trajan appointed his nephew Pliny the Younger governor of Bithynia, a Roman province of Asia Minor. Pliny and Trajan exchanged letters about how to deal with Christians living in Bithynia. These letters, dated 112, are perhaps the oldest extant writing about Christianity by non-Christians.

Having never been present at any trials concerning those who profess Christianity, I am unacquainted not only with the nature of their crimes, or the measure of their punishment, but how far it is proper to enter into an examination concerning them. Whether, therefore, any difference is usually made with respect to ages, or no distinction is to be observed between the young and the adult; whether repentance entitles them to a pardon; or if a man has been once a Christian, it avails nothing to desist from his error; whether the very profession of Christianity, unattended with any criminal act, or only the crimes themselves inherent in the profession are punishable; on all these points I am in great doubt. In the meanwhile, the method I have observed towards those who have been brought before me as Christians is this: I asked them whether they were Christians; if they admitted it, I repeated the question twice, and threatened them with punishment; if they persisted, I ordered them to be at once punished: for I was persuaded, whatever the nature of their opinions might be, a contumacious and inflexible obstinacy certainly deserved correction. There were others also brought before me possessed with the same infatuation, but being Roman citizens, I directed them to be sent to Rome. But this crime spreading (as is usually the case) while it was actually under prosecution, several instances of the same nature occurred. An anonymous information was laid before me, containing a charge against several persons, who on examination denied they were Christians, or had ever been so. They repeated after me an invocation to the gods, and offered religious rites with wine and incense before your statue (which for that purpose I had ordered to be brought, together with those of the gods), and even reviled the name of Christ: whereas there is no forcing, it is said, those who are really Christians into any of these compliances: I thought it proper, therefore, to discharge them. Some among those who were accused by a witness in person at first confessed themselves Christians, but immediately after denied it--the rest owned indeed that they had been of that number formerly, but now (some above three, others more, and a few above twenty years ago) renounced that error. They all worshipped your statue and the images of the gods, uttering imprecations at the same time against the name of Christ. They affirmed the whole of their guilt, or their error, was, that they met on a stated day before it was light, and addressed a form of prayer to Christ, as to a divinity, binding themselves by a solemn oath, not for the purposes of any wicked design, but never to commit any fraud, theft, or adultery, never to falsify their word, nor deny a trust when they should be called on to deliver it up; after which it was their custom to separate, and then reassemble, to eat in common a harmless meal. From this custom, however, they desisted after the publication of my edict, by which, according to your commands, I forbade the meeting of any assemblies. After receiving this account, I judged it so much the more necessary to endeavor to extort the real truth, by putting two female slaves to the torture, who were said to officiate in their religious rites: but all I could discover was evidence of an absurd and extravagant superstition. I deemed it expedient, therefore, to adjourn all further proceedings, in order to consult you. For it appears to be a matter highly deserving your consideration, and more especially as great numbers must be involved in the danger of these prosecutions, which have already extended, and are still likely to extend, to persons of all ranks and ages, and even of both sexes. In fact, this contagious superstition is not confined to the cities only, but has spread its infection among the neighboring villages and country. Nevertheless, it still seems possible to restrain its progress. The temples, at least, which were once almost deserted, begin now to be frequented; and the sacred rites, after a long inter-mission, are again revived; while there is a general demand for the victims, which till lately found very few purchasers. From all this it is easy to conjecture what numbers might be reclaimed if a general pardon were granted to those who shall repent of their error.

Trajan's Response

You have adopted the right course, my dearest Secundus, in investigating the charges against the Christians who were brought before you. It is not possible to lay down any general rule for all such cases. Do not go out of your way to look for them. If indeed they should be brought before you, and the crime is proved, they must be punished; with the restriction, however, that where the party denies he is a Christian, and shall make it evident that he is not, by invoking our gods, let him (notwithstanding any former suspicion) be pardoned upon his repentance. Anonymous information ought not to be received in any sort of prosecution. It is introducing a very dangerous precedent, and is quite foreign to the spirit of our age.

believing that a restoration of the ancient state worship would bring unity and political strength, Diocletian issued a series of edicts, beginning in 305, that ordered Christian churches destroyed, all bishops and presbyters imprisoned, and all Christians to choose between denying Christ and suffering death. Again the fires of persecution took the lives of many Christians and forced others to compromise.

Results of physical persecution. In general, the periods of persecution greatly affected the church. Abnormalities common to repressed minorities or underground movements developed. The situation caused many to center their religious devotion on relics of former martyrs and to believe in the magical efficacy of the vehicles of worship. Some became fanatical in their desire for martyrdom and ascetic sufferings. A serious problem arose after each persecution concerning what to do with those who had denied Christ or had in some other way compromised with the Roman power. Bishops acquired unusual prestige and sanctity during this experience. The bishops had become to the Roman state the symbol of the Christian movement and were singled out for special persecution. The many courageous bishops who died for their faith made the office of bishop a rallying point for Christian faithfulness.

The Decline of Imperial Opposition

Political factors finally brought an end to the long struggle of Christianity against the Roman state. Emperor Diocletian determined to set up a system of imperial succession in order to ensure capable leadership for the empire and at the same time prevent revolution from occurring whenever the emperor's throne became vacant. Consequently, he appointed Maximianus as co-emperor and, in addition, appointed two subordinate rulers with the title "caesar"—Constantine Chlorus in the West and Galerius in the East. He proposed that when an emperor died, the co-emperor would immediately become the sovereign, preventing an effort to seize the office by violence. One of the subordinate caesars would theoretically be elevated to the co-emperor's place and a new caesar would be appointed. The system appeared to be foolproof. When Diocletian retired in 305, the various armies nominated their caesars to be not only co-emperors, but sole emperor. Military considerations determined who should rule as emperor.

The rise of Constantine. The soldier who finally conquered all his rivals and became the sole ruler of the empire was Constantine, son of Caesar Constantine Chlorus in the West. Constantine's mother was already a Christian and his father had looked tolerantly on Christians, refusing to enforce the edict of Diocletian for their persecution. Copying his father's attitude, Constantine, on succeeding his father as ruler in the West, gladly united with the eastern rulers Galerius and Licinius in an edict in 311 that provided limited toleration for Christians. In the following year Constantine fought a crucial battle with Maxentius and claimed that he had seen a vision in the heavens that caused him to adopt Christianity and win the victory. In 313 Constantine and the eastern Emperor Licinius issued the Edict of Milan, granting full toleration to Christianity. In 323 Constantine defeated Licinius in battle and became the sole ruler.

Constantine and Christianity. Constantine's adoption of Christianity was more of a political than a religious decision. The Roman Empire was declining fast. Its greatest need was a strong internal unity that could engender loyalty and beat off attacks from without. Constantine proposed to achieve this unity by making Christianity the cement of the empire. This would supply a double bond for the citizenry—political loyalty supplemented and strengthened by religious unity. At the same time Constantine did not divorce himself from religious support of the pagan devotees; he retained the title of chief priest of their system and became one of their deities after his death in 337. Some question whether Constantine truly became a Christian. His considerable crimes, including murder, long after his alleged vision, seem hardly the acts of a Christian. Thinking that baptism washed away sins, he delayed receiving this rite until he was at the point of death.

Constantine showered favors upon Christianity. Almost singlehandedly he ended persecution. He destroyed pagan temples and filled official positions with Christians. Christians were exempted from military service, their churches were allowed to hold property without taxation, their day of worship was made a civil holiday, and their growth was encouraged. In 325 Constantine issued a general exhortation to his subjects to become Christians.

The effect of Constantine's adoption of Christianity on the movement has been widely debated. It led directly to the official declaration that Christianity was the state religion at the time of Emperor Theodosius (378-95). Constantine was not responsible for all of the corruptions of Christianity from the New Testament pattern, for these had developed long before his day. He did, however, introduce many new elements of corruption and greatly contributed to the rise of the Roman Catholic Church. Society will never know how Christianity would have developed if it had not been adopted by the imperial authority. Doubtless it would have escaped many of the evils that came to beset it.

□ □ □ □ □

The Christian movement developed during its most crucial period amidst an unfriendly environment. The literary attacks upon Christianity during the period were not an unmixed evil, for they made it clear to Christian leaders that an authoritative canon and a definition of beliefs were necessary. Physical persecution by the Roman Empire was local and intermittent until the middle of the third century, when

two worldwide efforts were made to exterminate Christianity. The
opening years of the fourth century witnessed the rise of Constantine,
a friendly emperor, who turned the Christian movement in a new
direction by providing secular support.

3

The Struggle for Purity

While Christianity was meeting its severest test from the outside, it was also struggling to retain its original purity of doctrine and practice. Of the two battles the second was more important; yet, while the first battle was won, the second, though not entirely lost, inflicted great and terrible wounds on Christianity.

Early Purity

The earliest Christian writings outside of the New Testament are of interest because they reveal the internal condition of Christianity and indicate the direction of thinking. Six early writings (apart from several fragments) have been preserved.

- *First Clement (A.D. 96).* A letter written by Clement, pastor at Rome, in reply to one addressed to him by the church at Corinth, is probably typical of many letters written by various influential bishops throughout the empire. The Corinthian church had deposed some presbyters appointed by the apostles. Clement urged the church to return these men to office and commented at length on the evils of jealousy and faction.

- *Epistle of Barnabas (about 135).* This letter, emphasizing the superiority of Christianity over Judaism, was probably not written by Barnabas, the fellow laborer of Paul.

- *Epistles of Ignatius (about 115).* Much controversy has arisen over the epistles of Ignatius. Scholars disagree about how many epistles Ignatius wrote, about the genuineness of many references in the epistles, and about the correct text of the letters. Some assign twelve epistles to him, some seven, and some follow a Syriac version with only three epistles. If authentic, these letters would appear to have been written about 115 after Ignatius had been condemned to death by the Emperor Trajan. These letters contain many exhortations to the churches to be faithful to the bishops, presbyters, and deacons whom God had given them. The letter to the church at Rome, in particular, constantly reiterates the desire of Ignatius to be devoured by the wild animals in the arena as a martyr for Christ.

- *Shepherd of Hermas (about 140).* This religious allegory was quite influential in the second century. Made up of five visions, twelve commands, and ten similitudes, it endeavored to promote purity and faithfulness.

- *Epistle of Polycarp (about 116).* Polycarp was pastor at Smyrna. He was quite important in that he was an intimate disciple of the apostle John and the teacher of Irenaeus, a prominent writer of the second century. His epistle consists mainly of scriptural quotations designed to inculcate purity in doctrine and steadfastness in service.

- *Didache or Teaching of the Twelve Apostles (about 140; discovered 1883)* Many have accepted the *Didache* as being a genuine writing of the first or second century. It seems to have been a manual prepared by Jewish Christians for use in a Jewish Christian community. The most controversial section is the seventh chapter, which describes baptism as true immersion, but allows pouring if there is not sufficient water to immerse.

These early Christian writings reflect a healthy and pure Christianity. The strong emphasis on obedience to the church officers in Ignatius (if these are actually the letters of Ignatius in 115 and do not contain interpolations by a later hand) shows a tendency that later became an actual corruption of the New Testament pattern. Later writings than those ascribed to Ignatius, however, show no evidence of that tendency. In the main, these writings show the use of Scriptures as authoritative, give good advice, and aim at producing a purity of life and faithfulness in service.

Later in the second and throughout the third century, Christianity faced several internal struggles, which may be outlined under four headings:

- The struggle against diluting Christianity;

- The struggle against inadequate views of Christ and the Trinity;

- The struggle against pagan corruptions;

- The struggle against lowering Christian standards.

The Struggle Against Diluting Christianity

Christianity would have been destroyed if, like the Roman religious system, it had incorporated other religions in itself. There were several efforts to alter the character of Christianity by attempting to add other religious systems in part or in whole.

Attempt to Dilute with Legalism

Jesus emphasized the impossibility of putting new wine in old wineskins. Later, the Judaizers who hounded Paul endeavored to mingle Jewish legalism with the spiritual Christian movement. How does a person become a Christian? The Judaizer answered that he or she must first become a Jew, meeting certain legal requirements, then move to the realm of what Jesus had added to Judaism. This perversion, which Paul addressed in Galatians, was the occasion of the first church council in Jerusalem in A.D. 50. Paul boldly asserted that a person need not become a Jew before becoming a Christian. He brought Titus, one of his converts, as proof. The council agreed that Paul was correct, and James, who presided over the council, prepared a decree to that effect.

Later a number of parties sprang up, using names like Ebionites, Nazarenes, and Elkesaites. They regarded Christ simply as a Jewish prophet and Christianity as an extension of Judaism. Because the Jews of Palestine had been badly scattered in the destruction of Jerusalem (A.D. 70) and in the Jewish War (A.D. 132-35), Jewish-Christian sects died in the first few centuries, but legalistic thinking, involving the merit of obedience and works, is still with us.

Attempt to Dilute with Gnosticism

Gnosticism had its source in Jewish speculation, although it was adopted by Gentile philosophers and in its developed state actually became anti-Jewish in its teachings. Gnosticism means knowledge. Followers claimed secret knowledge about God and the world that nobody else had. The roots of Gnosticism may be found in Jewish writings like those of Philo of Alexandria (20 B.C. to A.D. 40). As a system fully developed by Gentile philosophers, Gnosticism laid stress on the nature of evil, the nature of God and His relation to the world, and on the meaning of the present order of existence.

Gnostic View of Evil. Central to gnosticism was its definition of evil. The Gnostics tried to isolate evil by affirming that it resided in matter or material things. If something had mass, it was evil. Goodness was found in spirit. It followed that a chair is evil, a house is evil, our physical bodies are evil. Some far-reaching inferences, decidedly anti-Jewish in nature, followed this definition of evil. If the physical world is evil and the Jewish Old Testament taught that in the beginning God had created this physical world, then the nature of God was compromised, for how could a perfect God create an evil world? In reply the Gnostics took the position that the Jehovah of the Old Testament was not the true God, but was a lower creation of the true God.

At this point the many Gnostic systems offered various explanations of the creation. Most taught that evil broke into the completely spiritual existence before the creation of the world, growing out of envy and spiritual pride and resulting in the imprisonment of pure human souls in evil bodies. The good God, they continued, was too holy to create an evil world; but in order to provide a place for human habitation, this good God formed a divine being a little less holy than Himself. Finally after a series of descending gods or aeons, the Jehovah of the Old Testament was created. He was so much less holy at this stage that He found no difficulty in creating an evil world. In this way the Gnostics magnified the complete holiness of God and yet accounted for the creation of an evil world by the ultimate authority of the true God.

Gnostic view of Christ. Applied to Christianity, this system affirmed that Christ was the highest of the aeons—the divine being that the true God had created. Christ did not have a real body in the incarnation, they said, because He was too holy to be attached to an evil substance; rather, Christ was a spirit who appeared to be in human form. The Gnostics twisted the idea of Christian redemption to fit their idea that sin resides in all material substances. Salvation, they said, consisted of freeing the spirit from the evil body. Christ worked redemption by coming from the true world of spirit in a material, evil world in order to teach humankind this true knowledge. Of course, the Gnostics denied the fundamental Christian doctrines of an actual incarnation, an actual physical ministry, and an actual death on the cross. Gnostics thought the resurrection of the body was ridiculous, since every material body was completely sinful.

Gnostic view of ethics. This conception of the sinfulness of the body resulted in a twofold attitude toward morality. (1) Some Gnostics said that since the body was sinful anyway and would be cast away at the time of death, it was not wrong to live in a licentious way; the soul would remain pure in the midst of any physical debaucheries. (2) Others said that since the body was sinful, it should be starved, neglected, and mistreated. Licentiousness and asceticism branched from the same tree.

Anti-Gnostic writers. Evidences of the struggle by Christianity to keep this philosophical system from swallowing up the Christian message are found in the New Testament. Tradition has it that John the apostle had this group in mind when he wrote his Gospel and first epistle. His Gospel graphically describes the actual physical ministry of Jesus, particularly emphasizing the story of the cross. His epistle speaks of Christ as the One whom the disciples had "seen with our eyes, that we have looked upon, and our hands have handled" (1 John 1:1), and he identifies the Spirit of God as the one that "confesseth that Jesus Christ is come in the flesh" (4:2). The Book of Colossians combats the doctrines of the Gnostics, and the Nicolaitanes condemned in Revelation may have been Gnostics (2:6, 15).

Christian writers during the second and third centuries refuted Gnosticism. The principal anti-Gnostic writers were Irenaeus (about 130-202) and Tertullian (about 160-220). *Irenaeus* had been a disciple of Polycarp in Asia Minor, who had sat at the feet of the apostle John. Perhaps some of the fire that burned against the Gnostics in the heart of Irenaeus had been kindled secondhand by John. Irenaeus moved from Asia Minor to France, and in 177 he became bishop at Lyons. In 185, out of wide experience and painstaking scholarship, he wrote his principal work entitled *Five Books Against Heresies,* directed almost wholly against the Gnostics. His refutation of the Gnostic system was thorough and effective.

Tertullian was a hot-blooded Roman lawyer in North Africa before his conversion to Christianity about 180. He became a Montanist about 200. His writings are pungent and thought provoking. He attacked practically every opponent of Christianity—the pagans for

their idolatry, persecution, and bloodshed; the heretics for holding
inadequate views of the Trinity; the Jews for not coming to Christ; and
the Gnostic systems described above.

Gnostic influence on Christianity. The influence of Gnosticism on
Christianity was tremendous. On the surface the very fact that Christians answered the attacks of Gnostics provided a valuable source of
literature that mirrored the condition of Christianity in the second and
third centuries. Beyond this literary interest, Gnosticism forced Christianity to define itself. If, said the Gnostics in effect, Christianity is not
what *we* say it is, then what is it? Thus it became necessary for Christianity to define its essential elements; this was done in several ways.

1. Under the leadership of the Holy Spirit the various churches
    gathered the writings of the apostles and primitive Christians
    and formed the *canon* (rule) or the inspired writings. These writings had been tested in the crucible of daily living. It is true that a
    council of churches did not recognize this collection officially
    until some time later, but from the writings of the various Christian leaders it is apparent that Christians of this period recognized the books that are now included in the New Testament as
    inspired.

2. Christians began preparing short statements of faith that could
    be memorized easily. One of the earliest *creeds,* or statements
    of faith, dates back to about the second century, and reads as
    follows:

> I believe in God the Almighty Father,
> And in Christ Jesus his Son,
> Who was born of the virgin Mary,
> Crucified under Pontius Pilate and buried,
> Who arose from the dead on the third day,
> Ascended into the heavens,
> Sits at the right hand of the Father,
> From whence he shall come to judge living and dead,
> And I believe in the Holy Spirit,
> [and] the resurrection of the flesh.

It may be observed that this statement is a direct answer to the
claims of the Gnostics in that it emphasizes the actual earthly
body of Christ, His crucifixion, and the resurrection of the body

---

(Document 4)
Irenaeus: The Universal Faith

Bishop Irenaeus of Lyons in Gaul (present France) wrote an extensive refutation of Gnosticism. He constantly reminded his readers that Gnostic doctrine varied from teacher to teacher and from town to town but that the true worldwide church taught the same apostolic doctrine everywhere. In the following passage from Against Heresies, *Irenaeus described the church's "rule of faith," which resembled the creed that eventually emerged.*

The Church, though dispersed throughout the whole world, even to the ends of the earth, has received from the apostles and their disciples this faith: [She believes] in one God, the Father Almighty, Maker of heaven, and earth, and the sea, and all things that are in them; and in one Christ Jesus, the Son of God, who became incarnate for our salvation; and in the Holy Spirit, who proclaimed through the prophets the dispensations of God, and the advents, and the birth from a virgin, and the passion, and the resurrection from the dead, and the ascension into heaven in the flesh of the beloved Christ Jesus, our Lord, and His [future] manifestations from heaven in the glory of the Father "to gather all things in one," and to raise up anew all flesh of the whole human race, in order that to Christ Jesus, our Lord, and God, and Savior, and King, according to the will of the invisible Father, "every knee should bow, of things in heaven, and things in earth, and things under the earth, and that every tongue should confess" to Him, and that He should execute just judgment towards all; that He may send "spiritual wickednesses" and the angels who transgressed and became apostates, together with the ungodly, and unrighteous, and wicked, and profane among men, into everlasting fire; but may, in the exercise of His grace, confer immortality on the righteous, and holy, and those who have kept His commandments, and have persevered in His love, some from the beginning [of their Christian course], and others from [the date of] their repentance, and may surround them with everlasting glory.

---

of Christ, all of which were completely antagonistic to Gnostic doctrine.

3. Christians began formulating the entire Christian teaching as *Systematic theology* in order to answer Gnostic thinkers, and they began establishing Christian schools to teach Christian doctrine. Clement of Alexandria (born about 160) was one of the first systematizers of Christian doctrine. He was trained in a Christian school formed by Pantaenus at Alexandria and suc-

ceeded his teacher as head of the school when Pantaenus was
·forced to flee from persecution in 190. Clement's principal writings illustrate the importance of this type of literature. He prepared an elementary book of Christian instruction for children or
new converts. On a higher level he addressed an eloquent work
to the Greeks in an effort to win them to the gospel. He prepared some speculative discussions of the profound truths of
Christianity as a challenge for philosophers to accept the Christian faith.

The other important systematizer of Christian doctrine was Origen (about 185-254), who succeeded Clement as head of the
Alexandrian school. Origen gathered texts of the Scriptures in
various languages, wrote commentaries on virtually the whole
Bible, fought literary battles with paganism, set forth devotional
and practical exhortations on many aspects of Christian life, and
prepared the first systematic theology. His work abounds in
speculation, some of which is quite unsound. In particular he
went astray in teaching the eternity of matter, in advocating a
sort of human preexistence of each individual soul, in supposing that everyone (including rebellious humans and the devils
themselves) would finally be restored to divine favor, and in
holding several Gnostic ideas about humans and creation. Origen's two disciples, Gregory Thaumaturgus and Dionysius of
Alexandria, did much to popularize Origen's theology.

4. The Gnostic movement set in motion ideas and methods of
   argument that greatly influenced Christianity. The Gnostics wed
   philosophy and religion, suggesting intermediary beings
   between God and man. They claimed the authority of an
   unwritten tradition, handed down secretly from primitive times.
   Irenaeus refuted their claims by replying that true Christianity
   also had a tradition given by the Lord through the apostles and
   preserved by many churches that could trace their history back
   to apostolic days. Thus the Gnostic movement led to a *veneration of tradition* and antiquity; succession, more than conformity
   to the revealed Word of God, became the ultimate proof of
   authority and orthodoxy.

5. The Gnostic movement, along with other heresies, so emphasized the worthlessness of the material body that it paved the
   way for *asceticism* and *monasticism*. Asceticism teaches that

the soul may be purified and merit gained by punishing the body through neglect, isolation, or some positive discomfort. Monasticism, in effect, organized ascetical tendencies so that persons might cut themselves off from contact with the outside world and systematically discipline their bodies for the benefit of their souls. This movement will be discussed in a succeeding chapter.

Attempt to Dilute with Manicheanism

Christianity had spread to Persia early in the Christian era. In the middle of the third century a Mesopotamian known as Mani felt the influence of the many religious movements about him and from them he compounded a composite religion that took his name. Mani mixed elements from the older pagan religions of Persia with Judaism, along with the vocabulary of Christianity and a few of its teachings. He also adopted many Gnostic interpretations of Christianity. This religion did not greatly influence orthodox Christianity.

The Struggle Against Inadequate Views of Christ and the Trinity

The watchword of Judaism for over a millennium had been "Hear, O Israel, the Lord our God is one" (Deut. 6:4). The New Testament describes Christ as God and the Holy Spirit as God. Second-century Christians increasingly discussed how the incarnate Christ could be God without affecting the oneness of God. Five principal views that attempted to answer this question may be briefly summed up.

Alogoi

This view solved the problem by denying the eternal sonship of Christ. This group was known as the *alogoi* (that means literally "not the Word"—referring to John 1:1). As their name suggests, they denied Christ was the Word, the expression of God, insisting that there was no Trinity since God was one. Christ, they said, was a great teacher, but not God.

Adoptionism

This view asserted that Christ was born simply as a man but that God adopted Him. Although agreeing with the idea that Jesus was adopted of God in a special way, the followers of this view differed at various points from one another. A popular viewpoint asserted that

Jesus was adopted at His baptism when the dove descended from heaven and God's voice announced, "This is my Son, whom I love; with him I am well pleased" (Matt. 17:5). At this time divine power descended upon Jesus—for that reason the view is sometimes referred to as *dynamism,* meaning "empowered"—and remained with Him as a teacher and healer until the experience of the cross. His cry, "My God, my God, why have you forsaken me?" (Matt. 27:45) was interpreted as a sign that the divine power had departed from Him. After all, it was argued, God could not die on a cross, so whatever deity Jesus received at His baptism was taken from Him at the cross before His death. In this sense, Christ became the adopted Son of God only for a brief season of earthly ministry, and no doctrine of the Trinity was necessary.

Subordinationism

Another view said that Christ was divine but subordinate to the Father. This view eliminated the necessity for a doctrine of the Trinity, for while Christ was divine, He was less than God the Father and could not be one with the Father in essence.

Modalism

One group advanced the view that Christ was just another name for God. This school of thought argued that when Christ was born in the world in the incarnation, it was God the Father being born; there was no Father left in heaven. When Christ ascended again into heaven, He became God the Father. When the Holy Spirit was given in power at Pentecost, heaven was emptied again. In other words, this view said that the Son and the Holy Spirit were simply God the Father in another mode or function.

Orthodoxy

Many followed the orthodox view that Christ is of one essence with God and that the identification of the three persons in the Godhead in no sense affected the basic monotheism of the Old Testament.

These several views relative to Christ and His relation to the Trinity were gathered up in the Arian controversy to be discussed later.

The Struggle Against Pagan Corruptions

After the first century the principal converts to Christianity were Gentiles or pagans, most of whom were won to Christianity from other religious backgrounds. Many of the corrupting ideas of these contemporary religious systems were reproduced in the Christian movement. Several of these pagan tendencies will be mentioned.

Fetishism

All forms of paganism magnified the importance of religious externals, objects and acts. The early Christians were scornfully referred to as atheists because they had no material evidences of their religious zeal. Such externals began to be added to Christianity in the second and third centuries. Early Christians began to believe that the bones of saints were holy; that religious possessions and the sign of the cross evidenced piety. True religion was increasingly judged by participation in religious acts and possession of sacred relics.

Sacramentalism

Closely akin to this development was a new attitude toward the ordinances. The two symbolic ordinances of the New Testament were baptism and the Lord's Supper. These were given the name *sacrament* (from the Latin military oath of loyalty), which carried with it the idea that the physical elements were judged to possess salvation and spiritual grace. The water of baptism began to be viewed as having saving efficacy. According to Justin Martyr (about 165), baptism completes salvation. Irenaeus (about 185) boldly asserted that baptism is the new birth and brings regeneration. Irenaeus' writings contain the first hint that infants were being baptized. This would confirm the belief that water baptism without reference to repentance brings redemption. Ignatius (about 115) called the bread and wine of the Lord's Supper the "medicine of immortality." Perhaps Ignatius understood this as symbolic language, but by the time of Irenaeus the assertion was flatly made that after the bread has been consecrated it is no longer common bread. In some sense it has been given a new character that enables it to convey spiritual grace to men and women.

Sacerdotalism

The word *sacerdotalism* means "priestism." Not only the Jewish system but all of the ancient pagan cults included priests and ritual as a part of their religious worship. The introduction of pagan ideas of external magical efficacy in the rites of baptism and the Lord's Supper demanded that such "magic" be preserved by securing trained and qualified persons to administer them. People began to believe that only the bishop or those trained and authorized by him could effectively call forth the grace resident in these rites. Thus salvation became identified with the rites of baptism and the Lord's Supper, and these were effective only under the supervision of the bishop.

A Female Deity

Every pagan religion in the ancient world had its female deity. Converts from these systems emphasized the role of the virgin Mary until she became an object of adoration and worship.

Professionalism

Jesus said the kings of Gentiles exercised lordship over them, but among Christians, service and humility were to characterize the leaders. This Scripture was forgotten as bishops began to seek lordship and authority in the ecclesiastical sphere. Copying from practically every pagan religion, Christian leaders began to make a distinction between the sacred character of the inner group, who dispensed religion, and the rest of the mortals. The very names adopted in Christianity show the official attitude of superiority, for clergy means "those who have been called of God," while laity means "the people."

The Struggle Against
Lowering Christian Standards

There were three movements during the first several centuries which, although separate and distinct, overlapped and to some extent included one another. All accepted the contemporary corruption that viewed baptism as a saving ordinance, but all protested against allowing the unworthy—whether these had denied Christ in the persecution or had surrendered sacred Scripture to be destroyed—to receive or administer the benefits of a saving church and saving sacraments.

Montanism

Between 135 and 160 Montanus, apparently a recent convert from the heathen priesthood, suddenly began to upbraid the Christians in Asia Minor where he lived. He charged them with accepting Gnostic ideas, following human leadership instead of the Holy Spirit in church life and organization, and becoming criminally lax in Christian discipline. With two female helpers, Priscilla and Maximilla, he denounced the bishops in his area for their unspirituality and asserted that they were not qualified for office because they lacked the proper gifts of the Holy Spirit. Montanus emphasized two distinctive doctrines.

1. *Montanus emphasized the Holy Spirit.* At times the preaching of Montanus suggested that he was the Holy Spirit promised by Christ. He claimed an immediate inspiration for himself and his assistants so that their words were authoritative, beyond the written Scriptures.

2. *Montanus emphasized eschatology.* Montanus predicted that Christ was coming shortly to begin the millennial reign in the little Phrygian village where Montanus was preaching. Because this was true, Christians ought to be completely separate from the world and ready for Christ's kingdom. He drew up a list that distinguished mortal sins (that bring condemnation) from venial sins (that are forgivable). The clergy, in particular, must follow a stricter ethic than the ordinary Christian. At a time when Christians were being persecuted to the death, Montanus warned that if Christians fled from suffering or denied the faith, they would bring total and final condemnation on themselves. Physical suffering and similar hardships for Christ purified and strengthened the spirit. Such a rigid definition of worldliness, punctuated by the example of Montanus, had great influence in forwarding the monastic movement a little later. The outstanding convert of Montanus was Tertullian (about 200), the great writer of North Africa. Tertullian did not accept all of the doctrines of Montanus, but saw the inroads of worldliness and laxity on the Christian movement as most perilous.

Novatianism

In many respects Novatianism was the reappearance of Montanism. When Emperor Decius (249-51) attempted to root out Christianity from the world, there were two ideas about the treatment of those who had fled from persecution, surrendered sacred Scripture, or denied the faith. One party allowed these people to return to the bosom of the saving church after certain conditions had been met; the other party said that these should never be allowed to return. Since it was conceived that salvation outside of the church was impossible, this question was of more than academic importance. In 251, after considerable controversy, Cornelius, the leader of the lenient party, was chosen bishop at Rome. Novatian, leader of the strict party, withdrew from fellowship with the lenient party, saying the true church no longer existed. He was elected bishop by his followers. Churches following his leadership sprang up in various parts of the empire, particularly in North Africa and Asia Minor. Many Montanists saw in this movement the revival of their own ideas and flocked to Novatian. There are evidences that this movement persisted until almost the fifth century.

Donatism

The severe persecution by Diocletian brought the same problem to the front in the opening years of the fourth century. During the crisis Bishop Mensurius of Carthage and his deacon Caecilian made themselves quite unpopular by attempting to discourage overzealous Christians from seeking martyrdom. After the death of Mensurius in 311, Caecilian was ordained bishop of Carthage by Bishop Felix of Aptunga, who was accused by the strict party of having surrendered Christian Scriptures during the persecution. The strict party objected to this ordination on the grounds that Felix was a heretic. They asserted that a heretic's ordination did not transmit power to perform saving baptism or other episcopal acts. In 312 a council of about seventy bishops of the strict party assembled at Carthage and elected Majorinus bishop, causing a schism quite similar to that of Novatian. This controversy was named after Donatus, who was ordained bishop of the strict party after the death of Majorinus in 313. The doctrinal position of both sides was about the same, except the strict party insisted that when a bishop is personally unworthy (having denied the faith under persecution or surrendered Christian Scriptures) or has been consecrated by an unworthy bishop, any ecclesiastical acts of that bishop are invalid. In other words, he is unable to administer saving baptism. The Donatists claimed that they represented the true line of episcopal succession and were qualified to administer such saving baptism and perform other episcopal rites.

The Donatists attempted to consolidate their position by requesting an ecclesiastical hearing before disinterested bishops. In 313 the case was heard before six bishops (including the bishop of Rome), but the decision favored Caecilian. The next year the Donatists appealed the case to a council, but again the decision favored Caecilian. The Donatists appealed to the Roman emperor who had become sole ruler in the West. In 316, however, Constantine decided against them and threatened them with banishment if they did not cease this schism. Only after the Donatists had appealed to the secular power and been spurned did they finally come to the position that there ought to be no civil interference with religion. Donatism gathered strength and continued until about the fifth century.

During the period from 100 to 325, the Christian movement faced various internal forces that threatened to move it away from the New Testament pattern. Some of these internal problems were caused by the external forces of persecution and corruption. Christianity was affected in some instances by the very machinery it set up to deal with these problems. The next chapter will discuss some of the changes in character that came to Christianity because of the struggle against external and internal forces.

4

The Close of an Era

The second period of church history (A.D. 100-325) closed with the meeting of the first universal council. The universal council was held because of a doctrinal struggle over the person of Christ. That story will be told in the next chapter since it inaugurates a new direction on the part of Christianity—the beginning of the Roman Catholic Church. The close of this crucial period offers an opportunity to examine Christianity in 325 and to compare it with the kind of Christianity taught in the New Testament.

New Testament Christianity taught that salvation comes through simple faith in Jesus Christ. Nothing is required for salvation, declared Paul, but the regenerating work of the Holy Spirit that comes when one confesses Jesus as Lord and acknowledges Jesus' resurrection from the dead. Saving faith is an immediate experience with Christ, and all are capable of coming directly to Christ. No external institution, good work, human priest, or religious rite is required to qualify a person for coming to Christ and receiving the free gift of salvation. New Testament Christianity also taught that a New Testament church is a body of persons who have been born again, baptized, and gifted with the Spirit of Christ. The officers of the local body were two—pastors and deacons. The pastor had various names: bishop, shepherd, minister, presbyter, or elder. The ordinances were two: baptism and the Lord's Supper. All churches were on the same level, and each one had authority to govern its own affairs without outside interference.

By the close of this period (325) it is difficult to look at the general state of Christianity and recognize a picture like the one drawn from the New Testament. No longer were the people the church. The pastor or bishop, given a new office, was believed to constitute the church. The word *church* had come to mean the totality of bishops, not a local body or a local institution. Salvation was believed to come through the bishop as the custodian of the saving sacraments of the church. He alone was qualified, it was believed, to administer or authorize saving baptism and to serve the "medicine of immortality," the Lord's Supper. Churches and pastors were no longer equal under God and before men. Territorial divisions were marked off to show the boundaries of the authority of various strong bishops.

The nature of Christianity had been corrupted by 325. Changes had come in several overlapping areas.

- In the nature of faith

- In the nature of the New Testament Church

- In the nature of ecclesiastical authority

- In the nature of worship

Change in the Nature of Faith

By 325 faith had lost its personal character as the whole dependence of an individual directly on the person and work of Jesus Christ. Rather, while Christ was a part of the system, faith was to be directed toward the institution called the Church; and salvation did not result from the immediate regenerating power of the Holy Spirit, but was mediated by the sacraments of baptism and the Lord's Supper. Since the sacraments were under control of the Church and since salvation came only through them, it followed that a person must join the Church in order to be saved. That is what Bishop Cyprian meant in 250 when he said that no person can have God as Father who does not have the Church as mother. No wonder those who denied the faith in the time of persecution were so extremely anxious to be forgiven by the Church, for they believed that salvation outside of this institution was impossible.

During this period personal faith was eliminated entirely in some instances. In the writings of Irenaeus (about 200) there is a hint that in his generation infants were baptized in order to save them. Under these circumstances individual faith is considered unnecessary. With

---

(Document 5)
Cyprian: Christian Unity

Bishop Cyprian of Carthage strongly opposed the Novatian schism. Cyprian (about 250) taught that the church was a divinely ordained institution necessary for human salvation; faithfulness to this institution was necessary for individual salvation. In the following passage from his writing On the Unity of the Church, *Cyprian was the first to refer to the united church as the undivided robe of Christ (see John 19:23-24).*

This sacrament of unity, this bond of a concord inseparably cohering, is set forth where in the Gospel the coat of the Lord Jesus Christ is not at all divided or cut, but is received as an entire garment, and is possessed as an injured and undivided robe by those who cast lots concerning Christ's garment, who should rather put on Christ. Holy Scripture speaks, saying, "But of the coat, because it was not sewed, but woven from the top throughout, they said one to another, Let us not rend it, but cast lots whose it shall be." That coat bore with it a unity that came down from the top, that is, that came from heaven and the Father, which was not to be at all rent by the receiver and the possessor, but without separation we obtain a whole a substantial entireness. He cannot possess the garment of Christ who parts and divides the Church of Christ. On the other hand, again, when at Solomon's death his kingdom and people were divided, Abijah the prophet, meeting Jereboam the king in the field, divided his garment into twelve sections, saying, "Take thee ten pieces; for thus saith the Lord, Behold, I will rend the kingdom out of the hand of Solomon, and I will give ten sceptres unto thee; and two sceptres shall be unto him for my servant David's sake, and for Jerusalem, the city which I have chosen to place my name there." As the twelve tribes of Israel were divided, the prophet Abijah rent his garment. But because Christ's people cannot be rent, His robe, woven and united throughout, is not divided by those who possess it; undivided, united, connected, it shows the coherent concord of our people who put on Christ. By the sacrament and sign of His garment, He has declared the unity of the Church.

someone to act as proxy for the infant in order to make pretense of faith, the "saving water of baptism" was applied. There is evidence that the first instance of pouring for baptism took place about this time. Novatian, leader of the strict ecclesiastical party at Rome, became quite ill, and it was feared that his death was near. He had never been baptized. Since he was not strong enough to permit immersion in water, it was decided to pour a quantity of water upon his body. This was done and marked the beginning of a change in the form of baptism. Sprinkling soon developed, for if the water does the saving, a little water can be as effective as a great deal, and it is also more convenient.

With this view of church and sacraments, it is evident that complete dependence upon Christ, clearly the only requirement for salvation in the New Testament, was modified to require obedience to the institution and reception of the sacramentals. Thus faith alone, without church and sacraments, could not save; church and sacraments alone, as in the case of the infant, could save without faith by the individual.

Change in the Nature of the New Testament Church

Sacramentalism made a vast difference in the conception of a New Testament church. In the New Testament period the church consisted of the people in a local body. The leaders were on the same level with the people, but served because they had been given special gifts by the Spirit. The ordinances were not magical but symbolic. Suddenly however, this view was entirely changed. For one thing, the original equality among the various pastors, bishops, or presbyters serving in a church began to disappear. In the New Testament church there was no difference in office between a bishop and a presbyter, the two names simply described functions of the same office (Acts 20:17-35). Early in the second century, it was common for one of the ministers to assume leadership, sometimes because of unusual scholarship, strong personality, or maturity.

As early as 150 one of the writers speaks of a president of the ministers in a single church. There were several reasons why such an officer should develop rapidly. The earliest bishops or presbyters engaged in secular labor to make their living and performed the duties of their church office when not at work. As Christians increased in number and financial ability, the best qualified leader was asked to resign his secular labor and give full time to the religious task. It became his business to "oversee" (the word that means "bishop") the work of the Christian community. He received the title of bishop in a special sense and claimed the name as a unique dignity. The other ministers were called "presbyters," distinguishing them from the overseeing minister, the bishop. Early in the second century the churches at Antioch and Asia had developed such a leader over all other presbyters, but the churches in Rome, Philippi, and Corinth did not yet have this overseeing minister.

Another factor that brought authority and prestige to the new officer known alone as the bishop was the development of local councils for advice and discussion. Leaders of the various churches in a given geographical area began to hold councils or synods; and because of his place in the local congregation, the new bishop acted as spokesman for his church. He brought word to the congregation concerning the united action of all Christians in fighting heresy, in exercising discipline, and in other matters of common action. By the end of the second century, the office of bishop had become a third church office. In each local church, or diocese, there were three grades of ministers: one bishop to oversee all and exercise total authority, many presbyters, and many deacons.

The bishop soon began to exercise authority beyond the confines of a single congregation. When there were comparatively few Christians, one church could serve an entire city. As new congregations were organized in different sections of cities where a bishop was already serving, a significant departure from the New Testament conception occurred. The New Testament plan called for each congregation to have its own leadership and to be independent of any authority from another congregation. What actually happened was that in cities where influential bishops were already serving, their jurisdiction was extended to include new congregations. Under the authority of the bishop new presbyters were ordained to provide workers for the new congregations. In Rome, for example, by the end of the third century there were forty congregations; each congregation or parish had its own presbyter or—as he came to be known—priest. Over the entire city there was a single administrative officer who bore the title of bishop. Influential city bishops soon extended their authority in this fashion to include villages around the large cities.

Some late writings identify the bishop with a local congregation, but by the fourth century the separation of the office of bishop from presbyters and the development of a territorial authority over a large area was the normal situation. The strongest bishops (archbishop, ruling bishop, patriarch, ruling father, or pope—papa) presided at large councils attended by bishops and presbyters from adjacent territories and began trying to extend their jurisdiction even further. The extent of such development is shown by the sixth canon of the first universal council at Nicaea in 325. This canon stated that, according to custom, the bishop of Alexandria shall exercise authority over Egypt, Alexandria, and Pentapolis. The bishop of Antioch shall have similar authority in the area adjacent to his city; and the bishop of Rome shall exercise a dominant influence over the territory around his city.

The influence of the bishop developed in other directions. The church was conceived as a saving institution because it possessed the saving sacraments of baptism and the Lord's Supper. Who in the church controlled these sacraments? The bishop! The view became current that only the bishop could authorize or perform the sacraments; thus the bishop personally possessed the essential power of the church. Such a view was strengthened during the persecutions and the heretical movements. The bishop had been thrust in the position of embodying the Christian faith. The strongest Christians became bishops. During the persecutions bishops bore the brunt of the attacks; during the conflicts with heresy they had been looked to as the bulwark of orthodoxy. As a result, the bishop became the church in popular conception and was believed to hold authority to wield her sacramental powers. Bishop Cyprian of Carthage said in about 250 that where the bishop is, there is the church, and there is no church where there is no bishop.

Thus the original nature of a New Testament church was corrupted. It no longer consisted of the congregation, for the bishop was the church. It no longer was a fellowship; it had become a saving institution. Its ordinances had become saving sacraments, not symbolic reminders of Christ. Its ministry no longer was in two offices, but in three. It was no more a democracy in government, but a hierarchy.

Change in the Nature of Ecclesiastical Authority

As we have seen in the previous section, the literary remains of ancient Christianity show clearly a shift from the New Testament conception of the final authority of a local church to the idea that the final word of authority in all religious matters was the bishop. Christianity produced four general types of literature in the two centuries following the apostolic period.

Edificatory Literature

The earliest literature was primarily edificatory in nature. None of the writers of this early type of literature shows any evidence that the New Testament pattern for ecclesiastical authority had been altered. The letter of Clement of Rome to the Corinthians urges the church to restore some officers who had been disciplined, even though they had originally been appointed by the apostles. This means that the Corinthian church exercised authority even beyond apostolic appointment. Clement's letter gives advice, but claims no authority to require the Corinthian church to follow it. The morbidly ascetical writings of Ignatius (about 115) placed great emphasis on obedience to the pastor and the deacons. Because of the emphasis on these two ideas, there is considerable suspicion that interpolations by later hands endeavored to give early authority to matters developed later. At this early period, however, the bishop was simply one of the pastors of a local body. Although later than the writings of Ignatius, the Epistle of Polycarp and the *Shepherd of Hermas* reveal no episcopal development.

Apologetic Literature

The main purpose of apologetic literature was to defend Christianity against such charges as atheism, licentiousness, and cannibalism, leveled against it by the pagans. In the doctrinal discussions of this literature the ground of authority was the Scriptures, primarily the Old Testament. There was no appeal to episcopal authority.

Polemical Literature

The purpose of polemical literature was to fight heresy. Two important writers in this field were Irenaeus (about 130-202) and Cyprian (195-258). In the course of his arguments to discredit Gnosticism, Irenaeus (about 185) first refuted their doctrines from the Christian Scriptures. He then proceeded to say that the continuous existence of the various churches from the days of the apostles proved that they had not erred in interpreting apostolic teachings. Referring to Rome as an example of one such church, Irenaeus named its bishops in succession back to apostolic days (but his list poses problems in its disagreement with other lists). Irenaeus made historical succession of bishops the basis for confidence that orthodox Christianity was true Christianity, while Gnosticism was a perversion. Basically, then, the authority cited by Irenaeus was the Scriptures; but he attempted to prove the correct interpretation of the Scriptures through succession.

The other important polemical writer was Bishop Cyprian of Carthage (195-258), who did more than any other individual to forward the office of bishop as the ultimate Christian authority. Cyprian's theory grew out of practical problems in administrating his diocese. In his struggle over what to do with those who had denied Christ or surrendered Scriptures under persecution, he finally rested his argument on the fact that he, as the bishop, had authority over all churches and individuals in his diocese, because he was the successor of the apostles. He conceived of one universal (catholic) church in the world, composed of many bishops, the successors of the apostles. The unity of all the various bishops constituted the unity of the catholic (universal) church. Only those who were in fellowship with this universal episcopal unity (the catholic church) were saved. Thus if any person in any diocese refused to be obedient to his bishop, that person forfeited his or her salvation.

The interesting paradox about Cyprian is that while he firmly taught that all bishops were of equal rank (and practiced it when he fought the Roman bishops and told them to quit meddling in his diocese), he called the Roman Church the "mother and root of the catholic church." When the Roman bishop attempted to instruct Cyprian on the validity of heretical baptism and to exercise whatever authority was involved in the title Cyprian had applied to the Roman Church, Cyprian vigorously denied the right of any bishop, even the Roman bishop, to exercise jurisdiction in the diocese of another bishop.

It was Cyprian, then, who corrupted the New Testament pattern of authority. Instead of the local church, the territorial bishop became the final word of authority. The universal (catholic) church rested upon the sole sovereignty of the bishops as successors of the apostles. Local churches lost every vestige of authority.

Systematic Literature

This type of literature concerns the development of doctrine—not episcopal development.

Change in the Nature of Worship

In the New Testament the pattern of worship consisted principally of singing, Scripture reading, prayer, and preaching. Services required no altar or ritual, for the people recognized God as Spirit who could be reached through spirit. A change had occurred by 325. The idea that the sacraments were magical brought a change to the nature of worship. Instead of magnifying his prophetic or preaching ministry, the local presbyter began to function as a priest. In fact, after the fourth century, the very name *presbyter* began to drop out, and the title of this office became *priest*. This development could be expected when the sacraments became magical; administering this sort of rite required a priestly qualification. Consequently, the center of worship became the observance of the Lord's Supper, already being called *mass* (from the Latin word meaning *dismissal*, because those not qualified to partake of the Supper were asked to leave the church).

The magical nature of the sacraments also brought an emphasis on the proper form, words, and materials used in administering them. In the Roman religion, great stress was laid on pronouncing the ritual exactly as a means of making the service effective. If a word was mispronounced or omitted, the magical nature of the religious service could not be appropriated. This spirit began to prevail in Roman Christianity; the ritual must be repeated exactly according to formula in order to be efficacious. Furthermore, this corruption in the nature of the worship services contributed greatly to the development of the catechetical means of instruction in religious doctrine. Since the worship service was dedicated to a priestly ritual, it became necessary to instruct children and new converts in the proper ritual as well as in the rudiments of Christian doctrine on some other occasion than in the church services. Summaries of the ritual and doctrine were prepared, and newcomers were required to memorize these as a prerequisite to admission.

Finally, the purely spiritual nature of religious services was changed. Magnificent processions and external splendor, like pagan parades, became popular. Places identified with early Christianity became holy and were treated with unusual reverence. Early Christians sought the bones of martyrs and other material remains and attributed to them magical power. They named and observed holy days. Easter had been set apart from the time of the apostles, but new days were added. Both the baptism and the birth of Jesus had been celebrated in January during this period. In an effort to win the pagans, the celebration of Christ's birth was changed shortly after the close of the period to December 25, a Roman and Scandinavian feast day.

Reasons for Extensive Corruption of Christianity

We find it impossible to discuss in detail the various interacting factors that moved Christian development in the direction that it took. The suggestions that follow mention the most obvious of the elements that turned Christianity away from its original purity.

Rapid Growth

The growth of Christianity in the three centuries following the death of Christ was phenomenal. Figures cannot be given with any accuracy, but some think that Christians numbered from five to ten millions by the time of Constantine (323). From a human standpoint this tremendous growth may be explained by three general factors.

1. *Paganism had failed as an answer to needs.* Greek rationalism had emptied the pagan heavens. People thoroughly disbelieved the superstitious legends that had power neither to affect their daily lives nor promise good things to come. In the dizzy maelstrom of social, economic, and political foment that threatened persons in the early Christian centuries, pagan religious systems were of no help.

2. *The Christian message was positive and effective.* The content of Christ's teachings tugged at the hungry hearts of people everywhere. The pagans could see what Christianity meant by observing the lives of the Christians. Love was the theme of their living. When called on to die during periods of severe persecution, Christians responded with faith and courage. Such a spirit the pagans could account for only in terms of the power of God.

3. *Christian zeal in witnessing for Christ was overpowering.* Unlike the pagans, Christians insisted that all religions were not of equal value; either they accepted Christ as Savior or were lost. Every Christian was a missionary, every crossroad a pulpit, every person a prospect. There was a sense of urgency in the Christian witness. Conscious of Christ's injunction to be watchful and busy, Christians worked with a feeling that the Lord might return anytime. As a consequence, they pleaded with power and personal conviction.

The remarkable growth that followed was one of the factors that helped corrupt the original purity of the Christian movement. Without question the power and prestige of the bishop was enhanced when large numbers of converts made Christianity the religion of the majority of the people in many areas. These converts were not drawn entirely from the lower class of people. Education, wealth, and civil rule soon were enlisted in the Christian cause, bringing to the overseeing bishop powerful new weapons and influential friends.

This growth also enhanced the danger of sacramentalism. Large numbers of pagans flocked to the doors of the Christian church and were admitted through the use of magical sacraments. Great masses of unregenerated pagans were brought into the churches. Thoughtful Christians watched uneasily as pagans introduced ideas from the background of their early religious training. With other factors, this situation led to monasticism, as Christians fled from paganized churches to find purity and spirituality in the caves of the desert.

Finally, the influx of large numbers into the Christian churches furthered the institutional development of Christianity. Young children and uninitiated pagans required extensive instruction in ritual and doctrine. The sprinkling of water on them could not bring a new heart; it was hoped that extensive instruction would make them good Christians.

Pagan Persecution

The external opposition to Christianity, described in the second chapter, was also a contributing factor in the changes that occurred in Christianity. What should be the attitude of a church toward a member who, when brought to physical torture by secular authorities, denies Christ and surrenders precious Christian Scriptures to be destroyed? This happened many times in periods of severe persecution during the first three centuries. The two severest trials came about 250 and about 300 during the Decian and Diocletian persecutions. Many nominal Christians defaulted during these periods. In general, after each period of persecution five rather distinct groups could be named.

- *Martyrs* were those who were slain because they refused to put a pinch of incense on the altar of the Roman emperor and deny Christ.

- *Confessors* were true to Christ, but because of local influence or leniency were not put to death, although they were sometimes blinded or maimed.

- *Apostates* denied Christ and offered incense on the altar of the emperor.

- *Falsifiers*, by bribes or passive compromise, received certificates from the imperial officers stating they had offered pagan incense and had cursed Christ, although this was not actually the fact.

- *The unfaithful* surrendered true Christian Scriptures to the officers.

The early leaders were divided over how to treat the apostates, falsifiers, and unfaithful. Some, like Montanus, Novatian, and Donatus, wanted to bar them forever from the church. Others, like Caecilian and Callixtus, wanted to let them return to the church after evidence of repentance. Various plans were suggested for bringing such offenders back. One system permitted them to kneel outside the church and give evidence of grief for a full year(*weepers*). The second year they were allowed to come to the church and hear the service(*hearers*). The third year they could kneel during the service until the time for the Lord's Supper, when they had to leave (*kneelers*). The fourth year they were allowed to stand during the service(*co-standers*). Finally, in the fifth year, they were admitted as *communicants* to the Supper and restored to fellowship.

One can easily see how such a system would increase the influence of the church as a saving institution; otherwise such strenuous efforts to get back into its fellowship would hardly be worth the protracted ceremonies. The persecution fostered other elements that contributed to the corruption of Christianity, such as the deterioration that always comes from literary warfare, the centralizing of ecclesiastical authority in the bishop to meet the threats of the persecutors, and the development of the attitude that physical coercion was the best means of dealing with dissenters.

Internal Conflicts

One of the most important factors in the corruption of Christianity was the series of internal controversies described in the previous chapter. While officially condemning many of the heretical perversions, Christianity unconsciously assimilated some of the teachings. The doctrine of mortal and venial sins was lifted from Montanism, as well as ascetic and monastic emphases. Gnosticism had taught there was a series of mediating persons between humans and God; the idea of mediating saints who invoked the blessings of God became common in Christianity. The magical power of the ordinances that changed them to sacraments came unrefined from paganism. Jewish ideas hastened the development of the priestly system. The secular

Roman government provided a pattern for organization that was duplicated by the ecclesiastical monarchy that grew in later centuries. Expression of Christian truth in philosophical terminology was inevitable in the course of various controversies, but it served to glaze over spirituality with arguments. The various internal struggles played a large part in elevating the position of the bishop, since the bishop was called on to be the champion of orthodoxy.

Ecclesiastical Rivalry

The office of bishop had been separated from the presbyter or priest and successively became the governing power in a local church, the ecclesiastical head of a diocese (a city) and the spiritual prince of a territory, sometimes an entire province. The development of councils or synods for mutual help and advice introduced the bishops to one another and encouraged the opportunity for larger leadership by the more gifted bishops. One of the common practices during the controversies was for one of the parties to secure favorable response from one or more of the strong bishops before the outbreak of the conflict. This insured allies, but it also enhanced the prestige and influence of the bishops to whom appeal had been made, for it gave them the opportunity to act as judge. By 325 the three most influential bishops in the Mediterranean world were those in Rome, Antioch, and Alexandria. Already these bishops were sparring for the chief place, and other bishops were striving to elevate themselves to the place occupied by these bishops. This intense rivalry fanned the flames of ambition that normally did not lack fuel. This struggle between bishops was characterized by recrimination, condemnation, and outrageous forgery of official documents in an effort for one bishop to attain first place. What a contrast with the teachings of the humble Galilean!

Major changes in the nature of Christianity had taken place by 325. The developments brought a new movement that did not greatly resemble Christianity except in terminology. There was no Roman Catholic Church as yet, for the bishop of Rome was only one of several powerful bishops; but the direction had been taken. The church had become a saving institution centering in the bishops. A small group of strong bishops had been elevated to world leadership. One of them was already claiming first place and was working feverishly to secure it.

Bibliography

Cadoux, C. J. *The Early Church and the World.* Edinburgh: T. & T. Clark, 1925.

Gwatkin, H. M. *Arian Controversy.* London: Longmans, Green & Co., Inc., 1896.

Hardy, E. G. *Christianity and the Roman Government.* New York: The Macmillan Co., 1925.

Kelly, J. N. D. *Early Christian Creeds.* 3rd ed. New York: Longman, 1972.

Kelly, J. N. D. *Early Christian Doctrine.* 2nd ed. New York: Harper, 1969.

Pelikan, Jaroslav. *The Emergence of the Catholic Tradition (100-600).* Chicago: University of Chicago Press, 1971.

Ramsay, William M. *The Church in the Roman Empire Before 170 A.D.* Grand Rapids: Baker, 1954.

Uhlhorn, Gerhard. *The Conflict of Christianity with Heathenism.* New York: Charles Scribner's Sons, 1891.

Workman, Herbert Brook. *Persecution in the Early Church.* Cincinnati: Jennings and Graham, 1906.

III. Period of Papal Development (A.D. 325-1215)

Introduction to the Period

From A.D. 325 to 1215, the Roman Catholic Church, under the headship of the pope, developed and reached its height. The period begins in 325 when the first world council initiated a new direction. Another council marks the close of the period in 1215. This is the Fourth Lateran Council (also called the Twelfth Ecumenical Council by the Roman Church). The Fourth Lateran Council represents the highest pinnacle attained by the Roman Catholic Church. Between these two councils, the Roman Catholic Church developed, expanded, and reached its height.

The large historical movements of this period were political and military. In the fourth and fifth centuries, the German barbarians from the North and Northeast overran the Western world, ushering in the Middle Ages. The old Greco-Roman culture and economy were overwhelmed. The tribes in general, however, were either converted from paganism or indoctrinated away from Arian Christianity through efforts of the Roman Church. One of the tribes, the Franks, became the dominant military power, and with them the Roman Church made an alliance. In 800, Pope Leo III crowned the Frankish king, Charlemagne, emperor. The church and the secular government began a struggle for mastery that was to continue through this period.

The Eastern world was not invaded by the Germanic hordes, but it was overwhelmed by a worse fate. The Moslems of Arabia began their conquest for world domination in the middle of the seventh century. Almost the entire eastern section around the Mediterranean fell to the Saracens in little over a half century. By 732 they had conquered all of North Africa and Spain and were invading France. In that year Charles Martel defeated them at Tours. The threat that these Arabs and their successors offered to western Europe had a substantial effect on the movement of history.

The next seven chapters will describe this period from the viewpoint of ecclesiastical history. The first chapter in this section will intro-

duce the student to the new direction that began in 325, and the last
one will review the ecclesiastical development of the nine centuries.
The five chapters within this framework describe the laying of Roman
Catholic foundations between 325 and 451; the expansion of the
Roman Catholic Church between 451 and 1050; the religious and
secular opposition to this Roman Catholic expansion between 451
and 1050; and the achievement of complete supremacy, both secular
and religious, by the Roman Catholic system between 1050 and
1215.

Points of Special Interest

The student will notice several significant matters during this
period.

1. The Roman Catholic development was gradual and slow, but
   effective. Two groups opposed autocratic power: (1) those in
   the church who rejected Roman pretensions and (2) the secular
   governments outside the church who resented Roman domination. These two elements of opposition were never completely
   overcome. A special chapter has been devoted to each;
   although they overlap, they present in unified and topical form
   the struggle against the expansion of Roman power.

2. The records of dissenting movements are meager. The nature of
   the religious spirit of the time demanded dissent. Laxity always
   develops asceticism of some kind; rigor and repression always
   breed disobedience and dissent.

3. The long-range program of the Roman Church was its greatest
   strength. The ups and downs of Roman ecclesiastical power
   sometimes made it seem doubtful that world domination would
   ever come. The papacy followed its historic policy of never
   retracting a claim made in earlier centuries, however preposter-
   ous and arrogant it may have been. Asserting such claims when
   the occasion was favorable helped the church dominate the
   world of the twelfth and thirteenth centuries.

5

A New Direction

Developments sketched in previous chapters represent more than a departure from the New Testament pattern; they constitute a preparation for further significant changes. Church government no longer proceeded from the people, but from the officers. The two sacraments, endowed with magical efficacy, had made the church a saving institution; salvation came through admission into this saving institution, not from the power of a message by the institution. The bishop was separated from other local church officers to rule as a monarch, not only in the local church but also in large areas contiguous to his own. The new direction of the development that began with the first world council at Nicaea in 325 led directly to the Roman Catholic Church. Such a development would have been impossible without the friendly attitude and strong arm of the secular power. These elements were consolidated when Constantine chose to link his future with the growing and dynamic Christian movement.

Constantine's Purpose

Constantine was a political genius. From his comparatively meager understanding of Christianity and his brief contact with it, he concluded two things: (1) Christianity would become the dominant religious system of the world, and (2) the dying Roman Empire could be saved, or at least prolonged, by a union with this dynamic religion. Constantine wanted Christianity to become the cement of the Empire; he wanted religion to act as a unifying factor in the political system.

This was not an altogether new idea, for religion had been a part of the Roman system of government through the centuries. Constantine's innovation was in exchanging a state-projected syncretism that invited all who would to join for a widespread and powerful movement that was exclusive in its view of God and its requirements for admission.

(Document 6)

Etheria: Visit to St. Thecla's Church

In 1887 an Italian scholar discovered a manuscript detailing the pilgrimages of the holy woman Etheria. The account of her extensive travels in the Bible lands is unique in that it allows us to read firsthand about the ancient church from a woman's perspective.

So, setting out from Tarsus, I came to a certain city on the sea, still in Cilicia, which is called Pompeiopolis. Thence I entered the borders of Hisauria and stayed in a city called Coricus, and on the third day I arrived at a city which is called Seleucia in Hisauria; on my arrival I went to the bishop, a truly holy man, formerly a monk, and in that city I saw a very beautiful church. And as the distance thence to St. Thecla, which is situated outside the city on a low eminence, was about fifteen hundred paces, I chose rather to go there in order to make the stay that I intended. There is nothing at the holy church in that place except numberless cells of men and of women. I found there a very dear friend of mine, to whose manner of life all in the East bore testimony, a holy deaconess named Marthana, whom I had known at Jerusalem, whither she had come for the sake of prayer; she was ruling over the cell of apotactitae and virgins. And when she had seen me, how can I describe the extent of her joy or mine? But to return to the matter at hand: there are very many cells on the hill and in the midst of it a great wall which encloses the church containing a very beautiful memorial. The wall was built to guard the church because of the Hisauri, who are very malicious and frequently commit acts of robbery, to prevent them from making an attempt on the monastery which is established there. When I arrived in the Name of God, prayer was made at the memorial, and the whole of the acts of St. Thecla having been read, I gave endless thanks to Christ our God, who deigned to fulfil my desires in all things, unworthy and undeserving as I am. Then, after a stay of two days, when I had seen the holy monks and apotactitae who were there, both men and women, and when I had prayed and made my communion, I returned to Tarsus and to my journey.

This union of forces was something new, both for the Empire and for Christianity. Each developed differently because of its alliance. Christianity was not able to save the Roman Empire—it was too far gone; and Constantine was wrong in supposing that Christianity would cement the Empire. How could Christianity bring unity to the political world when Christianity was divided? Already three schools of Christian thought had developed and displayed antagonism to one another.

Alexandria formed the center of the earliest of these schools. A converted philosopher, Pantaenus, organized a school to instruct Christian converts. He was succeeded by Clement, and Clement by Origen—both of whom have been mentioned in connection with literary monuments of the second period of church history. These teachers looked on philosophy as the means of interpreting Christianity. In the best philosophical tradition, they read the Bible allegorically, placing great emphasis on redemption as a mystical union with God through Christ.

Antioch was the second center. This school was founded by Lucian in the closing quarter of the third century. Representing the tradition of the apostle John, this school of thought accepted the Scriptures as its own best interpreter. Because of the intensive struggle with the Gnostics, the teachers of Antioch mistrusted philosophy. They sought the literal meaning of a text, as understood in the light of its grammatical and historical background.

The Western school of thought claimed writers from both Europe and North Africa. Like the Antiochian center, it also mistrusted philosophy and placed its principal emphasis on the practical application of Christianity.

As controversies arose in Christianity, they followed the pattern of thought represented in the various schools. Although they used the same facts and Scriptures, the followers of the Alexandrian school, using the philosophical approach, reached different conclusions from the Antiochian school and the Western school. Often the search for truth was simply a secondary stimulus to the controversy; the intellectual rivalry spurred on the adherents of each type of thought far beyond the limits of Christian charity.

The Donatist split in North Africa thrust itself on Constantine at almost the time he had decided to make Christianity the cement of the Empire. How could a divided Christian church unite the Roman Empire? Donatism gathered up earlier schismatic movements like

Montanism and Novatianism. Constantine's treatment of Donatism was motivated by political factors. He did his best by argument, threat, and finally physical persecution to close the ranks of Christianity, all without success. This problem for Constantine was just a taste of what was yet to come. The cry of the Donatists later on, "What has the emperor to do with the church?" was one that symbolized the greatest dilemma of the new alliance between church and state. What should an emperor do in order to maintain political control when his Christian citizens insisted on forming hostile theological camps on the basis of scriptural interpretations? Whether or not it was his original intention to relate himself in such fashion, Constantine was forced to become "bishop of the bishops" in an attempt to restore unity. This position was accorded him by the ecclesiastical leaders of the Empire.

The controversy that brought Constantine to this place of doctrinal and ecclesiastical leadership was called the Arian controversy and concerned the interpretation of the person of Christ in relation to God.

The Beginning of the Arian Controversy

One of the earliest doctrinal discussions in Christianity centered on the nature of Christ and His relationship to God the Father. Was Jesus Christ completely God or was He less than God? This question had never been adequately answered, although many outstanding Christian writers had wrestled with the problem. If Jesus were completely God, do Christians have three Gods (including the Holy Spirit)? But, came the response, could Jesus save us if He were not God, as He had claimed?

Origen of Alexandria had probed deeply into this question during the third century. His writings contain two different views. In one place Origen affirmed that Christ is subordinate to God, is less than true God. In another he asserted that Christ was the eternally generated Son of God; Christ had always existed as the divine Son, both before time and since the temporal creation. Strange as it may seem, these two positions in Origen form the center of the Arian struggle. The first view set off the controversy, and the second view finally resolved it.

Arius, the man responsible for beginning the controversy, was a presbyter under Bishop Alexander of Alexandria. Although he was serving in Alexandria, he had been trained at Antioch to interpret Scriptures in a literal sense. About 318 Arius decided that it would compromise the dignity and honor of God the Father to say that Jesus

Christ was of the same divine, eternal essence as God. Consequently, he worked out a system that declared Christ a being who had been created before time and that through Christ God had created all other things. His theory made Christ greater than humans, but less than God—somewhere between the two, but fully neither.

The controversy spread rapidly beyond Alexandria and soon gripped the entire Eastern world. The Antiochian school of thought could see nothing wrong with the interpretation and added intellectual rivalry to the issue. Arius was a popular and able preacher who gained much support by his personal charm. As the controversy grew, Constantine acknowledged that some sort of action had to be taken. After becoming the sole emperor in 323, following the experience he had gained in dealing with the Donatists, he called a meeting of all Christian leaders to settle the issue. This universal (the meaning of the Greek word for catholic) council met at Nicaea with over three hundred bishops present. Since the bishops were considered to be the church and since this was a world gathering of bishops, in reality this meeting gave visible expression to the catholic (universal) church. Constantine dominated the council, addressing it when he desired and determining its doctrinal conclusions.

The Council of Nicaea

After preliminary matters had been addressed, a confession of faith by Arius was presented. It defined the nature of Christ as being different from that of God and viewed Christ as a created being, greater than humans and worthy of worship, but less than God. The council promptly and vehemently rejected this creed. Bishop Eusebius of Caesarea offered a creed that he said had been used previously in his church. The wording of this creed was ambiguous. When the orthodox party saw that the Arians were willing to accept the creed of Eusebius, they led a movement to reject it because it was not explicit enough. Athanasius, a young deacon from the church in Alexandria and the champion of the orthodox view, presented the following creed to the council:

> We believe in one God, Almighty Father,
> Maker of all things seen and unseen,
> And in one Lord Jesus Christ, the Son of God,
> Begotten of the Father and only begotten
> That is, from the essence of the Father,
> God from God, Light from Light,

> True God from True God,
> Begotten, not made,
> Of one essence with the Father,
> Through whom all things were made,
> both the things in heaven and the thing,
> upon the earth,
> Who for us men and for our salvation,
> Descended and became flesh and became man,
> Suffered and arose on the third day, and ascended into the
> heavens,
> And is coming to judge living and dead.
> We believe also in the Holy Spirit.

At the end of this creed the council attached a written condemnation of anyone denying its doctrine, mentioning specifically the assertion by the Arians that Christ did not exist in all eternity. This creed emphasized the oneness of Christ with God the Father. The key words were "of one essence with the Father." Constantine believed that this creed would bring political and religious peace, doubtless following the advice of Bishop Hosius of Cordova, his ecclesiastical adviser. With Constantine's approval the creed was adopted and a decree of banishment was issued against Arius and those who followed his view. Christians who had been victims of imperial power a few years before used imperial power to persecute one another. Constantine later changed his mind and recalled Arius, banishing Athanasius. This complete doctrinal reversal meant nothing to his political mind. Constantine probably had little grasp of Christian doctrine. His deferred baptism, moral and ethical standards, and retention of the pagan office that guaranteed his place as a Roman god after death were evidence of his spiritual character.

Later History of Arianism

There was much dissatisfaction in Christianity after the decision of the Nicene council. The language of the creed led some to fear *tritheism* (three gods) and others to fear *modalism* (the loss of individual personality). By political maneuvering and playing on the fears of sincere religious thinkers, Arians gained the upper hand for a generation. A semi-Arian school that took a position halfway between that of Athanasius and Arius developed, asserting that Christ was not of one essence with God, but was similar to God. This drew many followers from the strict Athanasian party. Athanasius was repeatedly banished for holding to the views of the Nicene Creed.

The political scene helped bring a temporary Arian triumph. When Constantine died in 337, his three sons (Constantine II, Constans, and Constantius) divided up the Roman Empire. Constantine II was killed in 340 in a battle with Constans, and Constans committed suicide in 350. These two men favored the Nicene view. The third son, Constantius, was an Arian. His reign (from 337 to 61, as sole ruler after 350) provided an opportunity for Arianism to develop with the blessing of imperial authority.

In addition to banishing Athanasius, Constantius dealt severely with pagan and Jewish adherents. He enacted the death penalty for offering pagan sacrifices and for becoming a Jewish proselyte. Partly because of this severity, a pagan reaction took place. Constantine had slaughtered his relatives, other than the three sons, in order to insure proper succession. He missed two intended victims. One of them, Julian, the son of a brother whom Constantine had killed, secretly embraced paganism and in 361 wrested control of the Empire from Constantius. He did everything he could to increase divisions in Christianity. Athanasius was brought out of banishment, and the other dissenters were encouraged. Julian also endeavored to introduce a reformed and refined paganism. After his death in 363, the succeeding emperors favored Christianity of the Nicene type. Arianism slowly receded in influence through the following centuries. The second universal council of 381 at Constantinople reaffirmed the position of the first council relative to the person of Christ.

Results of Arianism

One important result of the Arian movement was the spread of its doctrine of Christ through missionary activity. In 340 while Arianism enjoyed imperial favor, a young missionary, Ulfilas, trained in the Arian doctrine, was sent to the Visigoths. He served until his death in 383, apparently receiving much assistance. Ulfilas labored diligently, but the conversion to Arian Christianity of great masses of Visigoths and neighboring tribes could hardly have been the work of one person. Ulfilas is best remembered for reducing the Gothic language to writing for use in his translation of the Scriptures. During the late fourth and fifth centuries these Germanic tribes overran the Roman Empire. A remarkable number of the invaders had already embraced

Arian Christianity and required only instruction in the Nicene under-standing.

Another result of the Arian movement was Constantine's adoption of the general policy of physical persecution against ecclesiastical dis-senters. The Donatists had suffered physical persecution at the hands of Constantine in 316, following their refusal to accept the decision of the Council of Arles. After five years Constantine stopped closing Donatist churches and banishing their bishops, recognizing that the results of this use of force were unsatisfactory. Constantine resumed persecuting the Donatists because of his deep desire to secure exter-nal conformity.

Furthermore, the Council of Nicaea provided a precedent and pat-tern for future councils. Everyone knew that the decision of the coun-cil had been arbitrary. Constantine had determined what the council should decide. Decrees of the council were recognized as authoritative Christian pronouncements. Thoughtful leaders pondered this new development. They began to believe Christian motives and conduct were secondary; decisions were the authoritative matters and the goal to be attained. Many of the later universal councils reached their deci-sions through physical coercion and rough-and-tumble tactics. It is difficult to see what part genuine Christianity had in some of these councils.

Finally, the Council of Nicaea gave visible form to the catholic church. In the writings of Cyprian, in the previous century, it was asserted that the church existed in the bishops. The catholic church (universal Christianity) could become visible when all of the bishops gathered in council. This was effected at Nicaea, and it completed the ecclesiastical machinery for universal domination by a spiritual mon-arch.

The New Relationship

The beginning of an alliance between Christianity and the Roman Empire under Constantine profoundly influenced the history and development of religion and the state. Christianity was officially decreed the religion of the Roman state under Emperor Theodosius (378-95).

A New Area of Controversy

Before Nicaea, Christianity had no occasion to question relations to the state. Centuries of secular persecution followed the original antagonism of the Empire against an "illegal" religion. The attempt to adjust the relations between Christianity and the secular power forms a large part of the history of Christianity in the centuries to come. Some believed that the state should control the church; Roman history recommended toward this view. Constantine assumed this attitude, as did his sons. The emperor became the "bishop of bishops." Such a relationship became known as *caesaro-papacy*—state domination of the church. Others wanted the church to be above the system. Still others believed each institution had a peculiar stewardship from God and believed that the two should work alongside one another without undue interference. This problem has never been settled to the satisfaction of all. A new direction, tremendously significant in the history and development of Christianity from Nicaea to the present, was begun.

The Increase of Secular Influence

One finds it difficult to conceive how much secular influence was exerted upon Christianity through the alliance between church and state under Constantine. In the area of organization, for example, Christianity made use of the imperial pattern. In the terminology of American geography, Christianity organized on the basis of city, county, state, sectional, and national political divisions. After the development of the office of pope in the next century, the imperial organization and that of Christianity were strikingly similar.

The very motives of Constantine in adopting Christianity indicate the direction Christianity would head. He wanted to use Christianity as a political and social factor in building the state. This required him to use secular power to establish uniformity. The state must stamp out dissent and settle doctrinal and ecclesiastical disputes. The administrative officers of state devised ways to increase efficiency in Christian administration; Christian officers under Constantine began to use methods and ideas in church life that they had learned in government service.

Nicaea brought with it the problem of secular authority in filling important ecclesiastical offices. The Christian movement was too politically important to allow radicals of any kind to hold high office. A bishop had to please the state as well as God. In this sphere secular influence was widely exercised.

The Influence of the Unregenerate

All historians speak of the mass movement to join the church after Christianity had come into imperial favor. Although Christianity was not officially termed the religion of the state for about half a century, Constantine's appeal to his subjects to become Christians, his generous gifts to those who were Christians, and the ease with which Christianity could be embraced aided people to make their decisions. The similarity between the magical sacraments of Christianity and parallel rites in paganism gave the prospective members a feeling of familiarity in their initiation. In the army, especially, the influence of some sagacious leader might result in winning all his loyal followers in a short time.

An example of the ease with which this could be accomplished may be seen in the conversion of one of the Frankish chieftains in the next century. Clovis faced a crucial battle on the following day. He made a solemn vow that, if the Christian God of his wife would give victory in battle, he would become a Christian. Having won the victory, he kept his vow. When his army learned what was happening, they wanted to join. The soldiers marched alongside a river where priests stood with branches from trees. As the soldiers went by, the priests dipped the branches into the river and flung baptismal water on them, repeating the proper formula. As soon as the water touched the soldiers they supposedly were made Christians. It is not surprising that when these pagans entered the membership of the Christian churches, they brought pagan ideas with them. Consequently, Christianity was more and more infected with pagan corruptions as it became a popular movement.

Impetus to the Rise of Monasticism

The filling of Christian churches with sprinkled pagans was responsible in part for the rapid development of asceticism. Laxity in Christian life and ethics has always brought reactionary movements. Sometimes these did not develop into parties or schisms, but came from individual remorse that led to ascetical practices. Remaining in the regular churches, conscientious Christians found relief of soul through fasting, long hours of prayer, and rigorous spiritual discipline. Others chose a more radical method. In the East, where the climate was inviting during most of the year, men left their churches and homes and became religious hermits. They took literally the injunction of Jesus to the rich young ruler to "leave all and follow me." They

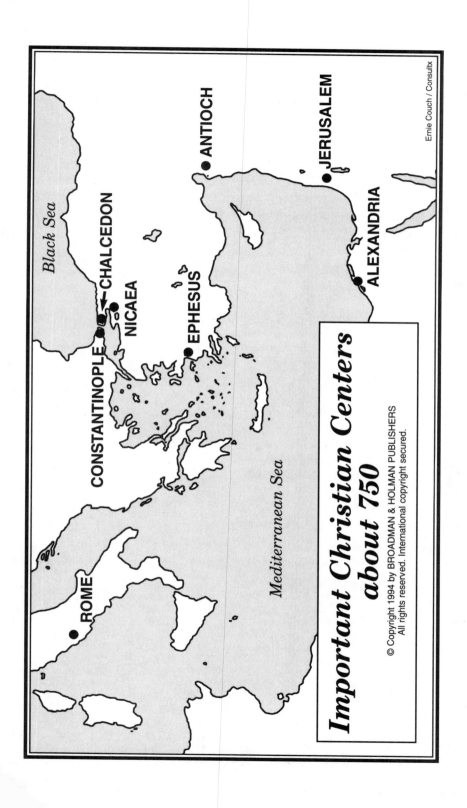

Important Christian Centers about 750

Ernie Couch / Consultx

ROME

Black Sea

CONSTANTINOPLE

CHALCEDON

NICAEA

EPHESUS

ANTIOCH

JERUSALEM

ALEXANDRIA

Mediterranean Sea

(Document 7)

Athanasius: Anthony of the Desert

Bishop Athanasius of Alexandria is famous as a defender of the Nicene doctrine of the Trinity, but he was also an early advocate of monasticism. In his Life of Saint Anthony, *Athanasius popularized the stories of the aged Anthony.*

The blessed Anthony was alone in that desert, for the place wherein he had his habitation was waste and desolate; and his mind therefore dwelt the more upon exalted things, and it was content therewith. Now the brethren who used to go to visit him besought and entreated him to allow them to bring him there month by month a few garden herbs and olives and oil; and although he contended with them about it they overcame him with their entreaty, and compelled him to receive them, and they began to pay him visits, one at a time, according to their entreaty to him. And the blessed man was exceedingly old, and he was far advanced in years. And in that desert also he endured strife, not with flesh and blood, but with devils and impure spirits, and we have learned this also from those who were going to visit him continually. They used to hear also there the sound of tumult and of outcry, and to see flashing spears, and at night time they would see the whole mountain filled with fiery phantoms, and those men were greatly terrified; but the blessed Anthony was trained in stratagems of war like a man of war, and he was prepared, and he stood up and rebuked the Evil One, who straightaway ceased according to his wont; and he encouraged the brethren who were with him not to be terrified or to tremble at such visions as these. For, he said to them, "They are only empty phantoms which perish as if they had never existed at the name of the cross"; and wonder and admiration laid hold upon every man at the greatness and at the manner of the righteousness which was found in the blessed man.

He was not terrified at the devils, he was not wearied by the desert, and his soul had no fear of the wild beasts which were therein; but Satan suffered torture from all these things. And one day he came to the blessed man, who was singing the Psalms of David, and he gnashed his teeth upon him loudly; but the blessed Anthony ceased not to sing, and he was comforted and helped by the Grace of our Lord. One night whilst he was standing up and was watching in prayer, Satan gathered together all the wild beasts of the desert, and brought them against him, and they were so many in number that he could hardly have left one beast in its den; and as they compassed him about on every side, and with threatening looks were ready to leap upon him, he looked at them boldly and said unto them, "If ye have received power over me from the Lord, draw nigh, and delay not, for I am ready for you; but if ye have made ready and come at the command of Satan, get ye back to your places and tarry not, for I am a servant of Jesus the Conqueror." And when the blessed man had spoken these words, Satan was straightaway driven away by the mention of the Name of Christ like a sparrow before a hawk.

felt that by secluding themselves in a cave away from others and engaging in prayer and spiritual contemplation they could "lose their lives in order to save them."

One of the most famous of these hermits was Anthony of Thebes, or Anthony of the Desert (about 250-355). Fleeing from society at about the age of twenty, he spent the next eighty-six years in a cave. He was venerated as a very old man, and his cave became a place for blessing. Others began leaving their homes and following his example. Before long, there were so many hermits in the deserts that the caves were all taken. Soon there came the formation of community or *cenobitic groups*. A number of hermits banded together under a common rule of organization. The earliest known movement of this kind was that of Pachomius that took place about 335 in Egypt.

Monasticism spread in Asia Minor, then westward. The western practical mind and the rigorous climate discouraged those Christians who would flee to caves, but by the sixth century Benedict of Nursia began an orderly and effective movement in Italy. This will be discussed in a succeeding chapter.

□ □ □ □ □

A new direction had come. The problem of imperial persecution had been replaced with the problem of imperial favor. The Christian ideal was greatly influenced by the pattern and patronage of the Roman government. The development of the universal council as an authoritative legislative body for all Christianity, coupled with Constantine's intense desire for universal conformity to a single Christian pattern of doctrine and practice, was a big step toward a monarchical government in Christianity. Christians had learned to persecute fellow believers in an effort to secure uniformity.

The succeeding chapters will tell the story of the rise of the Roman Catholic Church. All of the ingredients necessary to make such a system were now assembled: sacramentalism, sacerdotalism, episcopal government, Roman ambition, ecclesiastical rivalry, an authoritative world gathering, and the pattern and power of the secular state. The Roman bishop used all of these elements efficiently in the next period.

6

Roman Catholic Foundations

By 325 when the first catholic (universal) council met, the church may be called by the name "Catholic." By this time the church had assumed several characteristics not distinctly taught in Scripture. These characteristics include (1) the idea of a visible universal church composed of bishops, (2) the belief that the sacraments (as they will now be called) carried with them a magical kind of transforming grace, (3) the employment of a special priesthood (the clergy) who alone were qualified by ordination to act in the administration of those sacraments, and (4) the recognition of the bishops as the ruling officers (episcopal government). All of these characteristics may be seen at the present time in the Christian groups who call themselves Catholic—Roman Catholic, Greek Catholic, and Anglican Catholic.

After 325, foundations were in place for a new advance in hierarchical development. The oligarchy, the rule of many bishops, began to change to a monarchy, the rule of one bishop. The one ruling bishop was the bishop of Rome. This does not mean that the Roman bishops did not exercise strong influence before 325. As early as the year 58 the apostle Paul had complimented the church at Rome for their excellent reputation throughout the world. The earliest noncanonical writings tell of the great influence of the large, wealthy, and generous body of Christians at Rome. This church had benefited from the illustrious name and history of the city in which it was located, for Rome had been the center of the world for centuries.

Churches having problems often wrote larger and more experienced churches for advice in matters of discipline and doctrine. The Roman Church received many such appeals for help. A good example is the letter the church at Corinth sent to Rome in the last decade of the first century. The Corinthian church, exercising her prerogatives as an autonomous body, had removed several presbyters whom the apostles had appointed. In the controversy someone had written to the church at Rome for advice. The reply by Clement, a pastor or bishop at Rome, is probably typical of letters many bishops wrote to churches asking for advice in such matters. The Roman Church was slower than some of the other churches to place a single bishop above the remainder of its officers. Apparently Bishop Anicetus (154-65) was the first monarchical head of the Roman congregation.

About 185 Bishop Irenaeus of Lyons referred to the apostolic tradition of the Roman bishop. His reference carried with it an emphasis on the doctrinal rightness of Rome rather than the ecclesiastical authority of Rome.

In the middle of the second century a quarrel broke out between Rome and certain leaders in Asia Minor about the proper date for observing Easter. The Eastern churches reckoned the date of Easter according to the moon, regardless of what day in the week the celebration came. The church at Rome waited until the following Sunday. Bishop Polycarp (a disciple of the apostle John), representing the East, and Bishop Anietus, representing the West, could not agree, so each continued to observe Easter according to his own practice. The controversy touched all the churches and threatened the peace of the Christian world. Synods (or councils) were called at Rome and in Palestine. They debated the merits of each side. Most favored the practice of observing Easter on Sunday. When the Ephesian bishop and many churches in Asia Minor refused to change their ancient practice, synods or no synods, Bishop Victor of Rome (189-98) declared them excommunicated. Promptly, Irenaeus rebuked Victor for this action. This action raises doubts for us as to what Irenaeus actually believed about the orthodoxy and authority of the Roman bishop.

Tertullian, the Carthaginian presbyter often recognized as the first Latin Catholic theologian, had no sympathy with claims by the Roman bishop. He broke with him in 207 to join the Montanist movement. Tertullian's pupil, Cyprian, also wrote eloquently about the unique place of the Roman bishop, but about 250 Cyprian vigorously told the bishop to stop meddling outside of the Roman diocese. The only superiority he would allow to the Roman bishop was in dignity. The fourth century Donatists addressed their appeal to a council, then to the emperor, not to the Roman bishop.

By 325 the Roman bishop was undoubtedly considered to be one of the strongest bishops. Some writers of that period viewed the Roman bishop as possessing an unusual dignity among bishops, but he remained as one of many bishops, all of whom, according to Cyprian, possessed equal and apostolic authority.

The sixth canon of the Council of Nicaea (325) recognized the Roman bishop as being on a par with the Alexandrian and Antiochian bishops. A forgery was inserted in the Roman bishop's copy of this canon. This forged element alleged Rome had always held the primacy. This fraud was discovered when the Roman copy was compared with other copies of the Nicene records. It suggests the mindset of those in Rome as they sought by every means, fair or otherwise, to claim preeminence. No wonder many scholars doubt the texts of some of the older writings that have been preserved by Rome. Forged insertions and false decretals appear through the history of the Roman Church in an effort to forward their position.

Between the first universal council of 325 and the fourth council held at Chalcedon in 451, the Roman bishop laid the foundations for the ecclesiastical monarchy now known by his title. Many outstanding factors entered into this development.

Able Leaders

One of the most important reasons for the rise of the Roman bishop is the type of leaders who held the office. They recognized the dignity of their position and sought in every way to advance it. As evidenced by the forgery mentioned earlier, they wanted first place and actively sought it. Their immediate territory was well organized so as to consolidate their holdings. The marvelous organizational skill of the Romans was turned into ecclesiastical channels. Whole series of subordinate officers guaranteed discipline and uniformity.

Two of these men were quite vocal in their claims. Innocent I (402-17) was the first bishop of Rome to claim universal jurisdiction on the basis of the Petrine tradition. Leo I (440-61), who may be rightly called the first pope, asserted scriptural authority for Innocent's claims, secured imperial recognition of his claims to primacy, and by a confluence of political and ecclesiastical interests was able to dictate the doctrinal statement of the Council of Chalcedon, the fourth univer-

(Document 8)
The Nicene Creed

The Nicene Creed was first published by the Council of Constantinople, the second ecumenical council (A.D. 381). Today it is the most widely accepted of the Christian creeds, adopted by the Orthodox churches of the East, the Roman Church, the Anglican Church, and many Protestant churches.

The following English translation is taken from the older Anglican version of The Book of Common Prayer. *The words "and the Son" in the last paragraph were added to Latin versions during the Middle Ages; the Orthodox churches do not accept this addition.*

I believe in one God the Father Almighty, Maker of heaven and earth, And of all things visible and invisible: And in one Lord Jesus Christ, the only begotten Son of God, Begotten of his Father before all worlds, God of God, Light of Light, Very God of very God, Begotten, not made, Being of one substance with the Father, By whom all things were made: Who for us men, and for our salvation came down from heaven, And was incarnate by the Holy Ghost of the Virgin Mary, Also was made man, And was crucified also for us under Pontius Pilate. He suffered and was buried, And the third day he rose again according to the Scriptures, And ascended into heaven, And sitteth on the right hand of the Father. And he shall come again with glory to judge both the quick and the dead: whose kingdom shall have no end.

And I believe in the Holy Ghost, The Lord and giver of life, Who proceedeth from the Father and the Son, Who with the Father and the Son together is worshipped and glorified, Who spake by the Prophets. And I believe one Catholick and Apostolick Church. I acknowledge one Baptism for the remission of sins. And I look for the Resurrection of the dead, And the life of the world to come. Amen.

sal council in 451. "Peter has spoken," cried the bishops when Leo's *Tome* was read; and such recognition, imperial and ecclesiastical, laid the foundations for the papal system.

Geographical Position

The bishop of Rome had no rival in the Western world. Rome had been the ecclesiastical leader of the West long before the rise of strong bishoprics in North Africa and Europe. This was not true in the East. Ancient and powerful bishops in cities like Alexandria, Jerusalem, Antioch, and Ephesus disputed constantly. Rather than choose an umpire among themselves, they regularly appealed to the sole Western bishop. By so doing, they unconsciously increased the Roman bishop's stature.

Move of the Imperial Capital

In 330, the emperor Constantine moved the capital of the Roman Empire from Rome to Byzantium, which became known as Constantinople. Instead of weakening the position of the Roman bishop by this move, Constantine unknowingly aided the growth of the bishop's prestige. As long as the emperor resided in Rome, the bishop took second place. As "bishop of bishops," the emperor overshadowed his political subjects and dominated the ecclesiastical policies of the bishop. When the emperor moved to a new city in the East, he freed the Roman bishop from governmental influence and allowed him to operate without restraint. In fact, the move of the emperor made the bishop both an ecclesiastical and a secular sovereign. The Roman bishops became administrators of the secular affairs of the city, defending it against military aggressors, maintaining internal order, supplying its physical needs, and initiating its foreign policy.

Political Prestige

Rome had been the center of the political world for several centuries when the last of the apostles died. How much prestige this political situation brought to the church of Rome cannot be estimated. The importance of such political centrality is seen in the fact that Constantinople had no other claim to ecclesiastical prestige than that it was the seat of the emperor; yet in a little over a century it was Rome's greatest ecclesiastical rival because of its political importance.

History and Tradition

The church at Rome had a long and honorable history; it is impossible to find evidence of the present Roman claim that Peter was bishop of Rome. The tradition that Peter was pastor at Rome for a quarter of a century developed very late, and outstanding Roman Catholic writers admit that it can never be proved. Furthermore, Roman claims of authority based on this tradition were not made until the fifth century. After the Roman bishop had become powerful, he claimed right to such power because of the Petrine succession.

Bishop Leo I (440-61) gave the theory of Petrine succession a scriptural basis. Leo used three New Testament passages to prove that Peter was given the authority to rule all Christendom.

- *Matthew 16:18-19.* Christ would build His church upon Peter personally, for Peter was given authority to bind and loose souls in a spiritual monarchy.

- *John 21:15-17.* Peter was to be the chief shepherd and have the tasks of feeding, tending, and caring for all of Christ's sheep in the world.

- *Luke 22:31-32.* Peter, after having been turned from his errors by Christ, would become the chief teacher of Christendom. Peter wielded this authority over the other apostles and later passed this same authority down to his successors as bishop of Rome; thus, other bishops, like other apostles, were subject to the authority of the Roman bishop.

Doctrinal Wisdom

The bishop of Rome strengthened his position as leader of other bishops by handling himself well during doctrinal scuffles between 325 and 451. There were three controversies in the East (Apollinarian, Nestorian, and Eutychian) and one in the West (Pelagian) during this period. These controversies illustrate the speculative nature of the Eastern mind and the practical nature of the Western mind.

Was Christ Human?

Apollinaris, bishop of Laodicea in the middle of the fourth century, tried to explain how Christ could be both divine and human. He took John 1:14 literally: "The Word became flesh." Apollinaris argued that Jesus had no rational human spirit because the divine Word (Logos) took the place of the rational human spirit. Such a Christ would certainly be divine, but would He be human? Bishop Damascus of Rome condemned this view in 377 and gained added prestige when the second universal council at Constantinople took similar action in 381.

Was Christ's Human Nature
Separate from His Divine Nature?

The Nestorian controversy grew as much out of ecclesiastical rivalry between the bishops of Rome, Alexandria, and Constantinople as it did from an effort to find the truth. Nestorius became bishop of Constantinople in 428. Shortly later, he strenuously objected to applying the title "mother of God" to the virgin Mary. Nestorius asserted that Mary might be called the mother of Jesus' human nature, but certainly should not be viewed as the mother of Christ's divine nature, as the term might suggest. Bishops Cyril of Alexandria and Celestine of Rome promptly condemned Nestorius. They objected that the view of Nestorius disrupted the unity of Christ's person and deity, so separating Christ's nature to human and divine as to deny the deity of Christ. By physical and political force Bishop Cyril controlled the third universal council (at Ephesus in 431), which pronounced Nestorius guilty of heresy and deposed him. His followers fled to Persia and established a separate church that has continued through the centuries.

Did Christ Have
One Nature or Two?

The Eutychian controversy followed as a reaction to the Nestorian controversy. Eutyches, a zealous monk near Constantinople, profoundly moved by the differences between Bishop Cyril of Alexandria and the Nestorians, took the position that after the incarnation Christ had only one nature and that it was divine. Bishop Leo I of Rome sided with Bishop Flavianus of Constantinople in condemning Eutyches. In a long letter to Flavianus, Leo insisted that Christ had two natures. In 449, Bishop Dioscurus, who had succeeded Cyril at Alexandria, assembled a synod at Ephesus in which, by threat and violence, the theory of Eutyches was approved. Leo of Rome called this the "robber synod" and refused to accept its findings, but because Theodosius supported Eutyches, the Roman bishop was powerless to act.

In 450, Theodosius died, and his sister was favorable to the Roman view. With her approval another council was summoned (recognized as the fourth universal council) and met at Chalcedon in 451. The council heard the reading of the letter of Leo to Flavianus and the assembled clerics cried out, "God has spoken through Peter; the fisherman has spoken." The council accepted Leo's doctrinal definition of Christ's nature. Christ was the same as God as to His deity and the same as we are as to His humanity; Christ is one person in two natures united "unconfusedly, unchangeably, indivisibly, inseparably."

Bishop Leo of Rome revealed a feeling of superiority over even a universal council. In deference to the political power of Constantinople, the bishop of that city, although without apostolic tradition, had been recognized as a patriarch by the council of 381 in Constantinople, and the Chalcedonian council of 451 asserted in its twenty-eighth canon that the bishop of Constantinople had authority equal to that of

---

(Document 9)

The Christological Definition of Chalcedon

The Council of Chalcedon adopted the following definition of the person of Christ on October 22, A.D. 451. This is one of the most important theological documents of Christian history.

We, then following the holy Fathers, all with one consent, teach men to confess one and the same Son, our Lord Jesus Christ, the same perfect Godhead and also perfect in manhood; truly God and truly man, of a reasonable (rational) soul and body; consubstantial (coessential) with the Father according to the Godhead, and consubstantial with us according to the Manhood; in all things like unto us, without sin; begotten before all ages of the Father according to the Godhead, and in these latter days, for us and for our salvation, born of the Virgin Mary, the Mother of God, according to the Manhood; one and the same Christ, Son, Lord, Only-begotten, to be acknowledged in two natures, inconfusedly, unchangeably, indivisibly, inseperably; the distinction of natures being by no means taken away by the union, but rather the property of each nature being preserved, and concurring in one Person and one Subsistence, not parted or divided into two persons, but one and the same Son, and only begotten, God the Word, the Lord Jesus Christ, as the prophets from the beginning (have declared) concerning him, and the Lord Jesus Christ himself has taught us, and the Creed of the holy Fathers has handed down to us.

---

the Roman bishop. Leo refused to accept this decision by the ecumenical council, declaring that he would not recognize the bishop of Constantinople as his peer. He preferred to rule alone.

How Are Persons Saved?

The one Western controversy of this period centered on a very practical question and one that influenced church organization. The Western church was less interested than the Eastern in speculative matters, but it promptly and effectively dealt with practical concerns.

The British monk Pelagius and his disciple, Coelestius, raised such an issue. Can persons be saved without the special revelation in Christ and the Bible? Must special divine grace work on the soul in regeneration to attain salvation? Pelagius and Coelestius taught that newborns are innocent and need not be baptized because they have no sin to wash away. The two monks fled from Britain to Italy, then to North Africa about 411. Their rejection of the doctrine of original sin and other teachings brought them in direct conflict with the beliefs and practices of the churches in North Africa.

The Pelagian group said that every man could either choose to sin or choose to be righteous. They considered all of human environment to be God's revelation, including creation, friends, and circumstances; and they insisted that no special regenerating grace was necessary for salvation. They said it was quite possible to be saved without Scriptures and Christ's revelation; although these should not be minimized since they provided inspiration and guidance. There was no such thing as original sin, because, they said, God creates each soul at the time of birth and endows it with purity and freedom.

Because of his views Coelestius was excluded from the church at Carthage in 412 and fled to Palestine to rejoin Pelagius. In 415, an interesting incident occurred that illustrates the general attitude of Eastern bishops toward the Roman bishop. Bishop John of Jerusalem and his presbyters were assembled to hear charges against Pelagius. After the evidence had been presented, John gave the decision that since Pelagius was from the West, he came under the authority of the bishop of Rome. That is, all *Latin* Christianity was viewed as coming under the sway of the Roman bishop.

The Roman bishops intermittently took both sides of the Pelagian controversy. In 416, Bishop Innocent condemned the movement. After his death in that year, Bishop Zosimus publicly approved the teachings of Pelagius and Coelestius. In the following year, the North African bishops condemned the Pelagian movement. Even the Roman Emperor Honorius in Constantinople issued an edict condemning the Roman bishop and any others holding to this heresy. Finally Bishop Zosimus of Rome changed his position and approved the African view, ordering all Western bishops to make the shift in doctrine at the same time. Many eminent bishops refused to condemn entirely the views of Pelagius. The Pelagian view was officially condemned at the universal council in 431 at Ephesus. The Council also condemned the Nestorians, with whom the Pelagians had been friendly. Many of the bishops maintained a semi-Pelagian position, laying emphasis on good works and human initiative in salvation. This position was opposed to the alternative theory held by the great opponent of Pelagius, Augustine of Hippo.

Augustine (354-430) was the great theologian of the fifth century. Turning successively from philosophy to Manicheanism to skepticism to Neoplatonism to Christianity, he became the dominant figure in Christian thinking for a thousand years. His profound experience of finding God and his deep devotion to God gave richness to his theological ideas. His *Confessions*, deeply personal and mystical, explain his doctrinal point of view.

In the Pelagian controversy, Augustine asserted that Adam had been created faultless and with freedom, but that in Adam's fall humankind had lost its purity and freedom. Augustine believed that the baptism of babies or adults washed away the guilt of original sin, but not sin itself, and he taught that the sacraments of the church were necessary to preserve the individual from additional guilt and penalty of this sin. He insisted that humans cannot work for salvation, that even the ability to accept salvation is a gift of God. The helplessness of humans requires God to do everything. God both chooses those who should be saved (predestination) and enables them to be saved. Augustine's inconsistency may be glimpsed at this point. In his emphasis upon God's sovereignty, Augustine left nothing for humans to do in salvation, yet he demanded that infants be baptized in order to be saved from inherited guilt. If God predestined a child to be saved, apparently baptism would have little effect. Augustine's strong emphasis on God's total sovereignty repelled some of his contemporaries as much as Pelagius' doctrine of salvation obtained by cooperating with God. This gave rise to the semi-Pelagian and semi-Augustinian views already mentioned.

In addition to his *Confessions* and his opposition to Pelagius, Augustine made two other distinct contributions. He established the official doctrine of the Roman Catholic Church relative to the Donatist controversy. The Donatists had taught that when a bishop's character was unchristian or unrighteous, all the sacramental acts of that bishop was invalid. Thus, they had said, Bishop Felix could not properly ordain Caecillian and Caecillian could not administer saving baptism, because both were heretics; they had delivered up Scriptures to be destroyed during the time of persecution. Augustine reinterpreted the issue by teaching that a bishop's character had no influence on the validity of his sacramental acts, since the authority or insignia of the church guaranteed the validity of any official acts that a bishop might perform. This marked another advance in the direction of an authoritative Church.

Augustine also put in written form the ideal toward which the Roman Catholic Church was struggling. Although unfinished, his twenty-two books entitled *City of God* sketched the conflict between earthly rule and the heavenly rule. Remember, Augustine was writing at the time Germanic barbarians were overrunning the Western world.

In the very year that he died these pagans were pounding at the gates of Hippo, his own city. Augustine described the earthly city, maintained through war, hate, and evil; in contrast he pictured God's city, slowly but surely growing to cover the earth and overcome the secular rule of the earthly city. This idea of a conflict between the spiritual—identified with the ecclesiastical system—and the secular was a prophecy of events to come and did much to influence the thinking of Augustine's era and the Medieval period.

Thus, from 325 to 451, the foundations for the Roman Catholic Church were laid. Four world councils provided an arena where the Roman bishop was able to exert growing authority. Arguing on the same grounds that had proved effective against the Gnostics, the Roman bishops said that their tradition of succession to the apostle Peter endowed them with continuing authority. They quoted Scripture texts to prove that Peter had such authority. When wrong doctrinally, and even when snubbed by an ecumenical council, the Roman bishop showed his tremendous prestige and sagacity by shifting his position or standing firm, as circumstances warranted, and through it all was able to maintain his powerful place. The recognition by imperial and ecclesiastical authorities of Bishop Leo's pretensions to primacy, based upon the Petrine tradition, provides grounds for believing that Leo was the first of the Roman Catholic popes.

7

Roman Catholic Expansions

Between 325 and 451 foundations of Roman papal control of the Catholic Church were laid. Alleged primacy of Peter and the alleged apostolic succession through the Roman bishop gave Roman claims a scriptural tone. The period from 451 to 1050 was full of confusion and violence, but the historical movement that brought crisis to Roman Christianity—the barbarian invasions—also provided an opportunity for the papacy to expand its claims to include authority over secular powers and to widen the geographical extent of papal control.

Invasion by the Germanic Tribes

Even while the Council of Chalcedon (451) was affirming some of the claims of Bishop Leo I of Rome (440-61), great migrations were taking place. During the second century it had been necessary for the Roman government to maintain large garrisons across central Europe to keep the German tribes from spilling over into the Roman Empire. As other tribes wandered south and west from the broad steppes of what is now Russia, additional pressure was put on the tribes facing the Roman garrisons to move on to the empire. Throughout the third and fourth centuries of the Christian era, Roman rulers fought continuously to stem the invasion of the various tribes known as Goths, Visigoths (western Goths), Ostrogoths (eastern Goths), Vandals, Franks, Burgundians, Lombards, and so forth. The tribes began moving in during the fourth century. The date when the Ostrogoths finally overthrew Rome is usually given as 476, but Rome had fallen as early as 410 to Alaric the Goth. Attila (452) and Geisric (455) were subdued only by the sagacity of Pope Leo I.

Some of these tribes were already nominal Christians. Ulfilas and his movement had reached many of them with Arian Christianity. As these Germanic tribes overran the old Roman Empire, they broke down the old Graeco-Roman civilization. They also gave the Roman Catholic Church an opportunity to mold a new civilization. These tribes did not destroy and slay as they advanced to Roman territory. Rather, they adopted whatever elements of the old culture appealed to them and intermarried with the population. Because of these factors, the power of the Roman Catholic system was not harmed permanently by the invasions.

The Catholic Church secured lasting benefits. At least five of these benefits stand out.

1. The Germanic tribes provided new and numerous subjects for Roman Catholic control. They were awed by the beautiful and solemn services in the orthodox churches and were delighted with the magical sacramental system. The Arian Christians among the tribes were unskilled in doctrinal matters, and they were easily won to the orthodox point of view on the person of Christ.

2. The tribes gave the Roman Church an opportunity to enlarge and tighten its organization. There were new churches to establish, new priests to train, and new catechisms to provide. The untutored Germans brought no new doctrinal problems to complicate this tremendous expansion.

3. The Germanic tribes were rulers over the domains they had conquered but became subjects of the religious training of the Roman system. This meant that the Roman hierarchy quickly attained great prestige and extensive influence. This supported the point of view suggested by Augustine's *City of God*: that the heavenly city was superior to the secular and would one day become dominant.

4. The Western world was cut off from the influence of the Roman emperor in Constantinople. Except for a brief period, the entrance of the Germanic tribes made it impossible for the emperor to exercise secular or ecclesiastical power over the

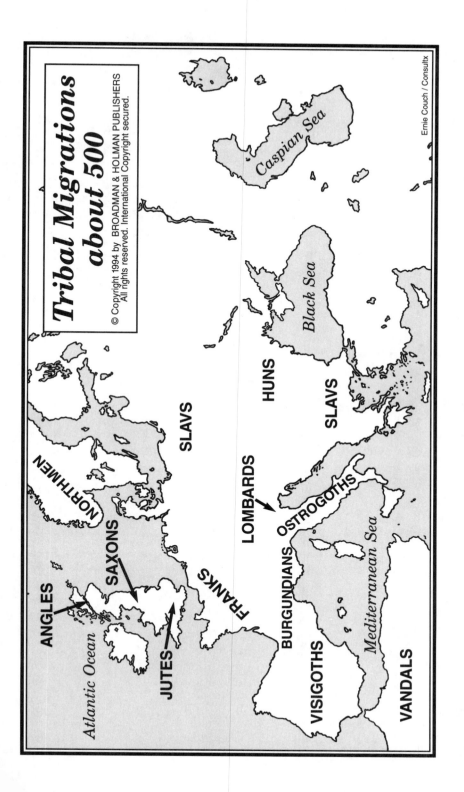

Tribal Migrations about 500

Ernie Couch / Consultx

Caspian Sea

Black Sea

Mediterranean Sea

Atlantic Ocean

NORTHMEN

ANGLES

SAXONS

JUTES

FRANKS

SLAVS

LOMBARDS

HUNS

SLAVS

OSTROGOTHS

BURGUNDIANS

VISIGOTHS

VANDALS

Roman Church. Before the invasion the emperor had still viewed himself as bishop over all bishops and with his army had held a threat over the Western world. With the barbarian wall surrounding the West, the emperor was helpless to interfere.

5. The winning of these barbarians to a recognition of the spiritual sovereignty of the Roman Church was a deathblow to the ambitions of any other Western bishop and brought gifts of territory and military protection.

Monasticism in the West

The barbarian invasions probably gave impetus to the monastic ideal in the West. In the Eastern world Anthony and Pachomius had begun hermit life and cenobitic organization. In the West the movement developed more slowly, but eventually became more influential. The example of the East doubtless motivated Western leaders to emphasize ascetical life. Leaders like Athanasius, Jerome, Ambrose, Augustine of Hippo, Martin of Tours, and Eusebius of Vercelli tried to convince others of the superior virtue of devoting their lives to monasticism. After persecution by the state ended, the monastic movement became increasingly popular. Martyrdom was now rare; the most rigorous means of self-denial and suffering for Christ was now monasticism. The triumph of the "lax" party over the "strict" party in dealing with those who had been untrue to Christ caused many to look askance at the regular means of worship and service and to go to caves or monastic seclusion. Some viewed the Germanic invasions as the wrath of God on Christianity for leaving its early purity and passion, and they determined to flee for safety to the rigorous monastic movement developing in the West. Others were dismayed by the pagan corruptions introduced to the thinking and practice of the church. Another group bewailed the formalism in worship that characterized Western Christianity and sought in monasticism a more personal communion with God. These and other factors help to explain the growth of monasticism in the West.

With the passing time, the Western movement modified the character of monasticism. Although monasticism had originally been a lay movement, Western monasticism made priests of all who took monastic vows. Furthermore, the Western movement used monasticism as an instrument to advance the very church system against which it was in part a protest. Monks became missionaries and front-line soldiers of Christianity. In fact, monastic orders have been at the forefront of every victory achieved by the Roman Church since the Middle Ages.

(Document 10)

The Benedictine Rule

Benedict of Nursia wrote a detailed code to govern monastic life. The following selection from Section 33 discusses whether monks should have anything of their own.

More than anything else is this special vice to be cut off root and branch from the monastery, that one should presume to give or receive anything without the order of the abbot, or should have anything of his own. He should have absolutely not anything: neither a book, nor tablets, nor a pen—nothing at all. For indeed it is not allowed to the monks to have their own bodies or wills in their own power. But all things necessary they must expect from the Father of the monastery; nor is it allowable to have anything which the abbot did not give or permit. All things shall be common to all, as it is written: "Let not any man presume or call anything his own." But if any one shall have been discovered delighting in this most evil vice: being warned once and again, if he do not amend, let him be subjected to punishment.

Benedict of Nursia was the best-known Western monk. About 500 Benedict became a hermit and in 529 founded a monastery at Monte Cassino, south of Rome. His system emphasized worship, manual labor, and study. In less than three hundred years monastic houses following his rule covered the European continent. Benedict was the person most responsible for shaping the monastic movement along practical lines and reconciling its ideals with those of the church.

The most important monastic reform occurred in the opening years of the tenth century. Duke William of Aquitaine funded a new monastery at Cluny in eastern France in 910. William wanted to free this monastery from the corrupting influence of secular control and interference from local bishops. He stipulated that the new monastery should be under the immediate jurisdiction of the pope. Earlier monasteries had been controlled by the bishop in whose diocese they were located. William began a new type of strict monasticism in a reform movement which brought his monasteries in direct loyalty and obedience to the pope. The new monastery followed the rule of

Benedict, strictly interpreted. This type of reform became popular and spread rapidly.

Developments during the next century changed the new type of monasticism even more. The abbots of Cluny began assuming jurisdiction over the new monasteries founded by Cluniac followers, as well as those embracing reform under Cluniac principles. The abbot of Cluny became the head of an extensive network of monasteries whose aims he could dictate and whose abbots he could appoint. Such an organization, whose head swore allegiance immediately to the pope, was greatly influential in undermining any episcopal and secular authority opposing the papacy.

Missionary Expansion

Rome did not promote missions to any extent until the sixth century. Reference has been made to the work of Ulfilas in the fourth century under the auspices of Eastern Christianity. Bishop Martin of Tours fought paganism vigorously in his country during the fourth century. Some missionary work was carried on in the British Isles. A Scotchman named Patrick, whose Christianity was not of the Roman Catholic type, evangelized Ireland in the early part of the fifth century, and an Irishman, Columba, preached extensively in Scotland in the latter part of the same century. Another Irish missionary, Columbanus (543-615), preached in southern Germany, in France, in Switzerland, and finally in Italy, where he died.

These missionaries were not under the direction of Rome, but they prepared the way for Roman Catholic authority. In 596 at the direction of Pope Gregory I (590-615), a Benedictine monk named Augustine and forty companions went to England as missionaries.

After a struggle with the differences in Christianity that they encountered in Ireland and Scotland, the Roman Catholic type of organization and worship prevailed. The Synod of Whitby (664) decreed that Roman Christianity should be practiced in all of England. The older type of Christianity disappeared.

From England, Roman Catholic missionaries moved to the Continent. Wilfrid, a Benedictine monk, who had been influential in establishing Roman Christianity in England, began mission work in what is now Holland about 678. He was followed by Willibrord about 690. The greatest of the Roman Catholic missionaries from England was Boniface. During the first half of the eighth century Boniface worked tirelessly in northwestern Europe to bring existing churches under

(Document 11)
Bede: Augustine Arrives in England

Pope Gregory I sent Augustine and a band of monks as missionaries to Britain. In his Ecclesiastical History of England, *Bede detailed Augustine's arrival in Kent in southern England. The king accepted Christianity. The missionary Augustine is known as Augustine of Canterbury to distinguish him from Augustine of Hippo, the African bishop and theologian.*

The powerful Ethelbert was at that time king of Kent; he had extended his dominions as far as the great river Humber, by which the southern Saxons are divided from the northern. On the east of Kent is the large Isle of Thanet, containing, according to the English way of reckoning, six hundred families.

In this island landed the servant of our Lord, Augustine, and his companions, being, as is reported, nearly forty men. They had, by order of the blessed Pope Gregory, brought interpreters of the nation of the Franks, and sending to Ethelbert, signified that they were come from Rome, and brought a joyful message, which most undoubtedly assured to all that took advantage of it everlasting joys in heaven, and a kingdom that would never end with the living and true God.

The king, having heard this, ordered them to stay in that island where they had landed and that they should be furnished with all necessaries till he should consider what to do with them. For he had heard of the Christian religion, having a Christian wife, of the royal family of the Franks, called Bertha, whom he had received from her parents upon the condition that she should be permitted to practice her religion with the bishop Liudhard, who was sent with her to preserve the faith.

Some days later the king came into the island, and sitting in the open air, ordered Augustine and his companions to be brought into his presence. For he had taken precaution that they should not come to him in any house, lest, according to an ancient superstition, if they practiced any magical arts they might impose on him, and so get the better of him. But they came furnished with divine, not magic, power, bearing a silver cross for their banner, and the image of our Lord and Saviour painted on a board; and singing the litany, they offered up their prayers to the Lord for the eternal salvation both of themselves and of those to whom they came.

Roman Catholic authority and to win the pagans. Other Roman Catholic missionaries pushed toward the north and east. Early in the ninth century Ansgar reached Denmark and Sweden. Cyril and Methodius, worked extensively in the Balkans during the same century. They were sent out by the Greek Church, but voluntarily transferred to the Roman Church.

As a result of this missionary activity the Roman Catholic Church brought vast populations under its control, instilling in them a loyalty that knew no ecclesiastical rivals.

Military and Political Aid

In the long run the barbarian invasions of the West brought new and important allies to the Roman Catholic Church. For a period the various marauding tribes caused considerable trouble, fighting with one another and with the Romans. By skillful and armed opposition, the popes at Rome were able to maintain some semblance of order during the death of one culture and the molding of another. They were the secular rulers of the city of Rome and through this gained prestige and power. Many of the barbarians were won quickly to Christianity. When Clovis, the great Frankish chieftain, decided to cast his lot with the Christian God in the closing years of the fifth century, his entire army made the same decision, although hardly on religious grounds. Furthermore, several of the popes, such as Gregory I (590-604), made alliances with tribal leaders nearby and secured a measure of political freedom.

The story of the alliance of the papacy with the Frankish kingdom will be told in more detail later. Notice, however, the papal alliance in the eighth century with the strongest military power in Europe greatly increased the expansion and development of authority of the Roman Church. First, the Frankish kings defeated the Lombards who were threatening Rome. Second, the Frankish leaders gave to the papacy a large territorial domain in the vicinity of Rome, marking the beginning of what became known as the "papal states." In 751 the pope crowned Pepin, the strong military leader of the Franks, king instead of crowning one of the hereditary line. What Pepin had asked for was simply the moral support of the papacy to forestall revolution in the Frankish kingdom during the change of the ruling house, but the prestige of a pope who could dispense, or at least ensure, kingdoms was greatly respected. When the pope crowned Charlemagne emperor in 800, there was a feeling that the pope had the authority to make or unmake emperors. The bishops of Rome and the king of the Franks were cooperating to revive the glory that was Rome.

Charlemagne

The greatest of the Frankish rulers was Charles the Great (Charlemagne) (771-814). As a military and political leader he had no peer in the Medieval era. He doubled the territory of his empire. More than that, the empire was consolidated and well administered during his reign. His contribution to the expansion of the Roman Church was greater than that of any of the popes. As he pushed his secular military conquests, Charlemagne carried Roman Christianity with him. By 777 he had destroyed the kingdom of the Lombards in northern Italy, replacing it with inhabitants who recognized the authority of the pope. He forcibly required the Saxons in northwestern Germany to accept Christianity. When he attacked countries already nominally Christian, he required them to come under the authority of the Roman pope, as in the case of the war against Bavaria.

Charlemagne made important contributions to education and literature. He combed Europe to secure scholars who would found schools and produce literature. He encouraged priests to widen their learning, in some cases to begin it. Charlemagne gave the Roman Church many gifts and great prestige.

Charlemagne viewed his relation to the church much as Constantine had. Even in matters of controversial theology he felt free to summon synods and issue authoritative decrees. At the Synod of Frankfurt in 794 Charlemagne took a position opposite to that of a general council—that of Nicaea in 787— and also that of the pope— by forbidding image reverence and worship.

Secular support of Charlemagne probably did more to advance the papal cause than any other single factor in this period.

Forged Documents

The Roman popes during this period effectively used two important forgeries. The first was known as the *Donation of Constantine.* This spurious document asserted that when the Emperor Constantine had moved his capital to Constantinople in 330, he had donated to the bishop of Rome sovereignty over the Western world and had ordered all Christian clergy to obey the Roman bishop. The forgery was a crude one, for it had literary and historical reflections of the eighth century. It was probably produced about 754 in an effort to induce Pepin the Short and his successors to recognize the secular claims of the papacy in the West. Yet it was a successful forgery. Not only did Pepin give to the papacy the land in Italy conquered from the Lombards, but his successors recognized the *Donation* as genuine and based their conduct on it. The forgery was not discovered until the fifteenth century, long after the document had served its purpose.

The other documents involved in the same forgery were known as the *Pseudo-Isidorian Decretals*. Isidore of Seville had collected genuine ecclesiastical laws and decretals in the seventh century and published them as a guide for future action. The forgery of some additional decretals took place about a century later. This was done to advance the office of the pope against the claims of the archbishops and metropolitans by quoting the primitive documents in papal favor. These were officially used by the popes after the middle of the ninth century. By the time they had been proved to be a forgery in the eighteenth century, this fraud also had been effective in establishing the power of the pope over the church.

Feudalism

Charlemagne's son and three grandsons continued his kingdom, but decay had begun to undermine it. The rule of the Carolingian line (the line of Charles) broke down in the closing years of the ninth century. With the decline of a strong central government, the movement known as feudalism developed. When there was no central king, local leaders organized themselves and those whom they could control in small armies and small kingdoms. The size of the kingdom depended on the strength of the leader. Sometimes it consisted simply of a city; sometimes it included large areas. Each kingdom became a complete monarchy. The sovereign, or ruler, required that all in the area of his kingdom swear personal fealty to him.

The lowest class in this system was the *serfs*. These men and women were the slave laborers and were treated as property, bound to the soil. Above them in dignity were the *freedmen*, who were not slaves, but had no privileges and very little liberty. The *leudes* held land by the favor of the sovereign, administering sometimes small tracts and sometimes vast areas. The *leudes* exercised complete supervision over the freedmen and the serfs beneath them. The more important of the *leudes* served as a sort of advisory council to the sovereign and assisted in community functions, such as administration of justice and community enterprises. When enemies threatened, all of these vassals took arms to protect the rights of the sovereign.

At first glance it might appear that feudalism would greatly harm the interests of the Roman Catholic system. Some of the petty sovereigns might be unfriendly to the pretensions of the pope. The immediate result of feudalism was a decline in the authority and prestige of the papal office. Bishops were *leudes* in many of these small kingdoms and were forced to take the oath of allegiance to the secular sovereign. Religious work was neglected because of secular duties.

When measured in terms of centuries, feudalism did not permanently injure the papal system. Bishops sometimes became sovereigns in small kingdoms or as vassals sometimes received large grants of land from the sovereign. Subsequently, much of this land fell into the hands of the Roman Church. In addition, a popular reaction against secular authority resulted in a feeling of affection and loyalty among the lower classes for religious leadership. All of these factors in feudalism worked to the advantage of the Roman system, even when papal prestige and authority were at a low ebb.

Internal Developments

Worship

During the period from 451 to 1050 the Roman Catholic method of worship began to be copied throughout the West. Variations in language, order, and liturgy were eliminated as much as possible. Worship centered on the observance of Mass (the Supper), described previously, and had become more than a sacrament to bring grace to the one partaking; it was now looked on as the sacrifice of Christ again—the shedding of His blood and the breaking of His body. The symbolism had become literal. The wine was not yet withheld from the people. Although the church had not made an official pronouncement on the subject, it was generally understood that something happens to the bread in the mass to change it to the body of Christ. An extensive system of mediating saints had grown up. People invoked martyrs by name, asking for their intercession. The worship of the virgin Mary also increased during this period. The story was spread that she had been taken immediately to heaven at her death. People began offering prayers to Mary for her help and intercession. Relics became an increasingly important part of religious life. The number of sacraments was not fixed. Some theologians argued for simply two (baptism and the Lord's Supper), some insisted upon five, while others would have a dozen. Auricular confession had been well established, and the idea of merit from external works became widespread. Monasticism of the Benedictine type covered Europe.

Doctrinal Controversies

Most of the doctrinal controversies Roman popes engaged in originated in the speculations of the East. These controversies were influential in establishing ecclesiastical and secular relationships. In this period the papacy directly asserted its authority, not only over ecclesiastical rivals, but over secular powers as well.

One of the first disputes occurred when the patriarch of Constantinople refused to banish a heretic. Pope Felix III (483-92) attempted to excommunicate the patriarch, dismissing him from the priesthood, cutting him off from Catholic communion and from the faithful. Felix asserted that his authority as the successor of Peter enabled him to do this. Even the Eastern bishops who had been loyal to the papacy informed Felix that he had no power of this kind, and they chose communion with Constantinople rather than with Rome. For thirty-five years this schism continued until a succeeding pope healed the schism with no loss of dignity.

Monophysite controversy. One very important doctrinal controversy remained unresolved from previous eras—the question of the nature of Christ. The Council of Chalcedon (451) had defined the nature of Christ as being twofold—completely divine and completely human. Conciliar action did not convince everyone in the East. The opponents of this decision took the name of Monophysites (one nature). Practically all of Egypt and Abyssinia, part of Syria, and most of Armenia took up Monophysitism and have retained it to the present. In an effort to mollify this large section of the Eastern World, Emperor Zeno (474-91) at Constantinople issued a decree that practically annulled the definition of Chalcedon, but the only result was to alienate the West.

In another effort to placate the Monophysites, Emperor Justinian (527-65) issued a series of edicts in 544 that also compromised the Chalcedonian definition in favor of the Alexandrian interpretation by saying that the human nature of Christ was subordinate to the divine. Pope Vigilius (538-55), who owed his office to imperial influence, at first refused to accept the action of Justinian, but imperial pressure in 548 induced him to consent. Two years later he changed his mind and refused to attend a council to discuss the question. At the conclusion of the council in 553, Pope Vigilius was excommunicated and Justinian's edicts were given conciliar authority. The pope apologized and accepted the council's action, and the excommunication was lifted.

Another attempt was made to conciliate the Monophysites. Through the influence of Patriarch Sergius of Constantinople, Emperor Heraclius set forth a doctrinal interpretation that brought favorable response from the Monophysites in 633. This interpretation shifted the area of discussion from the *nature* to the *will* or *energy* of Christ. Heraclius taught that Christ had one divine-human energy or will. Pope Honorius (625-38) was consulted and replied that Christ had one will, but that the expression "energy" should not be used because it was unscriptural. Succeeding popes took the other side of the question. One of them, Pope Martin I (649-55), defied the order of Emperor Constans II (642-68) not to discuss the question and assembled a Roman synod in 649 that, among other things, condemned the emperor's order. The emperor promptly seized the pope and sent him into exile to die. The Monophysites, meanwhile, had been overcome by the Islamic invasion; so to please Rome and restore unity, Emperor Constantine IV (668-85) summoned the sixth universal council at Constantinople in 680-81 that asserted Christ had two wills. Interestingly enough, this council condemned Pope Honorius as a heretic.

Iconoclastic controversy. Probably the bitterest of the doctrinal controversies began in the eighth century and is known as the "iconoclastic [image-destroying] controversy." The use of images in worship had become quite popular in both Eastern and Western Christianity since the time of Constantine, who died in 337. The earliest Christians had refused to keep any kind of idol or image either in the home or at church and for that reason were called atheists by second-century pagans. The influence of paganism ushered in extensive use of images, ostensibly at first, for the sole purpose of teaching through pictures and statues. These images soon began to be looked upon as possessing divine qualities. They were venerated, kissed, and, in some cases, worshiped by enthusiastic supporters. The Moslems objected strenuously to this idolatry and, partly as a political move to conciliate the Islamic caliph, Emperor Leo the Isaurian (717-41) issued an edict in 730 against the use of images. Despite the fanatical opposition of the monks, the images were removed from Eastern churches.

When the emperor commanded the churches in the West to remove images, he met further opposition. He argued with the pope that image worship is prohibited by both the Old and New Testament and by the early fathers, that it is pagan in its art and heretical in its doctrinal ideas. In reply Pope Gregory II (715-31) said that God had commanded the making of the cherubim and seraphim (images); that images preserve for the future the pictures of Christ and the saints; that the commandment against images was necessary to prevent the Israelites from idolatry, a danger that no longer existed; and that adoration and prostration before the images did not constitute worship, simply veneration. The controversy continued for more than a century.

Through political maneuvering by the regent Irene, the seventh universal Council of Nicaea in 787 upheld the right of image worship. Charlemagne flatly opposed the decree of this council and the position of the popes, insisting that images were for ornaments, not worship. During the controversy Pope Gregory III (731-41) pronounced the sentence of excommunication against anyone removing, destroying, or injuring images of Mary, Christ, and the saints. This position was upheld by succeeding popes, despite the opposition of Charlemagne. Emperor Leo the Armenian (813-20) voided the decrees of the Second Nicene Council of 787 as soon as he had taken office, but image worship won its final victory when the regent Theodora (842-67) ordered the images restored and the iconoclasts persecuted. A limitation was placed on images in the East, permitting only paintings and mosaics in the churches. Statues projecting beyond the plane surface were forbidden. No limitation of this kind was made in the West. Images were more venerated and widely used there as a result of the controversy.

Strong Popes

The expansion of papal authority during this long period (451-1050) rested, in the final analysis, on the able popes who occupied the chair at Rome. During the last years of his pontificate Leo I (440-61) showed his growing power by humiliating Archbishop Hilary of Arles by restoring a bishop whom Hilary had deposed legally and by having Hilary imprisoned for disobedience. He meddled with ecclesiastical rivalries in Greece and North Africa and claimed final authority for everything Christian.

Gelasius (492-96) asserted the primacy of the Roman pope in every church in the world; Symmachus (498-514) claimed that no tribunal on earth could try a pope. Gregory I (590-604) was probably the ablest pope of the Medieval period. By careful diplomacy he wooed imperial support. He established a practice of bestowing the pallium on every bishop, making the pope's consent necessary for a valid ordination or consecration. A part of his program emphasized the need for a celibate (unmarried) clergy. His theology was based on the sacramental system of the Medieval period and was notable especially for its emphasis on good works and purgatory. His missionary interest in England caused him to send Augustine, a monk. there in 596. He revised church music and ritual and worked toward making Rome's pattern uniform throughout the world. His encounter with the patriarch of Constantinople was not entirely successful (as will be seen in succeeding pages), but he did not allow this to diminish his exalted view of his office.

Nicholas I (858-67) was the last outstanding pope before the outbreak of anarchy. He expanded the missionary program, excommunicated the patriarch of Constantinople during a brief schism, required the emperor, Lothair II, to take back a divorced wife, and humiliated those archbishops who were tardy in obeying his instructions to the letter.

Anarchy and Confusion

The closing two centuries of this period provided a crucial test for the papacy. The events of this era will be discussed in more detail in chapter 9. Europe was in anarchy after about 880. The turmoil in Italy turned the papal office into a petty political prize. Between 896 and 904 there were ten popes, most of whom were disposed of by murder and treachery. The period from 904 to 962 is known as the "pornocracy," because the papal office was controlled by unscrupulous and wicked people. From 962 to about 1050 the popes were named and controlled by the German emperors of the reestablished empire. The papacy had reached its lowest point in prestige and authority, but a new day was dawning. Through an effective internal reform, the rise of orderly central governments, and the ability to use ecclesiastical weapons, the papacy reached new heights of power in ecclesiastical and secular realms.

Between 451 and 1050 the Roman Catholic Church and the papacy made remarkable advances. The barbarian invasions were disguised blessings. Monasticism provided militant and trained soldiers. Missions expanded Roman Catholic influence beyond the widely extended boundary of the new Roman Empire under Charlemagne. Doctrinal controversies generally worked to the benefit of the papacy, although Honorius was condemned as a heretic and Vigilius was humiliated by Eastern councils. The alliance of Rome with the Franks during the eighth and ninth centuries brought it land, prestige, and authority. The breakdown of that central government brought loss and humiliation to the papacy. The church had become so dependent upon the military and political strength of the state that it could not stand without them.

The struggle of the papacy to dominate ecclesiastical and secular authorities has been described in this chapter in terms of papal expansion. There was another side that should also be heard. The succeeding two chapters will deal with opposition from ecclesiastical rivals and from secular powers. The overlapping in the story will be justified by the different point of view that will be presented in these two chapters.

8

Religious Opposition
to Roman Authority

The Roman Catholic Church did not attain its dominant position without encountering strong opposition from other Christians. The dignity of the Roman diocese had always been recognized, but to create an ecclesiastical monarchy with the Roman bishop as its head was hardly in accord with the thinking of early Christian leaders. The earliest Roman bishops, about whom there is direct historical information, were rebuked by neighboring bishops for breaches in ecclesiastical and doctrinal matters. Before the close of the second century Roman bishops were condemned because they followed the Montanist heresy and were excommunicated for ecclesiastical laxity.

Weaknesses in Rome's Claims

Several definite weaknesses in the claims for primacy by the Roman Church existed, but three stand out as most important.

Relative to Apostolic Succession

Rome was not the only church with a strong tradition. Irenaeus (185) and Tertullian (200) point out that many churches were founded by the apostles and had apostolic writings. Corinth, Philippi, and Ephesus were mentioned in particular. Gregory I (590-604), one of the greatest of the Roman popes, admitted that the churches at Alexandria and Antioch had the same apostolic background as Rome. His letter said, "Like myself, you who are at Alexandria and at Antioch are successors of Peter, seeing that Peter before coming to Rome held the see of Antioch, and sent Mark his spiritual son to Alexandria. So, do not permit the see of Constantinople to eclipse your sees that are the sees of Peter." In other words, if the basis of Roman authority, as claimed, is succession from Peter, then Antioch and Alexandria should have a claim prior to that of Rome. As a matter of fact, if tradition constitutes the basis of authority, then Jerusalem, where Jesus established the first church, should have the primacy.

Relative to Peter

The claims of the Roman Church to universal dominion because of the alleged primacy of Peter were made very late in history. Innocent I (402-17) was the first Roman bishop to base his authority on the Petrine tradition. By that time, Rome was already recognized as one of the principal bishoprics in Christianity. Leo I (440-61) prepared the first scriptural exposition of later papal claims about the primacy of Peter, basing them, as previously discussed, on Matthew 16:18-19; Luke 22:31-32; and John 21:15-17.

In Matthew 16:18-19 the important words are "upon this rock," since the promise of binding and loosing is repeated to all the disciples on other occasions (see Matt. 18:18; John 20:23). What is the rock upon which Jesus would build His church? The greatest theologians of the first four centuries did not agree with the Roman view. Chrysostom (345-407) said that the rock was the faith of the confession; Ambrose (337-97) said that the rock was the confession of the universal faith; Jerome (340-420) and Augustine (354-430) interpreted the rock as Christ. Anyone wanting to be literal in interpreting this passage should also be literal in verse 23, where Jesus names Peter as Satan. The passages in Luke and John must be utterly twisted out of their meaning to support universal papal domination.

Furthermore, a reading of the New Testament fails to give the impression of any primacy on Peter's part. Apparently, Peter did not recognize it; he felt the need to give a labored explanation to the Jerusalem church for baptizing Cornelius. The other disciples apparently were ignorant of it, for James, not Peter, presided at the Jerusalem conference. Paul's sharp rebuke to Peter and Peter's admission of error suggest that Paul knew nothing of Peter's primacy.

The Roman Catholic claim that Peter was the first bishop of Rome and served in that capacity for twenty-five years is completely unsupported by Scripture or primitive tradition. Paul's letter to the Romans (about 58) makes no mention of Peter. Neither does the account of

Paul's residence in Rome in the Acts of the Apostles. The agreement made at the Jerusalem conference about 50 A.D. limited Peter's ministry to the Jews and Jewish Christians. The Roman Church was likely predominantly Gentile.

Relative to Primacy of the Roman Bishop

If antiquity and tradition possess any authority, the principle of the equality of all bishops should be upheld. This was a very ancient and universal belief. The New Testament shows that even the apostles respected the authority of the churches that they had established. Antioch did not ask Jerusalem for permission to begin the missionary movement, and Paul did not first consult Peter before preaching salvation to the Gentiles throughout the Roman Empire.

In the second century the same principle was followed. Bishop Irenaeus of Lyons condemned Bishop Eleutherius of Rome (174-89) for following after heresy and rebuked Bishop Victor of Rome (189-98) for intolerance, but he still recognized their ultimate right to have their own opinions. Origen (182-251) denied that the Christian church was built upon Peter and his successors. All the successors of the apostles, he said, are equally heirs of this promise. Cyprian (200-58) emphatically asserted the equality of all bishops, stating that each bishop holds the episcopacy in its entirety. Even Jerome (340-420), famous as a papal proponent and translator of the Greek and Hebrew Scriptures to the Vulgate (the official Latin version of the Bible), remarked that wherever a bishop was found, whether at Rome, Constantinople, Eugubium, or Rhegium, he had equality as a successor of the apostles with all other bishops. Pope Gregory I used a similar argument when protesting against the ecclesiastical pretensions of his rivals. If the patriarch of Constantinople was the universal bishop above all others, then bishops were not really bishops, but priests, wrote Gregory. Gregory argued that all bishops were equal, and if one was exalted above the others, the others would cease in reality to have the episcopal office.

The victory of Leo I at Chalcedon in 451 established him as the first Roman pope, at least in the thinking of many scholars. The victory grew out of the recognition of Leo's claims concerning Peter's primacy and the transference of that primacy to the Roman bishops through historic succession. Even this achievement did not destroy the ancient belief that one bishop is equal to another. Had it not been for the political and military support of the secular powers, the Roman bishop could never have asserted his claims, even in the West. Bishop Hilary of Arles fought strenuously to maintain this principle, but Leo humiliated him through political power. This was also true with Bishop Hincmar of Rheims in his struggle with Pope Nicholas in the ninth century.

Opposition to Roman Pretensions

Since Rome was the first and strongest bishopric in the West, opposition in that section of the Mediterranean world was nominal. Tertullian and Cyprian, bishop of Carthage, defied the Roman bishop, and through the Medieval era various bishops resisted the encroachments of papal power. Invasions by the Germanic tribes in the third and fourth centuries provided the opportunity for Roman Christianity to gain great multitudes of new followers who knew no rival loyalty; the Islamic seizure of North Africa in the seventh and eighth centuries eliminated any rivals from that area.

In the East the situation was different. Two outstanding religious centers vied for supremacy: *Antioch*, famous for its Pauline tradition, and *Alexandria*, viewed as Petrine in origin since it was thought that Peter had sent John Mark to that city as a leader. Even before the founding of Constantinople in 330 as the capital of the Roman Empire, and before the bishop of Jerusalem was strong enough to be recognized as a patriarch, these two cities had been ecclesiastical rivals. One of the causes for the influence of the bishop of Rome was that each of these rivals sought Roman support for his position against the other side. Consequently, appeals to the Roman bishop came frequently.

The Council of Nicaea (325) recognized the equality of the bishops of Rome, Antioch, and Alexandria. The Council of Constantinople in 381 raised the bishop of Constantinople to the dignity of a patriarch, and the Council of Chalcedon in 451 gave that position to the bishop of Jerusalem. Thus five strong bishops were potentially rivals for first place. The Roman bishop had the advantage. He was the only candidate from the West. Sharp and ancient rivalry kept the Eastern patriarchs constantly vigilant lest one should gain some favored place. Constant controversy and schism prevented careful organization and ecclesiastical consolidation in the East. The principal opposition to Rome came from Constantinople for two reasons: (1) the political situation of Constantinople ensured its prestige and power and (2) all of the rivals except Constantinople were overwhelmed by the Islamic invasion of the seventh century. These two elements deserve brief discussion.

The Rise of Constantinople

The move of the imperial capital from Rome to Constantinople in 330 brought it important ecclesiastical influence immediately. Within a half century after the establishment of the city as capital, Constantinople was the chief rival of Rome, mainly because of the work of Emperor Theodosius (378-95), who made Christianity the official state religion. The Council of Chalcedon in 451 reasserted the dignity of Constantinople and remarked that such eminence was due to the *political* importance of the city. Evidently, it took neither apostolic tradition nor religious orthodoxy to attain such a high place. By this time the bishop of Constantinople was simply a tool of the emperor in most respects. This situation is known as *caesaro-papacy,* the domination of the church by the emperor. The several controversies of the Eastern world made Christianity a potential political danger. So to preserve unity in the political sphere, it became necessary for the emperor to keep constant watch over the church. Doctrinally, Eastern Christianity developed the same sort of sacramentalism and sacerdotalism as Western Catholicism, although it practiced trine immersion for baptism.

Despite the inevitable clash between the strongest power of the East and that of the West, the day of reckoning was delayed because of invasions in each area. The Germanic invasion of the West and its far-reaching consequences have been described in chapter 7. The Islamic invasion of the East did not begin until the seventh century. Even before the Eastern collapse, it became apparent that the bishops in Alexandria, Antioch, and Jerusalem would not be able to stand up to the ecclesiastical power of Rome and Constantinople.

The bishop of Constantinople challenged the pretensions of the Roman bishop after the Council of Chalcedon (451) had placed special emphasis on the Constantinopolitan office. Reference was made in the previous chapter to the effort by Pope Felix III to excommunicate Patriarch Acacius of Constantinople in 484 and to the refusal of the Eastern world to accept such authority on the part of the pope. The story of Pope Vigilius and his humiliation by the East through imperial power in the Council of 553 has been told. The claims of the patriarch at Constantinople became more extravagant when Emperor Justinian (527-65) recaptured Italy from the barbarians in about 536 and began to control the pope. The ambitions of Constantinople were not different from those of Rome. No longer would Constantinople, the imperial capital, be second to Rome or even equal with Rome; it would supplant Rome.

In the last decade of the sixth century Bishop John of Constantinople claimed the title "ecumenical patriarch." At Rome, Pope Gregory I (590-604), unaided by military and political power, could only protest and scheme. He circulated letters among the bishops of the East, arguing that there could be no such thing as a universal bishop or pope, basing his statements on the principle of the equality of all bishops. He begged the patriarchs at Alexandria and Antioch not to recognize the claims of the bishop of Constantinople since they, like himself, were successors of Peter. The pope did not make any demands based on his alleged succession from Peter, nor did he excommunicate anyone. The battle of titles was temporarily won by the bishop of Constantinople, although Gregory assumed a new one—"servant of servants of God."

The Islamic Invasion

The opening years of the seventh century produced a religious and national movement that was destined to affect Christianity in East and West for almost a thousand years. Its founder was Mohammed (570-632). In his youth he was a camel driver and merchant of Mecca in Arabia. On his trips to Palestine, Mohammed had ample opportunity to observe the Jewish and Christian religions and to see the influence of Greek culture and Roman rule. In 610 he proclaimed a new religion that was a mixture of Jewish, Christian, Greek, and Roman elements, together with Arabian ideas and emphases. His system included prophets from Judaism (like Abraham and Moses) and Christianity (Christ) and outstanding military leaders from pagan history. The last and greatest prophet of God, however, was Mohammed, who supposedly was the Holy Spirit promised by Christ.

Mohammed's system was completely fatalistic, teaching that all things are already determined. An individual's good works prove that he or she is elected to a paradise of sensual and fleshly enjoyment. These good works include prayer, fasting, almsgiving, and war against the unbelievers. After Mohammed's death in 632, his followers planned to conquer the world. Striking westward, the Saracens overran Palestine and practically all of the East except Constantinople. Within a hundred years they had conquered all of North Africa, had

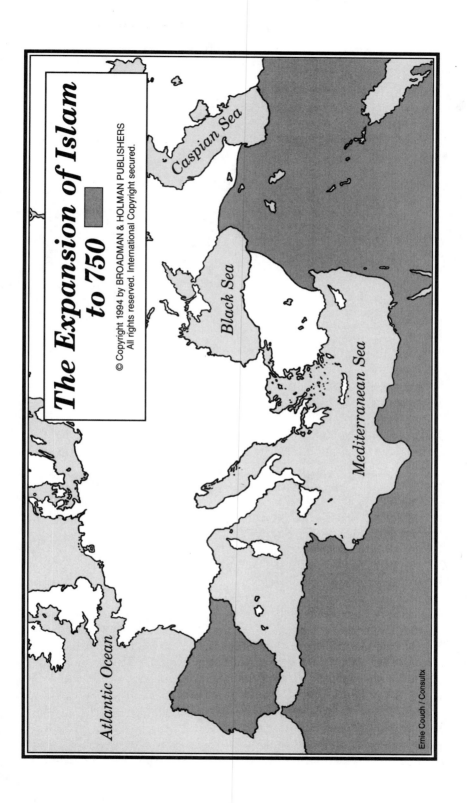

The Expansion of Islam to 750

© Copyright 1994 by BROADMAN & HOLMAN PUBLISHERS
All rights reserved. International Copyright secured.

Caspian Sea

Black Sea

Mediterranean Sea

Atlantic Ocean

Ernie Couch / Consultx

crossed the straits of Gibraltar into Spain, and were arrayed for battle near Tours, France. In 732 Charles Martel defeated them in a crucial encounter that determined the culture of Europe. Again, seven years later, Charles inflicted a severe defeat on them to save continental Europe from their devastations.

As a result of this movement, all of the Eastern rivals to Rome were swept away except Constantinople, which was under constant threat of capture. Wherever Islam ruled, Christianity became stagnant through rigorous repression. The invaders in Palestine and Alexandria destroyed priceless Christian manuscripts and books.

Renewed Controversy
Between East and West

The several doctrinal controversies of this period were discussed in the previous chapter. The bitterness of these struggles served to accentuate the ecclesiastical rivalry between Constanantinople and Rome. Added to these factors were ethnic differences, political distrust (especially after Charlemagne was crowned in Rome in 800), and doctrinal and ceremonial variations. It appeared that a permanent schism would occur in the ninth century. Patriarch Photius of Constantinople (858-76 and 878-86—twice in the office) rejected the claims of the Roman popes and instituted a vigorous program to win the bordering Slavic states to Greek Christianity. Photius charged that the Roman Church was heretical in doctrine and practice, particularly in amending one of the ancient creeds without calling a universal council to discuss the matter. Pope Nichols I (858-67) was one of the ablest of the Medieval popes and maintained Roman prestige. The issue was temporarily put on hold by the Synod of Constantinople in 869.

The controversy was renewed in the eleventh century, resulting in a permanent schism between Latin and Greek Christianity. Patriarch Michael Cerularius (1043-58) of Constantinople deliberately provoked the schism. He wanted to have more power and felt that a break with the West would offer the greatest opportunity for advancement. Without much difficulty, he was able to stir up the wrath of Pope Leo IX (1049-54).

In the conferences to discuss the situation, the ancient differences between Eastern and Western worship were debated. Rome used unleavened bread; Constantinople, leavened bread. Rome had added

---

(Document 12)
The East-West Anathema

The following section is from a letter that Pope Leo IX sent to Patriarch Michael Ceruliarius in 1053. During the following year the churches in the East and West separated from one another, a schism which still continues.

You are said to have publicly condemned the Apostolic and Latin Church, without either a hearing or a conviction. And the chief reason for this condemnation, which displays an unexampled presumption and an unbelievable effrontery, is that the Latin Church dares to celebrate the commemoration of the Lord's passion with unleavened bread. What an unguarded accusation is this of yours, what an evil piece of arrogance! "You place your mouth in heaven, while your tongue, going through the world," strives with human arguments and conjectures to undermine and subvert the ancient faith.

---

a word to the Nicene Creed teaching that the Holy Spirit proceeded from Father and Son; Constantinople denied that additions could be made to the creed without an ecumenical council. Rome required clerical celibacy; Constantinople allowed the lower clergy to marry. Rome allowed only bishops to anoint in confirmation; Constantinople allowed priests to do so. Rome allowed the use of milk, butter, and cheese during Lent. Constantinople did not. These differences were not the cause of the schism. By deliberate design the Roman representatives were irritated to the breaking point, and on July 16, 1054, East and West formally excommunicated one another. This division continues even today, but Rome and Constantinople have made progress toward reconciliation.

Dissent from Catholicism

Reference has been made in the previous period to dissenters from the Catholic and Roman Catholic Christianity. Montanism, Novatianism, and Donatism maintained themselves through several centuries of struggle. Nestorian, Monophysite, and Monothelite parties, denouncing both Roman and Greek Catholicism, have continued to the present day in considerable strength.

Jovinianus and Vigilantius

Two distinctly antipapal movements appeared in the Roman Church in the fourth and fifth centuries. One was headed by Jovinianus of Rome (about 378), who bitterly denounced the movement toward asceticism and righteousness by works. His main tenet asserted that a saved person does not need merits from fasting, celibacy, and withdrawal from the world. A similar movement was begun by Vigiliantius (about 395), who protested strongly against image worship, asceticism, and the honoring of relics. The first of these movements was condemned by Bishop Siricius of Rome (384-98) in a local synod, while the second was swallowed up in the barbarian invasions of the fifth century.

Paulicians

One of the important dissenting minorities during the Medieval period was the Paulicians. The origins of this group are obscure. Its general doctrinal position suggests that it grew out of primitive Armenian Christianity; its name came from veneration for Paul the apostle or from Paul of Samosata, bishop of Antioch until about 272. The Paulicians bitterly opposed the Roman, Greek, and Armenian churches as "satanic." They viewed Christ as the adopted Son of God. Their emphasis on the power of Satan has caused some to charge them with dualism. It is uncertain whether they observed the ordinances or viewed them as completely spiritual elements. They greatly venerated the apostle Paul and emphasized and practiced his ethical and moral teachings. Except under the iconoclastic emperors Leo the Isaurian (717-41) and Constantine Copronymus (741-75), the Paulicians were rigorously persecuted. In their zeal against images, they took the side of the Saracens and assisted in destroying and pillaging. During the eighth and ninth centuries, many Paulicians emigrated to Thrace and Bulgaria and from there to the lower Danubian regions. Some believe that the Bogomiles of the Balkans and the Cathari of southern France absorbed their teachings and continued their movement. Some think that the Anabaptists were a product of these influences.

Ecclesiastical opposition to Roman pretensions had Scriptures and primitive principles in their favor. The scriptural arguments for Rome's primacy were developed late in history and are unconvincing. The ancient principle of equality of bishops was overcome by Rome only through severe struggle and the use of military and political coercion.

Constantinople, the principal opponent of Rome, made a determined bid for first place. After numerous and bitter controversies, a permanent schism was effected in 1054. Other ecclesiastical rivals of Rome were overwhelmed by the Islamic invasion of the seventh century. These Arabic invaders succeeded in pushing to southern France before their defeat by Charles Martel in 732.

The record of ecclesiastical opposition to papal authority is very sketchy. Those within the hierarchical system who might oppose the domination of Rome would have thought twice before making outward protest or recording literary dissent. The only records were kept by those who looked on the dissenters as heretical schismatics. There must have been much dissent that had no voice, but during the centuries immediately following the eleventh, opposition to papal authority sprang up in every part of Western Christianity.

9

Secular Opposition
to Roman Authority

When Constantine assumed a friendly attitude toward Christianity and became sole emperor in 323, Christians hoped that tension between the secular state and Christianity was a thing of the past. Constantine issued imperial edicts making it possible for Christianity to develop in a favorable atmosphere. One reason for the removal of the capital of the empire to Constantinople was that Rome was crowded with pagan temples and memorials. At the Council of Nicaea (325) Constantine displayed a paternal attitude and until his death in 337, whatever his motives may have been, maintained a singularly constant devotion to the Christian movement. After Constantine's death, some segment of Catholic Christianity was conscious of the antagonistic or repressive aspect of secular power through the remainder of the period. Before discussing specific instances of this, it is well to give a summary of why secular opposition arose.

Reasons for Secular Opposition

Secular power struggled against Christianity for various reasons.

Religious antagonism. The Emperor Julian (361-63) opposed the Christian movement. His family was slain by the order of his uncle, the Christian emperor, and his personal resentment was transferred to the religion that his uncle professed. Julian had been interested in paganism as a student. On becoming emperor, Julian attempted to reintroduce a refined paganism, but the attempt failed.

A desire to control Christianity. For political or selfish purposes this desire led many secular rulers, both East and West, to impose severe restrictions on Christian leaders. As mentioned earlier, this condition was known as caesaro-papism.

Material possessions. The church's wealth was an excuse for attempts by some of the Germanic tribes to seize the land and goods of the Church.

Rivalry with secular powers. By the fifth century Roman popes were beginning to assert their right to rule not only the spiritual world, but the secular world as well. Such assertions, supported later on by ecclesiastical weapons, kept the papacy in constant struggle with secular power.

Internal controversies. Religious controversy, particularly in the East, caused secular restriction and repression and was very dangerous politically. Secular rulers considered it a political necessity to maintain control over Christianity.

Corruption and decay. Corruption and decay in Western Christianity brought the strong arm of imperial rule. Sometimes for religious reasons and sometimes for political considerations the late Medieval emperors appointed the occupants of the papal office and dictated their policies.

A brief summary of relations between the various secular powers and the developing Roman Church will provide historical examples of these several reasons for secular opposition.

Opposition from the
Roman Empire Before 476

The three sons of Constantine succeeded him in 337. One was killed in battle, one committed suicide, and the third, Constantius, ruled until 361. Constantius was an Arian Christian, and his long rule brought repression and antagonism to Nicene Christianity which included Rome. Athanasius, not the Roman bishop, was singled out as the target in the persecution of Nicene Christianity.

Emperor Julian (361-63) was anti-Christian in his attitude and actions. Had Constantine been a consistent Christian (or even a Christian at all), Julian might well have been reared to respect Christianity and to embrace it. Julian's brief reign and the fundamental weakness of the refined paganism that he tried to introduce blunted the force of his antagonism towards Christianity.

(Document 13)

Augustine: The Supreme Good of the City of God

Many skeptics blamed Christianity for the decline of the Roman Empire and the barbarian victories. Augustine replied that true reality was in the higher order of the city of God. Medieval church leaders used Augustine's arguments in their struggle for power against secular governments.

Since, then, the supreme good of the city of God is perfect and eternal peace, not such as mortals pass into and out of by birth and death, but the peace of freedom from all evil, in which the immortals ever abide, who can deny that that future life is most blessed, or that, in comparison with it, this life which now we live is most wretched, be it filled with all blessings of body and soul

and external things? And yet, if any man uses this life with reference to that other which he ardently loves and confidently hopes for, he may well be called even now blessed, though not in reality so much as in hope. But the actual possession of the happiness of this life, without the hope of what is beyond, is but a false happiness and profound misery. For the true blessings of the soul are not now enjoyed; for that is no true wisdom which does not direct all its prudent observations, manly actions, virtuous self-restraint, and just arrangements, to that end in which God shall be all and all in a secure eternity and perfect peace.

The basic rivalry between church authority and secular authority was made clear in this period. Augustine's very influential writing, the *City of God*, set secular and religious authority against one another and magnified their incompatibility. Fifth-century popes grasped the ideal, soon beginning to describe the relationship between the two powers as two swords—the *spiritual* sword as greater than the *secular* sword.

Struggle with the Germanic Tribes (476-800)

It is difficult to describe in a few words the complex story of the barbarian invasions of the West, but the movement can be summarized in six general periods.

The Breakdown of Old Roman Authority (About 392)

Since primitive times the Empire had maintained a string of garrisons across the northern frontier in order to restrain Germanic tribes to the north and east. Twice during the third century the Gothic tribes almost succeeded in invading the Empire. Finally, because of the increasing pressure of less civilized and stronger tribes pushing south and west from central Asia, the Empire allowed the Visigoths to cross the Danube and secure refuge in the Empire proper. Aroused in 378 by alleged mistreatment, the Visigoths met the Roman army in the Battle of Adrianople and inflicted a severe defeat. Emperor Theodosius (379-95) was able to control them, but at his death the deluge began. The Visigoths were beaten away from Constantinople, but moved westward to capture Rome in 410. They took Gaul two years later and began to rule in what is now France and Spain. The dikes had been breached, and barbaric tribes of every sort flowed into the Western empire. Vandals, Alans, and Suevi entered Gaul and Spain; the Franks and Burgundians settled in Germany; the Angles, Saxons, and Jutes occupied England; the Vandals moved through Spain to conquer North Africa.

The Rule of the
Army (Until About 493)

A century of confusion and conflict followed the barbarian invasions. Army chieftains became rulers. In 476 a mutiny by the Germanic tribes in the army resulted in the overthrow of the nominal Roman government; a German general became king. Although this was a minor event, it has often been considered the end of the Roman Empire in the West.

The Rule of Theodoric
the Ostrogoth (493-526)

In 493 a new wave of barbarians invaded Italy—the Ostrogoths, the eastern Goths from Russia. Their chief, Theodoric, ruled from Ravenna in northern Italy and was successful in maintaining order.

The Re-establishment of
Imperial Control (535-72)

Justinian the Great became emperor in Constantinople in 527 and immediately made plans for conquering the West. By 534 the Vandals of North Africa had been defeated and the Ostrogoth kingdom in Italy had been attacked. Justinian maintained imperial control of the West during his lifetime.

The Kingdom of the Lombards (572-754)

Late in the sixth century the Lombards swept south into Italy and captured the northern section. Although they did not take Rome, their strong military power prevented any other tribes from doing so. They were a constant threat to Rome's security, but their presence guaranteed the bishops of Rome a certain freedom from Constantinople.

The Rise of the Franks (754-800)

The tribe known as the Franks was destined to become the dominating power in all Europe. As early as the second century, Romans had fought to keep this tribe, along with others, from crossing the Rhine in northern Germany. With the breakthrough of the Visigoths in the fourth century, the Franks had fought their way into southern Germany and eastern France. An event of great significance for Christianity occurred in 496. Influenced by his wife, who was an orthodox Christian, and his great victory over the Alemanni at Strassburg in 496, the Frankish chieftain Clovis (481-511) adopted Christianity and was baptized, along with his army. Succeeding kings enlarged the Frankish kingdom until it included most of what is now France.

When the Lombards in northern Italy threatened to capture Rome in 739, Pope Gregory III appealed for help to Charles Martel, the military dictator (although not the king nor of the kingly line) of the Franks, without success. Charles' son, Pepin the Short, entered into friendly relations with the papacy after the death of his father. His plan was to seize the kingship from one of the weak descendants of Clovis who had succeeded to that office by right of inheritance. In order to forestall serious opposition and perhaps revolution, Pepin wanted to secure ecclesiastical approval, along with the good will of the Frankish nobility. In return, Pepin could offer ample protection against the Lombards. Gladly the papacy entered into this trade, and Pope Zacharias (741-52) arranged for the anointing of Pepin as king of the Franks in 751. The new line was known as the Carolingians, after either Charles Martel or Charles the Great.

Pepin kept his part of the bargain. By 756 he had forced the Lombards to recognize the pope as the sovereign over a large area of land in central and northern Italy. This was the beginning of the papal states that the Roman Church held until 1870. Perhaps the desire to secure those lands motivated the forgery at Rome at this time known as the *Donation of Constantine*. This forged document asserted that Emperor Constantine in 330 had given to the Roman bishop all of the western lands. At any rate, Pepin and his successors were greatly influenced by this forgery.

Empire Versus Church (After 800)

Pepin's son was Charles the Great (Charlemagne). His aid to the Roman Catholic Church was described in the last chapter. He dominated the Western world ecclesiastically, in addition to ruling it as sovereign. The climax, not only to his rule but to the Middle Ages, came in 800 when Pope Leo III (795-816) crowned him as Roman Emperor. This act, apparently done by the initiative of the pope, shaped ideas and history for a millennium. For one thing, it was popularly looked on as reestablishing the old Roman Empire in the West, an office unfilled since Constantine moved the capital to Constantinople in 330. Ethnic and sectional patriotism hailed the beginning of a day that would restore the ancient glory to Rome and the West. In the second place, this restoration was viewed as proceeding from divine purpose. God had provided a secular power that was the counterpart to the spiritual power in the Roman Church. In the third place, papal prestige was lifted to new heights. The crowning of Pepin the Short, bestowing the imperial title on him, marked the pope as the giver of the greatest secular blessings of the earth. This prestige was enhanced when the Eastern Emperor Leo V (813-20) recognized the validity of the transaction. Finally, the papacy had given birth unknowingly to its greatest rival through the remainder of the Medieval period. Perhaps Pope Leo had in mind the ideal described in Augustine's *City of God*. If so, the results must have been disappointing. The earthly ruler controlled the heavenly; Charlemagne dominated the church, appointing bishops at will and for the most part dictating papal policy.

After Charlemagne died, his weak son, Louis, ruled until 840; his three grandsons divided the empire among themselves in 843. The three divisions, carved out at this time, became the states of Germany and France and the intervening strip.

Anarchy and Papal Degradation

The Carolingian line collapsed about 880. Strong nobles ruled feudal kingdoms as well as the church. After the pontificate of Nicholas I (858-67), the papal office sank to indescribably low depths. Violence, murder, and mutilation were practiced on its occupants as various political factions intermittently seized control. New invasions terrified and devastated the population. Northmen and Hungarians swept the northern plains. The Arabs in North Africa and Spain were on the verge of winning the victory they had been unable to accomplish because of Charles Martel in 732. From bases in Africa, Egypt, and Spain, these raiders captured Corsica, Sardinia, and Sicily, then Palermo and Messina in Italy proper. Rome was sacked in 841.

The German Re-establishment of the Empire

A new direction was taken in the middle of the tenth century when Pope John XII (955-64) appealed to the German king Otto I (936-73) for aid against the military attacks of Berengar II, an Italian noble seeking the imperial title. Otto had already invaded Italy in 951 with considerable success; ten years later, complying with the pope's request, Otto completed the task. In 962, Otto was crowned Roman Emperor by John XII. He and his successors exercised complete control of the papacy for a century. Otto III (983-1002) appointed the first German pope in 996 and the first French pope in 999.

Before the middle of the eleventh century, the emperors were looking longingly for a church reform. Henry III (1039-56) attempted to introduce such reform by brusquely ending a papal schism involving three claimants and appointing German popes who agreed to reform measures. His last nomination was his cousin, a zealous reforming bishop, who became Leo IX (1049-54).

Thus at the close of this period the papacy was under the complete domination of secular authority. This situation, however, was about to be remedied. The reforming work of Leo IX and the rise of the monk Hildebrand, who became Pope Gregory VII (1073-85), began the movement to rid the Roman Church of secular control.

In its relations with secular powers the Roman Catholic Church came out second best during this period. Even when such power was friendly, as in the case of Charlemagne, it reserved the right to handle Christianity as a part of imperial administration. The various popes strongly asserted the ideal introduced by Augustine, namely, the spiritual power in the world is superior to secular power and one day will completely overcome it. This ideal was not attained during the period from 325 and 1050.

The papacy made significant advances, however, despite many hardships. The forgeries of the eighth century greatly increased papal prestige. The *Donation of Constantine* was doubtless influential in causing Pepin to make the donation of large areas of land in central and northern Italy to the pope. Forged decretals bearing the name of Isidore of Seville influenced the relationship of the papacy to the secular power in that they established Rome as the focal point of the Christian movement.

The papacy was undergoing one of its greatest humiliations during the centuries before the close of this period; however, the end of this situation was near. Within a century, the papal office would regain its dominant place in ecclesiastical life and be on its way toward dominating secular authority.

10

Roman Catholic Domination

The authority and prestige of the Roman Catholic pope reached its height from 1050 to 1215. Capitalizing on the claims made before the deluge of anarchy and feudalism and the domination of the two empires (800 and 962), the Roman Church not only regained its power, but it was victorious in new and greater conquests. Many contributing factors made this possible. One principal factor was the attitude of the people. Tired of war and violence, people were ready to follow any leader who promised peace and justice, the key words of the papal promise. There was universal rejoicing when the spiritual weapons of the papacy began to overpower swords and spears. Secular unity had been destroyed in feudalism and the hope of one universal spiritual government, resting on sure and eternal foundations, provided an almost irresistible appeal.

The Roman Catholic revival began from the inside with a thorough reform and regrouping of papal forces; the revived papal monarchy dominated the Western world, both secular and spiritual. A brief discussion of the most important movements contributing to this revitalization of the papacy and the Roman Church follows.

Monastic Reform

The Benedictine monks had been one of the foremost factors in the expansion of the papacy and the Roman system. They were skilled both as missionaries carrying the gospel and farmers tilling the soil. Augustine's success in winning England is more spectacular than the

work of many of his brethren who formed small bands and conquered nature in large sections of the European wilderness, but the
accomplishments of the latter were almost as important. Monasteries
sprang up all over Central Europe, bringing large tracts of land under
the control of the Roman Church and providing a place of refuge for
the needy, a retreat for scholars, and a conservatory of learning
through the period of the Dark Ages. These monasteries, however,
did not escape the secular spirit of their times. Even though monks
were required to take an oath of poverty, for example, nothing was
said about the material possessions of monasteries. Through valiant
community of effort, through gifts of admirers, through special religious offerings for services, and by other means, the monasteries
became wealthy. The monks could not *own* possessions, but they
could *use* them, and this distinction made it possible to circumvent
entirely the idea of personal poverty. Other abuses crept into the system. Feudal lords sometimes lavished goods on the monasteries,
demanding (and securing in return) the right to name the abbots and
direct their policies. Monasteries became places of pleasant and lei-
surely service by the closing years of the ninth century.

A reform was needed and soon came. Under the leadership of its
strong abbot, the monastery at Cluny began a reform in the opening
years of the tenth century. Strict ascetical living was emphasized once
again. Complete separation from secular favors and control took
place. The pope became the immediate superior rather than the local
bishop. Several monastic communities banded together under the
leadership of the Cluniac abbot to expand this reform movement. The
religious sincerity and fervor of the movement induced support and
admiration. Even the secular rulers in Germany, the emperors,
encouraged the reform after 962. One might find it a revealing commentary on the decayed condition of the papacy in those centuries
that the popes in Rome opposed this reform, even though its main
purpose was to strengthen the papacy through spiritual reform.
Emperor Henry III (1039-56) allowed no Roman opposition to the
Cluniac movement to blunt the reform, however, and in 1049
appointed his cousin, who supported the Cluniac reform tradition, as
Pope Leo IX. Without delay Pope Leo began reform in Rome along the
lines of the Cluniac movement, choosing as one of his assistants a
young and zealous reformer named Hildebrand. Together Leo and
Hildebrand brought the reform to the papacy and made possible the

tremendous upsurge of the Roman Church during the succeeding centuries.

The Crusades

The Crusades were another factor that figured into the rapid rise of the papacy. This movement began as an effort to recapture Jerusalem from the hands of the Moslems. For centuries the Roman Church had laid great emphasis on pilgrimages as a means of securing forgiveness for post-baptismal sins. A pilgrimage to Jerusalem was considered the great satisfaction for sin. During the seventh century the Moslems captured the Holy Land but allowed pilgrims to visit Jerusalem for religious purposes. In the eleventh century the land was overcome by the Seljuk Turks, a new Islamic power from Asia Minor. These Turks were completely unsympathetic to any pilgrimages by Christians. For centuries, Western Europe had played with the idea of a vast attack on the Moslems to rescue the Holy Land. Great impetus had come in 911 from the conversion of the Normans, a warlike people who enjoyed nothing more than fierce fighting. The Normans had conquered areas of France, England, and southern Italy, and they had been particularly effective in driving the Moslems out of Sicily, Sardinia, and Corsica. Because they were seafaring people, the Normans were especially equipped to attack the Holy Land; they could sail the Mediterranean almost in striking distance of Jerusalem. Furthermore, the conversion of Hungary had provided a point of departure at the very edge of the Turkish Empire and had shortened the distance through hostile territory by thousands of miles.

The popes had hinted at the idea long before it was carried out. Pope Silvester II (999-1003) had spoken of a grand crusade against the Turks; Gregory VII (1073-85) had actively planned the attack, but because of his struggle with Emperor Henry IV he was unable to secure the secular support necessary for such an undertaking. In 1095 the Greek Emperor Alexius appealed to the West not to delay such a crusade any longer. The Turks were threatening to take Constantinople. In that year Pope Urban II (1088-99) called on secular powers to devote themselves to this divine crusade, promising forgiveness of sin to those dying in the effort. Europe was swept with the passion of slaughtering for the cross (the word *crusade* comes from the word *cross*).

The first Crusade began in 1096 when about half a million soldiers moved toward Jerusalem. As this enormous and undisciplined army moved eastward, it lived off the countryside, devastating the areas through which it moved as though it were a hostile army. About forty thousand soldiers finally reached Jerusalem and captured it. There were about eight other Crusades, including the tragic Children's Crusade in 1212.

The results of the Crusades were manifold. In a sense they worked toward the immediate strengthening of the papacy. They brought an immediate prestige to the papacy that could give orders to princes everywhere and assume international leadership. The papacy profited enormously from the financial standpoint. The people lavishly bestowed gifts on the Roman Church, and they arranged to give their possessions to the church in the event that they did not return. The papacy used the Crusades as an excuse to levy a new ecclesiastical tax, which continued to be enforced long after the crusading movement had ceased.

Papal methods were both aided and shaped by the crusades. It became an accepted idea that the pope could call on all faithful secular rulers to march against heretics anywhere, including minority religious dissenters in Europe and secular princes who refused to be obedient to papal orders. A new and powerful weapon for coercion had been formed.

The Crusades were based on the idea that had brought relics and fetishism to popularity. Extreme reverence for, and even actual worship of, physical remains provided a substantial motive for the struggle to recapture the greatest of all relics, Jerusalem. During the period of the crusades almost every sort of relic was allegedly brought back from Jerusalem. When Jerusalem was recaptured by the Turks, the market value of relics went out of sight; cutting off the source of relics brought inflation. Fraud and misrepresentation were rampant in the trafficking of these items. The use of the rosary increased considerably in the Roman Catholic system during this period.

In the long run, the Roman Catholic Church was harmed by the Crusades. The popes weakened their prestige by continuing to press for new Crusades after the fad had gone out of style. The continuance of the Crusade tax did not increase papal popularity either.

The Crusades opened the eyes of many to a new world. Those who had invaded the Eastern world were exposed to new literature, new interests, and new ideas, and they brought these things back with them. Some of the popes became enamored with the ancient literary remains and forms and emphasized culture more than Christianity. The Renaissance was not far off when the minds and hearts of the people were stirred and enlightened. Such general diffusion of new ideas could not fail to undermine an institution based on superstition and fear.

The Crusades introduced new economic and social reforms. The reforms fostered trade and commerce. New items for manufacture created a need for industry. The middle class, neither peasant nor prince, developed. Those returning from the wars flooded the cities, modifying social and economic forms.

Politically the papacy was not permanently strengthened. The breakdown of feudalism resulted in the rise of nations, a potential threat to papal power. As the strong nobles were slain in the struggle, the monarchs in the various states became more powerful. Even the opposite situation in the German states did not work out to papal advantage. The German knights refused to go on the Crusades. The tardy decline of feudalism in the German states may have been an immediate help to the papacy in its effort to divide and conquer, but this situation brought general unrest among the Germans. When the struggle came, the papacy had to fight individual battles in scores of small feudal areas instead of simply winning over the monarch in a large domain.

Scholasticism

The third movement that made a distinct contribution to the rapid recovery of the Roman Church has been called *scholasticism*. The term refers to the teachings of the scholars. Charlemagne encouraged the education of the clergy and the upper class. Perhaps from this inspiration the universities of the twelfth century arose, principally in order to teach civil and ecclesiastical law. These institutions of learning became small, self-governing cities within cities. Every European city ardently longed for its own university during the thirteenth and fourteenth centuries. Two types of universities developed. In Italy, growing out of considerable political freedom, the students organized their own schools and administered them; in France, following the monastic system, the faculty constituted both the teachers and the administrators of the school. The curriculum included theology, medicine, canon and civil law, and the liberal arts (grammar, logic, rhetoric, music, arithmetic, geometry, and astronomy). The religious scholars of these schools developed the system known as "scholasticism." It was based on a method of thought (deductive reasoning) and a preconceived conclusion (the intellectual proof of papal doctrine). Deductive reason begins with a general truth that is authoritative and develops subsidiary refinements by applying valid principles. The important factor is the starting point. Scholasticism, expanding on the thought forms and philosophy of Aristotle and Plato, started with the Bible, the decrees of popes, the canons of councils, and tradition as authoritative; from these it reasoned out the doctrines of the Roman Church. Although the various schools of thought differed in their viewpoint relative to the place of reason and revelation, the total result of scholasticism was to undergird with philosophy the Roman Catholic system. Bible and tradition are so intermingled in the doctrinal development of the Roman Church that any attempt to eliminate tradition would require a complete redefinition of every doctrine.

Some of the leading scholastics were Johannes Scotus Erigena (about 800), Riescellinus (about 1090), Anselm (1033-1109), Abelard (1079-1142), Alexander of Hales (about 1245), Albertus Magnus (1206-80), Thomas Aquinas (1225-74), John Duns Scotus (1265-1308), and William of Occam (about 1349).

Strong Papal Leadership

Beyond the contributions of monasticism, the Crusades and scholasticism, the spectacular rise of the Roman Catholic papacy to the height of power in the period from the eleventh to the thirteenth centuries was the work of three strong popes. Had all the contributory factors existed, the Roman Church still could not have attained the place it did without the initiative and determination of the strong leaders who headed it.

Gregory VII (1073-85)

The first of these popes was Gregory VII, better known as Hildebrand. Under the reforming program of Leo IX, Hildebrand was appointed a cardinal in 1049. Soon he assumed leadership in the policies of the papal government and did not relinquish control until his death in 1085. He endeavored to carry out three principles:

1. To eliminate internal opposition to papal rule within the Roman Church;

2. To free the papacy from external influence in the appointment of bishops and the election of popes;

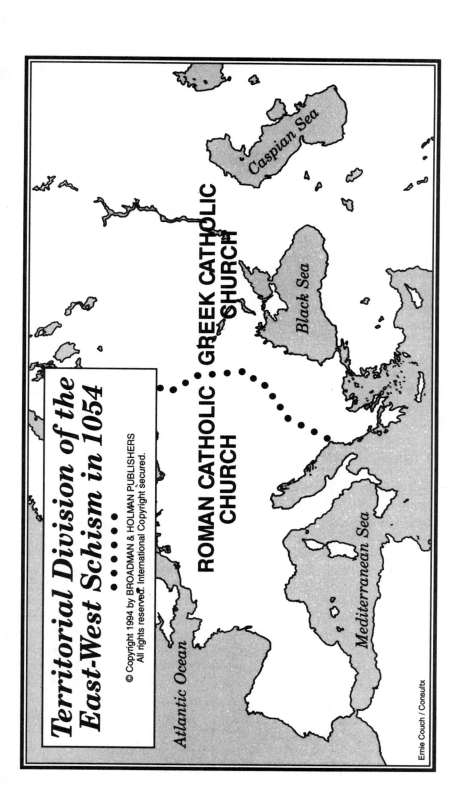

Territorial Division of the
East-West Schism in 1054

Atlantic Ocean

ROMAN CATHOLIC : GREEK CATHOLIC
CHURCH

CHURCH

Caspian Sea

Black Sea

Mediterranean Sea

Ernie Couch / Consultx

(Document 14)
Anselm: Faith Seeking Understanding

Anselm of Canterbury was one of the founders of Scholasticism and one of the most original thinkers of the Middle Ages. He tried to interrelate faith and reason, but he argued that we must believe in God if we are to understand Him. In the following passage Anselm argued that God is the Being of which we cannot imagine a greater. This has sometimes been called the ontological argument for the existence of God.

Therefore, O Lord, who grantest to faith understanding, grant unto me that, so far as Thou knowest it to be expedient for me, I may understand that Thou art, as we believe; and also that Thou art what we believe Thee to be. And of a truth we believe that Thou art somewhat than which no greater can be conceived. Is there then nothing real that can be thus described? For the fool hath said in his heart, There is no God. Yet surely even that fool himself when he hears me speak of somewhat than which nothing greater can be conceived understands what he hears, and what he understands is in his understanding, even if he does not understand that it really exists. It is one thing for a thing to be in the understanding, and another to understand that the thing really exists. For when a painter considers the work which he is to make, he has it indeed in his understanding; but he doth not yet understand that really to exist which as yet he has not made. But when he has painted his picture, then he both has the picture in his understanding, and also

understands it really to exist. Thus even the fool is certain that something exists, at least in his understanding, than which nothing greater can be conceived; because, when he hears this mentioned, he understands it, and whatsoever is understood, exists in the understanding. And surely that than which no greater can be conceived cannot exist only in the understanding. For if it exists indeed in the understanding only, it can be thought to exist also in reality; and real existance is more than existance in the understanding only. If then that than which no greater can be conceived exists in the understanding only, then that than which no greater can be conceived is something a greater than which can be conceived: but this is impossible. Therefore it is certain that something than which no greater can be conceived exists both in the understanding and also in reality.

Not only does this something than which no greater can be conceived exist, but it exists in so true a sense that it cannot even be conceived not to exist. For it is possible to form the conception of an object whose non-existence shall be inconceivable; and such an object is of necessity greater than any object whose existance is conceivable; wherefore if that than which no greater can be conceived can be conceived not to exist; it follows that that than which no greater can be conceived is not that than which no greater can be conceived [for there can be thought a greater than it, namely, an object whose non-existance shall be inconceivable]; and this brings us to a contradiction. And thus it is proved that that thing than which no greater can be conceived exists in so true a sense, that it cannot even be conceived not to exist: and this thing art Thou, O Lord my God, existest in so true a sense that Thou canst not even be conceived not to exist. And this thing is fitting. For if any mind could conceive aught better than Thee, then the creature would be ascending above the creator, and judging the Creator; which is a supposition very absurd. Thou therefore dost exist in a truer sense than all else beside Thee, and art more real than all else beside Thee; because whatsoever else existeth, existeth in a less true sense than Thou, and therefore is less real than Thou. Why than said the fool in his hear, There is no God, when it is so plain to a rational mind that Thou art more real than anything else? Why, except that he is a fool indeed?

3. To secure cooperation from secular rulers in attaining the ideals of the papacy.

The weapons used by Gregory to accomplish his program were spiritual and secular. In dealing with secular opposition, the spiritual preeminence of the papacy turned it into a political club. It was generally accepted that there was no salvation outside the external church. Salvation came through the sacraments, and no Western church could properly observe the sacraments unless it was in communion with Rome. Thus for all practical purposes, the pope controlled salvation. The manipulation of this power formed the basis of papal coercion. When any person, for example, refused to obey the Roman pontiff, an edict of *excommunication* was prepared and published. This officially cut the person off from the church, and this separation included the loss of salvation. A total excommunication was a fearful thing. Excommunicated persons were deprived of salvation. Mass could not be held in their presence, and those giving them refuge of any kind were subject to severe discipline by the church. If the one excommunicated was a ruler, the church had the power to release his subjects from all loyalty to him, opening the way for general political revolt. Loyal Catholic rulers were invited to crusade against the heretic and seize his kingdom for themselves, giving them a double incentive to support the papacy.

The second weapon based on control of the sacramental vehicles of salvation was the *interdict*. In a sense, the interdict was excommunication applied to a community, whether a small town or a large kingdom. An interdict closed the churches, which were viewed as the only means of salvation for the people. The only ministry that was carried on provided baptism (to bring babies in the church and salvation) and extreme unction (the sacrament at death to prepare the individual for judgment). The giving of these two sacraments during the period of interdict was a means of maintaining the strength of the church if the interdict was applied for a long period.

By these weapons—excommunication and interdict—papal power could be applied quickly in a practical and political way. Furthermore, when civil rulers were friendly, the popes used their influence to secure still another coercive weapon. This was known as the *ban*, by which civil rulers made an outlaw of the person involved in ecclesiastical disobedience. The machinery of secular punishment could then be applied to heretics.

Gregory VII freely used excommunication, interdict, and ban as weapons to reassert the claims of the pseudo-Isidorian decretals and the *Donation of Constantine*, and to invoke the authority of the apostle Peter. He quickly brought effective internal reform of the papal government and soon began speaking authoritatively to all secular rulers. Under his leadership Roman synods took the right of nominating or appointing popes completely out of secular hands and placed it in the power of the cardinal bishops and cardinal clergy. In addition, kings and secular princes were denied the power of appointing or installing any bishop. These measures were an attempt to eliminate all secular power in appointing church officials and to place that power directly in the hands of the papal government.

Furthermore, under Gregory an edict requiring clerical celibacy was ratified. This meant that deacons, priests, and bishops could not take wives. It eliminated the financial burden on the church of providing for the families of its officers; it enlarged the distinction between the clergy and the laity; it made the clergy more mobile, for without wife and family the priest or bishop could move quickly wherever he might be sent; it ensured the right of the church to appoint a bishop's successor without family influence in case the bishop's sons should be ecclesiastics and desire to fill empty posts; and it made the church heir to the possessions of most of its clergy, for clerics had no one else to whom they might leave their worldly goods when they died.

Pope Gregory used the interdict freely in an effort to establish papal power. He sent legates (or representatives) to every civil government

(Document 15)
Pope Gregory VII and Emperor Henry IV

Emperor Henry IV issued a decree deposing Gregory VII on January 24, 1076. He began with his decree like this.

Henry, king not by usurpation, but by the holy ordination of God, to Hildebrand, not pope, but false monk.
This is the salutation which you deserve, for you have never held any office in the church without making it a source of confusion and a curse to Christian men instead of an honor and a blessing....

Henry IV declared the papal throne vacant. Later, however, the emperor was forced to annul his decree against the pope in these words.

Henry, by the grace of God king, to the archbishops, bishops, margraves, counts, and to his subjects of every rank and dignity, greeting and good will. Our faithful subjects have convinced us that in our recent controversy with pope Gregory we were led astray by certain evil counselors. Therefore we now make known to all, that we have repented of our former actions and have determined henceforth to obey him in everything, as our predecessors were wont to do before us, and to make full reparation for any injury which we may have inflicted upon him or his office. We command all of you to follow our example and to offer satisfaction to St. Peter and to his vicar, pope Gregory, for any fault you may have committed, and to seek absolution from him, if any of you are under his ban.

After Henry IV repented at Canossa, Pope Gregory VII sent the following letter to the German Princes.

Before [Emperor Henry IV] entered Italy he had sent to us and had offered to make complete satisfaction for his fault, promising to reform and henceforth to obey us in all things, provided we would give him our absolution and blessing. We hesitated for some time, taking occasion in the course of the negotiations to reprove him sharply for his former sins. Finally he came in person to Canossa, where we were staying, bringing with him only a small retinue and manifesting no hostile intentions. Once arrived, he presented himself at the gate of the castle, barefoot and clad only in wretched woolen garments, beseeching us with tears to grant him absolution and forgiveness. This he continued to do for three days, until all those about us were moved to compassion at this plight and interceded for him with tears and prayers. Indeed, they marvelled at our hardness of heart, some even complaining that our action savored rather of heartless tyranny than of chastening severity. At length his persistent declarations of repentance and the supplications of all who were there with us overcame our reluctance, and we removed the excommunication from him and received him again into the bosom of the holy mother church....

in order to guard papal interests in various countries. Perhaps his greatest triumph came in his enforcement of synodical decrees relating to the appointment and installation of bishops by secular powers. In this struggle, the pope fought against an ancient and popular practice. In feudalism, it will be recalled, the sovereign, or lord of the manor, was the sole ruler in his own domain. If a bishop happened to serve in that domain, the bishop swore allegiance to this secular ruler. Should the bishop die, the sovereign usually appointed someone else to that office from his own domain. Since papal power was greatly weakened during the centuries of anarchy and feudalism following the breakdown of the Carolingian line, no protest was voiced over this situation for generations. Pope Gregory refused to allow the bishop to be appointed, installed, or controlled by the secular power. The Roman synod of 1075 reiterated this principle, denying the right of the emperor to appoint and invest bishops.

A test came quickly. Henry IV (1056-1106), the German emperor, could not understand the changed situation. Had not his predecessors appointed even the popes less than a century before? Had not the popes agreed solemnly that the emperor should forever have the right to appoint even the bishop of Rome? So when a bishopric became vacant in the northern part of Italy, the emperor immediately appointed a successor and installed him in office. When Pope Gregory denied the validity of the action, the emperor declared the papal office empty. A century had made a great difference. Now the pope, his prestige restored, hurled the dreaded weapon of excommunication against the emperor, freeing Henry's subjects from allegiance to him. More from political than religious motivation, the emperor made a pilgrimage southward to ask the pope's forgiveness and secure restoration to the church. Meanwhile, the pope had started northward toward Germany to carry on the struggle. They met at Canossa, where the emperor stood outside the castle in the snow, barefooted, for three days, begging the privilege of asking the pope's forgiveness. On being admitted, he made promises to be obedient and was restored to fellowship.

The emperor's humiliation strengthened his influence with his people; despite his reinstatement, the emperor declared war on the pope and succeeded in driving him into exile, where he died in 1085. The successors of the emperor and the pope continued the battle. In 1122 an agreement, known as the Concordat of Worms, was reached. This provided the church with control of the election of bishops and abbots, but the emperor exercised supervision over the elections. In case of a dispute the emperor would have the deciding vote. The pope should invest every bishop, or abbot, with the spiritual symbols of office—the ring and the staff—while the emperor should be allowed to touch the candidate with sceptre to indicate imperial approval. Neither popes nor emperors were true to this compromise.

Alexander III (1159-81)

The second of the strong popes who were responsible for bringing the papacy to the height of its power was Alexander III. He entered the papal office under fire. The cardinals elected him by a small majority. The minority of the cardinals, with the support of the Roman clergy and of the emperor, elected a rival pope, Victor IV. The emperor, Frederick Barbarossa (1152-90), disliked Alexander and supported Victor, going so far as to summon a church council, which obediently voted in favor of Victor. Alexander was supported by England, France, Spain, Hungary, and Sicily. For almost twenty years Emperor Frederick tried to force his way to Rome in order to set up Victor as pope, without success. In 1177, he submitted to Alexander.

Alexander continued the work and spirit of Gregory VII. His dealings with England were typical of his efforts to advance the power and prestige of the papacy. In 1163, after the death of the archbishop of Canterbury, King Henry II of England (1154-89) forced the appointment of Thomas à Becket, one of his cronies. To the king's dismay, Becket became a champion of the pope against the king. In 1164 the king called a national council in an effort to eliminate papal influence in England. This council passed all of the king's measures, known as the Constitutions of Clarendon. Ecclesiastical courts were shorn of extensive jurisdiction; no appeal could be made to Rome without the king's permission; the king could appoint abbots and bishops in England; the revenues from vacant episcopal offices in England would revert to the king. The archbishop was assassinated because of strong opposition to King Henry over this program. Popular feeling was so aroused by this act that Henry was forced to submit to the pope and renounce the Constitutions in 1172.

The Third Lateran Council was convened by Pope Alexander in 1179. It decreed that the cardinals alone should elect the pope, that Roman Catholics should take arms against heresy with the promise of full forgiveness of all sins if death should result, and that secular authorities should not meddle with internal affairs of the church.

Innocent III (1198-1216)

The third and greatest of the popes of this period was Innocent III. Gregory VII had made exalted claims concerning the dignity of the pope and the Roman Church: God alone had founded the Roman Church; the pope's feet should be kissed by all princes; emperors could be deposed by the pope; the pope could be judged by no man; and the Roman Church had never erred, nor would it ever err. Innocent III went further, making the pope God's only authoritative representative on the earth. With the work of Gregory VII and Alexander III to prepare the way, with the continuing spirit of the Crusades to foment religious passion and fanatical loyalty, and with doctrine and organization perfected, Innocent was able to dominate the entire world, secular and ecclesiastical.

Through his influence he deposed emperors, forced heads of states such as Spain and France to submit to his authority, required states to pay annual tributes of money, and most spectacular of all, humiliated King John of England. The English king had tried to defy Innocent and found himself excommunicated and his kingdom under interdict. Without papal support, King John was captured by his nobles in 1215 and was forced to grant the Magna Charta, a bill of rights for protection against oppression by the crown. The pope refused to admit the validity of the document because, he said, it was secured under duress. Meanwhile, by interdict and other coercive measures, Innocent brought every secular government into his orbit. He put into practical operation the claim that he was the immediate instrument of God for world rule.

The Fourth Lateran Council of 1215 marks the height of official Roman Catholic domination. This council was unrivaled as a picture of universal subjection to the pope by every ecclesiastical and secular power. The patriarch of Constantinople, once a strong rival, was there to bow his knee. The spectacle of this tremendous pageant was more important than what was done. A new Crusade was discussed, union with the Greek church was looked into, the punishment of heretics by the state was arranged, and a number of canons were enacted providing for ecclesiastical discipline. The doctrine of transubstantiation, which affirms that the bread and wine of the Mass lose their character and actually become the body and blood of a newly crucified Christ, was officially defined.

The universal dominion of the papacy had become an accomplished fact. Between the Council of Nicaea of 325 and the Fourth Lateran Council of 1215 the Roman bishop had become master of the spiritual and secular world. The structure was complete. Its builders thought that it was eternal. In less than a century it began to crumble.

The papacy accomplished a spectacular revival of authority and prestige in the eleventh and twelfth centuries. An internal reform through the agency of monasticism began the recovery. Papal prestige skyrocketed as a result of the Crusades, but the long-range results were not favorable. Scholasticism provided intellectual justification for papal doctrines. Three outstanding popes, using the ecclesiastical weapons of excommunication, interdict, and crusade, humbled every secular power.

11

Retrospect and Prospects

The Roman Catholic papacy had reached its height. Secular and ecclesiastical princes bowed to its authority. Until near the end of the thirteenth-century it appeared a new and permanent world order had been created. It is instructive to compare the Christianity of this golden age of Roman Catholicism with the Christianity of the New Testament. Beyond the external signs of glittering wealth, false pride symbolized in the kissing of feet and holding of stirrups by earthly princes, and the kneeling of men to men, a vast difference in character between the movement described in the New Testament and that in the Roman Catholic Church of the thirteenth century had developed.

Roman Catholic Domination

The New Testament picture of ministers (bishops) serving in an autonomous local church, theoretically equal with all bishops, had disappeared. Instead a few important bishops shaped the policies of all Christianity. The bishop of Rome was able to impress upon all other Western bishops not only his example but his authority. In addition, the Roman bishop, through spiritual and political coercion, managed to assume control over secular kings. Sometimes retreating, sometimes compromising, sometimes demanding, the Roman bishops constantly kept in mind their ultimate aim of universal rule, ecclesiastical and secular, and attained it after about a millennium of struggle.

Roman Catholic Organization

The simple local church government of the New Testament days was gone. In its place was the Roman hierarchy. The Roman bishop headed a vast network of ecclesiastical organization that controlled the sacramental vehicles commonly supposed to bring salvation. Such a widespread operation demanded a strong central organization. In the fourth century Rome was divided by the bishop into twenty-five parts, each headed by a presbyter or priest. Each was called a parish or *titulus*. In order to provide for the administration of charity, seven deacons, with a specific geographical section under his responsibility. were appointed for the city of Rome. This scriptural number of deacons was later augmented by seven subdeacons.

In the eleventh century these twenty-five priests, the seven deacons, and several bishops from the area around Rome formed the basis of the College of Cardinals. The name *cardinal* developed from a Latin word meaning "a hinge." Although the play on words has nothing to do with the original application of the word, it is true that the Roman system hinges on cardinals. Since the time of Gregory VII (1073-85), the cardinals have been entrusted with the most important organizational tasks of the Roman Church. Their duty is to elect and advise popes and determine administrative policy through committee functions. There are three types of cardinals: cardinal bishops, cardinal priests, and cardinal deacons. Cardinal priests are usually strong bishops from various parts of the world, while cardinal deacons are usually priests. Cardinals are appointed by the pope, who can also depose them, although that is unusual. The committee work of the cardinals increased rapidly after the thirteenth century. All of these committees and tribunals—the central core of Roman Catholic organization—are called the Roman Curia.

Roman Catholic Doctrine

We have discussed the corruption of New Testament teachings in the developing Roman Catholic system. The New Testament pattern of salvation emphasized faith in Jesus Christ without the mediation of a person or institution. Ordinances of baptism and the Lord's Supper were symbolical, not magical. In the Roman system the ordinances became sacraments, vehicles of grace. Salvation was conceived as coming from the Catholic Church alone through the administration of the sacraments. The question of the number of sacraments, argued by Catholic theologians for centuries, was finally resolved. Chief credit for establishing the official position should probably be given to Peter Lombard. About 1150 he prepared his *Four Books of Sentences;* the last division included a discussion on sacraments. Unlike earlier theologians such as Augustine (who died in 430) who believed that all ministries of the church were sacraments, and later theologians like Hugo of St. Victor and Abelard (contemporaries with Peter Lombard), who emphasized five sacraments, the *Sentences* named seven sacraments. Peter Lombard's *Sentences* were taught in practically all of the schools for theological training during the next few centuries. Thomas Aquinas (1225-74) provided the most influential synthesis of Catholic doctrine for the modern period and was in agreement with Peter Lombard in asserting that the church has seven sacraments.

The seven sacraments were baptism, confirmation, penance, the Lord's Supper (Mass), extreme unction, ordination, and matrimony. A brief description about each follows.

The *sacrament of baptism* is the initiatory rite. By it, the church taught that original sin and all acts of sin committed up to the time of baptism are forgiven. Sprinkling became the general mode of baptism in the West after about the ninth century, and infants began to be subjects of baptism in the second or third centuries. In order to maintain the appearance of baptism as profession of faith, the use of sponsors developed soon after the adoption of infant baptism. The priest administering baptism asked infants if they were willing to renounce Satan, if they believed the various points of the creed, and if they were willing to be baptized. The sponsors, or godparents, answered all questions for the undiscerning infants. The catechism says that this ceremony makes children Christians, children of God, and heirs of heaven.

The *sacrament of confirmation* claims to impart the Holy Spirit. Its scriptural basis is usually given as Acts 8:17 and 19:6. In the Western world this sacrament could be administered only by a bishop. Until about the thirteenth century it was conferred shortly after baptism; then the time was changed to allow the subject to reach the twelfth or thirteenth year. The age does not matter, since a sponsor is required and the sacrament works without reference to any understanding by the child. In this sacrament, which in a sense inducts the child into the duties and responsibilities of church life, the bishop anoints the candidate with oil that has been blessed.

The *sacrament of penance* provides forgiveness of sins committed after baptism. Scriptures like 1 John 1:9 are used to support this doctrine. The earliest confessions of sin were made to the congregation, but this practice could not continue, as increasing numbers of confessions made it difficult to have any other type of service. The intense persecutions of Christianity under Emperors Decius (249-51) and Diocletian (284-305) caused many nominal Christians to deny the faith. To meet this need, as well as the normal demand, a division of functions was required. Through successive developments, auricular confession (confession in the ear of the priest) became the custom. Not until the Fourth Lateran Council in 1215 was confession to the priest made a church law.

Under the theory developed by Aquinas and now generally accepted, the subject of this sacrament must first be moved by contrition, sorrow for sin, or attrition, a fear of the punishment of sin. With this motive, confession is made to the priest who in turn requires that the candidate must give "satisfaction." This idea probably grew out of the rigorous persecutions of the early period. The original purpose of satisfaction was to give evidence that the subject was really contrite and willing to do whatever possible to prove it. In a sense satisfaction originally had a twofold function: (1) it provided a basis for the forgiveness of eternal and deadly sins, and (2) it displayed contrition for sin in the temporal order. Sin was viewed as having eternal consequences and temporal disabilities.

This distinction became important in the development of various methods of making satisfaction and the exceptional extent of the effectiveness of such satisfaction. The method of making satisfaction before the tenth and eleventh centuries had been primarily through making religious pilgrimages to some shrine or through some means of revealing personal piety. After the eleventh century the temporal penalties could be remitted in whole or in part by the use of indulgences.

Indulgence was the name given to the remission of punishment because of temporal sins. After the eleventh century, instead of taking a pilgrimage as penance, it was possible to purchase an indulgence in order to give satisfaction for temporal sins.

In addition the interpretation of the large area in which temporal sins brought hurt increased the importance of the distinction between temporal sins and eternal. Temporal sins, it was taught, must be paid for in purgatory after death, if they were not completely canceled through satisfaction. The church, it was further taught, could issue indulgences for temporal sins because it possessed a treasury of merits bequeathed to it by the good works of Christ and the saints. This development was reflected in the order of the elements of penance. Earlier the order consisted of contrition, confession, satisfaction, and then absolution or forgiveness by the priest. Satisfaction was given before the priest pronounced absolution or forgiveness. The developed order was changed; contrition and confession formed the first part, but absolution came after confession, and satisfaction was placed last. Thus after confession, the priest, with authority granted him by the Roman bishop, would forgive the eternal sins of the confessor; then there was imposed on the person the necessity of giving satisfaction for the temporal guilt, if not expiated, required suffering in purgatory. The doctrine of purgatory was first taught as a matter essential to the faith by Gregory I (590-604).

The *sacrament of the Lord's Supper,* or Mass, is described as the unbloody sacrifice of the body and blood of Christ. By this means Christ's soul and divinity are reproduced in both bread and wine. This is the theological reason why the Roman Church refuses to allow the people to partake of the wine; they get all they need in the bread. The mass has become the central feature of Roman Catholic worship services, for through partaking of the bread, which allegedly has been changed to the broken body of Christ, and witnessing the transubstantiation of the wine to the blood of Christ, the subject actually partakes of Christ's body, which gives spiritual merit.

The *sacrament of extreme unction* is, as the name indicates, the last anointing. Its practice is based on James 5:14. In the administration of this sacrament the priest anoints the eyes, ears, nose, lips, palms of the hands, and feet to expiate sins contracted through any of these organs. A plenary, or full, indulgence is granted, but does not take effect until the time of death.

The *sacrament of orders* applies only to those entering in the service of the Roman Catholic Church. It sets them apart and qualifies them for the task they have assumed.

The *sacrament of matrimony* consists of the union of a man and woman in marriage. Ordinarily the sacraments of orders and matrimony mutually exclude one another.

Thus the Roman Catholic sacramental system, which had developed its present features by the thirteenth century aimed at controling the life of the subject. Individuals were touched by it at birth, in child-

---

(Document 16)

Hildegard of Bingen: Against Child Oblates

Medieval monasteries were cultural centers, and in them a few nuns became effective writers. Among these, Hildegard of Bingen (1098-1179) wrote criticizing parents who, according to custom, forced their children to enter a religious vocation.

And how did you dare so rashly to take hold of one dedicated and sanctified to me in baptism that you would hand him over to me against his will, to be bound in the most confining captivity to bear my yoke—when the result is neither parched nor green, so that he is neither dead to the world nor alive in it? And why have you oppressed him to such an extent that he is capable of neither? But that miracle of mine by which he must be examined in order to remain in spiritual life is not to be examinined by mortals. For I do not want the parents to sin in his consecration by offering him up to me against his will. But should some mother or father wish to offer their boy to my service, before presenting him, let that parent say: "I promise God that I shall protect my boy with expert care until he reaches the age of reason, by imploring, beseeching, exhorting him to remain devotedly in the service of God. And if he is in agreement with me, I shall immediately offer his service to God; or if he does not give me his assent, I may be innocent in the eyes of God's majesty."

But if the parents of the boy have attended him in these ways until he has reached the age of reason; and if, at that stage, the same boy, turning away from them, does not wish to give his consent, then the parents themselves, since they have shown in him the strength of their devotion, should not offer him up against his will; nor should they force the boy into that service which they themselves are unwilling to bear or perform.

---

hood, adolescence, and at death. Regular confession of sins and absolution at the hands of the priest were required as a means of escaping the purgatorial sufferings that the earthly church could remit. The Roman Church used every means of influence. An appeal was made through beauty to the eyes, through melody to the ears, through incense to the nose, through participation to the hands and knees. Solemn rites and incantations brought a sense of belonging and initiation, and a common language spoke of unity.

Roman Catholic Monasticism

Throughout the Medieval period the monastic movement retained its great popularity. That perfect life could only be found in monasticism was universally felt. The monks were viewed as persons who had lost their lives to save them again, who had given all to follow Christ. The strengthening of the papacy ensured great encouragement for monasticism, for monks were the strongest supporters of papal supremacy. Particularly after the new type of monasticism inaugurated by the Cluniac reform had developed, the pope was able to undermine the power of any antagonistic bishop. Since these monks were no longer under the control of the local bishop, the pope could send them to any diocese to hear confessions, forgive sins, baptize, bury, bless, or condemn. As a consequence, the bishop of that diocese would find himself bypassed and his functions taken over by the monks.

Monasteries provided a place of refuge for many: for the scholar who desired peace and quiet for study, for the pious who wanted a haven from worldliness, for the fearful who would flee from the misery and disorder of society. In a sense monasteries also provided a place for minor dissent. Some might disagree with the papal program, yet desire to remain in the ecclesiastical structure from either conviction or fear. Various monastic orders emphasized different areas in their organization. Many a monk doubtless found in the monastery a congenial atmosphere for ideas that would not have been generally acceptable outside it.

From the eleventh to the thirteenth centuries several new monastic orders arose. The Cistercians were one of the reform movements and became famous because Bernard of Clairvaux joined it in 1113. The Augustinian canons attempted to bring monastic discipline to the parish clergy. In 1119 an order known as the Premonstrants was founded, providing for communal living in a monastic house by the various priests of a particular parish. Another type of monasticism grew out of the Crusades. Three outstanding military orders developed. The Knights of St. John, or the Hospitalers, were organized in the twelfth century to aid sick and helpless pilgrims on their way to Jerusalem. The Knights Templars were a lay order organized in 1119 to protect Jerusalem pilgrims. The Teutonic Knights, with a similar mission, date from 1190.

The two most important orders of these centuries were the Dominicans and the Franciscans. Dominic (1170-1221) organized an order for the purpose of winning heretics back to the Roman Church through preaching. The pope recognized the order in 1216 and the movement spread rapidly. Before Dominic's death his order numbered sixty houses in every part of Europe. Doubtless copying the Franciscan movement, the Dominicans became mendicants or beggars. Because of their emphasis on education and preaching, the Dominicans produced some of the greatest theologians and scholars of the Roman Church.

Francis of Assisi was born about ·1182. At about the age of twenty-five he gave up his military and business pursuits because of a conversion experience, and two years later he determined to form an order that would endeavor to reproduce the spirit and work of Christ. This order received approval in 1221. The inclinations of Francis turned away from formal and effective organization, but through able friends, especially Pope Gregory IX (1227-41), the Franciscan movement developed and spread rapidly. After Francis' death in 1226 his followers became divided over the interpretation of his teachings.

The Dominicans, the Franciscans, and other medieval orders organized houses for nuns. Both as contemplatives and service-oriented nuns, many women found opportunities to participate in religious and community life they would have found nowhere else. Writings of a few of these nuns have been preserved and offer historical information on women in the church.

The Inquisition

The elements of Roman Catholic strength that have been mentioned—prestige, organization, doctrine, and passionate defenders—seemed to give promise of the continued domination of the world by the papacy. The picture would not be complete without examining factors that threatened, and finally overturned, universal papal domination. One of these factors was the extraordinary spread of religious dissent. In a succeeding chapter specific instances of dissent will be described. It is significant that Innocent III, the pope who symbolized the complete domination of Roman Catholic power, should find it necessary to institute special ecclesiastical measures to suppress dissent.

The inquisition of heresy had at first been made under the supervision of the local bishop. With the rise of the Roman bishop to power, it became his prerogative to dismiss those who refused to follow church teachings. The founding of the Dominican order followed the discovery of the strength of the Albigenses in southern France and constituted an effort to win these dissenters back to the faith. The Fourth Lateran Council of 1215 passed new decrees asking the various bishops to seek out heretics in their own dioceses. A new direction was taken in the thirteenth century. Emperor Frederick II (1215-50) offered the services of the civil government to the papacy to help suppress heresy and in 1252 a papal bull directed that civil magistrates be used in the detection and punishment of heresy. After 1233 the Dominicans were given the task of searching out dissenters and handling them. In 1262 the office of inquisitor general was set up at Rome to spearhead the fight against heresy.

The inquisitorial methods have been well publicized. Despite lurid descriptions it is doubtful that the stories exceeded the horrors of the actual movement, particularly in the Spanish Inquisition, which began in 1478. Christians were adept at devising ways to torture Christians. Informers were secured by promising them a part of the estate of the condemned. Torture was the principal method of securing evidence and no person was safe. Simply the accusation of heresy by anyone—personal hatred, greed, or other motive—was enough to start the machinery of torture, the pains of which almost anyone would confess to almost anything. Cynicism and bitterness filtered to all parts of the Continent. Things were not well with the dominating ecclesiastical system.

Political Developments

A new set of strong rulers was arising supported by the zeal of nationalism. Drawing new strength from the death of many powerful nobles in the Crusades and enriched by the increase of trade and the development of industry following the Crusades, these new secular sovereigns prepared to challenge the supremacy of the pope over civil government. That story will be told in a succeeding chapter.

Signs of Change

The Roman Catholic system reached its height through coercion because it allegedly controlled the only means of salvation. Superstition and fear played a large part in Christianity. Change of any kind constituted a threat to the system and changes were inevitable. The Renaissance was imminent. Already in the thirteenth century there were signs of spiritual awakenings and intellectual advance. When people learned that God was a Savior as well as a Judge, that they could find His love and blessings apart from the ecclesiastical organization known as the church, and that the service of God was not bound with merits and penance, the great sacramental system of the papacy was undermined.

❑ ❑ ❑ ❑ ❑

The difference between the New Testament pattern and the Roman Catholic Church in the thirteenth century was great. The Roman bishop had become dominant. His authority was recognized in spiritual and secular areas. His organization was strong and well disciplined. The doctrinal definition of Rome's principal tenants was almost complete. New monastic orders provided recruits for every kind of special service. The future seemed bright. There were elements that would have disturbed an observant onlooker. Dissent was widespread. The methods that were adopted to combat dissent only scattered the spirit across the Continent. New secular rulers were arising who were not afraid of papal excommunication and interdict. The foregleams of the dawn were casting light against which the Roman system could not continue to dominate minds and hearts.

Bibliography

Bede. *A History of the English Church and People.* Translated by Leo Sherley-Price. Revised by R. E. Latham. Harmondsworth, England: Penguin, 1968.

Bethune-Baker, J. *An Introduction to the Early History of Christian Doctrine to the Time of the Council of Chalcedon.* London: Methuen & Co., Ltd., 1951.

Bredero, Adriaan H. *Christendom and Christianity in the Middle Ages: The Relations Between Religion, Church, and Society.* Translated by Reinder Bruinsma. Grand Rapids: Eerdmans, 1994.

Duby, Georges. *The Knight, the Lady, and the Priest: The making of Modern Marriage in Medieval France.* Translated by Barbara Bray. New York: Pantheon Books, 1983.

————. *William Marshall: The Flower of Chivalry.* Translated by Richard Howard. New York: Pantheon Books, 1985.

Foakes-Jackson, F. J. *An Introduction to the History of Christianity A.D. 590-1314.* New York: The Macmillan Co., 1921.

Workman, Herbert Brook. *The Evolution of the Monastic Ideal.* London: The Epworth Press, 1927.

IV. Period of Western Reform (A.D. 1215-1648)

Introduction to the Period

The papacy could attain a higher prestige than it displayed in the Fourth Lateran Council of 1215. For a brief period it seemed that the papacy would be able to maintain its imposing position indefinitely. The claims of the popes who succeeded Innocent III (1198-1216) sounded like him, but they were not able to enforce these claims. The removal of the papal throne to France from 1305 to 1378 made it a tool of French national interests; the papal schism from 1378 to 1409 (with two popes) and from 1409 to 1415 (three popes) reduced papal prestige and authority. Strong attempts were made to reform the church in "head and members," but failed. From the Council of Constance (1414-18) to the theses of Luther (1517), papal abuses became more flagrant.

Various types of revolt against the Roman Church occurred between 1517 and 1534. The Council of Trent (1545-63) represented the Roman Catholic reform. The Reformation period closed with the Thirty Years War (1618-1648), which brought a measure of mutual toleration between Roman Catholics and their opponents.

Points of Interest

Roots of reform were imbedded deeply in medieval Christianity. For that reason it has seemed wisest to push back the traditional date of 1517 to the point at which the Roman Church reached its highest peak—the Fourth Lateran Council of 1215. Widespread dissent, the Avignon papacy, schism and confusion, and attempts at reform in the three centuries before Luther's theses justify our beginning the reform period with 1215.

The interaction of all factors in the Reformation—political circumstances, for example—should be noticed carefully.

Roman Catholic reform aimed primarily at modernizing its organization to meet the threats of the schismatics. No attempt was made to continue the radical reform measures taken by the councils of the fifteenth century.

The Renaissance and Reformation were important cultural periods in the history of Western Europe. Although these movements have also influenced Eastern Europe, Christians there were largely absorbed in a struggle for survival with advancing Islam.

12

Collapse of Papal Prestige

Factors that helped establish the prestige of the Roman papacy also helped to bring its downfall. The height that the papal monarchy attained for a few centuries was a guarantee that a decline must take place. Secular rulers could not fail to see that the papacy was an institution of this world, not of the next. Papal policies were often greedy and vicious. Despite assertions that the Roman leadership could not err, civil sovereigns saw many examples of mistakes in doctrines and policies. Papal avowal of the Crusades and the Inquisition were examples. The tragic slaughter of untold hundreds of thousands of men, women, and children in the fruitless march toward Jerusalem brought many to their senses. What could the will of God have to do with this sort of political undertaking?

The German nobles bluntly refused to participate in the Crusades, papal promises of complete forgiveness of sins notwithstanding. The popes were slow to see that the passion of the people had died down, and their continued pleadings for new Crusades and their collections of gifts and taxes, ostensibly for such Crusades, disgusted thoughtful and spiritual people. Furthermore, the Roman slaughter of the Albigenses and the use of crude and terrible tortures in the Inquisition were a shocking disclosure of the character of the papacy. As the Inquisition spread to all parts of Europe, the tyranny of the Roman system became more and more visible. Fear had always been a major part of the hold the Roman Church had on the people. Now, to the fear of purgatory, excommunication, interdict, ban, and zealous

Crusaders, the nightmare of accusation of heresy, against which there was no defense, was added. The brutality of the whole movement prophesied the downfall of such tyrannical monarchs, whether in the ecclesiastical or the secular sphere.

Financial Exploitation by the Roman Catholic Church

An important cause of rising resentment against the papacy was its financial demands. The tremendous expansion of the central organization of the church demanded immense revenues. When Rome set up the Rota Romana in 1234 as the supreme ecclesiastical court in Christendom, enough additional personnel were required to handle appeals from every part of the world. Subsidiary courts for special appeals were also necessary. An army of clerks was needed to maintain records. Worst of all, flagrant abuses characterized every step of the legal proceedings. Official records show that in some cases simply securing the briefs cost approximately forty times the legitimate amount. Litigants from all over Europe were encouraged to appeal their cases directly to Rome, and it was well understood that the highest bidder won the case.

The financial gain secured in this fashion was not enough to cover the vast expenditures, legitimate and otherwise, of the papacy. Especially during the fourteenth century the papacy used every possible means for increasing its revenue. Some of these methods were through annates, collations, reservations, expectancies, dispensations, indulgences, simony, commendations, the *jus spoliorum,* tithing, and special assessment.

Annates is the gift by a newly appointed bishop or abbot of his first year's income in the office to which he was appointed. *Collations* is the practice of shifting several bishops or abbots in order to secure annates from each one. For example, if the archbishop of Cologne were to die, the pope would not appoint simply one person, but he would shift the archbishop of Mainz to the open place, appoint the bishop of Trier to the Mainz office, another bishop to Trier, and so on. An effort would be made to give each cleric a better situation. Before exhausting his possibilities the pope could have a dozen annates paid because of one vacancy.

(Document 17)
The Franciscan Virtue of Poverty

The Little Flowers of St. Francis *is a medieval Franciscan narrative that promoted popular devotion to Francis of Assisi. The book portrayed Francis and his followers as faithful imitators of Jesus of Nazareth and especially emphasized their pursuit of poverty as a virtue.*

We must first consider that the glorious St. Francis, in all the acts of his life, modeled himself on Christ. Thus, as Christ at the beginning of His mission chose twelve Apostles who were to abandon all things worldly and follow Him in poverty and in the other virtues, so St. Francis at the founding of his Order chose twelve companions, who espoused the most high poverty. As one of the twelve Apostles of Christ, cast off by God, finally hanged himself by the neck, so one of the twelve companions of St. Francis, by name brother Giovanni della Cappella, apostate, finally hanged himself by the neck. And all this is for the elect a great example and cause of humility and fear, considering that no one is certain to persevere in the grace of God until the end. And as the twelve Apostles were to all men marvels of sanctity, and filled with the Holy Spirit, so those most holy companions of St. Francis were men of such marvelous sanctity as the world has not seen from the time of the Apostles: so much so that one of them was swept up to the third heaven, like St. Paul, and this was Brother Egidio; the lips of another, that is, tall brother Filippo, were touched by the angel with a burning coal, like Isaiah the prophet; one of them, Brother Silvestro, used to speak with God as one friend to another, as did Moses; another, the most humble Brother Bernardo, soared by flight of intellect into the very light of divine wisdom, like the Eagle, John the Evangelist, and expounded Holy Scripture most profoundly; still another was sanctified by God and canonized in Heaven while still living in the world, and this was Brother Ruffino, nobleman of Assissi. And thus all were privileged with unique signs of sanctity.

Reservations refers to the practice of reserving the best and richest offices for papal use. The pope did not serve the particular bishop or archbishopric, but would send a priest to minister to the needs of the people while the revenue was sent to Rome. *Expectations* mean the practice, by papal authorities, of selling to the highest bidder the right of nomination to an unusually desirable benefice before the person filling the office had yet vacated it. Ambitious men would keep a watchful eye on the health of the incumbents of the various desirable offices, and when there was any encouragement that an opening might soon become available, the bidding began. Occasionally several candidates paid huge sums in anticipation of securing the same office. Expectancies became almost a bid for the right to bid again when the incumbent of the desired office actually died.

Dispensations refers to the papal practice of excusing ecclesiastical violations on the payment of the proper amount of money. In one of his outbursts against the Roman Curia, Luther wrote that it was a place where vows could be annulled, monks could get permission to leave their orders, priests could buy a dispensation to get married, the illegitimate might be legitimatized, and evil and disgrace were knighted and ennobled. His closing sentence, in typical impetuous language, declared that at the Roman Curia there was "a buying and a selling, a changing, blustering and bargaining, cheating and lying, robbing and stealing, debauchery and villainy and all kinds of contempt of God that Antichrist could not reign worst." Even allowing for Luther's usual enthusiasm, it is evident that considerable income was secured by allowing dispensations for breaking canonical restrictions.

Indulgences were pardons for temporal sins. Individuals might buy them instead of taking a pilgrimage or showing some other evidence of contrition. The revenue from this source alone was considerable because of the widespread fear of spending a long period in purgatory.

Simony refers to the sale of a church office, and it takes its name from Simon Magus (see Acts 8:9 ff.), who tried to buy the power of the Holy Spirit with money. Closely associated with simony was the practice of *nepotism,* referring to the installing of relatives in lucrative churches offices.

Commendations has reference to the practice of paying an annual tax to the papacy in return for a provisional appointment year by year to a desirable benefice. The *jus spoliorum* was the name applied to the papal practice of demanding that any property secured by a bishop or other officer during the tenure of office should, on the death of the person, become the property of the church, since such property was judged to come to the deceased individual in consequence of holding the office.

Tithing applies to a levy against church property, the value of which formed the basis for the amount demanded. Special assessments were made under any pretext. The Crusades were an excuse for an annual tax. Unusual blessings, unusual sins, or any other situation might call for such assessments.

Beyond these various methods of raising money, gifts of every kind were solicited. Gifts for approving relics, for permission to view the papal rooms, for jubilees, for charities, or for other reasons swelled the revenue of the Roman Church almost beyond computation.

There were other factors that caused people to feel resentment toward the church. The Roman system reasoned carefully and made a distinct appeal to philosophical minds, but it was not meeting the needs of the people's hearts. Dissent was spreading. There was lack of union in the monastic system, as well as among the clergy. Some were openly skeptical. The enforcement of clerical celibacy promoted immorality and concubinage. The doctrinal teaching that the character of a priest or bishop was of secondary importance and did not affect his ability to forgive sins and administer valid sacraments played havoc with the morals of many.

It was the political aspect, however, that brought an end to the universal sway of the papacy. As on previous occasions, it became evident that papal prestige and authority could not be divorced from secular power.

The Beginning of Papal Humiliation

Pope Innocent III died in 1216, one year after the spectacular Fourth Lateran Council that marked the height of papal power. For about seventy-five years no direct challenge was made to papal domination in either ecclesiastical or secular spheres. With the election of Pope Boniface VIII (1294-1303), a new order of things began to appear—not that Boniface was less vocal in his claims for the papacy nor less aggressive in his demands on secular and ecclesiastical princes; if anything he was more vociferous and more arrogant than previous popes. His claims and demands were not heeded in the way that those of his predecessors had been. He was not very successful in his meddling with the political affairs of the Italian states. He attempted to end the Hundred Years War between France and England, but was ignored by both nations. Enraged, he threatened England and France with interdict and excommunication should they continue to levy war taxes on the Roman Church in their realms. King Edward I of England simply disregarded the pope; his parliament voted the taxes. King Philip IV of France, on the other hand, was not so kind. He promptly forbade the exportation of any revenues from France to the papacy. Hit at a sensitive point and with morale shaken, Boniface canonized Philip's grandfather in an effort to placate the

French king. The war had begun. In 1302, after a preliminary skir-
mish, Boniface issued his bull entitled *Unam Sanctam*—named, as
usual, after the first two words of the bull. The bull excommunicated
Philip and placed France under interdict. This famous bull plainly
stated that every person must obey the pope or forfeit salvation.
Philip was undisturbed, however; the weapons that brought Gregory
VII and Innocent III to power had lost their sting. Philip had the pope
seized and imprisoned. Boniface died the following year.

The Babylonian Captivity and Papal Schism

The successor to Boniface, Benedict XI (1303-4), lived only nine
months after his election to office. Benedict's successor, Clement V
(1305-14), was appointed through the influence of King Philip of
France. In his pontificate, papal headquarters were moved from
Rome to Avignon, France, in 1309. During the next seventy years
seven French popes filled the office. Because the papacy was absent
from Rome for about seventy years (just as the Southern Kingdom
was in Babylonian captivity for about the same length of time), this
period of papal residence in France has been called "the Babylonian
captivity of the Church."

Clement showed his subservience to Philip of France by acquiesc-
ing to the suppression of the Knights Templars. This action was dictated by the French king. The Templars had constantly opposed
Philip, and he feared the order would become a military rival.
Through promises and torture, enough evidence was secured to win
Pope Clement to Philip's side. In October 1311, Clement convoked an
ecumenical council (the fifteenth in Roman records), which voted to
suppress the order because of corrupt and immoral practices and
other crimes, including blasphemy.

The events of the next seventy years convinced the states of
Europe that the papacy had become a French institution. Enough
French cardinals were appointed to make up a majority. New methods of raising money were developed, particularly by John XXII
(1316-34).

The return of the papacy to Rome became an issue in each papal
election. Identification of the papacy with French interests was a serious blunder, particularly in view of rising nationalism everywhere.
Finally, in 1377 Gregory XI ended the fiasco by returning to Rome to

---

(Document 18)

Petrarch: The Papal Court at Avignon

Petrarch wrote this description of the papal court at Avignon sometime between 1340 and 1353. He was an Italian, and he wrote to condemn the excesses of the papacy under French control.

Now I am living in France, in the Babylon of the West. The sun in its travels sees nothing more hideous than this place on the shores of the wild Rhone, which suggests the hellish streams of Cocytus and Acheron. Here reign the successors of the poor fishermen of Galilee; they have strangely forgotten their origin. I am astounded, as I recall their predecessors, to see these men loaded with gold and clad in purple, boasting of the spoils of princes and nations; to see luxurious places and heights crowned with fortifications, instead of a boat turned downwards for shelter. We no longer find the simple nets which were once used to gain a frugal sustenance from the lake of Galilee, and with which, having labored all night and caught nothing, they took, at daybreak, a mul-

titude of fishes, in the name of Jesus. One is stupefied nowadays to hear the lying tongues, to see the worthless parchments turned by a leaden seal into nets which are used, in Christ's name, but by the arts of Belial, to catch hordes of unwary Christians. These fish, too, are dressed and laid on the burning coals of anxiety before they fill the insatiable maw of their captors.

Instead of holy solitude we find a criminal host and crowds of the most infamous satellites; instead of soberness, licentious banquets; instead of pious pilgrimages, preternatural and foul sloth; instead of the bare feet of the apostles, the snowy coursers of brigands fly past us, the horses decked in gold and fed on gold, soon to be shod in gold, if the Lord does not check this slavish luxury. In short, we seem to be among the kings of the Persians or Parthians, before whom we must fall down and worship, and who cannot be approached except presents be offered.

---

die. Urban VI (1378-89) was elected to succeed Gregory after promising to return to Avignon, but after his election Urban decided to remain in Rome. The cardinals met again and elected another pope, Clement VI (1378-94), who returned to France. Now there were two popes, each claiming to be validly elected—and each was. For a quarter of a century rival popes at Avignon and Rome anathematized one another and sought to undermine the work of one another. Of course, there had been antipopes before. In 251 Novatian had been elected bishop of Rome by a rival party. Other rival popes include Felix II (355-65), Boniface VII (974), and John XVI (997-98).

Probably the strangest papal schism occurred in the middle of the eleventh century. Benedict IX had been placed on the papal throne in

1032. In 1044 he was driven out of Rome and some local nobles placed Silvester III in the papal chair. Benedict returned to Rome and sold the papal office for about a thousand pounds of silver to an arch-priest in Rome, who took the name of Gregory VI. Benedict refused to abide by the agreement, and there were three popes, each with enough strength to resist his opponents, but not enough to conquer them. The situation was finally cleared up by Emperor Henry III.

During the fourteenth century the presence of two popes over a long period of time created a number of problems. The validity of almost every ecclesiastical act was questioned. Who should bestow the pallium on newly consecrated bishops? To which should the monastic orders swear their solemn vows? Who should be recognized by the various states? From an organizational standpoint, the situation was almost intolerable. Theoretically each pope, if he were the correct one, should oversee the appointment of bishops in every diocese, fill the numerous vacancies in the archbishoprics, maintain the number of cardinals, appoint administrative heads in the Curia, and perform other duties in the operation of a widespread ecclesiastical monarchy. With two popes there were likely to be two appointments to the various positions, rivalry in ecclesiastical law cases, and overlapping in jurisdiction. The Christian world was aghast. Protests came from everywhere.

In 1409 an ecumenical council was called by cardinals of the two popes to meet at Pisa. This council declared the papal office vacant and elected Alexander V (1409-1410) new pope. To the dismay of all, the two incumbents refused to recognize the authority of the council, and now there were three popes. By political maneuvering and liberal bribery, the several strong states were induced to support a new council, convoked this time by one of the popes. The Council of Constance (1414-18) deposed all three of the popes and elected another, who took the name of Martin V (1417-31). This time, however, the task was accomplished by political means. Once again the secular sword controlled the spiritual. The schism ended, but the prestige of the Roman papacy had been lowered. Voices everywhere were calling for a drastic reform of the whole system. The next chapter will discuss in some detail this clamor for reform.

The Roman Papacy had exercised world domination through the imposing ecclesiastical structure built between 1050 and 1215, but the building could not stand. Its essentially tyrannical and non-Christian character was seen in its initiation of movements like the Crusades and the Inquisition. The great increase in central organization, together with the squandering proclivities of the papal court, required vast revenues. Every papal policy appeared to be designed to raise money. Religious dissent was widespread. The popes could not read the signs of the times and endeavored to speak arrogantly to the strong monarchs of the developing states. Nationalism blunted the force of the ecclesiastical weapons wielded by Gregory VII and Innocent III, and the states paid little attention to papal demands.

King Philip IV of France gained control of the papal office, and for over seventy years papal headquarters were at Avignon. During this time the papacy was subservient to French interests, alienating the political rivals and enemies of France. The attempt to return the papacy to Rome in 1378 brought schism, which continued until 1417, when it was finally healed by conciliar action.

13

Clamor for Reform

The long "Babylonian captivity" of the church and the disastrous papal schism of about forty years dramatically demonstrated the need for papal reform. Many recognized that these tragic events were symptoms of the trouble and not its cause. Financial, political, and moral abuses by the papacy did not help the situation, but the basic problem was not abuse of the system, but the system itself. The clamor for reform did not merely address the immediate problem, but it challenged conceptions advocated by the popes for centuries. Some calls for reform had a distinctly biblical basis. The doctrinal and ecclesiastical tenets built up by the Roman Church over a long period were compared with the Scriptures and criticized from that viewpoint. Patriotic motives impelled some to demand reform. Rising nationalism of the late Medieval period brought conflicting loyalties to Europeans. Not a few of the protests against Roman domination grew out of resentment against French control of the papacy during the "Babylonian captivity." Wretched economic and social conditions and the Turks poised on the very border of the Empire in the Balkans led many to think that God was punishing the world because of the misdeeds of the papacy. Spiritual Christians in all countries were grieved to see the condition into which Christianity had fallen. Mysticism and dissent increased as men and women sought to find communion with God apart from the prevailing ecclesiastical system.

One of the greatest antecedents of reform was the movement known as the *Renaissance*. The throbbing of new intellectual life and the discovery of new worlds helped prepare the way for reformation. Humanism radically changed the way people thought, and their new vision discerned many of the superstitions that characterized the Medieval Roman Catholic system. Some writers have minimized the scope of the Renaissance, insisting that Western culture required no rebirth. The theological system of the Roman Catholic Church was partly responsible for the slow recovery from the barbarian invasions and the Dark Ages that followed. Because Medieval theology rested on the extensive unraveling of established propositions through the use of deductive reasoning, the sources of Roman Catholic doctrine were authoritative and traditional. There was little new grist for the mill, but a constant regrinding of the old. For this reason, truth and progress were actually impeded by the scholastic systems of Roman Catholic theology.

The Renaissance came. The Arabic scholars who followed the Islamic invasion of Spain in the eighth century helped to pry open the doors of learning in the West. Classical culture and the study of antiquity became the vogue. The Crusades helped introduce a new world. The fall of Constantinople (1453) gave impetus to the Renaissance when Greek scholars fled to the West for haven. A score of other factors—Italian nostalgia for the ancient glory of Rome, the appearance of genius in artistic and literary forms, economic developments, geographical discoveries, revolutionary inventions—made up what has been called the "rebirth" (Renaissance) of the West.

This awakening touched Christianity in many ways. The movement known as _humanism_, which will be discussed in the following pages, sprang directly from these elements. Humanism helped prepare the way for reform. The excellence of the ancient literary forms caused people to feel contempt for scholastic writings. The revival of interest in the ancients also renewed the study of the original Hebrew and Greek texts of Christian Scriptures, as well as the careful examination of the ancient Christian writings. The eyes of Europeans, so long focused only on the heavens, began to turn toward the world about them and on themselves. The very foundations of Roman Catholic authority were undermined by the new thought forms.

The centuries just before the sixteenth century resounded with calls for reform. Perhaps the best picture of this clamor for reform can be shown by discussing it from a geographical standpoint.

(Document 19)
Julian of Norwich: Reason, the Church, and the Holy Ghost

Julian of Norwich was a mystic, but her mysticism was contemplative and even intellectual. This is clear from the following selection from Revelation of the Divine Love.

By three things man standeth in this life; by which three God is worshipped, and we be speeded, kept and saved.
The first is, use of man's Reason natural; the second is, common teaching of Holy Church; the third is, inward gracious working of the Holy Ghost. And these three be all of one God: God is the ground of our natural reason; and God, the teaching of the Holy Church; and God is the Holy Ghost. And all be sundry gifts to which He willeth that we have great regard, and attend us to thereto. For these work in us continually all together; and these be great things. Of which great things He willeth that we have knowing here as it were in an A.B.C., that is to say, that we have little knowing; whereof we shall have fulness in Heaven. And that is for to speed us.

Italy

The strongest protests from Italy against the papal system were based on the intellectual revival and resulting humanism. *Humanism* was the name arbitrarily given to the classical and literary revival which began in Italy about the fourteenth century; it was patriotic as well as cultural. Many Italian humanists hoped that the glorious history of past days, spread before the eyes and minds of the present generation, might inspire a new unification of Italy and once again secure Roman supremacy in the secular sphere. The removal of the papal chair from Rome to Avignon, France, contributed to this longing.

The humanists collected manuscripts of classical writers of antiquity, learned to criticize ancient texts through internal study, reveled in imitating the literary style and social manners of the ancients, and viewed the world from a rich historical and literary background. They organized societies to study the Greek language, to read Plato and Cicero, and to gather libraries of the ancient authors. The movement spread from Italy rapidly into northern Europe through religious, intellectual, social, and economic ties. Development of the printing press helped spread the gospel of humanism, just as half a century later it reproduced the writings of the Christian reformers for transmission to every part of the world.

Humanism took a different turn in northern Europe. In Italy the interest was primarily cultural and patriotic, resulting in disdain for religious ideas and activity. It bred cynicism in many cases. Northern humanism, on the other hand, channeled its literary and cultural interest to religious antiquities. Scholars studied Hebrew and Greek in an attempt to interpret the Scriptures more accurately. Recovering the best text of the Scriptures encouraged the critical examination of ancient manuscripts; those interested in historical investigation republished the ancient Christian writings with critical interpretation. The northern emphasis looked toward uncovering the ancient origins of the faith and restoring the primitive purity of Christianity.

So far as reform was concerned, the influence of humanism in Italy and in the northern areas performed different services. In Italy its contribution was mainly negative; in the remainder of Europe it was more positive. The negative influences of humanism in Italy were twofold. First, humanism brought a widespread neglect of Christianity and enthroned ancient vices as well as virtues. Even the papacy was infected after its return from Avignon. In 1447 an out-and-out humanist scholar was elected pope and took the name of Nicholas V (1447-55). Under Nicholas religious matters became secondary to libraries, poems, and the classics. Pius II (1458-64) was an outstanding versifier before his election as pope.

Humanism also encouraged the application to Christian documents of the critical methods used on ancient classical manuscripts. Under Nicholas V, Lorenzo Valla, a young humanist scholar, was brought to the papal court to help translate Greek classics. While in and out of papal service he wrote a great deal about Christianity from the humanist viewpoint. His study of the Greek text of the New Testament was of great value to the reformers half a century later. He scoffed at the monastic movement and handled roughly the Vulgate translation, which is the official Latin version for Roman Catholics. One of his most spectacular feats was his convincing proof of the spurious nature of the *Donation of Constantine* by the application of internal criticism.

A product of this Italian patriotic revival was the celebrated poet Dante. Exiled to Ravenna in North Italy in the fourteenth century, Dante longed for the restoration of the glory of ancient Rome. His *On Monarchy* discusses the proper relations between the papacy and the empire. God has given each a sword, said Dante, and neither should control the other. The papacy should not control the empire or meddle in secular matters. While the idea was not new, its application would move the papacy back to an earlier stage of development. The fact that it was suggested by a thoroughly orthodox Catholic, in opposition to papal claims of several preceding centuries, together with the fact that Dante used biblical exegesis to controvert the papal interpretations, made the ideas of Dante quite significant.

The Empire

The loose collection of German states, known as the Empire, added their protest. Humanism played some part as the background for reform demands. The work of intellectuals like Rudolph Agricola, teacher of Greek at the University of Heidelberg, Sebastian Brant of Basel, Johann Reuchlin, and others was mainly negative. Their writings helped to undermine the Roman system with the populace and thinkers. They used both satirical verse and scholarly research in their protests. Some German humanists like Ulrich von Hutten, Franz von Sickingen, and Pirkheimer of Nuremberg actively supported the reform movement. Philip Melanchthon, nephew of Reuchlin and an accomplished humanist, became Luther's right-hand man.

The political situation provided the principal protest against papal power however. In 1314 Duke Louis of Bavaria became emperor following his military victory over a rival candidate. Louis became embroiled in a dispute with Pope John XXII at Avignon over the right of the pope to sanction the election of every emperor. French control of the papacy made it distasteful for Louis to submit. In 1324 the pope excommunicated Louis. Two scholars, Marsiglio of Padua and John of Janduno, collaborated to prepare the *Defensor Pacis* (Defender of Peace), one of the most unusual treatises of the day.

This document asserted that people are the final authority in all things, whether secular or ecclesiastical. Thus in ecclesiastical matters the whole body of Christians, following the principles of the New Testament, constitute the highest power. This remarkable document undermined the papal theory of government. Arguing from the New Testament, it denied that the pope had superior power over any other bishop and stated there was no scriptural evidence that Peter was ever in Rome. All spiritual power rests in the body of Christian believers, not in priests, bishops, or popes. Furthermore, in a Christian state, reflecting the character and will of the people, the civil ruler has the right to control ecclesiastical affairs, including the calling of ecumenical councils and the appointment of bishops. The ultimate authority resides in a general ecclesiastical council of the people, not simply the bishops.

Another powerful voice that supported Emperor Louis was William of Occam, the great English theologian, who took refuge with the emperor. Occam also insisted that the true church did not reside in bishops, but in the believers. He denied the infallibility of the pope and emphasized the Bible as a source of direction. He believed the papacy should never deal in secular matters and should be subordinate to a general council of all Christians.

France

French humanism made a distinct contribution to the protest against the unreformed papacy. The movement began later in France, but quickly gained strength. Through it the upper class in particular received considerable enlightenment as to the faults of the Roman system. Jacques Lèfevre Étaples (1455-1536) became an accomplished biblical scholar and antedated Luther in his advocacy of salvation by faith alone, without sacraments, and his emphasis on the authority of the Scriptures.

The University of Paris was an early center that called for reform. William of Occam had taught there and expressed his views. John Gerson (1363-1429) and the chancellor of Notre Dame, Pierre d'Ailly (1350-1420), inheritors of Occam's attitude and outlook, headed a scholarly group at the university who desired earnestly to reform the papacy. This group finally succeeded in ending the papal schism through the use of general councils.

England

Resentment against papal claims had deep roots in England. William Rufus, successor to William the Conqueror, notified the pope that he was unwilling to bow his knee, since his predecessor had not done so. The humiliation of England by Innocent III in 1215 produced a reaction against papal absolutism. One of the great reforming churchmen of England was Robert Grosseteste, who became bishop of Lincoln in 1235. As well as reforming his own diocese, Grosseteste addressed Pope Innocent IV about 1250 relative to the corruptions of the Roman Curia and of the Roman Church in general. Eight years later Grosseteste refused to accept Innocent's appointment of a relative to the Lincoln diocese. In the struggle between Boniface VIII and King Edward I in 1299, the English Parliament upheld their king and defied the pope. The "Babylonian captivity," which brought the papacy under French domination, occurred just at the time France and England were engaged in war. King Edward III (1327-77) secured the passage of two legislative blows against the papacy. In 1350 the Statute Against Provisors was enacted, which provided for the English to have free elections of archbishops and bishops—an attempt to eliminate foreign influence in filling high church offices. Two years later the Statute of Premunire was enacted, which made it treason for any English subject to accept jurisdiction of papal courts outside of England or to appeal cases to them.

John Wycliffe and the Lollards

In the latter years of his life, the patriot and teacher John Wycliffe (1320-84) was one of the outstanding opponents of the papacy. Before about 1376 Wycliffe withheld his attacks against the papacy, but the disreputable conditions surrounding the closing years of the Avignon papacy and the beginning of the papal schism in 1378 touched off his violent protests. Wycliffe urged that both of the popes be deposed. In his lectures at Oxford he suggested that if any secular or ecclesiastical prince were not faithful to his task, his right to hold the office was forfeited. If a bishop or pope proved unworthy, civil rulers, as agents of God's will, had the right to take away his temporal property. Probably encouraged by the protection given him by powerful English nobles, Wycliffe boldly continued his criticism of the papacy. Using the Bible—which he helped translate into English about 1382—as final authority, he vigorously attacked the Roman Catholic sacramental system, particularly the doctrine of transubstantiation. He also asserted that the New Testament made no distinction between the bishop and the presbyter (priest) and that consequently the Roman bishop had wrongfully usurped power that was not his. Wycliffe's views were greatly colored by his nationalism—he objected to papal extortion of English funds, to papal appointments of foreigners to English benefices, and to papal encouragement of mendicant monks in England who, he said, robbed the poor.

To give scriptural instruction, Wycliffe organized a group known as the "poor priests" who wandered about two by two (following scriptural injunctions) preaching and teaching. They were received joyfully by the people. Wycliffe was condemned by the pope in 1377, but he was protected until his death in 1384 by political influence. The Lollards, as his poor priests were called, continued to increase in number and influence until 1399. In 1395 they delivered a bold memorial to Parliament denouncing Romanism. The accession of King Henry IV (1399-1413), a staunch supporter of Rome, was the signal for persecution. Scores of Lollards were burned at the stake and their churches suppressed. Lollard followers went underground after 1417 and doubtless provided fertile soil for the reform movement that came about a century later.

English Humanism

English humanism also played a part in increasing antipapal sentiment. John Colet (1467-1519), dean of St. Paul's Cathedral in London, was an outstanding humanist. With William Grocyn and Thomas Linacre he formed a nucleus for the school of thought that despised scholastic methods and theology. Colet, a deeply spiritual and capable leader, was especially skilled in biblical interpretation. He was eloquent in constantly calling for reform. Colet was a great influence on Erasmus, the outstanding continental humanist, between about 1498 and 1514.

Bohemia

The clamor for reform in Bohemia was partly religious and partly patriotic. Bohemia was under German domination. Her Christianity had originally been received from the Greek Church, but the great Magyar invasion of the thirteenth century had forced the nation into a German alliance, and through the Germans the Roman type of Christianity had been introduced. The University of Prague was the center of religious and patriotic opposition. A number of eloquent preachers and teachers advocated stringent religious reforms. Among these was Conrad of Waldhausen, who openly denounced the Roman monks and clergy; Milicz of Kremsier; Matthias of Janow, a remarkably able teacher and writer; and Thomas of Stitny, a very popular preacher. Two events brought great impetus to the reform movement. One was the marriage of Anne of Bohemia to King Richard II of England in 1382. The other was the exchange of scholars and correspondence between the universities of Prague and Oxford, as a result of the closer ties between the two nations because of the marriage. The exchange of scholars and correspondence between the universities brought Bohemia into contact with the writings of John Wycliffe.

The head of the reform movement in Bohemia was John Huss (1368-1415). Huss was a native of Bohemia and educated at the University of Prague. A careful student of the Scriptures and of Wycliffe, he filled some of the highest offices at the University of Prague. Through his struggle against the Germans in the university he was able to secure from the king a change in the constitution of the school in January 1409. That change brought the native Czechs into a favored position over the German majority. As a consequence the German teachers and students withdrew.

Huss became increasingly bold in his attacks against foreign and papal usurpations. In 1410 he was excommunicated and his teachings were condemned. Huss published his treatise *Concerning the Church*, in which he repeated the views of Wycliffe, sometimes copying page after page from Wycliffe's writings. His preaching was directed against papal abuses and demanded reform. He was summoned to the Council of Constance in 1415 to discuss his views and he was promised safe conduct if he would attend. The Roman bishop violated the promise, however, remarking that the church did not need to keep its word with heretics. Huss was condemned by the Council and was burned at the stake in 1415. A follower, Jerome of Prague, suffered the same fate months later.

The burning of Huss and Jerome aroused Bohemia to open revolt. The Hussite wars, both political and religious in nature, lasted only until about 1435, but the influence of the strict party, the Taborites, led to the formation of the Bohemian Brethren.

The Netherlands

Probably the greatest continental humanist was Desiderius Erasmus of Rotterdam (1465-1536). The son of a priest and gifted in many ways, his life was profoundly affected by the death of his parents when he was thirteen. For a brief time he attended the school of the Brethren of the Common Life at Deventer, but he was shunted to a monastic school when his guardians squandered the money left for him. After splendid training at Paris and Cologne, he took his place as the outstanding humanist of his day, making his living by dedicating his works to the patrons who supported him. He had little inclination to break with the Roman system, but his writings are filled with ridicule of prevailing abuses and superstitions. His publication in 1516 of a critical edition of the Greek text of the New Testament was of double value—the text was quite helpful to reformation scholarship, and the preface spelled out the need for reform. He hoped for reform through the process of education and infiltration. Erasmus believed that if per-

---

(Document 20)
Thomas à Kempis: Of the
Few Who Love Jesus' Cross

Thomas à Kempis (1380-1471) is generally considered the author of Imitation of Christ. *This devotional book reflects the Christ-centered mysticism of the Brethren of the Common Life, a lay brotherhood of which he was a member.* Imitation of Christ *has enjoyed continuous popularity and is read in many languages.*

Seldom do we find a person so spiritual that he lives stripped of everything. Who can find someone truly poor in spirit and totally detached from all the things of this world? His price is well beyond that of anything on earth! If a person were to give up all his possessions, that would still be nothing. And if he were to do great penance, it would still be a little thing. And if he were to learn all knowledge, he would still be far off. And if he had great virtue and burned with passionate devotion, still much would be lacking in him;

that is, the one thing which is supremely necessary. And what is it? That having left all things behind, he must also leave himself—totally abandon himself—keeping nothing of his selfish, self-centered ways. And when he had done all that he knows must be done, then let him believe that he has done nothing. Let him not be deluded when others praise him, but let him admit in all honesty that he is only a humble servant of God. As Truth himself has said: "When you have done all that is asked of you, say to yourselves, we are unworthy servants." Then he will be truly poor and naked in spirit, and he may say with the Prophet: "I am alone and poor." Yet, no one is richer, no one more powerful, no one more free than the person who can give his whole life to God and freely serve others with deep humility and love.

---

sons simply knew the gospel of primitive Christianity, they would correct the prevalent ills and abuses.

Mysticism

A number of groups not specifically confined to one geographical area provided great impetus for the reform movement. The mystics were one of the most important. Mysticism viewed people as having an affinity with God that does not require an ecclesiastical organization to make contact. God's presence could be felt in the heart and soul without reference to sacraments. It may be observed that this attitude could completely bypass all of the organization of the Roman Church, for if one could have an immediate and intuitive vision of God, it would be unnecessary to use the services of the priest and the church. Most of the mystics did not actively oppose the external spiritual exercises of the Roman Church. They were willing to use these as aids to supplement their own consciousness of the nearness of God. They had a real concern about the corruptions and schisms in the church.

The principal leaders of this group were Meister Eckhart (1260-1327) in Germany and Jan van Ruysbroeck (1293-1381) and Gerhardt Groote (1340-84) in the Netherlands. Eckhardt's theology was simple: Christians should allow God to fill them until they are actually absorbed in God and become Godlike. The modification of this central idea in harmony with the sacramental system of the Roman Church accounts for differences in the thinking of Eckhart's successors, such as Johann Tauler (1290-1361) and Henry Suso (died 1366). The influence of these and other mystics went far beyond simply producing additional mystics. In fundamental conceptions their thinking modified the crass sacramentalism and formalism of many continental theologians. One anonymous mystic wrote a work that Martin Luther published and prized highly. Luther called this "German theology," as over against scholastic theology of the Roman Church. This writing was deeply influenced by German mysticism and scriptural theology.

The system of Ruysbroeck in the Netherlands motivated scholars to the study of the New Testament and helped prepare for the reform movement that broke out later. Gerhardt Groote, a lay mystic of the Netherlands, led in the formation of the organization called the Brethren of the Common Life, a group devoted to spreading the mystical and pious conceptions of Ruysbroeck. The Brethren established several schools in the Netherlands and Germany. Erasmus attended one of these schools for a period, as did Luther. Thomas à Kempis is credited with writing a devotional guide, *Imitation of Christ,* that is still valuable.

Many of the mystics were found in monasteries. Meister Eckhart was a Dominican monk. Doubtless the long hours of reflection and contemplation gave ample opportunity for the development of mystical tendencies or, as a matter of fact, for the rise of extreme ideas for ceremonialism. The tendency would be to reach either extreme—to develop a passionate love for excessive sacramentalism or a genuine attachment to God apart from any externals. One large party from the Franciscans broke with the majority in an effort to follow more closely the simple ethic of their founder. Their mystical and scriptural simplicity abhorred the luxurious and schismatic Christianity of the papacy.

They joined so zealously in the clamor for reform that they were condemned as heretics and many were martyred.

Popular Calls for Reform

The papal schism, extending to every diocese and raising serious
questions in the mind of every Roman Catholic about which pope
(and which bishop) was the valid one, stirred up on every side a popular desire for reform. The immediate goal was to secure the unity of
the papacy. Since the rival popes anathematized one another and all
supporters of one another—which really negated the effectiveness of
any sacraments and official acts of the false pope and his followers—
and since no one knew which was the correct pope, utmost confusion and widespread fear prevailed among the masses. Lay organizations sprang up, and orders of women arose emphasizing the need
for reform.

The desire to reform the Roman Church sprang from various
motives. The study of the Bible, intellectual awakening, patriotism,
economic and social conditions, military considerations, and religious
hunger all motivated people to seek reform. Voices could be heard
from practically all of the principal countries. Mysticism and dissent
increased considerably.

The next chapter will discuss the effort to bring reform, primarily by
the conciliar method. This did at least heal the papal schism, although
no progress was made toward reforming the papacy itself.

14

Efforts at Reform

The domination of the papacy by French interests from 1309 to 1378 and the schism lasting almost forty years after the attempt to return the papacy to Rome emphasized the necessity for reform. Circumstances and traditional beliefs, however, seemed to make any sort of reform completely impossible. There was no way to determine the proper occupant of the papal chair. Each of the popes was supported by a legitimately appointed and properly consecrated group of cardinals. Each had declared himself the rightful pope and had anathematized his opponent. Each had sufficient political backing to maintain himself in office. What could be done against a pope, assuming that one of the two or three was the proper one? As early as the fifth century, Pope Symmachus set forth a theory that the pope is responsible only to God. By 503 this idea had received dogmatic approval. As enlarged through the centuries, the doctrine was taught that even if the pope were in complete error, he could be tried only by God. No tribunal on earth could challenge the doctrines, morals, motives, or decrees of a pope. How could there be any action taken to heal the schism?

Individual Protests

Chapter 13 sketches some of the protests from every part of the Roman Church. Many people urged plans of reform; severe criticism was directed against the papal government and papal doctrines. In view of the traditional notion that no one could correct a pope and the doubt concerning which claimant actually was the true pope, no practical move was taken.

The Opinions of Scholars

Despite repeated appeals to both popes after 1378, neither would take the initiative to restore papal unity. Scholars in the various theological schools, whose views had often borne great weight in doctrinal controversies, were consulted about the best way to end the schism. It was inevitable that the idea of Marsiglio of Padua, written in 1324 in his *Defensor Pacis,* should be asserted, namely, that a general council possesses supreme authority in Christianity. This same suggestion was made by two other scholars, Conrad of Gelshausen in 1379 and Heinrich of Langenstein in 1381. By 1408 most of the scholars in the great universities of the Continent agreed that the only method of healing the schism was through a general council. The scholars could not agree about the makeup of the council. Some thought all true Christians should constitute the membership; others favored the precedent of earlier general councils, limiting membership to the bishops who, they said, constituted the visible church. There were other problems. Who should call the council? The emperor had called some of the early councils, but the popes had claimed that prerogative for many centuries. Neither of the popes was willing to call the council; however, the cardinals of the rival popes were convinced that a general council was necessary to restore peace and unity.

The Council of Pisa (1409)

The cardinals called a general council to meet March 1409 in Pisa. The council addressed three problems: the papal schism, reform, and heresy. The first of these problems was viewed as the principal purpose of the council. Many attended the council and took action by declaring the papal throne vacant. Cardinals representing both popes united to elect a new pope, who took the name Alexander V. Since neither of the two existing popes, Gregory XII and Benedict XIII, recognized the council as validly assembled or authoritative, the result was simply the addition of a third pope.

The Council of Constance (1414-18)

The mistakes of the Council of Pisa were evident. Many of the bishops wanted more information about the authority of a council, particularly in deposing a pope. Others felt that the council should have been summoned by a pope, not by the cardinals or by a secular power. Political factors would determine whether or not any action of a future council would be effective. As it was, each of the three popes had enough political and military support to remain in office. The new pope, Alexander V, was recognized by England, France, Hungary, and parts of Italy; Benedict XIII was called pope by Spain and Scotland; and Gregory XII had most of the Italian and German support.

(Document 21)

The Decree of the Council of Constance

The Council of Constance was perhaps the high point of conciliarism, the movement to limit the pope by the authority of a universal council. In April 1415, the Council issued the following decree.

This holy Council of Constance...declares, first that it is lawfully assembled in the Holy Spirit, that it constitutes a General Council, representing the Catholic Church, and that therefore it has its authority immediately from Christ; and that all men, of every rank and condition, including the Pope himself, are bound to obey it in matters concerning the Faith, the abolition of the schism, and the reformation of the Church of God in its head and members. Secondly it declares that any one, of any rank and condition, who shall contumaciously refuse to obey the orders, decrees, statutes, or instructions, made or to be made by this holy Council, or by any other lawfully assembled general council...shall, unless he comes to a right frame of mind, be subjected to fitting penance and punished appropriately: and, if need be, recourse shall be had to the other sanctions of the law.

Two leaders remedied these defects. John Gerson, one of the champions of the conciliar idea after 1408, determined to clothe a future council with express authority to take action in dealing with schism, reform, and heresy. The German emperor Sigismund (1410-37) determined to provide political support sufficient to make the decrees of the council effective. Sigismund had the first task and he worked diligently at it. He induced Pope John XXIII (successor to Alexander V) to call a general council to convene at Constance. By clever political tactics he secured the support of the Spanish, English, and Burgundian rulers for the council. He had chosen Constance in Germany as the meeting place in order to neutralize the influence of the Italian clergy, practically all of whom favored John XXIII. In addition, arrangements were made for the council to vote by nations rather than by individuals, in this way circumventing plans by some of the incumbent popes to "pack" the meeting. Each of the five nations—England, France, Spain, Germany, and Italy—had one vote and must vote as a unit.

Gerson and his supporters did their part. Through Gerson's influence the council passed a decree in April 1415, defining its authority. It claimed to represent Jesus Christ and asserted that its decisions on all religious matters were binding on every Christian, including the pope or popes. This decree, of course, cut directly across papal claims for centuries. Passed unanimously by the ecumenical council, it challenged ancient dogmas of the Roman Church that were alleged to be unchangeable and provided an example of an alleged infallible council and infallible papacy in conflict. Acting on this decree, the council forcibly seized Pope John XXIII and deposed him in May, 1415; Gregory XII then resigned; Benedict XIII was twice deposed, although he refused to accept this action.

Instead of having a new pope elected by the cardinals, it was agreed by the council that those cardinals present at the council, supplemented by thirty members of the council, should elect a new pope, with only a two-thirds majority required for election. They chose one who took the name Martin V. He took office immediately, and he had enough political support to guarantee his universal acceptance. The schism was almost over. Benedict XIII had refused to resign, but after his death in 1424, his successor was recognized only by Aragon and Sicily; and in 1429 the schism was completely ended.

The second problem of the Council of Constance was reform. After the election of Martin V the council passed another decree that denied papal claims of almost a millennium. This decree provided that a general council would meet again in five years and in seven years, and that thereafter a council would meet every ten years. Future popes would be subject to instructions from these councils. The ancient papal claims of superiority over the councils seemed doomed. However, the attitude of the new pope should have warned the conciliar leaders. Martin V had supported the conciliar idea until his election as pope; then he immediately became anticonciliar. When the council endeavored to bring reform, the new pope worked feverishly and successfully to prevent the adoption of antipapal measures.

(Document 22)
John Huss on Heresy

The Council of Constance condemned John Hus for heresy in 1415 and he was burned at the stake. Interestingly, however, Hus had his own ideas about heresy.

There are three kinds of heresy, namely, apostasy, blasphemy, and simony.... But know that these three heresies are not entirely independent of each other, but are connected with each other. Nevertheless, they are differentiated from each other so that apostasy is the rejection of the law of God; blasphemy is the defamation of the divine faith; and simony is the heresy of overthrowing the divine order. Thus with these three heresies the entire Trinity is contemned: God the Father is contemned by apostasy, for he rules mightily by a pure and immaculate law; he also has pro-vided a bride of Christ which is the congregation of the elect; God the Son, who is the Wisdom of God, is contemned by the second her-esy—blasphemy; and God the Holy Spirit, who in his supreme goodnesss wisely and humbly governs God's house, is con-temned by the accursed simony which is contrary to his order. For the simoniac opposes the Holy Spirit, intending to derange his good order, and thus also peac-e....simony is a spiritual leprosy which is difficult to be driven out from the soul save by God's spe-cial miracle....Simony, as the word signifies, is the trafficking in holy things. And since he who buys and he who sells is a merchant, a simoniac is both he who buys and he who sells holy things. Conse-quently, simony comprises both buying and selling of holy things.

The problem of heresy also occupied the attention of the council. The burning of John Huss and Jerome has already been mentioned. The outbreak of the Hussite wars shows that the council was not only religiously suspect but was also politically unwise.

Council of Pavia and Siena (1423)

The papal schism had been healed, but reform still had not begun. Martin V (1417-31) asserted traditional papal claims in an effort to neutralize the decrees of the Council of Constance, which claimed to be the supreme authority in Christendom. However, the pope felt it necessary to carry out the decree of Constance that provided for the calling of a general council in five years, especially since the Bohemi-ans were still threatening and the Ottoman Turks were winning new military victories. The plague at Pavia caused the removal of the coun-cil to Siena. The pope soon dismissed the council, however, alleging poor attendance as the reason.

Council of Basel (1431-49)

The Council of Constance had planned to call another general council seven years after the Council of Pavia. Pope Martin V agreed to call this council but he died before it assembled. His successor, Eugenius IV (1431-47), promised to support the conciliar program as a condition of election but violated his promise. When the council met and showed the spirit of the Council of Constance, Eugenius tried to dissolve the assembly before it took any action. Political pressure dissuaded him. Three problems faced this council: how to deal with the warring Hussites; what to do about a reform of the church; and how to effect a reunion of Eastern and Western Christianity, desired by some of the Eastern leaders as a means of driving away the Ottoman Turks who were threatening to capture Constantinople.

The council was partially successful in dealing with the Bohemians. It appeased the moderate party (the Utraquists or Calixtines), but caused a division between the moderates and the more radical Taborites. The result was another civil war in Bohemia, but the Catholics were able to defeat the Taborites and repress the spread of their ideas.

For a brief period it seemed that some effective ecclesiastical reforms might result from the deliberations of the council. After the council treated the question of the person of the pope and his authority, papal influence blocked further progress. Eugenius decided to deal with the council as the council had dealt with the Bohemians—to divide and conquer. The question of union between East and West was also pressed on the council. When sharp differences appeared, the pope denounced the council and in 1437 removed it by papal bull to Ferrara, thence to Florence in 1439. A substantial party refused to abide by the papal edict and continued to meet at Basel. They voted to depose Eugenius as pope and selected another who took the name of Felix V (1439-49). There were two popes again, but Felix had no political support, and there was widespread revulsion at the thought of another papal schism. Consequently, the Basel council was discredited and in 1449 surrendered to Nicholas V (1447-55), who had succeeded Eugenius. The council's efforts to reform the papacy had failed.

Council of Ferrara and Florence (1437-39)

The principal reason that Pope Eugenius had moved the council from Basel to Ferrara and then to Florence was to discredit the Basel reforming party. The pope was determined there would be no reform by a council. Because of this, considerable responsibility for the schismatic movement known as the Reformation must be laid at his door. The Council of Basel was eager to make reforms and doubtless would have done so along the lines of the Pragmatic Sanctions of France, to be mentioned later.

Representatives from the Greek Church preferred to meet in an Italian city, but this was of little importance. As a matter of fact, the question of uniting East and West was doomed before the Greek delegation arrived at Ferrara in 1438. A majority of the East definitely opposed union under any circumstances. The minority wanted union simply to secure military and political help against the Turks. In the council the pope agreed to organize a new Crusade against the Turks, in return for which the East would recognize the universal supremacy of the pope. This agreement was promptly repudiated by the Eastern clergy.

Reason for Failure of Conciliar Efforts

The collapse of the Council of Basel in 1449 brought an end to the movement begun about forty years before in the Council of Pisa. Some reasons for the failure of this effort to reform the church in head and members are apparent. There was a lack of unity in motives for reform. Some were interested in reform only from a political standpoint, others wanted personal advancement, while others were willing to go along with the movement as long as it was popular.

A partial solution of the immediate problem, the papal schism, blunted the desire for thorough reform. When the Council of Constance solved the most pressing problem facing it in 1417, even the brave statement of the authority of the council did not hide the fact that in the minds of many the council had gone as far as it should. With a single pope to deal with, leadership in a stringent reform brought danger of effective reprisals.

The active antagonism of the popes predestined to failure any attempts at reform. The several popes of the first half of the fifteenth century agreed in principle with the efforts of the conciliar reformers until they had been elected to the high office. Their sympathy for reform and their recognition of the authority of a council vanished immediately. The comparatively long period of time between the meetings of the reforming councils gave the papacy an opportunity to recoup much of its strength and prestige.

After the Reforming Council

Although an effective program of reform was not brought about, the battle had not been lost entirely. The various nations represented in the councils had seen firsthand the need for reform and the attitude of the papacy toward reform. They had caught a glimpse of the authority that political and military strength carried. Consequently, England, Spain, and France, already strong and unified, were able to secure important concessions from the papacy with reference to the control of the church within their boundaries. In fact, shortly after the failure of the Council of Basel, France assembled a meeting of the clergy and enacted the Pragmatic Sanctions in 1438, which accomplished the very thing for France that the conciliar proponents had hoped would happen for all Christendom. These Sanctions asserted that a general council was the supreme authority in Christendom and, among other things, claimed French autonomy in filling its ecclesiastical vacancies. The loosely organized German states, where the reform movement subsequently broke forth, were also unable to secure concessions and consequently felt the burdens of papal financial and ecclesiastical tyranny more heavily.

The failure of the conciliar movement seemed to increase the arrogance of the Roman popes. The religious and moral tone of the papacy from the close of the Council of Basel until the Lutheran Reformation was low. Two of the popes were humanists (Nicholas V, 1447-55), and Pius II, 1458-64); one of them a second-rate despot (Sixtus IV, 1471-84); two were shameless in their immorality and vice (Innocent VIII, 1484-92, who openly acknowledged and promoted his seven illegitimate children), and (Alexander VI, 1492-1503, noted for his immorality, vice, and violence); one should have been an army officer (Julius II, 1503-13); while the pope of the Reformation (Leo X, 1513-21) reportedly called Christianity a profitable fable and spent his time in his hunting lodge. Had there been wise and upright popes in this period, it is very likely that the next effort at reform would have been different in its direction and consequences. The succession of leaders of this caliber fostered rebellion against the church.

❑ ❑ ❑ ❑ ❑

The difficult problem of ending a papal schism was finally accomplished by the authority of a general council, buttressed by political and military support. Such action marked the council as superior to popes, a fact subsequently denied by succeeding popes, but that established them in their office and succession. To deny the authority of a council to depose popes would appear to deny the validity of their own succession.

The thorough reform of the Roman Catholic Church in head and members could not be accomplished by reforming councils, despite repeated efforts made during forty years. The occupants of the papal office in the half century immediately before the Reformation constitute ample evidence of the need for reform.

15

Ecclesiastical Dissent

A factor of great importance relating to the papal decline and the clamor for reform was the presence everywhere of antipapal dissent. To combine in one descriptive term all of the extensive movements that existed just prior to the Reformation is difficult. The only record of many of them comes from their persecution in the Inquisition. Some of the movements were distinctively medieval in their religious conceptions. Others held evangelical tenets. We find it is hard to interpret contemporary religious movements correctly despite the possession of extensive literature by their own adherents. The problem of attempting to give a true picture of movements whose only records are those of one testimony, an enemy to the cause and one unversed in differentiating objectively between evangelicalism and heresy, is far greater.

The same situation renders most difficult the matter of determining the relations and history of any such movement. Were these dissenters isolated and separate movements, or was there correspondence among them? Did they represent the fruits of earlier movements, or did they spring de novo from the earth? Such questions have passionate defenders at both extremes and cannot be settled completely. Conclusions in many cases are a matter of personal attitude and judgment.

Evidences of Unity and Continuity

Literary remains of concerted opposition to the Roman Church would naturally be quite scarce. We find indisputable evidence that

many of the movements that were at one time thought to be isolated and separate were, in reality, in close fellowship and correspondence. For example, evangelical parties in Germany, Austria,
and Italy assembled in convention as early as 1218 to discuss
points of mutual belief. Constant correspondence had taken place
long before the Reformation between evangelical dissenters
throughout Germany and in Bohemia. In the thirteenth century Pope
Innocent III denounced the translation of the Scriptures to the language of the people, and the possession of Scriptures in the vernacular tongue was looked on as heresy. Even before Wycliffe's version
in English in the late fourteenth century, dissenters were translating
the Bible in the language of the people. Dozens of German translations existed in the fifteenth century, some showing evidence of
independent work while others, betraying a common source, turned
up among widely separated groups. Long after the Reformation had
begun, the Anabaptists of Germany used these ancient translations
rather than the translation of Luther. An interesting reflection of connections among the dissenters is seen in the fact that the Waldenses
of Italy and France, the Brethren of the Common Life in the Netherlands and Germany, and the United Brethren of Bohemia used the
same catechism to instruct children in their movements. Editions of
the identical catechism are found in French, Italian, German, and
Bohemian.

We easily find convincing evidence that many of the dissenting
movements of the thirteenth and fourteenth centuries were the successors of more primitive groups. Peculiar doctrines, noticeable in the
system of the Eastern Paulicians of the early Middle Ages, for example, are reproduced in the Bogomiles of the Balkans and the Cathari of
France and Germany. The Western dispersion of the Paulicians is an
established historical fact. The name of the Cathari (Greek both in
form and in spirit) marks them as an Eastern movement transplanted
to the West, probably a reappearance of the Paulician and Bogomile
dissenters. There are evidences of the persistence of the older Christianity of Britain (discountenanced by the Synod of Whitby in 664), as
well as older Christianity on the Continent proper. The rapid spread of
Luther's reform and the sudden appearance of organized Anabaptist
congregations all over the Continent in the sixteenth century testify to
a widespread evangelical background.

Handicaps to Historical Certainty

We cannot be certain about the history of dissent in this period. The sparsity of historical material forbids it. Most of the literary remains were prepared by the enemies of dissent, secured through the most excruciating torture by inquisitors. Before the suppression of dissent through the central organization of the Roman Curia, this work was carried on locally by bishops or crusading preachers like Bernard, the Cistercian monk. Under these circumstances even inquisitorial records are lacking, and there is practically no evidence of any kind about the dissenters and their beliefs.

For example, although the Bogomiles of the twelfth century may have numbered as many as two million, one of the principal records of their beliefs comes from a Byzantine monk named Euthymius who died in 1118. He gave an account of how they rejected the Lord's Supper as the sacrifice of demons, called the churches the dwelling places of demons and the worship of images in them idolatry, and termed the "fathers of the church" false prophets against whom Jesus warned. Such charges doubtless were similar to the charges brought against the early Christians: they were called atheists because they had no idols, cannibals because they partook of the body and blood of Christ, and immoral because they spoke of Christian love. Perhaps the Bogomiles did reject the mass, reject the orthodox churches, and oppose images. From the entire description given, the Bogomiles appear to have been the product of missionary work by the Paulicians among the Bulgarians. At least, their alleged doctrines reflect some of the peculiarities of the Paulicians, modified by dualistic and Man-ichean tendencies.

Another example of the sparsity of records is seen in the story of the Petrobrusians and Henricians. These movements began sepa-rately but coalesced. Much of what is known about the Petrobrusians comes from the pen of a Roman Catholic enemy. Peter de Bruys was a priest of the Roman Church in the twelfth century. He had been a student of Abelard, the great freethinker. About 1104 he began a career as a reformer in southern France and was widely influential until his martyrdom about 1126. Henry of Lausanne, a Roman Catho-lic monk, associated with Peter as a reformer. After a long and active ministry, Henry died as a martyr in 1148. The evangelical nature of the things these men taught is evident in spite of the denunciation of their doctrines by their enemy biographer. (1) They denied that the christening of infants was baptism and said that only an intelligent and personal profession of faith without proxy brought salvation. (2) They vehemently rejected crosses in worship because Christ was slain on one. They believed that temples and churches were unnecessary for the worship of God. (3) They denied the doctrine of transubstantiation and perhaps refused to observe the Lord's Supper at all. (4) They recognized the Scriptures alone as authoritative, denying the authority of the church fathers and of tradition.

Innocent III and Dissent

Innocent III (1198-1216), the pope who closed the previous period and opened the present one, had contact with two dissenting groups, the Waldenses and the Cathari. These movements had a long history before that time. The origin of the Waldenses is disputed; even the source of their name is in doubt. Perhaps it was begun by Peter Waldo of Lyons, France, in the closing years of the twelfth century. He headed a movement in which laypersons traveled, teaching and singing Scriptures. The group was excommunicated in 1184, but continued to spread rapidly through southern France, Italy, Spain, and the Rhine Valley.

The inquisitors who sought information on the beliefs of the Waldenses testify that they had about the same doctrines as the Petrobrusians: the sole authority of the Scriptures, the necessity of believer's baptism, the denial of the authority of the Roman Church, the denial of purgatory and the merit of praying to the saints, and the refusal to believe that the bread and wine are changed to the body and blood of Christ by the priest. In addition, it was alleged that the Waldenses permitted preaching without proper ordination, vilified the pope, refused to make canonical confession, and rejected oaths and war. About 1212 Innocent III was approached by some of this group for permission to assemble and read the Scriptures. The pope gave this permission, but three years later initiated a decree of condemnation against all Waldenses. In an effort to cripple the movement, two successive Catholic synods forbade reading the Bible in the language of the people, either by laity or clergy. Although severely persecuted, the Waldenses continued and exist today.

The group known as the Cathari came to light in France in the eleventh century. Their doctrines were quite similar to those of the Bogomiles. In fact, the Cathari of France looked toward Bulgaria as their source and recognized a Bogomile leader as their spiritual head. Their dualistic view of God and docetic Christology suggest a strong Manichean influence, another indication that their doctrinal system might have originated in the East, where Manicheanism was strongest.

The dissenters known as the Albigenses (because they lived near Albi in southern France) were Cathari. Innocent III decided, in view of the great strength of the movement, that strong means must be taken to root it out. Accordingly, Innocent sent two legates to France to begin the effort. They were persuaded by the bishop of Osma and by Dominic to try religious measures first. Assuming the garb of beggars, the legates and others wandered about barefooted and presented an example of humility and poverty. Few Albigenses were convinced. Violent measures soon followed.

Count Raymond of Toulouse was the nominal ruler over the area where the heretics lived, but was indifferent to their religious views as long as they were good subjects. One of the legates was murdered in 1208, and Raymond was suspected and accused of complicity. Innocent III proclaimed a crusade against Raymond and the Albigenses. Whoever conquered them would have both territory and spoils from the war. For twenty years the war raged. As cities were captured, their inhabitants were either slaughtered or sold into slavery. The Albigenses fled throughout Europe, and others of the Cathari followed their example. Pope Innocent pushed through the Fourth Lateran Council in 1215 three canons relating to heretics: secular rulers must not tolerate heretics in their domain; secular rulers refusing to uproot heretics must themselves be driven out, either by their subjects or by Crusaders from the outside; crusading against heretics at home brings all the sacramental privileges and indulgences that accrue from crusading against the Turks in Jerusalem.

The Extent of Ecclesiastical Dissent

Between 1215 and the theses of Luther in 1517 it is possible to find sizable groups of dissenters in almost every section of the West. Dissent was also strong in the East, but that area was not involved in the domination of the papacy after 1054 and did not share in the Reformation.

England

In England the Lollards (the name given to the poor priests of Wycliffe) were a large and aggressive dissenting movement. A Roman

---

(Document 23)
John Wycliffe: On the Eucharist

John Wycliffe translated the Scriptures into English and helped promote Bible reading. At various points, his teachings resembled those of the Protestant Reformation, which began about 130 years after his death. In the following selection, Wycliffe explained his own interpretation of the presence of Christ in the Lord's Supper, a subject on which later Reformers were never able to agree.

(1) In dealing with the Eucharist it is necessary to set forth the more commonly known facts, and first to consider whether the sacrament of the altar is the real body of Christ. On this topic I have often said in public that there are three aspects of the sacrament of the altar to be considered, namely, the bare sacrament, apart from the matter of the sacrament, as the consecrated host; second, the sacrament and the matter of the sacrament as the true body and blood of Christ; and third, the matter of the sacrament, apart from the sacrament itself, as the union of Christ with his mystical body the Church. This is nowhere comprehensible by the senses, and consequently is not anywhere a sacrament. From this belief arise the objections of the pagans.

For they argue that a hog, a dog, or a mouse can eat our Lord, because they eat the body of Christ, that is, God.
(2) But we reply to them in accordance with this belief. Their assumption is false; beasts can eat the consecrated host, but it is the bare sacrament and not the body or blood of Christ. When a lion devours a man, it does not also devour his soul; yet his soul is present in every part of his body. Thus should one believe concerning the body of Christ in the sacrament of the altar. For this is whole, sacramentally, spiritually, or virtually in every part of the consecrated host, even as the soul is in the body.
(3) Secondly, they object on this account, that we priests break the body of Christ, and thus the head, neck, arms and other members; this would be an utterly horrible thing to do to our God.
(4) But we reply according to the prior belief that they falsely assume this. We break the sacrament or consecrated host, but not the body of Christ, which is something different, just as we do not break a ray of the sun, even though we break a glass or a crystal stone.

Catholic writer of the late fourteenth century said that one out of every two persons in England seemed to be a follower of Wycliffe. The Lollards were strong enough in 1395 to present a memorial to parliament attacking the Roman Church and its doctrines, in particular condemning the priesthood, celibacy, Roman transubstantiation, liturgies and prayers for the dead, auricular confession, and the crusades. Four years later, with the accession of Henry IV, who was under the influence of Archbishop Thomas Arundel of Canterbury, persecution of the Lollards began. After 1417 they were driven underground, but their influence and doctrines were not forgotten.

France and Spain

Reference has been made to the dissenting movements of Peter de Bruys, Henry of Lausanne, and the Cathari. Some historians believe that through these groups almost all of southern France was antipapal during the twelfth century. When the Albigensian persecution began in the thirteenth century, many of the Cathari fled to Spain and later became victims of the Spanish Inquisition. One of the letters of Bernard, the outstanding preacher of the twelfth century, remarks that the churches were without congregations because of the heretical movement.

Italy

Reformers were not unknown at the door of the papal see. One of the outstanding reforming figures was Arnold of Brescia in northern Italy. His strictures against the papacy were aimed mainly at the secular and financial activities of the clergy. He believed that freewill offerings alone should provide for the support of all religious leaders. He fled from Italy in 1139 to escape charges of heresy, but in 1145 he assumed leadership of a popular movement that expelled the pope and looked to the restoration of the ancient Roman republic. Ten years later, overwhelmed by the military alliance of Pope Alexander III, Arnold was martyred.

Arnold probably founded the group known as Arnoldists and inspired the development of the movement later known as the Poor Men of Lombardy. Little is known about these two groups, except that they are frequently mentioned as heretics in the Roman Catholic writings of the thirteenth and fourteenth centuries. They seem to have vigorously opposed the Roman Catholic system, denied that water in baptism brings forgiveness, and excoriated the Roman clergy for secularization and corruption.

Another Italian group known as the Humiliati arose in the twelfth century. Little is known about them, except that they were classed as heretics and mentioned in such fashion that they seemed to have been associated with the Waldenses.

The influence of these dissenters was extensive in northern Italy. In a document written about 1260, an anonymous author remarked that in northern Italy the Waldenses had more schools and more followers than the orthodox church. He further asserted that because of their large numbers, these heretics held public disputes against Catholicism and services in the marketplace or the open field.

The German States

The Waldensian movement was also popular in many areas of the Germanic states. The same author who described the large number of Waldenses in Italy spoke of the extensive spread of the Waldenses around Passau on the Danube River. He named forty-two places in the Catholic diocese of Passau that were affected by the heresy. In twelve of these places the Waldenses had schools and in one of them a bishop. Roman Catholic documents a century and a half later (1389) describe ninety-two points of papal doctrine and practice that the Waldenses rejected and provide evidence that this movement had became thoroughly evangelical in its doctrinal views.

In the fourteenth century two theologians in German schools openly taught at variance with the teachings of the Roman system. John of Wesel believed that the Scriptures alone were the final authority in Christianity. Wesel rejected the idea that priests control salvation and denied the doctrine of transubstantiation. Imprisoned by the Roman authorities at Mainz, he died in 1482. The other theologian was Wessel Gansfort, who died in 1489. Gansfort proclaimed the doctrine of justification by faith and attacked the doctrine of indulgences. Luther later confessed that his entire Reformation doctrine was so evident in the writings of Wessel Gansfort that, had Luther been acquainted with these writings, his enemies might have charged him with securing material from that source.

Netherlands and the Rhine Valley

The records also speak of heretical movements in the twelfth century in northern Europe. In the Netherlands, Tanchelm (1115-24) strongly denounced Roman Catholic churches and sacraments and in general followed the teachings of Peter de Bruys, with whom he was a contemporary. At about the same time Eudo de Stella carried on a similar ministry in the Rhine Valley. His followers were so stirred by his preaching that they destroyed Roman churches and monasteries. He was seized by the Roman Church and died as a martyr about 1148. Other dissenters, both evangelical and antipapal, left a record of their work along the Rhine Valley. They clearly denied the Roman doctrines of transubstantiation and infant baptism.

Bohemia

Perhaps of all the areas of Europe, Bohemia had the most widespread dissent movements. Historically Bohemia had looked to the Eastern world for her religious pattern and had only accepted the [11th] Latin Church because it was brought by the Germans who protected Bohemia against the Magyar invasions of the eleventh century. Religious resentment against foreigners formed a background of Bohemian dissent. The Waldenses were quite strong in southern Bohemia—so strong, in fact, that about 1340 they threatened to destroy their Catholic foes should an attempt be made to coerce them religiously. Out of the Hussite wars, following the burning of John Huss in 1415, came the two parties, the strict one (the Taborites) holding views much like those of the evangelical Waldenses. The Taborites fiercely opposed the Roman Catholic Church on every point save one, the retention of infant baptism. One of the outstanding [15th] leaders of Bohemian dissent in the fifteenth century was Peter Chelicky, a native Bohemian, born about 1385. He followed closely the doctrines of the evangelical Waldenses, and he allowed infant baptism in practice, although denying its validity in principle.

The Bohemian Brethren constituted the evangelical wing of the Hussite reform. This group was organized in an effort to bring a general reform within the national church in order to restore to Christianity the original purity that it had lost. This movement formed a community that endeavored to live according to the law of Christ. Specific organization was effected about 1457. Before the Reformation crisis of 1517 this movement had spread throughout Bohemia and Moravia and had become a considerable force for reform. Through extensive use of the newly invented printing press, the organization of schools, and the wide dissemination of their doctrines [16th] throughout Austria and Germany, the Brethren played a large part in preparing for the events of the sixteenth century.

❑ ❑ ❑ ❑ ❑

Dissent of some kind appeared in almost every section of Europe in this period. The sparsity of records makes it difficult to judge accurately either the doctrines or the extent of the movements. This description of these movements is not exhaustive. How many reformers lingered just below the surface of recorded history can never be known, but they were there. The rapidity with which the Reformation developed in the sixteenth century provides evidence of

this. How else is it possible to explain how a large part of the Continent and England embraced the reforming movements so rapidly
between 1517 and 1534? Such widespread defection from the
Roman Church was prompted by earlier dissent and dissatisfaction.

16

The Fullness of Time

The word *Reformation* describing the revolution of the sixteenth century is, in a sense, a misnomer. Principal events did not center in reform, but in schism. Those who participated in the organization of new ecclesiastical bodies conceived of their movements as true Christianity moving in, or toward, its primitive channel. In that sense there was a reformation of Christianity, but not of the Roman curia, for the curia refused to be reformed.

In 1517 a monk named Martin Luther, incensed by the recent sale of indulgences in a nearby German town, gave public notice on the door of the church at Wittenberg that he wanted to debate what the Catholic Church actually taught about indulgences. In this rather ordinary fashion the Lutheran Reformation began. What was it that brought comparative success to Luther's efforts when so many previous efforts had failed? Was it in the monk, in his environment, in the circumstances of his life, in his inheritance from previous generations? It was in all of these.

Political Factors That Aided the Reformation

Practically every political body in Europe contributed to the progress of the reform movement. In most cases it was done unwittingly. Spain was the strongest state in Europe during this period. The peninsula had been unified politically by the marriage between Ferdinand of Aragon and Isabella of Castile in 1469 and by the subsequent conquest of contiguous areas. The grandson of this couple, Charles I, became king in 1516 and in 1519 he was elected Holy Roman Emperor of the German nation. The latter succession titled him Charles V, by which he is best known. He inherited a strongly Catholic nation, made so by the work of Cardinal Ximenes, principal adviser of Queen Isabella. Ximenes had instituted a reform of the Catholic Church in Spain that abolished papal abuses and much papal control. Consequently, neither Charles nor his people were sympathetic with the continental reform movements. Emperor Charles V was the principal enemy of the Lutheran Reformation. He was more powerful and apparently more interested in suppressing it than were the popes. Only nineteen years old when elected emperor, his youthfulness was not marked by frivolity but by a zeal to restore to preeminence the ancient Catholic faith of his ancestors.

France was the principal rival of Spain during the Reformation period. France had achieved a strong centralized government through a succession of able kings. The rivalry between Spain and France flared up before the outbreak of the Reformation. Both King Ferdinand of Spain and Charles VIII of France had claims on the Kingdom of Naples in southern Italy. In 1495 Charles VIII was crowned king of Naples after leading a French army through central Italy and defeating the Aragonese claimant. King Ferdinand of Spain decided to assert his claim in Naples. In 1504 he drove Louis XII (1498-1515), successor to Charles VIII, out of Naples. Eight years later Ferdinand managed to drive Charles completely out of Italy. This marked the beginning of a series of wars between France and Spain, which in a sense saved the Lutheran Reformation. The chief opponent of Luther, Emperor Charles V of Spain, became so busy fighting France and the Turks that he could not devote himself to smothering the religious revolt until it had become strong enough politically to offer formidable opposition. The king of France during most of the Reformation was Francis I (1515-47), who did not favor the reform movement, but he helped it considerably by his political and military feuds with Spain.

The third of the centralized monarchies of this period was England. A military struggle among the nobles for royal succession almost eliminated them as a political factor, allowing the new king, Henry VII (1485-1509), to rule with a free hand. His son, Henry VIII (1509-47), was the sovereign during the principal portion of the continental movement. Henry VIII was a bitter opponent of the Lutheran reform during its early stage. He inaugurated a schism with the Roman

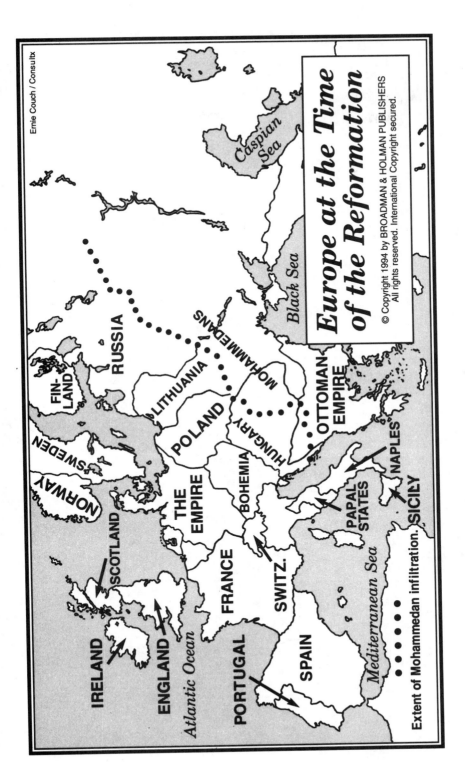

Europe at the Time of the Reformation

© Copyright 1994 by BROADMAN & HOLMAN PUBLISHERS
All rights reserved. International Copyright secured.

Ernie Couch / Consultx

Extent of Mohammedan infiltration.

Church in 1534 that was primarily external and governmental. He did not depart from most of the doctrines of Rome.

The fourth political power in Europe during the reform movement was the Empire. It will be remembered that the Western Empire was restored under Charlemagne in 800 and again under Otto the Great in 962. After about the middle of the thirteenth century the Empire began to decay again. A literary struggle over the right to bestow the imperial dignity (pope versus German electors) led to the *Defensor Pacis* of Marsiglio of Padua. The elective system won out. Although there were scores of small German states, seven strong sovereigns (three ecclesiastical and four secular) had named the emperor since 1356. The ecclesiastical electors were the archbishops of Mainz, Trier, and Cologne. The secular electors were the king of Bohemia, the elector of Saxony, the elector of Brandenburg, and the count palatine on the Rhine.

For generations the emperor had been chosen from the family of Hapsburgs. In the opening years of the Reformation the emperor was Maximilian I (1493-1519). Maximilian's son Philip was married to Joanna, the daughter of Ferdinand and Isabella of Spain. Through the efforts of Maximilian, his two grandsons Charles and Ferdinand controlled practically all of central Europe and Spain, with the exception of France. Charles became king of Spain through his mother's succession, and from his father he inherited the Netherlands and large portions of northern and eastern Europe. Ferdinand was married to Anne of Bohemia, by which the Hapsburgs acquired rule over Bohemia and Hungary. In a strong shuffling of political interests both the popes and the king of France, through their efforts to undermine the Hapsburg power headed by Charles V, hurt their own religious cause. The actual authority of the emperor over this loose confederation of German states was quite limited. The strong princes within the Empire ruled their own states as completely sovereign, often circumventing the wishes of the emperor through political sagacity. Such a situation allowed the elector of Saxony, for example, to protect Luther from the anger both of popes and of the emperor.

Another political and military power that played a large part in influencing the progress of Western reform was the Turks. After the capture of Constantinople in 1453, the Turks drove northwestward through the Balkans with an avowed purpose of overrunning all of Europe. During the Reformation the emperor's desire to stamp out Lutheranism was greatly affected by the Turkish menace. He could hardly afford to start a civil war when the Turks appeared to be on the verge of breaking into central Europe.

Italy had little political significance during the Reformation. Russia was rapidly becoming a strong political power, but it played no part in the Western reform. Christianity from the East had begun work in Russia, and later on Russia formed her own national church, loosely in fellowship with Constantinople. The Eastern world from Palestine to the Balkans had been overrun by the Moslems in the Medieval period, and it neither influenced nor was affected by the Western reform. Although not directly related to the movement, the states of Transylvania on the southeast of the Empire and Poland on the northeast were involved indirectly, since these areas, lying outside of the boundaries of the Empire, were havens for dissenting leaders.

Economic and Social Factors That Aided the Reformation

New economic and social patterns were greatly influential in fostering the reform movement. The German states entered into a period of economic and social transition in the fourteenth and fifteenth centuries. The merchant, or capitalist, class had arisen because of trade and commerce in the Mediterranean area. Geographical discoveries of the period opened a new economic world. The Portuguese discovery of a new route to India and the development of colonies provided new opportunities for the profitable investment of capital.

Furthermore, the discovery and development of German mineral resources threatened to supplant agrarian interests, pyramiding economic and social problems. Withdrawal of many peasants from agricultural labor and the increase of mineral production resulted in inflationary food prices. Harvest failure in Germany occurred for almost thirteen successive years, beginning about 1490, bringing starvation and malnutrition everywhere. There was universal discontent. Because of the necessity for harder work on the part of the peasants still working the land, resentment by the middle and upper classes at the sudden skyrocketing of food prices that nobody could explain or control, and the devaluation of wages due to economic inflation, the entire social and economic attitude was antagonistic. Peasant revolts became common, particularly after the attempt to supplant the old German legal customs by principles of Roman law. No wonder the inordinate avarice of the Roman Church in demanding tithes and indulgences was looked on as tyranny.

Intellectual Factors That Aided the Reformation

One reason for failure of earlier reform movements was the general lack of knowledge. Fear and superstition were obstacles too great for any antipapal movement to hurdle. The intellectual renascence that followed the Crusades gave a great deal of impetus to popular enlightenment. Development of the printing press in the middle of the fifteenth century made it possible to reproduce the spoken message for thousands of audiences. Luther's reform could not have been so effective had there not been widespread information and interest through the use of pamphlets and books. Furthermore, the movement known as humanism, while not always religious in its emphasis, provided enlightenment and leadership that contributed greatly to Luther's reform.

Finally, the attitude of the common people toward the papacy had undergone a profound transformation. No one, including Luther, would have dared to take the steps that might sever them from the visible Roman Catholic Church if it had been believed that such a schism would result in the loss of salvation. Foreign to philosophical realism and the claims of the Roman Church, there had developed a widespread conception that salvation could be attained apart from the Roman system.

Some followers of Luther abandoned him when he deliberately turned away from the Roman Church; but the fact that the German multitudes followed him in a schismatic movement, sharing with him the anathematizing by the church, speaks of a new point of view. The principal events that inculcated such a conception may only be guessed, but it is likely that the recollection of the papal schism had shaken the implicit faith of many in a visible and unrent body of Christ. The defiance of papal excommunication by the secular states revealed the popular mind and strengthened the idea that salvation did not rest solely with the Roman system. The presence for centuries of strong movements of dissenters like the Waldenses and Bohemian Brethren discounted Roman claims. Constant conflict between the church and the empire brought confusion and doubt concerning the claims of the church. Whatever the reasons may have been, it is evident that millions were willing to leave the body that claimed to be the only font of salvation. They were convinced that salvation could be found elsewhere.

Religious Factors That Aided the Reformation

Almost inseparable from the intellectual factors described were the religious elements that moved the multitudes toward reform. Some of the dissenting movements have been described in the previous chapter. We cannot measure the influence exerted by these groups, but it must have been tremendous. Either a great historical phenomenon occurred without sufficient antecedents or the masses of people were extensively prepared for a break with the dominant church before Luther and others called them out. Negative factors undoubtedly helped, such as the extremely low tone of religion and morality of the popes just before the Reformation and the unspeakable abuses of the entire Roman Catholic system as epitomized by the selling of indulgences. That these alone account for the tremendous revolution of the sixteenth century is difficult to believe.

Luther the Man

Without the factors that have been mentioned, even a Luther could not have accomplished what he did. He would have suffered the same fate that had befallen John Huss a century before. Yet a Luther was required to complete or weld together all of the factors already mentioned. In a real sense Luther combined all of the motives for reform that had previously been shown. Some had wanted reform on the basis of their devotion to the Bible. Luther, their leader, was an outstanding Bible scholar and attempted to fashion his reform on the Bible. Patriotism had been a motive for reform. Luther's reformation gathered up all the love that a German could have for his race and exploited it to the utmost. Many mystics longed for reform that would emphasize the ability to approach God without human priests and institutions. Luther read and published their literature and spoke in the language they understood. Humanism clamored for reform on the basis of a new intellectual approach. Luther sympathized with their general point of view.

Beyond these unifying elements in Luther's life, he stood as a symbol of the German peasant who had been aggrieved by papal tyranny

(Document 24)
Erasmus of Rotterdam: *In Praise of Folly*

Erasmus of Rotterdam, a great Northern humanist, criticized Catholic abuses in his satirical classic In Praise of Folly *(about 1511). Protestant Reformers later made similar criticisms, but Erasmus refused to join the Reformation. He remained a Roman Catholic until his death.*

And what shall I say of those who comfortably delude themselves with imaginary pardons for their sins, and who measure the time in purgatory with an hourglass into years, months, days, and hours, with all the precision of a mathematical table? There are plenty, too, who, relying upon certain magical little certificates and prayers,—which some pious imposter devised either in fun or for the benefit of his pocket,— believe that they may procure riches, honor, future happiness, health, perpetual prosperity, long life, a lusty old age,—nay, in the end, a seat at the right hand of Christ in heaven; but for this last, it matters not how long it be deferred; they will content themselves with the joys of heaven only when they must finally surrender the pleasures of this world, to which they lovingly cling.

The trader, the soldier, and the judge think that they can clean up the Augean stable of a lifetime, once for all, by sacrificing a single coin from their ill-gotten gains. They flatter themselves that all sorts of perjury, debauchery, drunkenness, quarrels, bloodshed, imposture, perfidy, and treason can be compounded for by contract and so adjusted that, having paid off their arrears, they can begin a new score.

How foolish, too, for religious bodies each to give preference to its particular guardian saint! Nay, each saint has his particular office alloted to him, and is addressed each in his special way: this one is called upon to alleviate a toothache; that, to aid in childbirth; others, to restore a stolen article, bring rescue to the shipwrecked, or protect cattle,—and so on with the rest, who are much too numerous to mention. A few indeed among the saints are good in more than one emergency, especially the Holy Virgin, to whom the common man now attributes almost more than to her Son.

And for what, after all, do men petition the saints except for foolish things? Look at the votive offerings which cover the walls of certain churches and with which you see even the ceiling filled; do you find any one who expresses his gratitude that he has escaped Folly or because he has become a whit wiser? One perhaps was saved from drowning, another recovered when he had been run through by his enemy; another, while his fellows were fighting, ran away with expedition and success; another, on the point of being hanged, escaped, through the aid of some saintly friend of thieves, and lived to relieve a few more of those whom he believed to be overburdened with their wealth....

As for the theologians, perhaps the less said the better on this gloomy and dangerous theme, since they are a style of man who show themselves exceedingly supercilious and irritable unless they can heap up six hundred conclusions about you and force you to recant; and if you refuse, they promptly brand you a heretic,—for it is their custom to terrify by their thunderings those whom they dislike....

St. Paul, they admit, was distinguished for his faith, but nevertheless when he said, "Faith is the substance of things hoped for, the evidence of things not seen," he defined it but inaccurately. He may have excelled in charity, yet he fails to limit and define it with dialectic precision in his first letter to the Corinthins, Chapter xiii. The disciples administered the eucharist reverently, and yet they had been asked about the terminus a quo and the terminus ad quem of transubstantiation; as to how a body can be in two places at the same time; of the differences which exist between Christ's body in heaven, on the cross, and in the holy wafer; or at what point does transubstantiation occur, since the prayer through which it is effected is, as a quantitas discreta, in a state of flux,—asked of these matters the apostles would not have replied with the acuteness with which the followers of Scotus distinguish and refine these subtleties.

for half a millennium. He was a champion who could speak the language of the people. His personal experience in moving slowly step-by-step from protest to disputation to condemnation and schism probably mirrored the experience of the average German who followed him. They understood him because they were so much like him. Without Luther, reform in the Germanic states would have been handicapped or impossible at the time. Somewhat similar historical and personal factors thrust forth Zwingli and Calvin in their particular areas. The time was ripe for reform.

The fullness of time had come. Reform was in the minds of many and on the lips of a few. A pioneer was required to inaugurate a successful revolt against the Roman Catholic system. Luther was that pioneer. Zwingli and Calvin were not far behind.

17

The Lutheran Reform

After centuries of preparation the movement that led to the shattering of the Medieval Roman Catholic system and the formation of some of the principal branches of the Christian movement began. The first of these reforms was that of Martin Luther.

Luther's Early Life (1483-1517)

Martin Luther was born in Eisleben, Saxony, a small Germanic state, on November 10, 1483. We are not surprised that the one who was to break through the heavy crust of the Medieval ecclesiastical tyranny should spring from this geographical area. German people were suffering a great deal from papal avarice. Luther came from peasant stock, which is not surprising. This class of people above all others bore the brunt of oppression and mistreatment from both secular and religious authorities.

Luther's parents were like most other peasants, poor and religious to the point of superstition. Luther never got away from some of their primitive ideas about witches and goblins. Shortly after Luther's birth his parents moved to Mansfeld, a nearby village, where his father engaged in the new mining industry. Luther attended elementary school here and further prepared for the university by enrolling at Magdeburg in the spring of 1497 and at Eisenach in the following year. In 1501 he entered the university of Erfurt, where he received the bachelor of arts degree in 1502 and a master's degree in 1505.

Up to this point Luther's life had not varied greatly from that of any other young man preparing for a professional career in law. He abandoned his legal career because of a tremendous religious crisis. The religious tensions deliberately induced by the Medieval Catholic system caused Luther, like every typical person of his day, to feel a constant religious unrest. The Roman Church demanded obedience to the earthly institution as the price of salvation. When people became careless, the threat of purgatory was used to bring dread and subservience. The sacramental wealth of the church was offered as a means of limiting the sufferings of the netherworld. God was pictured as completely inaccessible; Christ was portrayed as a dreaded judge. Only the benefits sold by the Roman Catholic Church could free one from the pangs of purgatory. The best opportunity of escaping divine wrath was to be found in the monasteries.

How long Luther had been thinking about these things cannot be determined. After he received his second degree at Erfurt, he had an overwhelming feeling to get right with God. He had experienced several frightening incidents that caused him to think about eternal things. While Luther was walking near Stotternheim on July 2, 1505, he became unnerved when a bolt of lightning struck near him. He vowed that if spared from death, he would become a monk. This was Luther's first step in an effort to find peace with God. Against the wishes of his father he kept his vow and fifteen days later entered the Augustinian monastery at Erfurt.

To his dismay Luther found no lasting peace in this surrender. When he attempted to perform his first mass in May 1507, his fear of God almost prostrated him. Following the precepts of the Medieval church, he sought relief through performing good works. His reputation for self-denial spread across the land, but still he found no peace. Obediently, he did everything prescribed by the Roman Catholic Church. He sought the merits of the saints; he engaged in almost obsessive confession of every type of sin, whether in thought, word, or deed; he performed regular religious duties feverishly; he even walked to Rome, the center of the Catholic religious world, where the greatest sins of every sort could be forgiven with the least effort. The merits of the saints reminded him of his own need. Confession only spoke of unremembered sins not yet forgiven. His work as a priest increased his trepidation at approaching God. His trip to Rome brought him into contact with cynical and greedy leaders. Through all of these tumultuous experiences Luther was approaching the object of his search.

Luther never related when his burden was lifted, but he described how it happened. John Von Staupitz, the vicar of the Augustinian monasteries, counseled with Luther and pointed him to the study of the New Testament. Equally important was the theological study that he found teaching at the University of Wittenberg, a position assigned him by Staupitz. Luther received the doctorate of theology degree in October 1512. His lectures during the next five years on Psalms, Romans, and Galatians helped him discover things that the entire sacramental system of the Roman Church could not accomplish. He discovered the true scriptural insight that salvation is a gift. Earlier he had tried to deserve salvation. He learned to accept salvation by faith without deserving it. He seized on the text, "The just shall live by faith," believed it, and found the peace for which he had long sought.

Luther's Reform Movement (1517-46)

Luther's discovery of a new relationship with God eventually caused him to urge others to find peace in the same way. Apparently Luther did not recognize the logical conclusion to which he must surely go: to challenge the validity of the system that could not bring him peace. Step by step his experience led him away from the obedience that he had exercised formerly. Luther did not always know when he took these steps and perhaps was not fully aware of the tremendous strides he had taken until he paused to look around. The first of these steps centered in his opposition to the Roman doctrine of indulgences.

Luther's Question About Indulgences

The Roman Church taught that all sins before baptism were washed away in that rite. The sacrament of penance was provided to care for postbaptismal sins. When persons sinned, they had to present themselves to a priest with sorrow in their hearts for the sin, confess their sins to the priest, receive absolution (in which the priest on behalf of God forgave the eternal guilt of this sin), and perform some good work to take care of the earthly penalty. Every sin gave offense in two directions: (1) it brought guilt before God, and (2) it wronged the earthly church. The priest pronounced God's forgiveness. The hurt to the earthly institution had to be atoned for by specific prayers, gifts of money, a religious pilgrimage, or some similar act of devotion. To neglect the earthly penalty, it was taught, brought additional suffering in purgatory after death.

The most popular way of paying this earthly debt in Luther's day was through the purchase of writs of indulgence from papal representatives. These indulgences were written statements announcing a specified remission of penalty to the purchaser. Indulgences were sought by those who wished to escape extensive residence in purgatory after death, as well as by those who had loved ones supposedly in purgatory and wished to apply this credit to the account of the one suffering there.

As early as 1516 Luther questioned the doctrine of indulgences. His own ruler, Frederick, the elector of Saxony, had a vast collection of relics. Should a person view these relics and make the proper offering, a writ of indulgence granting remission of specified canonical penalty was given. The genuineness of Luther's spiritual change was verified when in 1516 he endangered his own livelihood to question the correctness of the doctrine of indulgences, because a part of his own salary came from the proceeds of indulgence sales. In 1517 Luther had reached the point of exasperation. Pope Leo X had sold the archbishopric of Mainz to Albert of Brandenburg. To allow Albert to repay the money borrowed for the purchase of this office and to gain money allegedly to help build the Cathedral of St. Peter at Rome, Leo declared a special sale on indulgences. To attract buyers the older Catholic doctrine of indulgences was perverted, and it appears that some claimed that pardon for sin could be obtained through them. The Dominican monk Tetzel was given the task of hawking these indulgences.

The thing that infuriated Luther was the suggestion that both guilt against God and the penalty against the earthly church could be taken care of by indulgences. Since Frederick, Luther's prince, was also engaged in selling ecclesiastical indulgences to the people, Tetzel was forbidden to enter electoral Saxony for the purpose of selling these new indulgences. Tetzel, however, crowded the very borders of electoral Saxony in order that those who might be interested could cross over and buy the indulgences. On October 31, 1517, Luther prepared ninety-five statements for debate and, according to university custom, tacked them on the door of the church at Wittenberg, which was in a sense the university chapel. These statements (or theses) invited debate on three general statements: (1) the traffic in indulgences, which Luther avowed was unscriptural, ineffective, and dangerous;

(2) the power of the pope in the forgiveness of guilt and noncanonical penalties, which Luther denied; and (3) the character of the treasury of the church, alleged to consist of the merits donated by Christ and the saints. Luther denied that the merits of Christ and the saints constituted such a treasury to be used by the church.

The widespread storm following this protest seems to have been a surprise to Luther. Printing presses brought a new method of intellectual warfare. Luther's protest was reproduced, translated from Latin into German for all of Germany. Luther's language was plain and direct, written in the vocabulary and spirit of a typical German. From various angles the protest gathered popular antagonism against the papacy from many classes: biblicists, patriots, mystics, humanists. Pope Leo X was not alarmed by the protest at first. When he did take notice specifically, his first direct action was to appoint a new general of the Augustinian order with instructions to discipline Luther. At a meeting of Luther's chapter in April 1518 at Heidelberg, however, Luther found some support. Thereafter, he began to assume a bolder attitude. He soon began to question the continuous historical primacy of the papacy and completely denied the power of the pope over purgatory.

In July of 1518, Silvester Prierias, a Dominican official in Rome, attacked Luther as a heretic. Luther's reply went even further toward the evangelical position. He asserted that the pope and the ecumenical council could err and had done so, and that only the Scriptures are an infallible authority. Luther was ordered to report to Rome to answer to accusations of heresy, but through the influence of his prince, Frederick, the consultation was referred to Cardinal Cajetan in Augsburg. This interview in October 1518 drew from Luther the direct denial of the authority of the papal bull, for Luther asserted that the voice of the Scriptures outweighed the voice of the pope.

In November Luther appealed to a general council as the ultimate earthly authority in Christianity to pass on his views. This constituted a direct act of hostility to the pope, since previous popes had for a century described such an appeal as open heresy. Luther's precarious position was greatly aided by the influence of Frederick. The Holy Roman Emperor died on January 12, 1519, and Frederick was one of the seven electors who would choose a new emperor. The pope earnestly wanted to dictate who should be elected and consequently was quite deferential to Frederick. This probably accounts for a reversal of the antagonistic papal policy.

Karl von Miltitz, a German, was sent to conciliate Luther until after a new emperor had been chosen. Miltitz asked Luther to refrain from debating the question. Luther agreed on the condition that his opponents would do likewise. But professor Johann Eck of the University of Ingolstadt did not keep this truce and attacked Luther without calling him by name. Through Eck's influence a debate was arranged and took place in Leipzig early in July 1519. Here Luther was driven to approve doctrines of John Huss, who had been condemned and burned by the Council of Constance a century before. On July 15, 1520, a bull of excommunication against Luther was issued, commanding him to recant within sixty days. Luther later burned it publicly.

During the remainder of that summer and fall, Luther wrote the principal tracts that described his beliefs. In August he published his *Address to the German Nobility.* In this tract Luther urged a reform of the church by the Christian magistrate. He attacked the claims of the papacy that spiritual power is above the temporal, that the pope alone can interpret the Scriptures, and that ecumenical councils can be assembled only by a pope. His proposals for reform included eliminating the material wealth and possessions of the pope and emphasizing a spiritual ministry. Luther also attacked monasticism and celibacy. He believed that abuses and corruption within the church had to be corrected.

In October Luther's tract *On the Babylonian Captivity of the Church* was printed. In this tract Luther denied the efficacy of indulgences and boldly attacked the sacramental system of Rome. He insisted that both the wine and bread of the Supper should be served to the people and dwelt on the necessity of faith by the partaker in order to assure its efficacy. In his discussion of baptism, he created a continuous tension in his theological system by eliminating the necessity of personal expression of faith as a prerequisite to baptism. He demanded personal faith for the Supper, but he made no provision for such faith before baptism. He continued with a critical discussion of penance, confirmation, matrimony, orders, and extreme unction. He would eliminate all sacraments except baptism and the Lord's Supper, but praised part of the sacrament of penance. In the following month his tract on *The Freedom of the Christian* appeared. This writing emphasized the freedom and priesthood of every believer, whether layperson, priest, bishop, or pope.

(Document 25)

Luther: From *Address to the German Nobility*

Luther challenged the laity to assume Christian leadership. He believed that princes should lead in reforming the church, but he struggled to define the role of the common people.

It has been discovered that the pope, bishops, priests, and monks should be called the "spiritual estate," while princes, lords, artisans and peasants form the "temporal estate,"—a very fine hypocritical invention. But let no one be made afraid of it; and that for this reason: All Christians are truly of the spiritual estate, and there is no difference among us, save of office alone. As St. Paul says (1 Cor. 12), we are all one body, though each member has its own work to do, whereby it may serve the others. This is because we have one baptism, one gospel, one faith, and are all Christians alike; for baptism, gospel, and faith,—these alone make spiritual and Christian folk. Therefore a priest should be nothing in Christendom but a functionary. So long as he holds his office he takes precedence; if he is deprived of it, he is but a peasant or a burgher, like the rest. Therefore a priest is verily no priest when he is deprived of his office. But now they have invented their "indelible characters," and pretend that a priest can never be anything but a priest,—that is, that he can never become a layman again. But all this is nothing but mere talk and ordinance of human invention. We see then that those we call churchmen, be they priests, bish-ops, or popes, are not set apart from or above other Christians, except in so far as they have to do with the word of God and the sacraments, for that is their calling and office. And moreover the temporal authorities wield the sword and the rod to chastise the wicked and protect the good. A cobbler, a smith, a peasant—every man has his own calling and office, just like the consecrated priests and bishops: and every one in his office or calling must help and serve the rest, so that all may work together for the common good, as the various members of the body all serve each other.

See now what sort of Christian doctrine is this,—that the temporal power is not above the spiritual, and may not punish it. That like saying the hand shall do nothing to help, however grievously the eye may suffer. Is it not unnatural, not to say unchristian, that one member may not help another, even to shield it from destruction? Nay, the nobler the member, the more the others are bound to help it. Therefore I say, forasmuch as the temporal power has been ordained by God for the chastisement of the wicked and the protection of the good, therefore we must let it exercise its functions, unhampered, throughout the whole Christian body without respect of persons, whether it strikes popes, bishops, priests, monks, nuns, or whatever.

These writings and others in a similar vein, progressively becoming bolder in their attacks on the central doctrines supporting the papacy, completely alienated Luther from the Roman Church and made compromise impossible. On April 17, 1521, following a summons by Emperor Charles V, Luther appeared before the Diet of the Empire, meeting at Worms. After two hearings in which Luther boldly defended his views, he was kidnapped by his friends (perhaps under secret orders from Frederick) and on May 4, he arrived in disguise at Wartburg. Meanwhile at Worms on May 26, after Luther's supporters had returned home, the papal forces were able to secure an edict banning Luther as an outlaw. Thus by the middle of 1521 Luther had been excommunicated by the Roman Church and banned by the Empire.

Delay in Suppressing Lutheranism (1521-29)

History seemed destined to add the name of Martin Luther to the long list of victims of ecclesiastical intolerance. The kidnapping of Luther by his friends, however, removed him from possible physical danger for about a year. In addition, Emperor Charles V became engaged in war with King Francis I of France shortly after the close of the Diet of Worms in 1521. This war continued intermittently for the next eight years. Furthermore, the hands of the emperor, the chief opponent of Luther, were withheld from Luther because of the menacing Turks, who were driving through the Balkans with the intention of overthrowing the Empire. Emperor Charles V was also delayed from suppressing the Lutherans by the political maneuvering of the pope who was afraid of the amount of power Charles had.

During this time, with the aid of Melanchthon and others, Luther prepared a great deal of literature, including an excellent German translation of the Scriptures. Luther also began to put some of his beliefs into practice. In 1522 at Zwickau several religious radicals attempted to carry out a system that seemed to be based on Luther's ideas. The Roman Catholic priestly system of conducting the Supper was altered. The common people were given both elements—bread and wine. Roman liturgy, chanting, and altars were eliminated. The city was in an uproar. Luther voluntarily left his haven at Wartburg to take personal command in fighting these radicals. Luther may be described as a conservative reformer; that is, he retained those elements of Roman Catholic tradition that in his judgment were not specifically prohibited by the Scriptures. Thus infant baptism, robes, candles, and similar Roman Catholic characteristics appear in Lutheranism.

In 1525, the year of Luther's marriage, a great peasant's revolt occurred. For half a century there had been increasing tension between the nobility and the peasants who tilled the soil. The attempt to apply Roman law in place of the ancient Germanic law, the breakdown of feudal estates with the resultant suffering and confusion, and economic turmoil incident to the rise of the third estate (commercial and financial princes) fanned the flames of dissatisfaction among the peasants. In addition, Thomas Müntzer, a radical millenarian, accelerated the outbreak of violence by injecting a religious note. "God will not let you fail; on to slaughter!" was his cry. Thousands of peasants were mercilessly put to death in the revolt of 1525. Luther lost his faith in the common people and looked to the nobility as the hope of the reform movement.

Because of the preoccupation of the emperor, the annual meetings of the German diet had practically left the task of adjusting the religious situation in the hands of each prince or ruler for his own hand. By 1529, however, the situation was changed. The Lutherans faced a new crisis. The emperor had soundly defeated King Francis of France, had seen the Turks driven back from Vienna, and had permitted the pope to be imprisoned for a period. The diet met at Speyer that year; Ferdinand, brother of the emperor and a strenuous opponent of the reform movement, presided. By his direction the diet passed an edict that planned to annihilate the Lutheran reform and recatholicize Lutheran areas. A minority protested this action, receiving the name *Protestant*. This is the first occurrence of the name in ecclesiastical history. The Lutherans were required to answer the edict within one year.

The Crisis (1530)

At the meeting of the diet in 1530 at Augsburg, the Lutherans were fearful concerning events to come. In the previous year Philip of Hesse, one of the Lutheran princes, had endeavored to secure a military alliance between the Lutherans of Germany and the Zwinglians of Switzerland. At a meeting in Marburg in 1529, however, Luther refused to have any sort of connection with Zwingli, despite the fact that the only point of disagreement in their theology centered on the interpretation of Jesus' words, "This is my body." Luther, of course, being under the ban of the Empire, could not appear at the diet in

(Document 26)
The Augsburg Confession

The Confession of Augsburg is the most significant Lutheran confession. In 1530 Luther was considered an enemy of the Empire, but Philip Melanchthon wrote the Confession and presented it to the Imperial Diet. It is still the most important Lutheran confession.

VII. The Church

It is also taught among us that one holy Christian church will be and remain forever. This is the assembly of all believers among whom the Gospel is preached in its purity and the holy sacraments are administered according to the Gospel. For it is sufficient for the true unity of the Christian church that the Gospel be preached in conformity with a pure understanding of it and that the sacraments be administered in accordance with the divine Word. It is not necessary for the true unity of the Christian church that ceremonies, instituted by men, should be observed uniformly in all places. It is as Paul says in Eph. 4:4-5, "There is one body and one Spirit, just as you were called to the one hope that belongs to your call, one Lord, one faith, one baptism."

VIII. What the Church Is

Again, although the Christian church, properly speaking, is nothing else than the assembly of all believers and saints, yet because in this life many false Christians, hypocrites, and even open sinners remain among the godly, the sacraments are efficacious even if the priests who administer them are wicked men, for as Christ himself indicated, "The Pharisees sit on Moses' seat" (Matt. 23:2). Accordingly the Donatists and all others who hold contrary views are condemned.

IX. Baptism

It is taught among us that Baptism is necessary and that grace is offered through it. Children, too, should be baptized, for in Baptism they are committed to God and become acceptable to him. On this account the Anabaptists who teach that infant Baptism is not right are rejected.

X. The Holy Supper of Our Lord

It is taught among us that the true body and blood of Christ are really present in the Supper of our Lord under the form of bread and wine and are there distributed and received. The contrary doctrine is therefore rejected.

Augsburg. He aided Melanchthon in preparing the confession for presentation to the diet. The confession and a subsequent defense were rejected by the diet, and the Lutherans were given one year to forsake their heresies or bear the consequences. The Lutheran princes formed a military alliance known as the Schmalkaldic League. The Catholic princes had also joined together for military action. Emperor Charles did not find it expedient to attack the Lutherans. The Turks were threatening, the Lutherans were fairly strong, and King Francis I of France was ready to fight again.

Luther's Death

This uneasy truce between Protestants and Catholics was still in effect in February 1546 when Luther died. His death was not a great blow to his movement. Others had taken responsibility.

The Schmalkaldic War and the Peace of Augsburg (1555)

The Schmalkaldic War broke out in 1546 when Pope Paul III declared a crusade against the Protestant princes. Within a year the Protestants had been utterly defeated. Jealousy between Emperor Charles and the pope prevented the immediate destruction of the Protestants, however, and in 1552 after a period of political maneuvering the war erupted again. In a few months the Protestants regained all that they had lost.

The Peace of Augsburg admitted the right of the Lutheran religion to exist within the Empire. Each prince was to determine the religion of his state, and if anyone desired a different faith, the right of emigration without loss of honor or goods was guaranteed. In case a Catholic prelate desired to become a Lutheran, he had to resign his ecclesiastical position so that it might be filled from Rome. In the free cities where both faiths had adherents, each should be permitted to continue.

The Spread of Lutheranism

Before 1540 most of northern Germany was officially Lutheran. In the border states (Bohemia and Poland) and in the earlier years of reform in Hungary, Lutheranism was very strong. Denmark adopted the Reformation by 1536 through its rulers and the preaching of Hans Tausen. Sweden adopted Lutheranism in 1527 due to the preaching of Olaf and Lars Petersen and Lars Andersen and the work of King Gustavus Vasa. Finland, a Swedish satellite, adopted Lutheranism principally through political action, the most important preacher being Michael Agricola.

Martin Luther was the pioneer reformer who broke the power of the Roman Catholic system. He acquired sufficient political influence among the Germans to maintain his system despite coercion.

We must not forget that during the latter years of Luther's life, other reform movements were in progress. Ulrich Zwingli at Zurich, John Calvin at Geneva, the radicals and Anabaptists in various parts of the Continent, and Henry VIII in England presented other instances of reform. These will be considered in the following chapters.

paypal

The Zwinglian and Calvinistic Reforms

The second of the attempted general reforms of the Roman Catholic Church during this period began in two Swiss cities but spread extensively and soon rivaled the Lutheran movement. The Swiss republic offered unusual opportunity for the reform movement, but it also presented unusual obstacles. Almost three hundred years before, the several independent cantons, as the small county-like states were termed, had entered into a confederation, each canton, regardless of size, having one vote in the diet or congress. This made it possible for a minority of the people (in the less populated cantons) to prevent the majority of the people (in the cantons made up of larger cities) from embracing the Reformation movement by political vote. The struggle between the country cantons and the city cantons characterizes the course of the early Reformation efforts.

The country cantons had good reasons for opposing the reform. The Roman Catholic Church had for centuries employed strong young men from the Swiss rural cantons to be used as mercenaries in the papal army. They did not find papal abuses to be burdensome. The rural cantons possessed considerable independence of spirit and little money and so were hardly aware of papal exploitation. The more wealthy city cantons, on the other hand, had long fought papal financial exploitation and political domination. Humanism had made vast inroads into the larger cities, particularly Basel, where educational and printing facilities helped to spread information and agitate for reform.

The two cities of Switzerland which became leaders in the reform were Zurich and Geneva. Ulrich Zwingli was the principal figure in beginning the reform at Zurich; later John Calvin played the chief role in Geneva. Calvin's movement swallowed up the Zwinglian reform in one generation, so the two will be discussed as one movement.

The Zwinglian Reform in Zurich

Ulrich Zwingli was born in 1484 at Wildhaus in Switzerland. His uncle, a priest in the Roman Church, supervised his education in some of the outstanding schools of the Continent. From 1502 to 1506 Zwingli taught school at Basel while finishing his education. In this active humanist center he was greatly influenced by enlightened views and was brought to the study of theology. The lectures of the humanist Thomas Wyttenbach, in particular, gave the young teacher a passion to do all he could to eliminate the superstitious elements in Christianity and to restore the ancient authority—the Scriptures.

Through the influence of his uncle, in 1506 Zwingli was appointed parish priest at Glarus, where he served for ten years. From 1516 to 1519 he was priest at Einsiedeln. Here his pungent preaching and reforming tendencies attracted widespread attention. In 1519 he was appointed the chief preacher at the great cathedral church in Zurich. He had been moving already toward the application of scriptural principles. While at Einsiedeln in 1518, with the approval of his bishop, he had opposed the sale of indulgences by Bernard Sampson. On beginning his work at Zurich, Zwingli caused a sensation by preaching an exposition of the Gospels in the language of the people, scorning the traditional lessons assigned and the Latin tongue of the Roman Church.

Several experiences apparently kindled his reforming zeal. By 1520 he had become familiar with the reformatory works of Luther. Zwingli always insisted that he was not indebted to Luther for the principles of reform in Zurich. An analysis of the reforms instituted by Luther and Zwingli partly bears out Zwingli's contention. Zwingli's reform was intellectual, biblical, and political. He approached religion as a humanist seeking truth. Luther, on the other hand, was moved by a great experience which convinced him that the Roman system could not bring peace to the soul. So while Zwingli through reform sought to satisfy his *mind* with respect to the truth of Christianity, Luther aimed at satisfying his *heart* through true Christianity. Thus while Luther's writings doubtless encouraged Zwingli, it is possible that Zwingli's reform developed somewhat independently.

In addition to the writings of Luther, other factors turned Zwingli more zealously toward an active reform. The dreaded plague struck Zurich and Zwingli was stricken. At the very door of death he had a mystical experience in which he was conscious of the strengthening presence of God. From this and his bereavement in the loss of a brother, Zwingli seemed to deepen considerably in his spiritual life. For years he had been receiving a pension from the pope, a retainer for encouraging young men to engage in mercenary military service. In 1520, consistent with his new insights, he resigned this pension and took a firm stand against hiring Swiss lads as mercenaries.

His preaching began to emphasize the authority of the Scriptures alone. Acting upon this principle, some of his followers in Zurich in 1522 refused to fast during Lent on the grounds that the Bible did not forbid eating. Zwingli defended them against the strictures of their bishop and wrote a tract *On Choice and Freedom in Eating.*

In July 1522, Zwingli attacked clerical celibacy. He knew firsthand the terrible evils involved in this system, openly admitting in his writings that he was unmarried but not chaste. In 1524 he announced his marriage to a woman with whom he had been living in common-law relations for some years.

Exercising great influence over the city government at Zurich, Zwingli was able to develop his program of reform. The city council adjudged him to be victorious in two public disputations with Roman Catholic representatives in January and October 1523. Zwingli presented sixty-seven brief articles of faith, which went beyond Luther toward an even more evangelical position. In these Zwingli emphasized the Scriptures in contrast with the teachings of the Roman Church. Salvation is by faith. Roman sacraments, intercession of saints, and purgatorial sufferings are unscriptural. All believers are priests. Clerical celibacy must be abolished.

At one point, Zwingli had disagreement within his own ranks. It has been pointed out that his movement was partly political because he had to work through the government of the Zurich canton. When the question of baptism arose, the political aspect weighed considerably. Zwingli knew that if he denied the validity of infant baptism he would "unchurch" the Zurich city council, for all of them were sprinkled as babies. Apparently this factor caused him, after considerable hesitation, to retain infant baptism. He did not teach that infant baptism brought salvation, after the fashion of the Roman Church; rather, said he, infant baptism simply identifies the child with the Christian covenant, much as the rite of circumcision identified the Jewish child with the covenant of Israel. He viewed the Lord's Supper as a symbol of the body and blood of Christ. Zwingli was able to justify to the Zurich government eliminating images, relics, monasteries, and the traditional observance of mass.

By 1524-25, however, because he retained infant baptism, Zwingli was obliged to defend his movement against the attacks of a group which had stood with him in the early days of reform. Conrad Grebel, Feliz Manz, and others among his early supporters insisted that Zwingli must abolish infant baptism if he wanted to be consistent in his main principle—to restore the scriptural pattern. Even political circumstances, they said, should not prevent steadfast allegiance to scriptural injunctions. At first it appeared that Zwingli might move in this direction, but soon he vigorously resisted the movement.

Zwingli's reform transformed Zurich by 1525. His influence also aided in the reform of other Swiss and south German cities like St. Gall, Basel, Bern, and Strassburg. The rural cantons of Uri, Schwyz, Unterwalden, and Zug, however, completely satisfied with the old Roman Catholic relationship, formed with Lucerne a league to withstand the reform. Most of the other Swiss cantons and some of the southern German cities confederated in a reform league. Both groups sought outside alliances. In 1529 civil war seemed imminent, but by negotiation hostilities were postponed in a peace favorable to the Zwinglians.

In the fall of 1529 at Marburg an important meeting between the Lutherans and the Zwinglians was held. The Second Diet of Speyer had recently condemned all dissent from the Roman Catholic Church. The church demanded conformity within one year. Philip of Hesse, an influential Lutheran, wanted to secure a political and military alliance between Lutheran and Zwinglian forces in order to withstand the Catholics. Luther insisted that there must first be agreement in doctrine. On fourteen articles of faith Luther and Zwingli were in general agreement, but in a part of one article Luther rejected Zwingli. The point of difference lay in the interpretation of the presence of Christ in the Supper. Luther contended that Christ's physical body was present for the faithful in the true observance of the Supper. Zwingli objected that a physical body could not be everywhere at the same time. Zwingli said that the bread symbolizes or represents Christ's body.

This single point of disagreement outweighed all else. The dream of an alliance was shattered.

Zwingli returned to his task of endeavoring to secure acceptance of his reform throughout all of the thirteen cantons of Switzerland. The five Catholic cantons, however, alert for an opportunity to take the initiative, raised an army in 1531, and in the ensuing battle Zwingli was slain. His successor in Zurich, Henry Bullinger, respected the treaty signed with the Catholics and limited his work to his own canton. In less than a generation the Zwinglian movement was swallowed up by the larger and more influential movement of John Calvin.

The Calvinistic Reform at Geneva

The city of Geneva first felt reform as an indirect result of the Zwinglian movement. The winning of Bern to reform in 1528 brought additional impetus through the increased evangelical interests of this, the strongest Swiss city in the South. It was through the encouragement of Bern that William Farel, an impetuous reformer from France, made his way to Geneva in 1533. Geneva had felt already the political pressure of Bern to accept evangelical reform. Political factors, as a matter of fact, played the most important role in winning Geneva to the reform movement. The city was ruled by a bishop and an administrator, both of whom were controlled by the duke of Savoy, monarch over an adjacent kingdom. The citizens shared in local government through a general assembly and an elected committee known as the Little Council. Larger committees were appointed by the Little Council to resolve questions involving fundamental principles. Beginning about 1527, the ancient hostility between the citizens of Geneva and the duke of Savoy erupted into open war. The citizens were able to beat off the duke's attacks with the help of Bern and a Catholic neighbor, Freiburg, and to establish Geneva's freedom. With the encouragement of Bern, William Farel and Antoine Froment, two French preachers, infiltrated Geneva in the interest of the evangelical cause. About 1535 the reform movement took a strong foothold, and Geneva entered the evangelical fold. In July 1536, John Calvin paused in the city en route to Strassburg, and Farel enlisted him in the task of making Geneva a strong Protestant city.

The Work of John Calvin

John Calvin was born in Noyon, France, on July 10, 1509. His father was an influential ecclesiastical functionary and secretary of the

bishopric. As a result, Calvin's education was provided through benefices in the Roman Catholic Church. In 1528 he received the Master of
Arts degree from the University of Paris. At the request of his father
Calvin studied law at Orleans and Bourges, receiving the doctorate in
law at Orleans in 1532. His first love was literary, not legal, however,
and after the death of his father Calvin was free to forsake the practice
of law.

Calvin was familiar with reforming ideas. Jacques Lefèvre Étaples, a
French scholar living in Paris, had favored evangelical ideas as early
as 1512 in a commentary on Paul's epistles. He also translated the
New Testament a decade later. The writings of Luther were circulated
freely in France, and Calvin became familiar with them. Calvin's conversion to evangelical views was sudden, as his own testimony
asserts. Perhaps the full explanation will never be known, but various
factors were involved. His father and brother had been excommunicated by the Roman Church, which may have loosened the hold of
that system upon Calvin. His cousin, Robert Olivétan, was already a
full-fledged reformer. The humanistic atmosphere of Calvin's university training and teachers doubtless moved him toward evangelical
convictions. In May 1534, he resigned his benefices and for some
reason was imprisoned for a brief period. This is the first definite indication that Calvin had now entered the evangelical fold. With the outbreak of widespread and severe persecution in France in 1534, Calvin
fled here and there in France, then to Strassburg and later to Basel.
While at Basel in 1536 Calvin published the first edition of his outstanding work, *Institutes of the Christian Religion,* which brought him
immediate fame. His dedication of the *Institutes* to King Francis I of
France is a masterpiece of argumentation from the Scriptures and history. Calvin visited for a short time in Italy and Paris and on the journey to Strassburg passed through Geneva. Here William Farel
convinced him that it was God's will for them to set up the evangelical
standard in Geneva.

For the next two years Calvin labored in this important city. In January 1537, he presented to the Little Council of Geneva a series of
articles about reform. The Lord's Supper was made central in church
discipline. Moral lapses and the neglect of divine services without
excuse brought exclusion from participation in the Lord's Supper. A
confession of faith was submitted to the council for their approval,
after which all citizens were required to assent to it. The purpose was
to require total conformity to evangelical doctrines. The next logical

step was to train the growing children in the doctrine. Calvin provided a catechism for their use. A system of lay inspectors was installed to observe the conduct of the citizens. Immediate opposition to Calvin's program came from both political and religious dissenters. Calvin was attacked as a foreigner and a meddler. The annual city election in 1537 favored the Calvinistic supporters, but a year later the opposition succeeded in taking over the reins of government, and in April Calvin and Farel were banished from Geneva.

Calvin went to Strassburg, a city already strongly evangelical, and became pastor of the French refugees. He had a remarkably free hand in preaching and administrating the church. He was called upon after January 1539 to lecture to the advanced classes in the schools. He laid the groundwork for his famous expositions of biblical books, which subsequently were printed in commentary form. He also had opportunity to prepare a greatly enlarged edition of the *Institutes*.

(Document 27)

John Calvin: Divine Predestination

Calvin's name is associated with the doctrine of predestination, though this was only a part of his teaching. He explained his view in Institutes of the Christian Religion *(1559).*

Predestination we call the eternal decree of God, whereby he has determined with himself what he will to become of every man. For all are not created to like estate; but to some eternal life and to some eternal damnation is forordained. Therefore as every man is created to the one or the other end, so we say that he is predestinated either to life or to death....Foolish men do divers way quarrel with God, as though they had him subject to their accusations. First, therefore, they ask by what right is the Lord angry with his creatures by

whom he hath not first been provoked by any offense; for to condemn to destruction whom he will agreeth rather with the willfullness of a tyrant than with the lawful sentence of a judge. Therefore they say that there is cause why men should accuse God if by his forewill, without their own deserving, they be predestinated to eternal death. If such thoughts do at no time come into the mind of the godly, this shall suffice to break their violent assaults, although they have nothing more, if they consider how great wickedness it is even so much as to inquire of the causes of the will of God....For the will of God is the highest rule of righteousness, that whatsoever he willeth, even for this that he willeth it, ought to be taken for righteous.

While Calvin was absent from Geneva, Cardinal Sadoleto appealed to the city to return to the Catholic fold. Since no one in Geneva felt qualified to respond to this appeal, it was finally handed to Calvin in Strassburg. His *Reply to Sadoleto* in 1539, justifying the evangelical position, added to his reputation.

Calvin was married at Strassburg in August 1540 to Idelette de Bure, widow of an Anabaptist convert. Calvin spoke in highest terms of his wife and their happiness. She died in 1549. Their only child, born in 1542, lived but a few days.

In 1541, after considerable persuasion by his friends, Calvin returned to Geneva. He faced a difficult task. The party which had ousted Calvin had been overthrown in the elections of 1540 but were still formidable. The relations of Geneva with Bern were threatening, and the internal situation was bad. It appeared that rioting and disorder would soon break out in Geneva. Calvin returned with the assurance that he would be allowed to institute his reforms. A committee from the Little Council helped Calvin prepare his *Ecclesiastical Ordinances*. These provided for four offices in Genevan church life—pastors, teachers, elders, and deacons. The most distinctive aspect to this program was the office of elder or presbyter, from which the name *Presbyterian* is derived. Twelve laymen were chosen by the Little Council to serve as ruling elders in the Genevan church. This was a departure from the general idea that the presbyters were to be ordained and should preach rather than govern. These twelve presbyters were combined with the regular ministry (at first numbering but six ministers) to form the consistory, which had supervision over all ecclesiastical discipline. Calvin apparently had wanted the Genevan church to exercise its own discipline apart from the secular authorities but was forced into the compromise that allowed the Little Council to take a large hand in this sphere. The Consistory exercised detailed and extensive authority over Genevan ecclesiastical life.

Calvin's system of doctrine, as set out in the *Institutes*, began with the sovereignty of God and, following the general order of the creeds, discussed Christ, the Holy Spirit, and the church. His emphasis upon the predestination of God was attacked by several people and his retention of infant baptism reflected the importance he placed upon the sociological aspect of the sacramentals. His view of baptism was quite similar to that of Zwingli, and he taught the real presence of Christ in the Lord's Supper.

Because of entreaties of the Genevan authorities in 1541, Calvin returned to Geneva. There were still many opponents. By 1553 it appeared that Calvin's supporters might be defeated in the popular vote and that another banishment might result. However, in that year Michael Servetus, an exasperating and unorthodox Spaniard, made his way to Geneva. An old opponent of Calvin, Servetus already was under condemnation by Catholics and evangelicals alike for his attacks upon the doctrines of the Trinity and the person of Christ. Calvin vigorously prosecuted Servetus, and the opposition party unwisely gave indications of favoring Servetus. Consequently, when Servetus was condemned and burned in October 1553 Calvin's victory was complete. The elections of the following year gave him a resounding triumph. From 1555 until his death in 1564 Calvin ruled Geneva with little opposition.

The Spread of Calvinism

It will be remembered that after the death of Zwingli in 1531 his reform spread no farther. The aggressive system of Calvin and his thorough training of preachers soon began to bear fruit in the Zwinglian cantons. By 1566 Calvin's doctrines were acceptable to most of the Zwinglian cantons, and thereafter these became identified with the Calvinistic system.

The government of France was centralized under the control of the king. King Francis I (1515-47) had a working agreement with the papacy whereby each would profit by maintaining the Roman Catholic system. In cooperation with the pope, France had warred against Spain intermittently from 1521 to 1529, and for purely political reasons France and Spain had continued the struggle from 1536 to 38 and 1542 to 44. These wars forced Francis to adopt a policy which would best serve his immediate plans. As a result, a considerable foundation for reform in France was laid without extended persecution.

Reference has been made to Jacques Lefèvre Étaples, who spread evangelical views long before Luther. A number of his pupils continued to propagate evangelical views. Reform ideas appeared among the faculty of the University of Paris, long a Catholic stronghold. Calvin fled from France in the latter part of 1534, just as the full weight of royal persecution was beginning. Despite the frequent martyrdoms that occurred, large numbers of French preachers attended Calvin's school at Geneva and returned to their homeland to preach what was known as the Huguenot gospel. By 1559 there were forty-nine congregations of Calvinists in France, and in that year a synod was held in Paris that formed a national organization and adopted a Calvinistic confession of faith. Within two years the number of congregations had increased to 2,150. Between 1562 and 1598 a series of wars between the Huguenots and the Catholics took place. On the latter date through the efforts of King Henry IV (who had become a Roman Catholic in order to secure the French crown) the Edict of Nantes was enacted, providing certain "perpetual" liberties for French Calvinists. As a result of continued struggle in the seventeenth century, those liberties were eliminated in 1685.

The Netherlands consisted of about seventeen provinces in what is now Belgium and Holland. They had long been known as a center of opposition to Roman Catholic doctrine. The Waldenses, the Brethren of the Common Life, mysticism, and humanism were represented in this region. Between 1517 and 1520 Lutheranism spread rapidly in the Low Countries. The Mennonites made great progress until about 1540, when Calvinism began to become influential. One reason why many left the Mennonite ranks to become Calvinists was that the former demanded pacifism. Spain was waging a determined war against the Netherlands for both political and religious reasons. Many inhabitants embraced the militant Calvinistic movement in preference to the pacifistic Mennonite belief. By 1550 the Calvinists began organizing churches in homes. By 1559 a national synod was held, the Dutch Reformed Church (Calvinistic) was organized, and a Calvinistic confession adopted. From 1566 to 1578 the patriots under William the Silent (1553-84) fought the Spanish overlords, and in 1581 the northern provinces declared their independence.

Scotland had been evangelized very early by British missionaries. The Roman Catholic system gained control of Scotland in the eleventh century. The fight with England in the thirteenth and fourteenth centuries, which resulted in Scottish independence under Robert Bruce, brought Scotland into close alliance with France. Reform movements had begun in Scotland under the inspiration of the work of Luther, Tyndale, and others. Patrick Hamilton, trained in the University of Paris, voiced evangelical doctrines and was burned in 1528. As a result many nobles, both from political and ecclesiastical motives, turned toward Protestantism. In 1546 George Wishart was also burned. His martyrdom inflamed John Knox. Subsequently, Knox attended Calvin's school in Geneva in 1554 and served as pastor there after 1555. In 1559 Knox returned to Scotland and was victorious in establishing the Presbyterian system.

Calvinism did not attain great influence in the German states in this period. It was excluded from toleration in the Treaty of Augsburg in 1555. Melanchthon became increasingly sympathetic toward Calvinistic doctrine, particularly after 1546, when Luther died.

England was not greatly affected by Calvinism in this period, although the regents of Edward VI (1547-53) were familiar with it tenets. Its greatest influence in England came in the next period.

Reform erupted in Switzerland under the leadership of Ulrich Zwingli and John Calvin. The untimely death of Zwingli radically turned his reform into different channels. His movement was later swallowed up by that of John Calvin.

Both of the Swiss reformers condemned and persecuted the radicals and Anabaptists. By the time of Calvin's death in 1564, his movement was known in every part of Europe and England and was very influential in Scotland and Switzerland.

19

Anabaptists and the Radical Reformation

For centuries the principal historians either ignored or grossly misunderstood what is now recognized as one of the important movements of the Reformation period. This movement was called Anabaptism for centuries, although with some reservations by those most familiar with it. A. H. Newman, for example, recognized—as scholars of other denominations now agree—that the name "Anabaptist" was an epithet of reprobation or condemnation. It was long identified with fanaticism, schism, and lawlessness. As early as the fifth century the Theodosian Code decreed the death penalty for any who rebaptized another. This law was aimed at the Donatists, who sometimes were referred to as Anabaptists because they insisted on performing the rite of baptism on anyone coming from the corrupted Catholic churches, which, said the Donatists, had lost the power to administer saving baptism. With this sort of background, the name *Anabaptist* came to be applied to any religious iconoclast or fanatic.

To find someone referred to as an Anabaptist in the sixteenth century does not necessarily mean that such a person rebaptized; it may simply mean that the person's views were considered radical. For this reason, the name *Anabaptist*—emphasizing the single doctrine of believer's baptism—can hardly be applied properly to all religious radicals who were threatened or condemned by being classed in this category.

George Hunston Williams has discussed the Reformation under two categories: the Magisterial Reformation and the Radical Reformation. Luther and the other magisterial reformers used governmental authority to reform the doctrine and practice of the established churches. The radical reformers gathered believers into local fellowships based on intentional community. The radical reformers wanted to free their churches from state control in order to return to New Testament doctrine and practice.

These radical reformers will be discussed under four categories: (1) radical biblicists, (2) radical chiliastics, (3) radical mystics, and (4) radical rationalists. Before discussing each of these groups, a word should be said about the possible origins of these movements.

Origins of the Radical Reformers

In general, there are two points of view concerning the origin of these reformers and their extensive constituency. One is that they began because of the immediate historical situation and the renewed study of the Scriptures. This view would deny that there were any antecedents before the sixteenth century.

It might be more consistent to believe that the sudden appearance of these reformers over such a large area and embodying such varying doctrinal emphases cannot be explained in terms of a single or localized factor. History does not turn corners suddenly or reveal multiform expressions without antecedents. A movement as complex and widespread as this one would seem to demand a variety of factors: the lingering of medieval ideas, the immediate economic and religious commotion of the sixteenth century, the restudy of the New Testament in terms of contemporary interpretations, and perhaps other elements that cannot be classified.

Types of Radical Reformers

These classifications of the various types of radicals are totally arbitrary. Often one person could be put into several categories and another person would fit into none. There is value, however, in pressing some sort of outline on the material in order to provide a better context.

Radical Biblicists

This group has recently been termed the "Anabaptists proper" by one author, with good reason, for they demanded personal faith before baptism as a basic element of their belief. They were radical in the sense that they eliminated all traditions in favor of biblical authority. They used this as the source of their ideas about believer's baptism, separation of church and state, the elimination of sacramental and sacerdotal grace, the Christian spirit of love and the New Testament pattern of organization, and holy living as the result of an experience of regeneration through God's Spirit.

In his reform at Zurich, Ulrich Zwingli advocated the view that the Scriptures alone must constitute the basis for faith and practice. In 1523 in conferences with Zwingli, Balthasar Hübmaier (then pastor at Waldshut, Austria), Feliz Manz, and others discussed with him the necessity of rejecting infant baptism. Zwingli seemed to look favorably on the doctrine of believer's baptism at first, since it followed his avowed principle of following only scriptural injunctions and since already the elaboration of his Sixty-Seven Articles had pointed to the primitive practice of baptizing only after faith and confession.

His theory of Christianity's relation to society, however, finally drew him away from this position. Zwingli felt that he must have his reform. The denial of infant baptism would have forfeited that civil support, for the city council, on whom he depended for aid, would have been unchurched. Consequently, on January 17, 1525, in a disputation at Zurich, Zwingli denied the principle of believer's baptism. He was opposed by many of his former associates, stalwart men like the able and respected Conrad Grebel. The city council, acting as judge, decreed Zwingli victorious in the debate and gave orders that all babies must be baptized. The Anabaptists were to be banished or imprisoned. A second disputation in November ended similarly. In March 1526, Anabaptists were ordered to be drowned if they persisted in their heresy, and Felix Manz, Jacob Faulk, and Henry Riemon were early victims of this sentence.

The Anabaptist movement gained multitudes of adherents in Switzerland between 1525 and 1529. On being banished from Zurich, Anabaptist leaders like George Blaurock, William Reublin, Hans Brötli, and Andreas Castleberg went everywhere preaching. Great numbers of people were baptized in Schaffhausen, St. Gall, Appenzell, Basel, Bern, and Grunigen. Not only were numerous Anabaptist churches formed, but the movement helped purge unworthy ministers from other groups. Anabaptist preachers rigorously attacked their evil lives.

By 1529 the Swiss Anabaptist movement had declined greatly, but it did not die. Preachers like Pilgrim Marbeck worked extensively in Switzerland and later in south Germany. Particularly at Bern the Anabaptist congregations continued their struggle. Like other persecuted movements, Anabaptism went underground, and its influence cannot be judged.

One reason for the decline of Anabaptist activity in Switzerland was the beckoning of an adjacent country. Anabaptism had spilled over to contiguous areas like Austria and Moravia. Many Anabaptist leaders left Switzerland for Moravia. Moravia had been sown with radical seed by the Hussite and Taborite revolts. In June 1526 Balthasar Hübmaier fled to Nickolsburg, Moravia, after being persecuted in Austria and Switzerland. He experienced instant success, within a year baptizing between six and twelve thousand people. He was also able to publish several excellent works in defense of the Anabaptist position. His work in Nickolsburg, however, was undermined by Jacob Wiedemann and others who advocated strong pacifism (not only refusing to engage in war but declining to pay taxes to support those so engaged) and a communistic sharing of personal goods. Perhaps the bitterness of this controversy may have stripped Hübmaier of enough friends that the Austrian authorities were able to seize and burn him in March, 1528. He died one of the greatest and wisest of the Anabaptists.

The pacifistic and communistic party grew rapidly in Moravia. Jacob Huter assumed leadership, and a large community practicing communal economy became an Anabaptist haven for refugees from all Europe. Despite almost continuous persecution in the succeeding two centuries, Moravian Anabaptists increased and prospered. Their church government was similar to that of the earlier Waldenses of this area. The growth of the group in nearby Tyrol and Austria was at first rapid, but because of severe persecution the movement there was drastically curtailed.

The third principal group to advocate a rigid biblicism were the Mennonites, who took their name from Menno Simmons (1496-1561). Menno was born and reared in the Low Countries, received a good education, and was ordained a priest in the Roman Catholic Church in 1524. The atmosphere of reform prompted him to make a careful study of the Bible, especially after the execution of an Anabaptist near his home. The radical fanatics at Münster between 1533 and 1535 repelled him, but also impelled him to leave the Roman Church under the pressure of conviction. In 1536 he received the new baptism and became an Anabaptist minister. With Obbe and Dietrich Philips, Menno gathered and organized the biblicists of the scattered Anabaptist flock. He spent the remainder of his life as a

---

(Document 28)
Menno Simons: Appeal to Corrupt Sects

Anabaptists were publicly disgraced by their association with the Münster rebellion of 1535. In sharp contrast, Menno Simons emerged as the leader of Dutch Anabaptists. Simons taught pacifism and a high moral code. Soon the Dutch Anabaptists became known as Mennonites.

Christ said, "False christs and false prophets shall rise, and shall show signs and wonders, to seduce, if it were possible, even the elect. But take ye heed, behold, I have foretold you all things," Mark 13:22,23. O, You backsliding, erring children! Mind, had you taken to heart this faithful warning of our Lord and Savior, Christ; had you acknowledged his Spirit, doctrine and holy life as a perfect Spirit, doctrine and holy life, and acknowledged him as the true Prophet, promised in Scripture; and had you received him as the true and living Son of God; you would never have been led so far from his ways, nor would such frightful errors have taken place. But, O Lord! I fear that some of you are so enchanted, that you will nevermore come to Christ, the true Shepherd; for you, through a perverted and obscure understanding of the Scriptures, defend, as just and right, the abominable works of ungodliness, which are not only contrary to the Spirit, word and will of Christ, but also contrary to reasonable modesty, nature, and reason.

Is it not a grievous error, that you suffer yourselves to be so sorely bewitched by such worthless persons, and so lamentably misled from one unclean sect to another; first to that of Münster, next to Battenburg, now Davidists; from Beelzebub to Lucifer, and from Belial to Behemoth? Ever learning, but never able to come to the knowledge of the real truth. You suffer yourselves to be led about by every wind of doctrine. You choose out a way for yourselves, as do also the priests and monks; you hold not to the head, Christ, from which all the body, fitly joined together, cometh unto a perfect man, unto the measure of the stature of the fullness of Christ. I fear that your sins will be punished; for you are earthly, and carnal minded, whereby you thrust from you the pure knowledge of Christ, and hate his cross; and against all admonition of Scriptures, against the undeceiving example of Christ and his saints, you conform yourselves in the splendor, pomp, eating, drinking, folly, hypocrisy, and false worship, of this proud, useless, vain and idolatrous world, which you should, by right, instruct and admonish by a pious, humble, sober and godly walk.

fugitive from Catholics and Protestants alike. Traveling and writing extensively, Menno preserved the heritage of the biblical Anabaptists.

Menno Simmons, doubtless because of the intense repugnance he felt for the fanatics of Münster, disclaimed any historical connection with early Anabaptism, tracing his movement through the Waldenses back to apostolic days. He also followed the Waldensian pattern in several key doctrines.

Radical Chiliastics

The chiliastic wing of the radical movement turned their faces away from the ideal of restoring the primitive pattern in gathered congregations. Instead, taking their text from apocalyptic writings, securing training and inspiration from earlier fanatical fires still burning in Bohemia, and counting themselves chief actors in God's drama of restoring a millennial kingdom, these radicals sought to bring heaven to earth by means of sword and coercion.

The Waldensian and Taborite ideas found everywhere in Bohemia were reproduced in many details in the work of Nicholas Storch. Influenced by his early contacts in Bohemia, Storch displayed a fiercely denunciatory spirit toward those dissenting from him. He aligned himself in 1520 with Thomas Müntzer, a highly educated Lutheran pastor at Zwickau, who like Luther was attacking the monastic and priestly establishment of the Roman system. Storch set up a distinctive type of church organization after the model of the Taborite church which he had known in Bohemia. In the following year Müntzer turned up at Prague; apparently the indoctrination he received there put him into the party of irrevocable radicals.

Storch, meanwhile, who seems to have influenced Müntzer toward Bohemian polity and principles, remained at Zwickau, where he almost made radicals out of several of the Wittenberg faculty, despite the fact that he was holding "Bohemian" errors. Carlstadt, Cellarius, and Melanchthon were greatly impressed with Storch. The latter confessed to be greatly perplexed about how to answer Storch's arguments against infant baptism. After returning from Bohemia, Müntzer settled as pastor at Alstedt. There his revolutionary preaching against religious and social inequalities did much to prepare the way for the Peasant Revolt. Driven from Alstedt in 1524 by the authorities, he hastened to Mühlhausen, where his doctrine of social revolution, mingled with apocalyptic and fanatical rabble-rousing, hastened the Peasants War. Although Müntzer was put to death shortly, his influence did not die with him. Two other leaders, Hans Hut and Melchior Rinck, attracted by Müntzer's chiliastic ideas, preached millennial ideas far and wide across the German states.

The successor to the spirit of Müntzer, and a man who resembled him in many respects, was Melchior Hofmann (about 1490-1543).

Some of Hofmann's chiliastic ideas were possibly gained at Strassburg from Nicholas Storch, the teacher of Müntzer. After the disaster of the Peasants War, many of the radicals made their way to Strassburg in south Germany, where a measure of toleration prevailed. Leaders like Storch, Jacob Gross, Hans Denk, and Michael Sattler had given chiliastic coloring to Strassburg radicals. In 1529, after a riotous ministry in Sweden and Denmark, Hofmann turned to Strassburg and perhaps was baptized there in 1530. Hofmann boldly set the year 1533 as the date of the beginning of Christ's millennial reign and named the city of Strassburg the "new Jerusalem." He ordered that baptism be suspended for two years to prepare for the event. For most of the two years he traveled in the Netherlands, gaining a disciple in Jan Matthys, who would outdo his master in chiliastic fanaticism. Hofmann was sent to jail in May 1533 at Strassburg, where he died ten years later. Matthys announced in 1533 that he was the prophet Enoch who had been promised by Hofmann, and he assumed leadership of the fanatical party.

Matthys set the stage for the Münster fiasco. The people in Münster, a city of northern Germany, had reacted favorably to the evangelical preaching of Bernhard Rothmann between 1529 and 1532. Many radicals flooded the city, and in 1534 John of Leyden and Gert tom Closter, representing Matthys, arrived to take charge. Matthys announced that Münster, not Strassburg, was to be the "new Jerusalem." The seizure of the city by the radicals brought the troops of the Roman Catholic bishop. In the siege and war that followed, John of Leyden, who became leader when Matthys was slain, introduced polygamy and required baptism or banishment. The city held out for almost a year. The few leaders that were captured were tortured and hoisted in a cage to the tower of the principal church of Münster. Their bones remained there for centuries, a constant reminder of the dire effects of the radical movement.

Radical Mystics

The extreme emphasis on sacramental observances and the cold, strictly intellectual scholastic theology brought a reaction from those who looked within themselves for the witness and illumination of the Spirit. Moving in an atmosphere that scorned both Roman Catholic and Protestant sacramental systems, these mystics often found themselves attracted by nonsacramental Anabaptist and radical doctrines.

One of these was Hans Denk (1495-1527), a humanistic scholar and reformer associated with Zwingli for a period. In 1525 he organized an Anabaptist church in Augsburg but was successively driven to Strassbug, Worms, and Basel, where he died of the plague in 1527. His writings link him with earlier mystics. His friend Ludwig Hetzer (1500-29) had a somewhat similar experience with his persecutors before his execution in 1529. Sebastian Franck (1499-1542) moved from Romanism to Calvinism and was accused of turning to Anabaptism. His pronounced mysticism and defiant admiration of heretics who had dared to follow the truth make it difficult to classify him under any single category. He doubtless influenced Kaspar Schwenkfeld (1487-1541), who moved similarly out of Lutheranism, although Schwenkfeld's doctrines remained closer to orthodoxy than did those of Franck.

Jacob Kautz and John Bunderlin should be classed among these mystics; perhaps even Heinrich Niclaes (about 1501-60), the founder of the "House of Love" or the "Familists," should be included. Niclaes went from Roman Catholicism to Lutheranism, finding in neither what he desired. His mystical nature was stirred by David Joris (1501-56), and he seems to have felt that he had been given a special divine revelation beyond anything humans had yet known. He spent much time in England, and the influence of his movement was found there during the next century.

Radical Rationalists

Both Catholicism and Protestantism in the Reformation period abhorred the radical rationalists, whose reasoning not only led them out of orthodox churches but also developed doctrinal aberrations that put them "out of bounds." As a matter of fact, all types of radicals (biblical, chiliastic, mystical, and rationalistic) were averse to orthodox symbols and creeds. The mystics in particular often followed recognizable heresy in their doctrines of the church, of salvation, and of Christ. Franck, Hetzer, Denk, Kautz, and Bunderlin approached the views of rationalists, and in some cases went beyond them in their radicalism, but their methods and course of travel were different. One well-known rationalist was John Campanus (about 1495-1575). Influenced by Erasmus and the atmosphere of the radicals in the duchy of Julich, Campanus moved from Catholic and Lutheran views and fell into anti-Trinitarianism. His influence was widespread in Julich, and many followed his antipedobatistic ideas. He was jailed about 1555 and died there about twenty years later.

The best known of the radical rationalists was Michael Servetus (1509-53), a brilliant but erratic Spaniard. In 1534 he met John Calvin at the University of Paris, beginning a long relationship of mutual distrust and dislike. From 1546 until his death, Servetus greatly irritated Calvin through provocative correspondence and ill-tempered criticisms. In the year of his death Servetus published his *Christianismi Restitutio*, which asserted anti-Trinitarian and other doctrines abhorrent to Calvin and the rest of the orthodox world. He was seized in Geneva by Calvin and after an ecclesiastical trial was burned.

His influence may have survived in the work of Laelius Socinus (1525-62) and Faustus Socinus (1539-1604). The former was an Italian lawyer whose extensive skepticism about contemporary orthodoxy was not fully known until after his death. In 1547 he left Italy, already being suspected of heresy. He traveled widely and was an attentive observer at the trial of Servetus in Geneva in 1553. At his death in 1562 he left his manuscripts and his skepticism to his nephew Faustus, who became an outstanding propagator of anti-Trinitarian doctrines. In 1579 Faustus moved to Poland, a haven for liberal thinkers, where he met others of similar views like Peter Gonesius, George Biandrata, and Gregory Paulus. Here he founded a college and disseminated rationalistic views over a wide area until his death in 1604.

The strong anti-Trinitarian movement in Italy was snuffed out by the Roman Catholic Inquisition. Such figures as Renato and Tiziano characterize these radicals, who seem to have grasped evangelical ideas in general but held to an adoptionist Christology, with its consequent weak notions of sin and the atonement.

Other Radicals

The principal effort in this discussion has been to furnish a workable outline of the radicals and to name some principal figures. Many other radicals of this period were not mentioned. For example, Sebastian Castellio (1515-63), Pierre Paolo Vergerio (d. 1565), and Bernardino Ochino (1487-1564) are typical of those who found themselves out of step in their day. Some continued their seeking pilgrimages all of their lives.

The Significance of These Reformers

Some historians believe that twentieth-century Christianity reflects more of the ideas of the Anabaptists and the radicals than of any of the other reformers. This may be true. Because of their efforts to restore the primitive New Testament order, these movements, unfettered by political and social commitments that tied the hands of Luther, Zwingli, and Calvin, simply without inhibition tossed aside old and traditional ideas on the grounds that the New Testament did not specifically contain them.

From one point of view, most of the struggle between the radicals and the traditionalists, both Catholic and Protestant, centered in the relationship between Christians and the world or community about them. The true Anabaptists and many of the radicals insisted that the world or community cannot make Christians. This basically was the significance of rejecting infant baptism. Traditional Christianity, including the Protestant reformers, used proxy or community faith—spelled out in terms of "godfathers" and "godmothers"—to induct the newborn child to the Christian fold. Both Luther and Zwingli faced problems at this point. Luther's theme of "faith alone" was compromised by his final solution. Unwilling to divorce his movement from the traditional community tie of infant baptism, he made laborious efforts to justify it in terms of proxy faith for the infant or subconscious faith in the infant. His final result was to introduce a basic tension into his system by demanding personal faith for the Lord's Supper, but eliminating personal faith for the induction of the person into the Christian life.

Furthermore, the world or community cannot constitute a true church. There must be a gathered church in the sense that only believers, those with a faith baptism, may participate. At this point, also, Luther struggled heroically. He earnestly desired in the early days of his reform to separate the church from the world. His theme of "faith alone" demanded it. He finally turned away from this ideal in order to retain the church-community solidarity. In thus turning away from a gathered church, Luther destroyed the possibility of attaining another of his ideals: separation of church and state. A gathered church cannot be a part of the secular state. Abandonment of infant baptism drew a sharp line between world and church. Even heresy was not punishable by the state, because individuals are accountable only to God for their spiritual response. Religious liberty could not be simply a privilege but must be a right and a duty. Pope and emperor could no longer rule all mankind in different spheres. A gathered church eliminated the pope as completely as the rising national states eliminated the emperor. A gathered church also eliminated church-community solidarity and brought separation of church and state.

In addition, the world cannot determine the ethics and attitude of Christians. These must come from God but are more demanding than secular laws. The concepts of a disciplined community, an ethic of love, and a spiritual brotherhood were common ideas among the radical groups.

Finally, the world cannot satisfy the longings and impulses of the spirit. All of the radicals were to some extent mystics. For them God was near and His demands were personal. God's purposes seem to have been often misinterpreted, and eschatological schemes of frightful magnitude were developed. This is partly understandable in the light of the disorderly and violent world faced by these radicals. All of them, however, seemed to feel a personal participation in the eternal plans of a watchful and omnipotent Lord.

In the large sweep of history these radical ideas, designed to restore the primitive Christian pattern, have come to be understood and appreciated more than they were when they were voiced.

The radicals and Anabaptists were the most hated religious groups on the Continent in the sixteenth century. Roman Catholics and Protestants persecuted them. They present a complete picture of uninhibited persons who in some groups endeavored to reproduce primitive Christianity, in others sought to find God's presence in the temporal order, and to still others tried to bring in the millennial kingdom. Their contributions have been varied and significant.

20

The Anglican Reform

The last of the great reform movements occurred in England. British people received Christianity at a very early period, perhaps from the lips of soldiers who had been chained to the apostle Paul in Rome and who, after their conversion to Christianity, had been stationed on the island. The Romans had first invaded the British Isles in 55 B.C. under Julius Caesar. After the withdrawal of Roman troops in the fifth century because tribal invasions threatened Rome, the island was overrun by the Angles, the Saxons, and the Jutes. Seven principal states evolved (the Heptarchy) until they were united under Egbert in 827 into one kingdom—Angle-land or England.

Meanwhile, the Roman Catholic Church had sent Augustine the monk as a missionary in 596, and by 664 the Roman type of Christianity became dominant. After a period of struggle in which English and Danish kings intermittently ruled, the island was invaded in 1066 by William I of Normandy, who attained the kingship by defeating King Harold at the Battle of Hastings. William set the pattern for the attitude England would have toward papal supremacy. In a letter to Pope Gregory VII he refused to render fealty to the pope, although he agreed to send financial gifts. He carefully limited the influence of Rome on the English church, almost to the point of denying the ecclesiastical authority of the pope. Between William (d.1087) and Henry VII (d. 1509), English kings alternately obeyed and defied the popes. During the Hundred Years War, when the popes were living in France and under the influence of the enemy of England, King Edward III and parliament passed the statutes of provisors and praemunire in 1351 and 1353, respectively, limiting papal influence in England. In the same century John Wycliffe and his Lollards actively opposed the Roman papacy. In 1450 the War of the Roses erupted. This was a civil war among the nobles to determine who should succeed to the throne. The victor in 1485 was Henry Tudor. He attained considerable royal power because the strong nobles had been slain in the civil war and because he married the heiress of the House of York, his principal rival. He became Henry VII and the head of the English line that gave direction to the reform in that land.

Roots of Reform

The reform in England was not caused by the divorce of Henry VIII, as some suggest. That provided the occasion, but as mentioned in the previous paragraph, England had for centuries tugged at the strings binding her to the papal see. The outbreak of reform in England cannot be described as coming from doctrinal conviction. The leaven of the teachings of Wycliffe and the Lollards and the oblique attacks on Rome by the English humanists helped prepare the people for a non-Roman Catholicism. The strong nationalistic spirit that enveloped England played an important part in preventing strong opposition to the ecclesiastical changes that Henry VIII introduced.

The Occasion for Reform

The principal mover in the English revolt against papal control was the sovereign himself—Henry VIII. Despite his later fondness for changing wives, there were factors other than the flashing eyes of Anne Boleyn that pushed Henry toward a break with the papal see. The trouble began when Henry's father arranged for a marriage between Arthur (Henry VIII's older brother) and Catherine, youngest daughter of Ferdinand and Isabella of Spain. Such a union would strengthen the hold of the Tudor line on the English throne and was felt to be necessary. The wedding occurred November 14, 1501, but Arthur died on April 2, 1502. A union between the two nations was still desired, so it was arranged that young Henry should marry Catherine. The pope, Julius II, under pressure from England and Spain, granted a dispensation with serious doubts, and the wedding was celebrated on June 11, 1509. Catherine later in solemn oath asserted that she had never in fact been Arthur's wife.

Apparently Henry VIII never got away from feeling that the marriage was a sin, since canon law and Leviticus 20:21 forbade one to marry his brother's widow. The only child to survive the marriage was Mary, born in 1516. Four children before Mary's birth and several thereafter were either stillborn or died in early infancy. This meant that Henry had no male heir. Since the Tudor line had just won the throne and since England might resent a female sovereign, it was feared that the lack of a male heir would bring revolution. Henry determined to have the pope declare the marriage to Catherine invalid and permit another marriage in an effort to secure a male heir. The pope delayed accommodating Henry because Catherine's nephew was Charles V, who was both Holy Roman Emperor and king of Spain. Charles refused to permit the pope to take that action. When in 1529 the papal representative gave clear evidence of the papal refusal, Henry moved deliberately to break England away from Roman ecclesiastical control. By false accusation and coercion Henry secured legislation from Parliament in 1534 separating England from papal control and declaring Henry the supreme head of the Church of England. Meanwhile, in January 1533, Henry married Anne Boleyn, and as soon as Thomas Cranmer was consecrated as archbishop of Canterbury, the marriage to Catherine was declared invalid.

In addition to Anne Boleyn, between 1533 and his death in 1547 Henry married Jane Seymour (1536), Anne of Cleves (1540), Catherine Howard (1540), and Catherine Parr (1543). The principal events during the closing years of Henry's reform were: (1) the confiscation of monastic property; (2) the publication of Tyndale's Bible and later, through the influence of Thomas Cranmer and Thomas Cromwell, the wide circulation of an English translation of the Bible based on the works of Tyndale and Miles Coverdale; (3) the preparation by Henry of the Ten Articles, which attempted to wean the people away from Roman superstitions; and (4) the issuance of the Six Articles, which identified the Church of England as entirely Roman Catholic in doctrine although in all things (save ordination) under the headship of the sovereign of England. Such was the condition of the reform when Henry died on January 28, 1547.

The Continuing Reform
Under the Tudors (1534-1603)

Henry VII began the Tudor line in England. The children of his son (Henry VIII) completed that line. They were Edward VI (Henry's son by Jane Seymour), who reigned from 1547 to 1553; Mary Tudor (Henry's daughter by Catherine), who reigned from 1553 to 1558); and Elizabeth (Henry's daughter by Anne Boleyn), who reigned from 1558 to 1603. The beginning of the reform under Henry VIII has been sketched above.

Reform Under Edward VI (1547-53)

Henry VIII apparently looked toward further ecclesiastical reform, for the Council of Regency that he provided in his will for his nine-year-old heir, King Edward VI, was composed of men known for their reforming views. The new Duke of Somerset was made Lord Protector and moved cautiously in the direction of continued reform. The clergy was instructed to preach against the usurpations of the Roman bishops, and visitation showed a deplorable religious illiteracy among the established clergy, making it impossible for them to carry on an effective preaching ministry. The Six Articles of Henry VIII were repealed, along with most of the other heresy laws. Clerical marriage was permitted; royal control over the Church in England was tightened. In 1549 the first prayer book of King Edward VI, along with an Act of Uniformity prescribing its use, was prepared and circulated, reflecting Roman Catholic doctrine and ritual. After the Duke of Northumberland replaced Somerset (although without the official title of Protector), a revision of the prayer book was made (1552) that reflected Protestant thinking. In the next month a creed known as the Forty-Two Articles was prepared, which was more Protestant than the prayer book. Edward died July 6, 1553. Despite plotting by Northumberland, Mary, oldest daughter of Henry VIII, succeeded to the throne as England's queen.

Reform Under Mary (1553-58)

Mary came to the throne determined to take vengeance on those who had declared her mother's marriage to Henry invalid, to return England to the Roman Catholic Church, and to inflict God's judgment on those who loved England more than Rome. In 1553 the pope sent Cardinal Pole as legate to England. Under Pole's guidance every vestige of ecclesiastical reform set in motion by Henry VIII and Edward VI was expunged from the law books. England was restored to the Roman Catholic Church on November 30, 1554; suffering and death had already begun. A few months later, Bishops Ridley and Latimer were burned for heresy, and soon after Archbishop Thomas Cranmer suffered the same fate. Historians judge that the burning of these three leaders, along with about three hundred others during the five-year reign of Mary, made England a Protestant nation. Mary married Philip II of Spain (soon to become the Spanish king) in July 1554, but she died without heir.

Reform Under Elizabeth (1558-1603)

Elizabeth, daughter of Henry by Anne Boleyn, was the last sovereign of the Tudor line. Surprisingly she remained alive to secure the throne. The reason for sparing her life was purely political. Philip of Spain recognized that if anything happened to Elizabeth, then Mary, Queen of Scots and wife of Francis II of France, would be the successor to the English crown. This would have meant that England, Scotland, and France would unite under one crown. Philip greatly feared that this would destroy the continental balance of power. His father, the emperor, felt that Elizabeth should be slain regardless of possible succession, and too late to accomplish it, Philip came to the same conclusion. Elizabeth was anti-Roman, since the pope had declared that her mother was not properly the wife of Henry VIII. She was trained under Bishop Hooper, who was strongly Calvinistic in his doctrinal ideas.

Elizabeth moved slowly at first, but in 1559 with considerable opposition Parliament passed legislation acknowledging Elizabeth as supreme governor of the church and possessing even more ecclesiastical power than her father had known. She worked carefully to finish demolishing the entire pro-Roman structure that Mary had built. In 1559, by an Act of Uniformity, Elizabeth required again the use of the second prayer book of Edward VI with a few revisions.

Less than two hundred of the nine hundred Roman Catholic clergy refused to take the oath of allegiance to Elizabeth, but all of the Marian bishops were included in the minority. Cardinal Pole died shortly after Mary. For a non-Roman succession Elizabeth secured four bishops who had been consecrated under Henry VIII and Edward VI to ordain Matthew Parker and consecrate him as archbishop of Canterbury. The Church of England claims that this continuance of succession was valid under church law, while the pope has officially ruled that this succession is invalid. In 1563 the Forty-two Articles of Edward were revised and issued as the Thirty-nine Articles (although the twenty-ninth article was suppressed until 1571 because of political consider-ations). These articles have become the official doctrinal statement. They show a tendency toward Calvinism.

(Document 29)

Thirty-Nine Articles of Religion

The English Reform sought a middle path between Protestantism and Catholicism. The Thirty-Nine Articles of the Church of England (1562) reflect Protestant influence.

XI. Of the Justification of Man

We are accounted righteous before God, only for the merit of our Lord and Savior Jesus Christ by Faith, and not for our own works or deservings. Wherefore, that we are justified by Faith only, is a most wholesome Doctrine, and very full of comfort, as more largely is expressed in the Homily of the Justification.

XII. Of Good Works

Albeit Good Works, which are the fruits of Faith, and follow after jus-tification, can not put away our sins, and endure the severity of God's judgement; yet are they pleasing and acceptable to God in Christ, and do spring out neces-sarily of a true and lively Faith; insomuch that by them a lively Faith may be as evidently known as a tree discerned by the fruit.

XXIV. Of Speaking in the Congregation in such a Tongue as the people understandeth

It is a thing plainly repugnant to the Word of God, and the custom of the Primitive Church, to have public Prayer in the Church, or to minister the Sacraments, in a tongue not understood of the people.

XXV. Of the Sacraments

...There are two Sacraments ordained of Christ our Lord in the Gospel, that is to say, Baptism, and the Supper of the Lord. Those five commonly called the Sacraments, that is to say, Confir-mation, Penance, Orders, Matri-mony, and Extreme Unction, are not to be counted for Sacraments of the Gospel, being such as have grown partly of the corrupt follow-ing of the Apostles, partly are states of life allowed in the Scrip-tures; but yet have not like nature of Sacraments with Baptism, and the Lord's Supper, for that they have not any visible sign or cere-mony ordained of God.

In 1570 Elizabeth was excommunicated and deposed by the Roman Church. Rome declared her kingdom a proper target for cru-sades by the faithful. In 1587 Mary, Queen of Scots, was executed for alleged complicity in a plot to overthrow Elizabeth. As a result of these events, Philip II, now sovereign of Spain, assembled a fleet of ships. On July 12, 1588, the Spanish Armada set sail to capture England. They were defeated by the superior seamanship and equipment of the English navy; storms later helped destroy many of the invading vessels.

By the time Elizabeth died in 1603, England had a strong Protestant government. This did not mean that dissent would be permitted, for religious dissent could not be differentiated from civil rebellion in a realm where church and state were united in one sovereign.

Rise of the Puritans

With the rapid oscillation of the royal religious ideas, it is not surprising that the people did not quickly change their religious convictions to match. This was particularly true in the case of those who had been exposed to continental reform movements, for convictions were much deeper and more influential among Continental Protestants than they were on the English side.

As early as 1550, Bishops Hooper and Ridley (both later burned by Mary Tudor) revealed their repugnance toward some Roman beliefs and practices they regarded as superstitious and unscriptural. The reversal of royal religious demands under the Catholic rule of Mary Tudor (1553-58) sent scores of Protestant leaders fleeing to the Continent for safety. Many of them came in contact with Calvin's system in Switzerland. From this doctrine they were convinced that worship should contain only those elements that were distinctly enunciated by the Scriptures. This principle undercut the many Roman Catholic practices that rested on tradition and would in many cases dispense with some Lutheran retentions, for Luther chose to leave traditional practices and regalia in worship unless they were expressly prohibited by the Scriptures. Thus when a Protestant sovereign ascended the English throne in 1558, many of these exiles returned to their own country favoring a more radical Protestantism than the moderate English reform.

Those under Calvinistic influence demanded the elimination of Roman elements in worship, such as the adoration of the wafer in the Lord's Supper through kneeling, the retention of the priest as over against the minister, and other such practices not contained in the Scriptures. By 1564 these reformers were known as Puritans in popular vocabulary because they sought to purify the English reform. They

---

(Document 30)

Book of Common Prayer: Two Prayers

The following English prayers reflect both Protestant and Catholic influences on the English prayer book and the Church of England.

A General Confession

To be said by the whole Congregation after the Minister, all kneeling.

Almighty and most merciful Father; We have erred, and strayed from thy ways like lost sheep. We have followed too much the devices and desires of our own hearts. We have offended against thy holy laws. We have left undone those things which we ought to have done; And we have done those things which we ought not to have done; And there is no health in us. But thou, O Lord, have mercy upon us, miserable offenders. Spare thou them, O God, which confess their faults. Restore thou them that are penitent; According to thy promises declared unto mankind in Christ Jesus our Lord. And grant, O most merciful Father, for his sake; That we may hereafter live a godly, righteous, and sober life, To the glory of thy holy Name. Amen.

The Absolution, or Remission of Sins

To be pronounced by the Priest alone, standing; the people still kneeling.

Almighty God, the Father of our Lord Jesus Christ, who desireth not the death of a sinner, but rather that he may turn from his wickedness, and live; and hath given power, and commandment, to his Ministers, to declare and pronounce to his people, being penitent, the Absolution and Remission of their sins: He pardoneth and absolveth all them that truly repent, and unfeignedly believe his holy Gospel. Wherefore let us beseech him to grant us true repentance, and his Holy Spirit, that those things may please him, which we do at this present; and that the rest of our life hereafter may be pure, and holy; so that at the last we may come to his eternal joy; through Jesus Christ our Lord.

The people shall answer here, and at the end of all other prayers, Amen.

---

were encouraged by several of the archbishops of Canterbury who were Puritans in fact, if not in name. One of the Cambridge teachers was Thomas Cartwright. He became outspoken in asserting that Calvin's system was of divine origin and authority and, although ejected from his post by Archbishop Whitgift, was quite influential after about 1572 in converting persons to Puritan views and in rallying them to the standard.

From this time until many of them joined the Wesleyan movement of the eighteenth century, the Puritans played a large part in English religious life. They, along with the Separatists and the Baptists, are introduced here because references to them will be made in the reign of the first Stuart king, beginning in 1603.

The Development of Separatism

Some in England wanted to do more than simply purify the established church. Across the channel on the Continent, Lutherans had separated from the Roman Church and by the treaty of Augsburg in 1555 were officially recognized in their separation. The radicals, the Zwingians, the Calvinists, and many others across the Continent had denied the claims of authority by the Roman Church and had appealed to the Scriptures as their sole guide. Already the Scriptures had been provided in the English tongue. In 1525-26 William Tyndale, from his exile on the Continent, made an English translation of the New Testament and smuggled it into England. Apprehended and killed in 1535 by the Roman Catholic Church for this translation, his last words prayed were for God to open the eyes of the king of England.

The prayer was answered the next year. Henry had now broken with the Roman Church and permitted Miles Coverdale to translate the entire Bible into English. Matthew's Bible was published in 1537 and the Great Bible in 1539. Fittingly, these last three English translations almost reproduced Tyndale's. Perhaps God had opened the eyes of the king to permit the extensive circulation. The reading of the Scriptures in the English tongue by the common people sowed seeds for what amounted to a second reformation in England.

As early as 1567, after Archbishop Matthew Parker had demanded conformity to the symbols of the established church in England, the authorities apprehended a group of London Separatists under the leadership of Richard Fitz. They were of the congregational type, although it is difficult to estimate how far their organization had progressed. About 1580 an outspoken Puritan minister, Robert Browne, adopted separatist principles and with Robert Harrison founded an independent church in Norwich in the next year. Browne fled from persecution to the Netherlands and published three treatises that have remained an exposition of the basic views of the Congregationalists, although he returned to the established church. In 1587 Henry Barrowe and John Greenwood were imprisoned for separatism, and through their tracts Francis Johnson, a Puritan and an enemy of separatism, was won to their principles. In 1592 Johnson became pastor of an organized Congregational church in London, but in the following year, because of increasing persecution that brought death to Barrowe and Greenwood, Johnson was forced to flee to Amsterdam, where he became pastor of a congregation.

Soon a second Separatist church came to Amsterdam. A group of Separatists in Gainsborough, England, among the leaders of which were Thomas Helwys and John Murton and later John Smyth, fled about 1607 to Amsterdam and formed another independent church in that city. Out of this there came a new type of biblicism, which will be discussed under the heading of English Baptists. A third independent congregation to flee from England about 1607 settled in Leyden, after first stopping in Amsterdam. This group had come from Scrooby Manor, not far from Gainsborough and was led by men with familiar names: William Bradford, William Brewster, and John Robinson. From them came the Pilgrims who emigrated to New England in 1520.

English Baptists

The pastor of the second Separatist church in Amsterdam was John Smyth, who had been a pupil of Francis Johnson, pastor of the first Separatist church in the same city. Smyth had been reared in the Church of England under Elizabeth and in 1600 had been appointed preacher in the city of Lincoln. After serious study of the Scriptures he decided in 1606 to leave the established church and join the Separatists.

James I had determined to harry the nonconformists out of the land. Smyth joined the Gainsborough group and with them fled to Amsterdam about 1607. Here Smyth came to the conviction that the Scriptures must be the sole guide for faith and practice and that the Scriptures demanded the baptism of believers only. This, of course, went far beyond what the other Amsterdam independent church believed and helped bring alienation between the two churches. About 1609 Smyth baptized himself (by pouring) and thirty-six others and formed the first English church adhering to believers baptism. Smyth and a small following doubted his authority to baptize, so they appealed for admission to the Mennonite church nearby. Smyth died before being admitted to their communion, but eventually some were received.

On the other hand, Thomas Helwys and John Murton with the minority returned to England to form the first Baptist church on English soil about 1611-12. Here Helwys published his famous plea for liberty of conscience in a little book, *A Short Declaration of the Mystery of Iniquity.* He addressed his dedication to King James I, boldly asserting that the king was a human and not God and that while political fealty was due him by his subjects, every person was responsible only to God in spiritual things. Helwys was imprisoned at Newgate and probably died there. Murton became the pastor and leader of this first English Baptist church. By the time James I died in 1625 there were six or seven Baptist churches and by the close of the period (1648) about fifty churches containing perhaps ten to fifteen thousand members. Because of the influence of their environment in Holland they held to what is known as a "general atonement," that is, the doctrine that Christ died for all, not for just a particular few. For this reason they have been known as General Baptists. They were at first called Anabaptists because of their rejection of infant baptism, but they rejected the name. They were the first English group to champion complete religious liberty. After 1644 they were called Baptists.

(Document 31)
London Baptist Confession: The Local Church

The London Baptist Confession, the oldest Baptist confession, was published by an association of five London churches in 1644. The confession included the following explanation of church.

And although the particular congregations be distinct and several bodies, every one a compact and knit city in itself; yet are they all to walk by one and the same rule, and by all means convenient to have the counsel and help one of another in all needfull affairs of the church, as members of one body in the common faith under Christ their only head.

English Calvinistic or Particular Baptists generally are dated from 1638. A Separatist or independent church was organized in London by Henry Jacob in 1616. Several schisms came under succeeding pastors. In 1638 a group separated because of their conviction that only believers should be baptized. With others these formed the first Calvinistic Baptist church in England in 1638 under the pastoral leadership of John Spilsbury. They were later called Particular Baptists because of their belief in a limited atonement: Christ died only for the elect. By the close of the period there were more than seven Particular Baptist churches in England. Some of their outstanding leaders were William Kiffin, Hanserd Knollys, and John Bunyan.

(Document 32)
John Bunyan: Christian Visits the Interpreter

Bunyan's allegory Pilgrim's Progress remains the most popular of Puritan writings. When visiting the house of the Interpreter, Christian was a picture of an ideal Christian pastor.

Then [Christian] went on till he came to the house of the Interpreter, where he knocked over and over. At last one came to the door, and asked who was there. **Christian.** Sir, here is a traveler who was bid by an acquaintance of the good man of this house to call here for his profit; I would therefore speak with the master of the house.
So he called for the master of the house, who, after a little time, came to Christian, and asked him what he would have.
Christian. "Sir," said Christian, "I am a man that am come from the City of Destruction, and am going to Mount Zion; and I was told by the man that stands at the gate at the head of this way, that, if I called here, you would show me excellent things, such as would be helpful to me on my journey."
Interpreter. Then said the Interpreter, "Come in; I will show thee that which will be profitable to thee." So he commanded his man to light the candle, and bid Christian follow him; so he had him into a private room, and bid his man open a door; the which when he had done, Christian saw the picture of a very grave person hung up against the wall; and this was the fashion of it: it had eyes lifted up to heaven, the best of books in its hand, the law of truth was written upon its lips, the world was behind its back; it stood as if it pleaded with men, and a crown of gold did hang over its head.

Reform Under the Stuarts

James I (1603-25)

Elizabeth reigned for a long time, but it was evident when she died in 1603 that she had not lived long enough to stabilize the religious settlement that she had provided for England. The succession to the English crown went to King James VI of Scotland, the great-great-grandson of Henry VII of England. Both the restless Roman Catholics and the vocal Puritans were heartened by the prospects of the Scottish king's accession as James I of England. He was the son of Mary, Queen of Scots, and had displayed his rancor toward the dominant Presbyterianism of his native Scotland. Since James had married a Roman Catholic wife, and since his mother was executed by Elizabeth, Catholics reasoned that their cause would be close to the new king's heart. The Puritans, on the other hand, felt that James' experience with Scottish Presbyterianism had conditioned him to favor them in the new realm. Meanwhile, the leaders of the Church of England felt that the subservience of their church to royal supremacy would recommend them to the new king. The Church of England won the tug of war. The other contenders for royal favor were spurned.

Two plots against the king's life were attributed to Roman Catholics. This led to a demand that Roman Catholics conform. The Puritans met James in 1603 with a petition to purify English Christianity from Roman superstitions (by adopting Calvinistic doctrines), but James curtly refused. In the following year at the Hampton Court Conference, James again spurned Calvinism but granted a request for additions to the catechism and a revision of the English Bible. From the latter permission came the famous King James Version of the English Bible in 1611. By 1604 the king had rejected all Puritan bids and made it his policy to harass them constantly. An example is seen in the Declaration of Sports in 1618. James knew that the Puritans were careful to keep Sunday as the holy day of God. As a repressive measure, he required every clergyman to announce from the pulpit the sports program for the entertainment of the people on Sunday. This was a severe trial for any conscientious Puritan.

Charles I (1625-49)

On James' death in 1625, his son Charles succeeded to the throne. Charles was inferior to James both in ability and diplomacy. Protestants suspected Charles when he was installed because his mother was a Roman Catholic and because he had married a Roman Catholic princess. Charles tried to continue his father's policies, but the mounting resentment carried over to him from his father's reign was ominous. The situation was not eased by the persecuting tactics of William Laud. As archbishop of Canterbury, Laud used spies, the Star Chamber, and the Court of High Commission to suppress all dissent. The Declaration of Sports was again pressed.

Parliament resented his rigorous tactics, but Charles dismissed the Parliament in 1629 and ruled without their aid until 1640. He called them into session only because of a crisis that he was unable to handle without the cooperation of the people. The crisis sprang from Scotland; the Scots resented royal interference with their Presbyterianism. Since 1603 (when James became sovereign of both countries) the Church of England and the crown had desired to extend the establishment of episcopacy into Scotland. By wily diplomacy James had been able to make considerable progress in that direction. In 1637, however, Archbishop Laud attempted to force on Scotland a replica of the English establishment, including a drastic revision of the liturgy. Opposition was immediate. The struggle of the Scots to maintain Presbyterianism against royal policy became rebellion, but the king had insufficient funds and men to wage war against the Scots. Thus in April 1640, Charles was forced to call Parliament into session. Members of Parliament were in no mood to acquiesce in the face of royal flaunting of English law and equity. When Parliament demanded political and religious reform, Charles dissolved the body. Having met for only three weeks, it is known as the Short Parliament. Charles alienated his people by illegally holding convocation (the assembly of the clerical leadership) after the dissolution of Parliament. Under Archbishop Laud's direction a number of canons were adopted, declaring that the king had unlimited power over the persons and possessions of his subjects by divine right, without respect to their consent. The clergy were required to sign an oath never to change the government of the English church. In describing their submission, the canon ended a list of surrendered privileges with the words "et cetera" (and so forth), which could be interpreted in almost any sense. This legislation aroused such feeling that Charles suspended it; it showed the people what they might expect from their king.

Meanwhile, the Scots had invaded England. Charles was forced to call Parliament to secure funds and men. Parliament assembled November 1640, and it quickly showed that Puritanism was in the majority. Religious and political reforms were begun. When Charles attempted to seize several members of the House of Commons in January 1642, civil war broke out between the king and Parliament. Drastic alterations took place. The episcopal and liturgical (prayer book) forms were abolished, and the Westminster Assembly, made up principally of Puritans, was summoned to advise Parliament on the creed and government of the new English church. Parliament badly needed Scottish aid in their fight with Charles and agreed to work for uniformity in ecclesiastical organization and doctrine in England, Scotland, and Ireland, and to oppose episcopacy. This Westminster Assembly recommended the Presbyterian type of church government; this was established in 1646 and provided a Presbyterian liturgy for public worship in place of the prayer book. The famous Westminster Confession was adopted by Scotland in 1647 and by England in 1648.

Meanwhile, Parliament's armies were winning substantial victories, bringing into prominence a new leader, Oliver Cromwell. The new Presbyterian establishment and intolerance were no more attractive to Cromwell than the episcopal intolerance. Cromwell and most of his leaders were independents and favored no intolerant government, whether Presbyterian or episcopal. In December 1648, dissatisfied with the Presbyterian Parliament, the army purged Parliament of those members who refused to carry out the army's wishes. King Charles had been defeated in the field and had surrendered to the Scots. He convinced them that if they would take his side, he would favor Presbyterianism in England. The Scottish leaders, noting that the army of Cromwell was opposed to the Presbyterian Parliament and fearing that Cromwell would overthrow the Presbyterian reforms that had been made, agreed to support Charles.

In August 1648, however, the Scottish army, endeavoring to invade England, was soundly defeated by Cromwell. After the purge of Parliament under the influence of the army, Charles was tried for treason and beheaded. The period closed with the temporary defeat of royal power in England; with the Tudor reforms, the work of the early Stuarts, and the Presbyterian revolution swept away through the military power of Oliver Cromwell and his army of independents; and with considerable uncertainty about the outcome of the struggle in both political and ecclesiastical life in England.

These events in England had considerable impact in the English colonies of North America. That story is in a succeeding chapter.

The occasion of the English reforms was the caprice of Henry VIII (1509-1547), but the causes were much deeper. In 1534 the Church of England was established; it maintained Roman Catholic doctrine in most respects, although denying the headship of the pope. The regents of Edward VI moved toward Protestant doctrine, but Mary returned the English church to Rome in 1554. Five years later Elizabeth permanently wrenched it away. James VI of Scotland became James I of England (1603-25) to institute the Stuart line. His son Charles I (1625-49) was beheaded for treason at the close of the period. The decade before his death was a stormy one. Civil war took

place. Episcopacy and Presbyterianism were disestablished successively, and scores of tracts advocating religious liberty and toleration
of dissent appeared. Oliver Cromwell and the army assumed control
of the government at the close of this period.

The Roman Catholic Revival

The term "Counter Reformation," sometimes used to refer to the activity of the Roman Catholic Church during this period, is not entirely accurate; it is best to call it the Roman Catholic revival. This was more than a reaction against the Protestant Reformation; it was also a response to the Reformation of Luther and others. In fact, it is difficult to judge whether the Roman Catholic Church was hurt or blessed by the movement known as the Reformation. The events of this period may have saved the Roman Catholic Church from complete inner decay and provincialism at a time when the world was expanding rapidly. Without the stimulation and redefinition that grew out of conflict with the reformers, the Roman Church would have been ill prepared to face what lay in store for it in a new and larger world.

Background of Roman Catholic Revival

National Reform Movements

Reforming councils of the fifteenth century failed because of papal opposition. Popes never again have had to deal with antagonistic reforming councils like those of Pisa and Constance. They have been able to control succeeding councils and their decisions.

A new world was being born in the fifteenth century. Before, the principal struggles of the Roman Catholic Church had been with the Holy Roman Empire. The ideal of a universal political empire was dying, however, and in its place came the rise of a strong nationalistic spirit. The papacy was now forced to reckon with sovereign states. To a large degree the French king during the Reformation, Francis I (1515-47), was able to control both church and state in his country. After the breakdown of the Council of Basel, Charles VII of France, together with the nobles and clergy, had in 1438 enacted the Pragmatic Sanction of Bourges, providing sufficient state control to offset some papal abuses. England under Henry VIII (1509-47) exercised considerable state control over the church before breaking with Rome in 1534. The German states, honeycombed by ecclesiastical princes and retarded by papal divide-and-conquer tactics, possessed no national political unity and continued to suffer under papal abuses, all the while observing the more fortunate states about them. No wonder the reform spread like wildfire in this atmosphere.

The rise of Spain as a national state was particularly rapid. In 1469 it was united by the marriage between Ferdinand of Aragon and Isabella of Castile and enlarged by their subsequent conquests. Repressing all dissident forces within the peninsula and moving with boldness and firmness in European politics, Ferdinand and Isabella helped by leaving to their grandson, Charles I, the strongest government on the Continent. Although there was no hint of revolt in Spain against papal control, Ferdinand and Isabella as dual sovereigns recognized the need to maintain the integrity of the state in dealing with the Roman Church. They assumed control of the Roman Church in their state, directing their efforts toward purifying and strengthening the clergy and maintaining as far as possible the medieval conception of papal suzerainty. King Charles I of Spain became the Holy Roman Emperor in 1519 and declared at the Diet of Worms his determination to maintain the medieval standards of Roman Catholicism that his forefathers had known. The history of the Roman Church during this period was greatly colored by conflicts between the emperor, determined to protect the ancient Roman Catholic Church and its pure doctrine, and practically every other power, including the popes.

Preparing the way for Charles, and in many respects inspiring the Spanish type of reform, was Ximénes de Cisneros (1436-1517). Trained in Spain and Rome, Ximénes, despite seemingly sincere protests against holding high office, was appointed archbishop of Toledo and chancellor of Castile. Uniting ecclesiastical and royal authority, Ximénes founded the University of Alcala (Complutum) and arranged for the production of the Complutensian Polyglot, in which the Old Testament was printed in Hebrew, Greek, and Latin, and the Targum on the first five books of the Bible, while the New Testament had the text in Greek and Latin. Erasmus published his Greek New Testament in 1516. Ximénes had printed his text in 1515, though papal permission for publication delayed its appearance until 1520.

Ximénes demanded that all of the Moslems in Spain—who had settled there after Charles Martel had thrown them back from France in 732—either become Christians or be banished. In addition, Ximénes' rigid discipline is said to have driven over a thousand monks out of Spain before his death in 1517. His zeal inspired a theological revival and complemented the work of Torquemada in enforcing the Inquisition, which the crown had begun in 1478. Thus Spain had already instituted a type of reform of the Roman Church in the closing years of the fifteenth century, but it was nationalistic, strongly medieval, and intolerant. No Protestant reform movement either began or survived in Spain during the Reformation period.

Humanism and the Roman Church

Another factor that affected the Roman Catholic Church in its relation to the reform movement was the work of the humanists. Delving as they did into the ancient writings, Christian as well as classical, the humanists recognized wide differences between primitive Christianity and the church of their day. There can be little doubt that humanists in every country helped prepare the way for the Protestant reform. Some of them joined it. Some stayed within the framework of the Roman Catholic Church and encouraged the church to eliminate abuses and superstitions.

Desiderius Erasmus of Rotterdam (1466-1536), doubtless the outstanding humanist of the Continent, even suggested a plan for the proper kind of reform. For years he had been assailing the Catholic legends, and his writings sounded so much like those of Luther that he was later forced to disclaim authorship of some of Luther's tracts. Erasmus wanted a reform without violence or ill feeling. He suggested that the priests simply be trained in the right way and then teach the people a pure type of Christianity. His efforts did not succeed. For the most part, humanists were unwilling to plunge into revolution to attain reform, and apparently revolution was required.

Papal Response to
Reform Efforts Before 1540

The strong efforts to reform the papacy through councils were unsuccessful. Popes seemed to consider the failure of the councils as a vote of confidence in the unscrupulous methods and careless lives of the previous popes, as well as an evidence that widespread abuses in doctrine and practice were of minor concern. The looseness of Pius II (1458-64), Sixtus IV (1471-84), and Alexander VI (1492-1503) has already been mentioned. Julius II (1503-13) found it necessary to call a general council as a means of defeating a reforming council of the king of France and the emperor in 1510. The council met in Rome in 1513, shortly before the death of Julius; it had happy results for the papacy. French cardinals who had sharply criticized papal corruptions were pacified. More important, in 1516 Pope Leo X (1513-21) and Francis I of France reached a new understanding, abrogating the Pragmatic Sanction of 1438. King and pope agreed to share the ecclesiastical spoils of France. After approving this agreement, the general council dissolved in March 1517. In October of that year the Lutheran reform erupted.

Although tardy in appearing, a papal bull on November 9, 1518, corrected some of the worst abuses. The marrow of Luther's early protest consisted of his denial that indulgences could forgive guilt without repentance. The papal bull conceded this pivotal point and fixed papal authority as immediate on the earth only, although allowing considerable influence to the petitions of the pope for souls in purgatory, because of the merits of Christ and the saints. This bull did not represent a concession to Luther or a revision of official Roman Catholic doctrine; the reverse was true. The pope had made explicit declarations of Roman Catholic orthodoxy, and unless he conformed, Luther could be condemned for ecclesiastical anarchy as well as doctrinal defection. Lines began to form for each side in the controversy. A considerable body of literature appeared, some attacking and some defending Roman Catholic government and doctrine. Even Henry VIII of England and, later on, Erasmus wrote as defenders of the faith.

The brief pontificate of Hadrian VI (1522-23) accomplished little but lip service toward reform. Clement VII (1523-34) attempted the time-honored customs of crushing ecclesiastical dissenters by branding them as heretics fit to be burned and of countering Protestant princes by resorting to political alignment. His judgment was often poor. His support of King Francis I of France actually tied the hands of Emperor Charles V of Spain, when Charles was willing and able to kill the young and weak Lutheran movement. Pope Clement's policy sought to maintain a balance of power and opposed the growing Hapsburg influence during the critical period of reform; the pope's fear of the Hapsburgs may have saved the Protestant Reformation. In 1527, angered by the tactics of Clement, Charles allowed an army to invade Italy and take the pope prisoner. Hardships from this imprisonment probably hastened Clement's death.

His successor, Paul III (1534-49), worked carefully. From the ranks of the Oratory of Divine Love and others known to favor limited reform to suppress abuses, he appointed several new cardinals (Caraffa, Sadoleto, Pole, and Contarini) and set up a commission under their leadership to investigate and report on the need for reform. This report was of great significance, even though its approval in 1538 did not result in immediate action. Preparing this report helped train Caraffa, Sadoleto, Pole, and Contarini for the highest positions of authority in the Roman Church. Many of the ideas in their report were later included in the action taken by the Council of Trent.

Final Roman Catholic Decision on Reform

The Roman Church hesitated briefly. Should it attempt to conciliate the Lutherans or condemn them unequivocally? Some, like Contarini, remembered the effort of Philip Melanchthon at Augsburg to minimize differences between the Lutheran and Roman Catholic viewpoints and the abortive plan of Philip of Hesse to unite all reform movements against the Roman Church. They wanted to see if it were possible to work out an agreement that would be satisfactory to Lutheran leaders without compromising traditional Catholic dogma. Others, like Caraffa (who had been trained in the Spanish reformation), simply wanted to condemn the schismatics and organize to meet the challenge of the evangelicals. Besides, this party argued, what could be done with the Zwinglians, the Calvinists, the Anglicans, and others? Conciliation would lead far from the historic position of the Roman Church. Under pressure from Emperor Charles, a series of conferences was held. One was held at Hagenau in 1540, one in Worms in the same year, and one in Regensburg in 1541. Despite some strong efforts at compromise, these conferences failed to reach common ground for agreement.

After the conference at Regensburg (Ratisbon) in 1541, the Roman Church hardened its position against the Protestants. Roman Church leadership began to bend all efforts toward halting the inroads of Protestantism and toward getting its own house in order so that it could best wage its war. Again the quarrels between the pope and Emperor Charles V saved the Lutherans. The Schmalkaldic War, begun in 1546, resulted in the early defeat of the Lutherans. The pope had a vigorous controversy with Charles over the place of meeting for a proposed general council. Perhaps the quarrel was necessary, for the pope might not have been able to control a council under the shadow of Charles. Perhaps the papacy came out as well as it would have otherwise in the "calculated risk" taken by Paul III. At any rate, the Lutherans fought again and were successful.

Two movements greatly aided the struggle of the Roman Church with the reformers: the rise of the Society of Jesus (known more familiarly as the Jesuits) and the Council of Trent.

The Society of Jesus

Ignatius Loyola, founder of the Society of Jesus, was born in 1491 in Spain. At the battle of Pampeluna with the French in 1521, he was so severely wounded that he could no longer pursue military service. While convalescing he read legends that described Francis and Dominic as Christ's soldiers. Loyola determined to become a knight of the virgin Mary. After his recovery he entered the Dominican monastery at Manresa. His deep devotion drove him as a pilgrim to Jerusalem in 1523. Unable to carry on mission work as he desired, he sought an education and returned to a school at Barcelona. He was thirty-six and sat in classes with boys ten years old. He made rapid progress and in 1528 entered the University of Paris. There he gathered a small group of like-minded followers, chief among whom was Francis Xavier. In 1534 the group took solemn vows to work in Jerusalem or anywhere the pope might direct.

Three years later the expedition to Jerusalem began, but because of the Turkish War they were stopped at Venice. Here Loyola met Caraffa and attracted the attention of Contarini. Pope Paul III (1534-49) was impressed by the ability of Loyola and his devotion to the Roman Church. On September 27, 1540, the pope authorized the Society of Jesus; a membership of only sixty was permitted originally. Two years later this limitation was removed. Loyola was chosen as the first general of the order and held that position until his death in 1556.

(Document 33)

Ignatius Loyola: The Examination of Conscience

Loyola founded the Jesuit order as a disciplined force of militant Christians. The following selection from his Spiritual Exercises *spells out his understanding of self-discipline.*

Man is created to praise, reverence, and serve God our Lord, and by this means to save his soul. All other things on the face of the earth are created for man to help him fulfill the end for which he is created. From this it follows that man is to use these things to the extent that they will help him to attain his end. Likewise, he must rid himself of them in so far as they prevent him from attaining it.

Therefore we must make ourselves indifferent to all created things, in so far as it is left to the choice of our free will and is not forbidden. Acting accordingly, for our part, we should not prefer health to sickness, riches to poverty, honor to dishonor, a long life to a short one, and so in all things we should desire and choose only those things which will best help us attain the end for which we are created.

Particular Examination of Conscience to be Made Every Day

This exercise is performed at three different times, and there are two examinations to be made.

The first time: As soon as he arises in the morning the exercitant should resolve to guard himself carefully against the particular sin or defect which he wishes to correct or amend.

The second time: After the noon meal he should ask God our Lord for what he desires, namely, the grace to remember how many times he has fallen into the particular sin or defect, and to correct himself in the future. Following this he should make the first examination demanding an account of his soul regarding that particular matter which he desires to correct and amend. He should review each hour of the time elapsed from the moment of rising to the moment of this examination....

The third time: After the evening meal he will make a second examination, reviewing each hour from the first examination to this second one, and on to the second line of the same diagram he will again make a mark for each time that he has fallen into a particular sin or defect.

Organization and Doctrines

This new order had great impact. Only five years after the pope first authorized the Society, Jesuits were already playing a leading part in the Council of Trent. This Society has been at the forefront of some of the Roman Catholic Church's greatest achievements. From the first, the Society bore a military simplicity: a general at the head, provincials over geographical districts, and a careful system of recruitment and training. As early as 1522-23 Loyola had begun preparing a series of spiritual exercises for Christian soldiers. The manual outlined a four-week course—twenty-eight general divisions with five hourly meditations covering the entire redemptive drama. Novitiates were tested by difficult service for a two-year period, then were promoted to be scholars, trained in both ecclesiastical and secular learning. The next step was the coadjutor. This office was given to those who were chosen and carefully trained for particular service; it included teachers, priests, missionaries, authors, consultants, and advisers. After long and faithful service, a few coadjutors could be admitted to the inner circle of the Society—the professed from which the general officers would be chosen.

The thorough training and ethical standards of the Jesuits quickly brought them into places of leadership throughout Europe. As confessors and ecclesiastical lawyers, they greatly influenced the Catholic princes in their affairs of state. Jesuit schools, their compromising nature at the confessional, their crafty preaching, and their missionary zeal gave them a wide following. Perhaps *obedience* is the most important word in Jesuitism. Loyola wrote in his *Spiritual Exercises:*

> That we may be altogether of the same mind and in conformity with the Church herself, if she shall have defined anything to be black that to our eyes appears to be white, we ought in like manner to pronounce it to be black. For we must undoubtingly believe, that the Spirit of our Lord Jesus Christ, and the Spirit of the Orthodox Church His Spouse, by which Spirit we are governed and directed to Salvation is the same. . . .

And again, in the constitution, the statement is made:

> And let each one persuade himself that they that live under obedience ought to allow themselves to be borne and ruled by divine providence working through their Superiors exactly as if they were a corpse which suffers itself to be borne and handled in any way whatsoever; or just as an old man's stick which serves him who holds it in his hand wherever and for whatever purpose he wishes to use it. . . .

This blind obedience demanded renunciation of individual conscience. Other unacceptable moral standards of the Jesuits were the doctrine of probablism (any course may be justified if one authority can be found in its favor), intentionalism (if the intention is good, other considerations may be overlooked), and mental reservation (the whole truth does not necessarily have to be told, even under oath). Two other doctrines have been ascribed to the Jesuits, but they have been denied by some of their responsible leaders. One is that the end justifies the means; if the result is for the greatest glory of God, then any means used to accomplish it are permitted. The other is the assassination of tyrants. Despite Jesuit protests, there is evidence that these last two principles were acceptable at an earlier period of the Society's history and, as a matter of fact, are implicit in the first three of these moral standards.

The Progress of the Society

The Society made rapid progress in Italy, Portugal, Belgium, and Poland. Its greatest victories were won in Germany and Austria where, coupled with the Lutheran controversies, the Roman Catholic Church won back almost all of the territory in southern Germany that the Reformation had alienated. The Society's activities were only partly successful in France until the death of Henry IV (1589-1610), but Jesuit influence then increased. In Venice, England, and Sweden their program was not at all successful during this period. True to the original purpose for which the Society was founded, the Jesuits entered wholeheartedly into missionary work. Although he was unable to go to Jerusalem, in 1542 Francis Xavier (1506-52) was sent to India and Japan, where for ten years he labored sacrificially and heroically; in 1549 José de Anchieta traveled to Brazil; in 1581 Matteo Ricci (1552-1610) went to China; in 1606 Robert de Nobili (d. 1656) sailed to India; and in 1685 Jesuits began work in Paraguay.

Council of Trent (1545-64)

Background

The second great weapon of the Roman Church against the Protestant movement was fashioned in a well-controlled general council. When Luther was condemned by Pope Leo X he appealed from the pope to a general council. This appeal infuriated the supporters of the pope. The reforming councils of the fifteenth century had only been suppressed by the boldest action and good fortune. Pope Martin V, after his election by the Council of Constance in 1417, ending the terrifying papal schism, had promulgated a bull condemning any person who appealed the decision of a pope to a general council. Leo X (1513-21), however, had dealt with an ecumenical council and was confident that the best method of suppressing Luther would be to call such a council and let it, under his control, repress him. The death of Pope Leo X in the opening years of Luther's reform prevented this action. Despite clamor for a general council from all sides—Lutheran, Catholic princes, and even Emperor Charles V—the popes and their advisers had not felt it to be a propitious time to summon a general council. Paul III (1534-49), familiar with the demands of all groups and confident that he could control a general council, began preliminary negotiations soon after assuming the pontificate. At this stage he still had hopes of conciliating the Protestants, so his legates conferred with both Catholics and Protestants about attending such a council. Neither desired to have a council in Italy, where the pope could dictate to it. Twice Pope Paul issued a call for a council to assemble in Italy, and twice he was ignored. Finally, in conference with Emperor Charles, it was agreed that the council should meet in Trent, a small Austrian city, and after a delay caused by another Spanish-French war, the council was set for March 1545. The emperor hoped that this council would unite Europe religiously and politically, not through suppressing Protestantism but through conciliation. The pope, on the other hand, had determined by 1545 to have no part in the conciliation of the Protestants and looked to the council to define and declare Catholic doctrine for the purpose of confuting and condemning the Protestants.

The Sessions

Seven sessions of the council were held at Trent during the first two years (1545-47). When pestilence threatened at Trent, Pope Paul ordered the council to meet in Bologna, Italy, but this aroused the hostility of the emperor. The council met in Trent again in 1551 with some Protestant princes attending by invitation from the emperor, but when they saw that papal control of the agenda and committees robbed the council of any autonomous action, they soon withdrew. Another outbreak of the Schmalkaldic War ended this meeting of the council. Finally, after the death of several popes and numerous Protestant gains, Pope Pius IV (1559-65) negotiated for the reopening of the council as a weapon against Protestantism. In 1561 the council again assembled at Trent and met there until 1564, when its work was finished, mainly under Jesuit leadership.

The Results

The results of the council show that the papal party was in control most of the time. Occasionally uninhibited dissenters raised their voices relating to some of the more fundamental problems. For the most part, however, Trent was a complete victory for the ultramontane party. The hopes of Emperor Charles V for religious and political unification of Europe were shattered. He retired from office in 1556.

The council's recommendations included some elements of reform aimed at meeting the challenge of Protestantism. Priests were required to know their Bibles and be able to preach; stronger episcopal control in the parishes was ordered; arrangements were made for better education of clergy and for more care in making appointments; morality and discipline were emphasized. These were attempts to gird the Roman Church to fight back at Protestantism.

The doctrinal decrees of the council were aimed in the same direction. Doctrines of Lutherans, Zwinglians, Calvinists, Anabaptists, and other dissenters were specifically anathematized. An authorized canon of Scriptures was announced, which included the Old Testament Apocrypha. The Latin Vulgate was pronounced inspired in all its parts. The seven sacraments were defined. Scriptures and tradition were combined for authority; good works were judged to aid in justification; and it was reaffirmed that the church alone can interpret doctrine. These were strengthening measures taken by the church.

Inquisition and Piety

Two other factors, looking in opposite directions, completed the Roman Catholic response to the challenge of Protestantism. The first was the establishment in 1542 of the Roman Inquisition. This intensive ferreting out of heresy was effective only in Italy, where Caraffa and Loyola, who had charge of the inquisitorial reorganization, strongly enforced it. By driving out or destroying evangelicals like Bernardino Ochino, Pietro Martire Vermigli, Galeazzo Caraccioli, Vergerio, and Aonio Paleario, the Inquisition gave the Roman Church in Italy more freedom from dissent than it had ever known there.

At the same time, there was a revival of a medieval type of piety within the Roman Catholic Church in Spain and Italy. Mysticism and asceticism combined to popularize a sort of oriental "union with God" experience of exaltation in Spain. New monastic orders arose, and stringent reform occurred in some of the older orders. This renewed

---

(Document 34)

Teresa of Avila: The Fourth Degree of Prayer

Teresa of Avila was a mystic of the Barefoot Carmelite order who became famous for her ecstatic experiences. At one time the Inquisition suspected her of heresy, but the Roman Catholic Church later recognized her as a saint. In the following passage from The Interior Castle, *Teresa explained her ideas on mystic experience:*

While seeking God in this way, the soul is conscious that it is fainting almost completely away in a kind of swoon, with a very great calm and joy. Its breath and all its bodily powers progressively fail it, so that it can hardly stir its hands without great effort. Its eyes close involuntarily, and if they remain open, they see almost nothing. If a person reads in this state he can scarcely make out a single letter; it is as much as he can do to recognize one. He sees that there are letters, but as the understanding offers no help, he cannot read them, even if he wants to. He hears but does not understand what he hears. In the same way, his senses serve no purpose except to prevent the soul from taking its pleasure; and so they tend to do him harm. It is the same with the tongue, for he cannot form a word, nor would he have the strength to pronounce one. The whole physical strength vanishes and the strength of the soul increases for the better enjoyment of its bliss. The outward joy that is not felt is great and most perceptible.

However long this prayer lasts, it does no harm. At least it has never done me any; however ill I might have been when the Lord granted me this grace, I never remember an occasion when I experienced any bad effects from it. On the contrary I was left feeling much better. But what harm can so great a blessing possibly do? The outward results are so evident that there can be no doubt some great thing has taken place. Nothing else could have robbed us of our bodily strength, yet have given us so much joy that it is returned to us increased....

---

earnestness and zeal helped the Roman Church face the challenge of Protestantism.

□ □ □ □ □

The sixteenth century brought an active revival of the Roman Catholic Church. Unquestionably the Protestant Reformation provided a stimulus to much of this revival. The Roman doctrine was clarified and standardized. A powerful new order, the Jesuits, became the assault troops against Protestantism. A strong missionary program was launched. Most of the territory wrenched away from the Roman Catholic Church by the Protestant Reformation now became a new ecclesiastical battleground because of revived Catholic strength. In fact, before 1648 the Roman Catholic Church had won back most of the territory in southern Europe. The Roman Church retained or won back that area that had once been the old Roman Empire. This struggle by the Roman Church, with other factors, led directly to the wars over religion that will be discussed in the next chapter.

22

The Continuing Conflict

Nothing could illustrate better the secularized condition of Christianity in the sixteenth century than the fact that efforts to reform the Roman Catholic system brought two centuries of the bloodiest fighting in history. The antecedents to the use of military force for suppressing religious dissent were many and ancient. Neither Jesus, the New Testament, nor early Christians supported the use of force to spread the faith. Beginning with Constantine, however, Christianity increasingly used political methods and weapons to suppress religious dissent.

Wherever it could control secular rulers, the developing Roman Catholic Church followed Constantine's example of suppressing dissent with the sword. During the Medieval period it is likely that the secular sword did more for the growth of Roman power than all of Rome's missionaries combined. The Crusades represented on a large scale the foul spirit of military coercion in the name of religion. Heresy-hunting by torture and punishment by burning occupied the attention of most orthodox bishops in the Roman Catholic system until 1243, when special inquisitorial machinery was set up by the papacy to locate and forcibly suppress religious dissent.

The Hussite Wars of the fifteenth century brought a foreglimpse of the horrors to come in the next century. Julius II (1503-13), the warrior pope who boasted of his prowess with the sword, is a typical figure in an age when might made right. In the sixteenth century the attempts to reform the Roman Church brought repressive wars in four countries—Switzerland (against Zwingli), Germany (against Luther), France (against the Huguenots), and the Netherlands (against Calvinism)—while the Thirty Years War of the seventeenth century ravaged most of the continent.

Causes of the Thirty Years War (1618-48)

The first phase of the reform movement was completed by 1555 when the Peace of Augsburg ended the struggle between the Roman Catholics and the Lutherans (now called Protestants). The immediate result was a victory for Lutheranism. The secular empire recognized the legal right of Lutheranism to exist and expand. This was in marked contrast with the story two decades before, when the Lutheran movement, its leader officially judged a heretic and an outlaw, continued to exist because Emperor Charles V was too busy fighting France, the pope, and the Turks to suppress it. Despite vehement protests by the pope, Lutheranism could propagate its faith boldly. The use of the sword as a means of settling religious jurisdiction, it seemed, had come to an end.

Glancing back at this period from the present vantage point, however, it can be seen that all factors pointed to another war. In general, the following matters led to the outbreak of a new war between Roman Catholics and Protestants.

Lutheran Disunity

While Lutheranism was being threatened with extinction in the Schmalkaldic Wars that began in 1546, the Lutheran theologians were fighting vigorously among themselves over doctrine. We are not surprised that doctrinal controversies occurred among the followers of Luther. His break with the Roman Church led him to push out into new directions of thought. Sometimes his impetuous nature prompted him to emphasize certain aspects of theology to an extreme. At other times he expressed himself in terms that seemed to contradict what he had previously said. He hardly had time to meditate on a complete and consistent scheme of theology, but he was forced to produce it piecemeal in various writings. Furthermore, as he developed and matured in his reforming ideas, he often changed the views he had expressed just a few years or months before.

In addition, the diverse backgrounds and ideas of his prominent followers sometimes did not truly represent Luther. Philip Melanchthon, for example, after Luther's death in 1546, introduced new elements and attitudes into Lutheranism that diverged from Luther's general position. As a result, violent internal controversy rocked Lutheranism in the sixteenth century after Luther's death. Various secular princes supported the doctrinal views of this or that theologian. These Lutheran princes used force to suppress what they believed to be erroneous Lutheran doctrines. No wonder the Roman Catholics were encouraged.

The Roman Catholic Resurgence

Meanwhile, the Roman Catholic Church was also busy. Unified and strengthened by the internal readjustments of the sixteenth century, the Roman Church steadily won back territory and followers. The Society of Jesus provided trained and zealous soldiers who infiltrated Protestant lands and schools with subversive effect. In addition, Catholic princes soon began to persecute the Protestants in their lands; this was particularly true in Bavaria, Austria, Bohemia, and Hungary. Not only did this halt the defection of Roman Catholic princes and ecclesiastics to Protestantism, but it even helped the Roman Church regain extensive and important territories.

The Challenge of Calvinism

The Peace of Augsburg (1555) had granted recognition to Lutheranism as a legal religion, but no recognition was given to the followers of John Calvin, who were becoming numerous and powerful. Calvinism became a rival not only of Catholicism but also of Lutheranism. While the Roman Catholics were strengthening their forces in the closing years of the sixteenth century, Lutherans became engaged in a bitter struggle with the Reformed Church (Calvinism). In many instances Calvinism partly supplanted the Lutheran movement, as in Poland, Hungary, Bohemia, and the Palatinate. Perhaps one explanation why Calvinism made such vast inroads was that Lutheranism retained much of the medieval Roman system. While Calvinism was strongly anti-Roman, it had no Melanchthon to seek areas of compromise with the Roman Catholic system. Rather, Calvin rejected all tradition and insisted on a fresh start from the direct teachings of the Scriptures. In addition, the Calvinistic system was more nearly self-consistent in its teachings and its methods. Its emphasis on God's predestination in human experience put iron into the souls of those who fought the Roman system.

Violations of the Augsburg Treaty

The pope had never agreed to the Treaty of Augsburg in 1555. Naturally his followers were not at all scrupulous in observing the legal right of the Lutherans. Nor was the papacy alone at fault. The Lutherans were also guilty. The union of church and state, practiced through the centuries by the Roman Catholic Church, was also adopted in Lutheranism, Zwinglianism, Calvinism, and Anglicanism, making it necessary for them to use military and political weapons in advancing any movement that was a part of national interest. Under this philosophy, religious differences were viewed as political and military threats. Flagrant violations of the Augsburg Treaty were excused on the ground of national interest. They led unerringly toward war.

Political Rivalry

When war finally came, it presented a confusing scene. Political interests often took precedence over religious beliefs. Catholic France and Catholic Spain took opposing sides because of political rivalry. Protestant princes looked first at political factors before choosing sides and taking up arms. Consequently, although the struggle was basically between Roman Catholics and Protestants, the Thirty Years War brought strange alliances and questionable motives.

Outbreak of War

The immediate occasion for the Thirty Years War occurred in Bohemia. The emperor Matthias (1612-19) forbade Protestants to erect certain churches, despite his initial oath that he would tolerate the numerous Protestant subjects of Bohemia. To add fuel, the dyspeptic Matthias arranged for his cousin Ferdinand, a militant Roman Catholic, to succeed him as the king of Bohemia. The Protestant reform flared into violence in Prague in May 1618, and war was made certain when the Bohemian Protestants rejected Ferdinand as their king in the following year, choosing instead a Protestant.

The war that followed had four distinct phases.

Struggle in Germany (1618-23)

The Roman Catholic policy of continued preparation was quickly rewarded. By 1620 the Bohemian Protestants were crushed. All Protestant schools and churches were closed in Bohemia, Moravia, and Austria. Their pastors were driven into exile. The Catholics were not generous in victory, taking immediate steps to re-Catholicize the

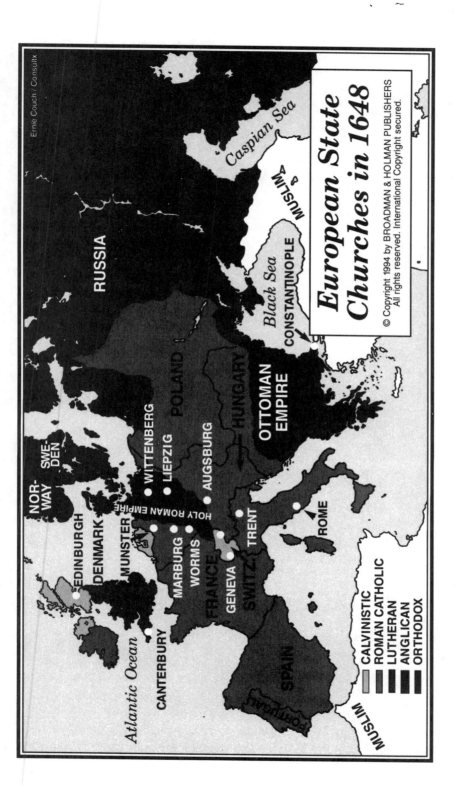

European State Churches in 1648

Ernie Couch / Consultx

RUSSIA

Caspian Sea

Black Sea

MUSLIM

CONSTANTINOPLE

OTTOMAN EMPIRE

HUNGARY

POLAND

WITTENBERG

LIEPZIG

AUGSBURG

NOR-WAY

SWE-DEN

HOLY ROMAN EMPIRE

EDINBURGH

DENMARK

MUNSTER

MARBURG

WORMS

FRANCE

GENEVA

SWITZ.

TRENT

ROME

CANTERBURY

Atlantic Ocean

SPAIN

PORTUGAL

MUSLIM

CALVINISTIC

ROMAN CATHOLIC

LUTHERAN

ANGLICAN

ORTHODOX

conquered lands. The Calvinistic government of the Palatinate was overwhelmed in 1623, and Protestants were required to conform or leave. This victory was especially significant because the prince of the Palatinate was one of the seven electors of the emperor. With the Catholic victory in the Palatinate, the pope controlled a majority of the electors, guaranteeing emperors subservient to the Roman Catholic Church.

The European Phase (1623-29)

Thoroughly alarmed by the rigorous repression of Protestantism in the newly won lands, Lutheran princes in northern Germany prepared themselves for conflict by seeking aid from nominally Protestant states—Denmark, England, and Holland. The Roman Catholics, however, defeated the new foes. Victorious Catholic forces imposed severe terms in the Edict of Restitution in March 1629. All Protestants were to be banished from Catholic lands, and it appeared that all of the gains of the Protestant Reformation would be wiped out under the Roman program.

Gustavus Adolphus (1629-32)

In this dark hour for the Protestants, two developments changed the picture. The first was the quarrel among the various Catholic leaders, secular and ecclesiastical, over the division of the spoils. The second was the intervention of Gustavus Adolphus, the sagacious and brilliant king of Sweden. In 1630 he began his invasion of Germany. At first other Protestants paid him scant attention, but within two years he had rallied Protestant forces and put Catholic armies on the defensive. In his moment of victory at Lützen in 1632, however, he fell in battle.

Indecisive Fighting (1632-48)

The next sixteen years brought terrible slaughter and great destruction of property, but neither side could secure victory. Germany, in particular, served as the battleground and suffered greatly. Despite the opposition of Pope Innocent X, the exhausted armies on each side agreed to end the war.

Results of the War

The Peace of Westphalia in 1648 is a landmark in religious history; it closed the last of the general wars over religion. By the terms of the treaty, Lutherans, Calvinists, and Roman Catholics were recognized as equally entitled to civil and religious rights. The year 1624 was designated as the normal year; by the terms of the treaty, each state or territory reverted to its religious status as of that date.

There can be little question that France won the war. The long battle between that nation and the Hapsburg line was finally resolved. The German states would not recover from devastation of the land for over a generation, and many of Germany's finest leaders were slain. The Holy Roman Empire continued to exist in name only. The pope protested the cessation of hostilities and, in fact, paid little attention to the terms of Westphalia. He continued actively his efforts to re-Catholicize through subversion and diplomacy. Generally speaking, southern Europe remained Roman Catholic, northern Europe remained Protestant. The German states and Switzerland included both Catholic and Protestant territories. Protestants in Bohemia and Austria, who had begun the great battle thirty years before, received no relief in the final terms. This exhausting war apparently convinced the Roman Catholic Church that Protestantism could not be defeated with arms.

Other Conflicts

Arminianism in the Netherlands

The theological system of John Calvin stressed God's predestination. Many objected to this system because they believed it involved human fatalism and compromised God's righteousness. Jacob Arminius (1560-1609) was the leader of the group opposing Calvin's doctrine. He denied unconditional election, asserted a universal atonement for all believers, taught that humans could cooperate with God in achieving regeneration, insisted that persons would resist God's grace, and believed that persons could fall from grace. Arminian views were condemned in the Synod of Dort in 1618, and dissent was dealt with vigorously.

England and Scotland

During this period there was a fierce struggle in England and Scotland over the religious establishment. Although that story is told in connection with the English reformation, it is referred to here to complete the picture of the confused and violent situation during the first half of the seventeenth century.

(Document 35)

The Arminian Articles

The Remonstrants were Dutch Protestants who followed James Arminius in rejecting some Calvinist teachings. The Synod of Dort (1618-19) rejected Remonstrant teaching outlined in the five Arminian Articles.

Article 1

That God, by an eternal, unchangeable purpose in Jesus Christ his Son, before the foundation of the world, hath determined, our of the fallen, sinful race of men, to save in Christ, for Christ's sake, and through Christ, those who, through the grace of the Holy Ghost, shall believe on this his Son Jesus, and shall persevere in this faith and obedience of faith, through this grace, even to the end; and, on the other hand, to leave the incorrigible and unbelieving in sin and under wrath, and to condemn them as alienated from Christ, according to the word of the gospel in John 3:36: "He that believeth on the Son hath everlasting life: and he that believeth not the Son shall not see life; but the wrath of God abideth on him," and according to other passages of Scripture also.

Article II

That, agreeably thereto, Jesus Christ, the Saviour of the world, died for all men and for every man, so that he has obtained for them all, by his death on the cross, redemption and the forgiveness of sins; yet that no one actually enjoys this forgiveness of sins except the believer, according the word of the Gospel of John 3:16: "God so loved the world that he gave his only-begotten son, that whosoever believeth in him should not perish, but have everlasting life." And in the first Epistle of John ii.2: "And he is the propitiation for our sins; and not for ours only, but also for the sins of the whole world."

Article III

That man has not saving grace of himself, nor of the energy of his free will, inasmuch as he, in the state of apostasy and sin, can of and by himself neither think, will, nor do any thing that is truly good (such as saving Faith eminently is); but that it is needful that he be born again of God in Christ, through his Holy Spirit, and renewed in understanding, inclination, or will, and in all his powers, in order that he may rightly understand, think, will, and effect what is truly good, according to the Word of Christ, John 15:5: "Without me ye can do nothing."

Article IV

That this grace of God is the beginning, continuance, and accomplishment of all good, even to this extent, that the regenerate man himself, without prevenient or assisting, awakening, following and co-operative grace, can neither think, will, not do good, not withstand any temptations to do evil; so that all good deeds or movements, that can be conceived, must be ascribed to the grace of God in Christ. But as respects the mode of the operation of this grace, it is not irresistible, inasmuch as it is written concerning many, that they have resisted the Holy Ghost. Acts 22 and elsewhere in many places.

Article V

That those who are incorporated into Christ by a true faith, and have thereby become partakers of his life-giving Spirit, have thereby full power to strive against Satan, sin, the world, and their own flesh, and to win the victory; it being well understood that it is ever through the assisting grace of the Holy Ghost; and that Jesus Christ assists them through his Spirit in all temptations, extends to them his hands, and if only they are ready for the conflict, and desire his help, and are not inactive, keeps them from falling, so that they, by no craft or power of Satan, can be misled nor plucked out of Christ's hands, according to the Word of Christ, John x.28: "Neither shall any man pluck them out of my hand." But whether they are capable, through negligence, of forsaking again the first beginnings of their life in Christ, of again returning to this present evil world, of turning away from the holy doctrine which was delivered them, of losing a good conscience, of becoming devoid of grace, that must be more particularly determined out of the Holy Scripture, before we ourselves can teach it with the full persuasion of our minds.

These Articles, thus set forth and taught, the Remonstrants deem agreeable to the Word of God, tending to edification, and, as regards this argument, sufficient for salvation, so that it is not necessary or edifying to rise higher or to descend deeper.

❑❑❑❑❑

The Peace of Augsburg of 1555 did not end the struggle between Roman Catholics and Protestants. Strife continued for half a century. In 1618 war erupted in Bohemia and spread across the continents. The Peace of Westphalia in 1648 marks the close of the last great Roman Catholic-Protestant conflict on the Continent. Legal recognition was accorded to the two most extensive continental reform movements—Lutheranism and Calvinism. Political motivations began to outweigh religious differences, though religious persecution was by no means a thing of the past.

23

American Christianity

American Christianity will be discussed in three sections. The first covers the period from the discovery of America in 1492 to the year 1648, an arbitrary date in American history but quite significant in European history. The second section covers the remainder of the American colonial period, while the third section begins with the founding of the American Republic (1789) and continues to the present. This chapter will cover the first of these sections.

Importance of American Christianity

American Christianity deserves extended treatment for several reasons.

- In a comparatively short time—by the standard of continental Christianity—American Christianity developed and achieved great vitality and influence. The United States is now the strength of the Roman Catholic Church as well as of the Reformation groups.

- In the twentieth century American Christianity has become the principal base for world missionary efforts.

- The gradual loss of vitality of Christianity in Europe has accentuated the extraordinary progress made in North America.

- Christianity in the United States has assumed forms diverging from the historic pattern.

Even the physical characteristics of the earth and rivers in what became the United States have tended to unify the nation, minimizing the sharp demarcations that characterized European states and racial groups. This underlying unity, along with the considerable resources of the great expanse of land providing an economy of plenty, produced a new type of person. Self-reliant, independent, suspicious of coercion, and conscious of the opportunities afforded by personal worth and industrious application, the colonial American was a new factor in the complex religious picture of the world.

Significance of the Time

The discovery and settlement of America came at a peculiarly opportune time. Reformations in Europe and England were working their purifying effects to provide an evangelical base for gospel extension. There was great improvement in the Roman Catholic Christianity that was transplanted, in that many of the medieval abuses of doctrine and morals had been repressed. Most of the Roman Catholic immigrants in the formative years came from the British Isles, where they had been tempered by their minority position and their contact with other persecuted minorities. Roman Catholicism in the United States has not shown the harsh and vindictive spirit that it has shown elsewhere. Tremendous growth of Roman Catholicism in the United States (with its different spirit in many respects) into a dominant power in the entire Roman movement gave hope that some day Roman Catholicism would abandon persecution and coercive tactics.

Not only the Roman Catholics but all Christian groups in early colonial America had contact with the sweeping religious currents of seventeenth-century England. Thousands had fled to America to escape the intolerable policies of Archbishop William Laud. The avalanche of tracts and books in the last years of Charles I advocating religious toleration and even religious liberty were known in colonial America. The harshness of the reactionary legislation of the restoration Parliament conditioned English colonists for the exultant national and anti-Roman surge that brought William and Mary to the throne and gave homeland and colonies the Act of Toleration in 1689.

With this background and the comparative isolation of the American colonies from English interference, the men and women who fled

---

(Document 36)

Christopher Columbus: On Discovering America

On first arriving in the New World, Christopher Columbus sent a written report to Queen Isabella of Castile. In this and other of his writings, Columbus spoke of strong spiritual motivations for his work. His religious motives have been extensively discussed and variously interpreted.

Indeed this outcome was manifold and marvelous, and fitting not to my own claims to merit, but rather to the holy Christian faith and the piety and religion of our sovereigns, for the human mind could not comprehend, that the divine mind has granted to men. For God is accustomed to listen to his servants, and to those who love his commands, even in impossible circumstances, as has happened to us in the present instance, for we have succeeded in that to which hitherto mortal powers have in no wise attained. For if others have written or spoken of these islands, they have all done so by indirection and guesses; no one claims to have seen them, whence it seemed to be almost a fable. Therefore let the King and Queen, the Prince, their happy realms, and all other provinces of Christendom give thanks to the Savior, our Lord Jesus Christ, who has granted us so great a victory and reward; let processions be celebrated; let solemn holy rites be performed; and let churches be decked with festival branches; let Christ rejoice on earth as He does in heaven when He foresees that so many souls of peoples hitherto lost are to be saved. Let us too rejoice, both for the exaltation of our faith and for the increase in temporal goods in which not only Spain but all Christendom together are to share. As these things were done, so have they been briefly narrated. Farewell.

---

to a new world planted a new kind of Christianity that could not have been understood or tolerated a century or two before.

Characteristics of American Christianity

This new kind of Christianity flowed from the activity and efforts of the religious dissenters, aided at some points by philosophical and humanistic idealism. A strong democratic spirit and the principle of separation of church and state greatly influenced and directed the religious life of the United States. These distinctives encouraged the rise of religious individualism, of denominationalism, of religion by conviction rather than coercion, of competition in religion, of a sharpened sense of lay obligation, of zealous and extensive missionary activity, of the organization of nonecclesiastical ethical and philanthropic bodies or societies, and of the secularization of public benevolences and institutions.

(Document 37)

Antônio Vieira: The Horrors of Slavery

Padre Antônio Vieira (1608-1697) was a Portuguese Jesuit missionary to Brazil. This sermon, preached about 1635, was one of Vieira's many denunciations of slavery.

If after their arrival we look at these miserable persons and at those who call themselves their masters, what one saw in the two states of Job, is what here represents destiny, putting happiness and misery together in the same theatre. Few masters, many slaves; the masters in festive dress, the slaves stripped and naked; the masters banqueting, the slaves starving to death; the masters swimming in gold and silver, the slaves burdened down with chains; the masters treating them like animals, the slaves worshipping and fearing them as gods; the masters standing and pointing at the whip, like statues of arrogance and tyranny, the slaves bowed down with their hands tied behind them like wicked images of slavery and spectacles of extreme misery. O God! How much thanks do we owe to the faith of those who, because they only enslave our understanding, in order that we see these inequalities, we recognize in everything God's righteousness and providence! Are not these men sons of the same Adam and Eve? Were not these souls ransomed with the blood of the same Christ? Are not these bodies born, and do they not die like ours? Do they not breathe the same air? Does not the same heaven cover them? Does not the same sun warm them? What star is that which reigns over then, so sad, so hostile, so cruel?

Early Struggle for Domination

The discovery of America was not mere chance; explorers did not just happen to stumble upon it. Solid financial reasons sent ships from various maritime nations scurrying westward. A very profitable trade with the Far East had been funneled through the eastern Mediterranean countries, but in 1453 the Turks seized Constantinople, and their conquests successively swallowed up all of the former points of trade. Development of the compass, astrolabe, and maps, making possible navigation when both stars and land were obscured, encouraged adventurous voyages. Many believed that the world was round and that the vast ocean bordering China, described by Marco Polo almost two centuries before, was probably the western terminus of the same ocean that washed the shores of Spain. That there might be land within the ocean between Spain and China was not at first considered.

Portuguese explorers began poking into inlets and harbors in west Africa, thence southwestward as far as the Cape Verde Islands. Christopher Columbus was possessed with the great dream that he could reach the profitable markets of the East by a voyage, not too hazardous or distant, due west. He sailed on August 3, 1492, arriving on October 12 at what is probably one of the Bahama Islands. The race was on! Spain, Portugal, France, and England soon claimed large sections of the Western Hemisphere. The Spanish led the way, a series of explorers touching land from North Carolina south to the Straits of Magellan. Portuguese explorers visited Labrador, Newfoundland, and Brazil. England paid scant heed at first to the explorations of the East Coast of the United States by John Cabot (perhaps accompanied by his son), but a century later England made them the basis for claims in the New World. France entered the field later, touching the northern section of the continent through the work of Varrazano and Cartier.

Spain made the first efforts at colonization. Within half a century after Columbus, the explorations of Cortez, Balboa, Ponce de Leon, de Soto, and Coronado made claims for Spain in Florida, Mexico, and what is now the southern United States. Priests and monks accompanied explorers and set up the Spanish type of Catholicism; but as soon as the Spanish sword was withdrawn, the movement deteriorated.

The Spanish colonial efforts focused on Mexico and Peru, the most advanced and populous regions of the New World. Spanish conquistadors dominated the Native American populations with surprising ease and colonial officials soon established Spanish administration, aided by the army and the missionary orders. The Portuguese colonization of Brazil began in 1532 and was similar in many ways to Spanish colonization.

The French government invested little in colonial efforts in America. Instead, French explorers conceived their own grand design. Their design involved no less than the complete control of America by straddling "the core of the continent"—the Saint Lawrence, the Great Lakes, and the Mississippi to the Gulf of Mexico. For a century and a half it appeared that this grand scheme would be successful. By 1754 the French flag floated unchallenged in the very areas of the grand design. Major diplomatic and military struggles on the Continent in what is called the Seven Years War (1756-63) blasted this great dream when France surrendered to Great Britain all French possessions in

---

(Document 38)

Rose of Lima and Her Crown of Thorns

Rose of Lima (1586-1617), a Peruvian nun, was the first Latin American recognized as a saint by the Roman Catholic Church. Not long after her death, Juan Menléndez described her life in True Treasures of the Indies. *Among her many acts of self-inflicted suffering, Rose secretly wore a metal crown.*

As this tin is a soft metal, and obedient to the hands, it lacked the firmness that the Virgin Rose needed to hold the nails in place, for they would come loose and not wound her as she wanted them to. She decided to make one of harder, stronger metal and found silver to be the best, both because of its cleanliness as well as for the purpose she had in mind. She ordered a narrow strip of silver to be beaten out and thirty-three nails to commemorate the years of Christ Our Lord, making ninety-nine nails all together, and this crown she wore with great delight of her heart.

And because her hair might interfere and prevent the nails from piercing her head as she wished, she shaved off all her hair, and this she did whenever it grew back, leaving a few locks on her forehead to cover the crown, for the rest of it was covered by her wimple, so she was a crowned victim under the folds of her wimple. It is difficult to understand or even conceive the pain and suffering she underwent with this strange penitence. How it wounded her delicate head! How sharply the nails pierced her! If one alone was more than enough to pierce her brain, for as all the senses and acts of the body are dependent upon that higher force by which they are governed, all the members and parts of the body feel the pains suffered by the head....

Ninety-nine strong immovable nails pierced her delicate head day and night; and to this cruel martyrdom she added still another.

Every day she changed the crown around so the nails would open new wounds each day. On Fridays she pushed it toward the back so it would encircle her ears, which, after her eyes, were the most sensitive part, and there she would leave it until Sunday, thus accompanying the Blessed Virgin, the mother of anguish and suffering, who lies pierced with grief at the foot of the cross.....

North America. France wanted to focus attention on obtaining military supremacy on the Continent.

English Colonies in America (1607-48)

The Spanish quickly dominated the large and prosperous Native American populations of central Mexico and Peru. The Spanish colonial administration focused its efforts on these two regions because their wealth was vastly greater than that of any other region. From the

Spanish perspective, the lands today known as Chile, Argentina, Canada, and the United States were lightly inhabited and of relatively little value.

English colonists who came to North America, unlike the Spanish colonists, came to the New World with their families to work the land. Although some of them imported African slaves, most English settlers worked their own lands. English colonies were inhabited not only by Anglicans but by dissenters and by immigrants from other parts of Europe.

The six denominations involved in early American colonization were the Church of England (1607), Congregationalists (1620), Calvinists (1623), Lutherans (1623), Roman Catholics (1634), and Baptists (1638).

Church of England in Virginia (1607-48)

English attempts to colonize the American continent began during the long reign of Queen Elizabeth (1558-1603). Adventurous sea captains had discovered a profitable venture in preying on Spanish ships sailing to and from colonial areas with valuable cargoes. Meanwhile, the English seafarers explored the lands along the southern coast of the North American continent and published glowing accounts. Sir Humphrey Gilbert and his half-brother, Sir Walter Raleigh, secured patents from Queen Elizabeth enabling them to colonize new lands. After Gilbert's untimely death, Raleigh endeavored unsuccessfully to establish a colony on Roanoke Island in Virginia in 1587. Profiting considerably from his experience, in 1607 the first permanent settlement was established at Jamestown, Virginia. Despite great hardships, the colony survived. Jamestown's religious background was in the Church of England. A church was established there; however, it was handicapped by the lack of a resident bishop.

Congregationalism in Massachusetts (1620-48)

English independents, or Brownists, who had fled to Holland in 1607 under the leadership of John Robinson, William Brewster, and others, determined in 1620 to sail to Virginia in the New World. Their ship, the *Mayflower*, was driven northward by the elements and landed instead in November 1620, in what is now Massachusetts. A large colony of Puritans under John Endicott entered the area in 1629, causing misgivings among these Pilgrim Separatists, but through the medical skill and gracious spirit of Samuel Fuller of the Separatist colony, hostility and misunderstanding between the Separatists and Puritans were removed. From a common council the group united into a single church system in which the authority lay in the congregation, banded together by a covenant, guided and instructed by ministers whom they set apart, and supported as a part of a theocratic government. In 1631 the colony enacted a regulation that only members of the established Congregational churches could be freemen. Thus the ministers in the local congregations were able to regulate suffrage on the basis of religious orthodoxy. By 1648 this colony had increased considerably, swelled by the Puritan exodus from England between 1630 and 1640.

(Document 39)

William Bradford: The Pilgrims Depart for America

William Bradford (1589-1657), first governor of Plymouth Plantation, wrote a history of the early years of the colony. Borrowing imagery from the eleventh chapter of Hebrews, Bradford described the journey to the colonies as a pilgrimage. They are still remembered as "the pilgrims."

When they came to the place they found the ship and all things ready, and such of their friends as could not come with them, and sundry also came from Amsterdam to see them shipped and to take their leave of them. That night was spent with little sleep by the most, but with friendly entertainment and Christian discourse and other real expressions of true Christian love. The next day (the wind being fair) they went aboard and their friends with them, where truly doleful was the sight of that sad and mournful parting, to see what sighs and sobs and prayers did sound amongst them, what tears did gush from every eye, and pithy speeches pierced each heart; that sundry of the Dutch strangers that stood on the quay as spectators could not refrain from tears. Yet comfortable and sweet it was to see such lively and true expressions of dear and unfeigned love. But the tide, which stays for no man, calling them away that were thus loath to depart, their reverend pastor falling down on his knees (and they all with him) with watery cheeks commended them with most fervent prayers to the Lord and His blessing. And then with mutual embraces and many tears they took their leave one of another, which proved to be the last leave to many of them.

The Massachusetts Bay Colony did not tolerate Separatism for both religious and political reasons. The Bay Colony was born with a "divine right" sense that transformed them from dissenters in England

to the established church in America (and curiously enough transformed the Anglicans into dissenters). Those dissenting in the American colony were viewed as abhorring God's revealed will and
rebelling against God's appointed order. Massachusetts Bay was to be
an ideal theocracy. Furthermore, the colony was schismatic from the
Church of England. Noisy strife, particularly any that might seem to
favor a radical Separatism in the colony, could have brought the ire of
Archbishop Laud and Charles I and had serious consequences.

When Roger Williams arrived in 1631 and immediately denounced
the Massachusetts Bay theocratic system, every effort was made to
silence him. He was banished in 1636, and in 1638 he organized
Providence plantations. Similarly, Anne Hutchinson introduced variant
ideas in 1637, and she was also banished. By the end of this period
the Massachusetts Bay Colony was engaged in a struggle to maintain
both theocracy and political independence.

Calvinism

The Dutch Republic also made explorations along the North American coast and made subsequent claims of territory. In 1609 Henry
Hudson inspected the North American coast from Newfoundland to
Virginia in an effort to locate a passage to the Far East. Although he
failed in this, Hudson explored the river that bears his name and
secured the adjacent area for the settlement in 1623 of New Amsterdam (later to become New York). The Dutch Reformed Church (Calvinistic) was organized there in 1628, although many other different
religious groups found a foothold. Until the close of the period there
was little religious persecution. Peter Stuyvesant became governor in
1647 and changed this policy.

English and Scotch-Irish Presbyterianism also began to infiltrate
the colonies during the latter part of this period. We sometimes find
it difficult to distinguish between the Presbyterians, the Puritans
from the Church of England, and the Congregationalists, all of
whom were greatly influenced by Calvinistic doctrines and organization. Between 1637 and 1639 there was considerable correspondence between English Presbyterian leaders and leaders of
Massachusetts Bay Congregationalism respecting the new type of
Calvinistic modification in the American colonies. Sometimes, as in
Connecticut generally, Presbyterianism was integrated without friction, and even Massachusetts Bay Congregationalism absorbed
some Ulster Presbyterian immigration. Other Presbyterians had con-

siderable trouble over doctrine with Congregational neighbors in 1640 but were well received by the Dutch Reformed leaders in New Amsterdam. The large Calvinistic immigration came after the close of this period.

Lutheranism

The first Lutherans to arrive in America came about 1623 among the early colonists in New Amsterdam. In addition, Swedish Lutherans began colonizing New Wilmington, Delaware, in 1638 and established the first Lutheran congregation in America. There was little Lutheran immigration during this period.

Roman Catholicism

The first permanent English Roman Catholic colony was established in Maryland in 1634. Sir George Calvert, a secretary of state under James I (1603-25), embraced Roman Catholicism in 1623. Calvert had long been interested in colonization and wanted to found a colony for his own personal affluence and as a religious refuge for Roman Catholics. Calvert secured grants to Newfoundland in 1622 (under James I) and to what now includes Maryland and adjacent areas in 1632, although he died before the transaction was completed. His son Cecil proceeded with the plan, and in March 1634 the colony was founded near the Potomac River. Jesuit priests worked actively in settling the colony and in converting the inhabitants to Catholicism. Lord Baltimore (Cecil Calvert) became uneasy at the zeal of the Jesuits and their ability to secure land and special immunities. He issued surprisingly repressive orders, doubtless because he feared the effect on public opinion in Protestant England should it be learned that the new American colony was dominated by the feared and disliked Jesuits.

Considerable improvement in the treatment of Roman Catholicism in England after the death of James I forestalled the expected immigration to the new Catholic colony. Consequently, Cecil, anxious to guarantee the success of the colony, welcomed settlers of all faiths and refused to establish the Roman Church with civil support. An admirable toleration was provided. This fell short of complete religious liberty, however, for the famous Act of Toleration of 1649 enacted the punishment of death for speaking against the Trinity and assessed heavy penalties for not believing in Jesus Christ, for breaking the Sabbath, by swearing and disorderly recreation, and for similar offenses.

Baptists

American Baptists trace their early ancestry to England. During the reign of Charles I (1625-49) numerous dissenters fled from the stringent persecuting measures of Archbishop William Laud. One of these was Roger Williams, a highly educated and talented "godly minister," according to the first description of him by Governor Winthrop in Massachusetts Bay Colony. He arrived in February 1631, about six months after Boston was settled and named. Williams is significant not only as the organizer of perhaps the first Baptist church in America but because of his advanced views. Religious liberty, separation of church and state, and democracy were condemned almost universally on both sides of the Atlantic in 1631, save by a few General Baptists in England and Williams in America. There was a decade more of time and political and constitutional revolution in England before dissenters there of any kind, apart from the Baptists, championed such ideas.

Where did Williams get such notions? Perhaps a clue is found in his writings. He preserved a story about the second pastor of the first Baptist church in London, John Murton, an early contemporary of Williams. This tale speaks of how Murton wrote Baptist tracts from prison by using milk and paper bottle stoppers for writing paper. A confederate outside browned the dried milk to rescue the writings of Murton. Murton died in London about 1626 when Williams was about twenty-seven years of age. Perhaps there is a larger context for this anecdote that Williams alone remembers from Murton, for some of the ideas of Williams were those of Thomas Helwys, first pastor of the church, and John Murton.

Williams was banished in 1636 from Massachusetts Bay Colony for holding such opinions. His critics in America thought that he had "windmills" in his head. In 1638 he founded a colony at Providence based on his advanced concepts of democracy and religious liberty, and in the following year he organized what was perhaps the first Baptist church in America. He soon began to doubt the validity of his baptism—a question that plagued others of the Baptists in England— and became a Seeker.

No such doubts assailed John Clarke, founder of the Baptist church at Newport, Rhode Island, perhaps in 1644 or before. His warmhearted and unselfish spirit, expressing itself in extensive and sacrificial labors on behalf of the gospel, religious liberty, and separation of church and state, marks him as the outstanding Baptist of this period.

A few Baptists also appeared during this period in New Hampshire and Connecticut and perhaps elsewhere, in addition to Massachusetts Bay Colony and Rhode Island.

From the beginning the religious forms and tensions of the Old World were projected into the tiny English colonies scattered along the eastern seaboard of America. Before the Peace of Westphalia (1648), American Christianity was already providing an early glimpse of the rich and complex development of denominations that was to characterize later American history. In half a dozen colonies there were that many different religious groups. Already a wide ocean and a seemingly limitless frontier were shaping a new society in America.

Bibliography

Bainton, Roland. *Here I Stand*. New York: Abingdon-Cokesbury Press, 1950.

Binns, Elliott. *The Reformation in England*. London: Gerald Duckworth & Co., Ltd., 1937.

Estep, William R. *Renaissance and Reformation*. Grand Rapids: Eerdmans, 1985.

George, Timothy. *Theology of the Reformers*. Nashville: Broadman Press, 1988.

Grimm, Harold J. *The Reformation Era*. 2nd ed. New York: Macmillan, 1973.

Lang, Andrew. *John Knox and the Reformation*. Washington, New York: Kennikat, 1967 reprint.

Manschreck, Clyde L, ed. *A History of Christianity*. Englewood Cliffs, New Jersey: Prentice-Hall, 1964.

Manschreck, Clyde L. *Melanchthon: The Quiet Reformer*. Nashville: Abingdon Press, 1958.

McNeill, John T. *The History and Character of Calvinism*. New York: Oxford University Press, 1957.

Noll, Mark. *A History of Christianity in the United States and Canada.* Grand Rapids: Eerdmans, 1992.

Tuckman, Barbara. *A Distant Mirror: The Calamitous 14th Century.* New York: Knopf, 1978.

Williams, George Hunston. *The Radical Reformation.* Philadelphia: Westminster, 1962.

V. Period of Encroaching Rationalism
(A.D. 1648-1789)

Introduction to the Period

At the beginning of this period the world was badly disorganized. The Thirty Years War on the Continent had ravaged most of the German states and the continuation of sporadic struggle projected the misery of the earlier catastrophe. In England the fratricidal war between the people and the house of Stuart ended dramatically in 1649 with the beheading of Charles I and the assumption of power by Oliver Cromwell. Throughout this period the Continent was dominated by France, although the political and religious repression of the people laid the foundations for the great revolution at the end of the period that was to sweep France out of her high place among the nations. England, meanwhile, moved toward the democratization of her monarchy. Parliament increasingly assumed more responsibility for government and policy. The Wesleyan revival doubtless saved England from a revolution similar to the one in France.

During this period the intellectual world threw off traditional restraints in its theological and philosophical systems. The formulations of Francis Bacon (1561-1626) and René Descartes (1596-1650) brought a new emphasis on rationalism in interpreting the world. This emphasis was continued in Spinoza and Leibnitz. The empiricism of John Locke (1632-1704) turned in a different direction, giving inspiration for the idealism of Berkeley and the skepticism of Hume. Immanuel Kant (1724-1804) brought the age of reason to its height. By making human's mind the dominant factor in categorizing the world of experience, Kant demolished older rationalism while introducing a new type. He laid the foundations for later systems of thought that developed more fully the truth that humans are not simply thinking creatures but have other facets in their nature.

Points of Special Interest

In this period the successive thrusts of Christianity against militant rationalism and skepticism are evident. On the Continent this took the form of Pietism. This movement was quite important in its immediate contributions, as well as in its influence on the revival both in America and England during the following century. The dominating theme in English Christianity in this period was the Wesleyan revival. Every part of English life was blessed by it, and the rise of England to a dominant place in world affairs in the next century stems in large part from the saving character of this revival, both in social and political life. The Great Awakening in the American colonies, evidently sparked by pietistic antecedents, did much to lay the foundations in religious and political life for the rise of the new nation.

24

Continental
European Christianity

The Peace of Westphalia (1648) marked the close of the Protestant Reformation. The principal European nations during the Reformation were England, Spain, France, and Sweden, with the loosely confederated Holy Roman Empire and the threatening Turks in southeastern Europe completing the picture. New nations were beginning to develop—Austria, Brandenburg-Prussia, the Dutch, and Russia.

The purpose of this chapter is to trace Christianity on the Continent from the close of the Reformation to the French Revolution. England will be considered in a separate chapter.

Political Background

Francis I of France and Charles V of Spain battled intermittently during the Reformation and, unintentionally, greatly helped the success of the Protestants. These wars were not incidental. National aspirations rose sharply in the sixteenth century; the old order was changing. The empire was decadent, and as though sensing their destiny, each of the several states endeavored vigorously to secure an advantage in the new order. Although Spain was the dominant power in the Reformation period through colonial discovery and early centralization, the leadership soon passed to France. A century of exhausting wars, a fatal weakness in maintaining a strong succession to her throne, and the inability to exploit her colonial empire toppled Spain from her high place. On the other hand, King Louis XIV of France (1643-1715) was a shrewd, heavy-handed man who ruled long enough to carry out an extensive and energetic program of aggression and expansion. The Holy Roman Empire, so potent a factor during the Reformation, was rapidly declining. Political decay and economic stagnation pulled down this imposing medieval edifice and delivered its opportunities and duties to the individual German states, principally Bavaria, Saxony, Hanover, Austria, and Brandenburg-Prussia. Italy remained divided into small states.

The Turks moved off the principal stage of events. Once more in the latter half of the seventeenth century the armies of the Turks threatened Vienna, as they did during Reformation years, but thereafter the tide subsided. Sweden also, after a brief period of glory through the work of Gustaphus Adolphus (1611-32), was defeated by a coalition of her enemies in 1709.

This was the golden age of the Dutch Republic, for a time undisputed mistress of the seas. During this period the Russian giant began to bestir itself. Peter the Great (1689-1725) made a start toward westernizing the nation, and under Anna (1730-40) and Catherine the Great (1762-96), Russia added considerable territory and moved toward assuming a larger place in the European family of nations.

Roman Catholic Church

The new nationalistic spirit sweeping the world demanded complete control by the state. The Roman Catholic Church continued to claim the immediate allegiance of clergy and people. The replacing of the power of the medieval empire by that of the individual states meant the weary repetition of conflict between overlapping powers. Strife between universal empire and anti-universal church was replaced by the battle between many strong national states and the militant Roman Church. Particularly in France and Austria on the Continent this was true. In France Louis XIV (1643-1715) attained absolute authority, while later on, Marie Theresa (1740-80) in Austria sought the same ideal.

The principal story of the Roman Church between 1648 and 1789 is the interaction between the ecclesiastical and diplomatic aims of France and Rome. The religious attitude of Louis XIV was governed by his nationalistic aims at the particular time, for he apparently had little religious conviction. In 1682 Louis XIV forced France's Roman Catholic clergy to issue the Gallican Articles, a direct strengthening of national interests by limiting the pope to spiritual things only and by putting all ultimate spiritual authority in the hands of ecumenical councils. Pope Innocent XI (1676-89) was one of the ablest and most conscientious pontiffs of the entire period, but he saw instantly the subversive nature of this legislation and fought it bitterly. His hatred of Louis XIV of France was so great that he may have consented to the overthrow of Catholic King James II of England partly because of James' friendship with Louis XIV. Innocent's successor, Alexander VIII (1689-91), tried to work out a compromise with Louis but did not succeed. Innocent XII (1691-1700), the next pope, found Louis in a trading mood, and in return for favors from the pope, the French king allowed his bishops to disapprove the Gallican Articles.

Persecution of the Huguenots

The Huguenots (French Calvinists) had received the "perpetual and irrevocable" promise of certain liberties in the Edict of Nantes (1598). The Roman Church regarded this toleration as deplorable and worked continually and effectively to undermine it. Catholic sovereigns of France during most of the seventeenth century were bitterly hostile to the Huguenots and waited to smite them. In the arena of practical politics the Huguenots improved their situation by standing firm for the government amidst popular uprising and received in turn the commendations of Louis XIV. In 1656 the Catholic clergy remonstrated with Louis XIV about the privileges granted the Huguenots. The king showed his true distrust of the Huguenots by persecuting them, particularly after 1659.

In October 1685, the original charter of French Protestant liberty (the Edict of Nantes) was revoked by the same meaningless words that brought it into being: a "perpetual and irrevocable edict." All Protestant houses of worship were to be destroyed and schools abolished, all Protestant religious services halted, and all Protestant ministers were to leave France within fifteen days. If Protestant ministers would become Catholics, they could continue with a substantial raise in salary and other specific rewards. Torture, prisons, and galleys now became the rule. Over a quarter of a million Huguenots fled from France, despite border guards positioned to halt them. As a result, France lost perhaps one fourth of her best citizens. Those who remained defiled their consciences, and their children were reared as skeptics or actual unbelievers. The established Roman Catholic Church shamelessly exploited state and people in such fashion that the first strong blows of the French Revolution a century later were aimed at the church. The monarchy became so impervious to the rights of the people that the foundations were laid for the great deluge.

Persecution of the Jansenists

Jansenists received their name from the founder, the French bishop Cornelius Jansen (1585-1638), who revered the theological system of Augustine. Augustine magnified the sovereignty of God in all areas of grace and salvation. Jesuits, on the other hand, were for the most part Pelagian, emphasizing human ability to aid in the redemptive transaction.

After the death of Jansen in 1638, his friends published his theological masterpiece lauding the Augustinian system. Naturally the Jesuits did their best to get this work condemned by the pope. The whole matter came to be a test between the Jesuits and their enemies. In 1653 the pope condemned five propositions that apparently contained the marrow of Jansen's views on grace. Prominent leaders like Blaise Pascal and Antoine Arnauld were arrayed on the Jansenist side. Pope Alexander VII and Louis XIV joined hands to require the Jansenists to conform. Persecution and coercion continued for over half a century, finally virtually overthrowing French Jansenism, although it survived in the Netherlands. The significance of this controversy rests in the fact that it represents the Roman Catholic condemnation of the teaching of Augustine, one of its early fathers, and a victory for the Pelagian ideas of the Jesuits. Pelagians deny original sin and believe that humans are freed to do either right or wrong. The synergism of the Roman Catholic system is more favorable to Pelagianism than to Augustinianism.

Persecution of the Salzburgers

In the mountainous areas of upper Austria the people, inaccessible for regimentation, had long been followers of evangelical doctrines. The Waldenses, the Hussites, the Lutherans, and the Anabaptists had disciples there. Outwardly, most of the people conformed to the Roman Catholic Church, but they met secretly for evangelical worship. By the time of the Peace of Westphalia (1648) many of these had become staunch Lutherans. Since the Westphalian treaty provided that Lutherans in the territory of a Catholic prince had the right of peaceable emigration, the Protestants of Europe were shocked when Lutheran congregations in the territory of the Bishop of Salzburg were harshly imprisoned for their faith. The archbishop conveniently died and stopped both the persecution and the furor. In 1728, however, a new archbishop was appointed who vowed to destroy the heretics. Persecution began again, and in 1731 about twenty thousand Lutherans were driven from the country in the midst of winter. Most of them went to Prussia, where they were gladly received.

Suppression of the Jesuits

The Jesuit order was probably the most influential party in the Roman Church during the first century after Loyola founded the society. Its tightly knit organization, clear-cut objectives, oscillating ethics, and overwhelming zeal brought it to the front rapidly, but these same characteristics also incurred enmity from many.

In the opening years of the eighteenth century, the Dominicans charged that the Jesuits in China were allowing the Chinese to continue worshiping pagan idols with a thin veneer of Christian vocabulary. In 1721 one of the men whom the Jesuits had driven from his assignment in Portugal, Innocent XIII (1721-24), was elected pope. He promptly withdrew from the Jesuits the right to conduct mission work in China and nearly abolished the order. Benedict XIV (1740-58) also condemned the heathenish practices of the Jesuits on the mission fields. Clement XIII (1758-69), a staunch supporter of the Jesuits, brought the final blow by the issuance of two bulls praising the Jesuit order. Portugal had already expelled the Jesuits in 1759; France had done likewise in 1764; and in 1767 Spain and Sicily took similar action.

The storm of protest against papal support of the Jesuits resulted in the election in 1769 of an anti-Jesuit pope, Clement XIV (1769-74). France, Spain, and Naples demanded suppression of the Jesuits as a condition of their continued relations with the papacy. After several preliminary steps, Clement abolished the Jesuit society in 1773 in vitriolic language. No Protestant has ever condemned them more unequivocally. Frederick of Prussia, a Lutheran, and Catherine of Russia, a Greek Catholic, gave the Jesuits haven in the hope of profiting by Jesuit resentment. Restoration came forty-one years later.

The Approaching Storm

A glance at the history of the popes during this period shows that in the eighteenth century they faced a hostile world. Bitter rivalry with nationalism and the trading of blows with Protestantism account for only part of the struggle. The other part came from the Enlightenment. The first enthusiasm of discovering an orderly world—one operated on the basis of fixed and determinable laws—was almost uncontrollable. In the minds of many, authority was the measure of all things. In the eruption of the revolution in France, the Roman Catholic Church and Christianity in general were looked on as enemies of human rights and opponents of the highest human achievements.

The Lutheran Church

The Lutheran lands bore the brunt of the war that ended in 1648. The frightful results of this war impoverished these German states for a century. The male population was decimated, and the constant march of armies that lived off the land brought devastation from enemy and ally alike.

Doctrinal Controversies

The harsh controversies among the Lutherans following the death of their founder barely subsided before the outbreak of the Thirty Years War in 1618. War partially stopped most theological disputation, but the torrent of angry words soon erupted again. This time it began with George Calixtus (1586-1655), a spiritual descendant of the party of Philip Melanchthon. The training and experience of Calixtus qualified him to play his role. Through extensive traveling and diversified study he learned to appreciate other Christian groups. About 1630 he began to minimize distinctively Lutheran doctrines and to suggest plans for Christian union. His opponent was Abraham Calovius (1612-86), whose temperament and training inspired a strong loyalty to Lutheran confessionalism and made him abhor all that Calixtus advocated. This controversy, foreshadowing a similar but less bitter division among American Lutherans, engaged much of the vitality and attention of continental Lutheranism in this period.

Pietism

Within Lutheranism one fruit of the depressed economic and religious conditions following Westphalia was an attempt to bring a vital renewal of practical Christianity. Pietism represents a reaction against rigid intellectual scholasticism and an effort to return to biblical principles. England had somewhat of a counterpart in her Puritan and Wesleyan revivals. The leaders of Pietism among the Lutherans were Philip Jacob Spener (1635-1705) and August Hermann Francke (1663-1727). Spener was the pioneer, while Francke carried the movement to its greatest success. Neither of these men desired to leave the Lutheran church but wanted to reform it from within. As a pastor in Frankfort in 1666, Spener saw the difference between true Christianity of the heart and the formal and intellectual acceptance of doctrine that characterized church life about him. He introduced Bible and prayer classes to his church in an effort to revitalize Christian living. In 1675 he published *Pious Wishes,* which urged that Christianity should be more personal, scriptural, practical, and loving. Fellow Lutherans accused Spener of leaning toward Calvinistic doctrines and turning away from the Lutheran faith.

Francke had a conversion experience in 1688 and became strongly evangelical and pietistic. His great work was done at the University of Halle. While there he translated Christianity into practical living, founding an orphanage and providing educational opportunities for thousands of boys from grade school through university. From this center came the early gleams of the modern mission movement when in 1705 it supplied the first missionaries for the Danish mission in India. Likewise, Henry M. Mühlenberg, probably the outstanding early American Lutheran, came from Halle in 1742.

In addition, the work of Spener and Francke resulted in the founding of the Moravian Brethren. Count Nikolaus Ludwig von Zinzendorf (1700-60) was reared by his Pietistic grandmother and received his schooling at Francke's institution in Halle. Zinzendorf permitted two families of Bohemian Brethren to settle on his estate in Saxony. Becoming interested, he joined their group and assumed leadership. He secured episcopal succession through both Lutheran and Reformed sources. Zinzendorf wanted to establish an association of all true Christians of all churches. He was banished from Saxony in 1736 by the state authorities and used the occasion to visit Moravian Brethren, as his group was called, in England and America. In 1742, much to his displeasure, his community in Saxony in his absence organized into a separate church. He was allowed to return to his home in 1749. The zeal and missionary activity of the Moravian Brethren were quite pronounced during the eighteenth century.

Beyond its own organizational life, Pietism had a considerable influence; it gave a renewed emphasis to study of the Scriptures and emphasized the importance of the conversion experience. In a reaction against its views, some of its opponents prepared the way for rationalism.

(Document 40)
Philip Jacob Spener: Circles of Piety

Pastor Philip Jacob Spener formed small groups in his Lutheran congregation to promote individual piety. These circles spread throughout Germany in a movement known as Pietism. John Wesley later organized similar groups in England known as Methodist societies.

It would perhaps not be inexpedient (and I set this down for further and more mature reflection) to reintroduce the ancient and apostolic kind of church meetings. In addition to our customary services with preaching, other assemblies would also be held in the manner in which Paul describes them in I Corinthians 14:26-40. One person would not rise to preach (although this practice would be continued at other times), but others who have been blessed with gifts and knowledge would also speak and present their pious opinions on the proposed subject to the judgement of the rest, doing all this in such a way as to avoid disorder and strife. This might conveniently be done by having several ministers (in places where a number of them live in a town) meet together or by having several members of a congregation who have a fair knowledge of God or desire to increase their knowledge meet under the leadership of a minister, take up the Holy Scriptures, read aloud from them, and fraternally discuss each verse in order to discover its meaning and whatever may be useful for the edification of all. Anybody who is not satisfied with his understanding of a matter should be permitted to express his doubts and seek further explanation. On the other hand, those (including ministers) who have made more progress should be allowed the freedom to state how they understand each passage. Then all that has been contributed, insofar as it accords with the sense of the Holy Spirit in the Scriptures, should be carefully considered by the rest, especially by the ordained ministers, and applied to the edification of the whole meeting. Everything should be arranged with an eye to the glory of God, to the spiritual growth of the participants, and therefore also to their limitations. Any threat of meddlesomeness, quarrelsomeness, self-seeking, or something else of this sort should be guarded against and tactfully cut off especially by the preachers who retain leadership in these meetings.

Rationalism

During the Medieval period Christian philosophers struggled with the question of the relationship between human reason and divine revelation. Particularly when reason seemed to conflict with some area of revelation did this problem become acute. Many Christians looked on the synthesis of Thomas Aquinas as setting forth the proper relationship. Aquinas took the position that reason should go as far as it could, forming a base for knowledge, and that revelation should then complete the structure, thus providing a capstone or completion for the whole. Other forces, however, continued to raise the original problem. For one thing, the Renaissance opened up new worlds of knowledge and understanding. Furthermore, during the late fifteenth and sixteenth centuries humanism turned many toward faith in their rational powers. In a sense the Protestant Reformation, by fighting superstition and appealing to human reason as well as by formulating rational confessions and debating over doctrine, aided the swing toward reason. Some leaders of the Reformation glorified human reason and drastically attenuated the field of the supernatural, but generally the struggle was in bounds with respect to basic supernaturalism.

During this period, however, the onslaught against supernaturalism in favor of radical rationalism became critical. Strangely enough, the severest blow was doubtless delivered by one who was endeavoring to protect Christianity against the deism of England and the skepticism of France. Christian Wolff (1679-1754) was reared in the tradition of the philosophers Descartes and Leibnitz, who emphasized that all truth is capable of clear demonstration and is basically harmonious. Wolff tried to bring all philosophical concepts into self-evident and incontrovertible clarity and then turned to theology with the same purpose. Believing that he could do so, he asserted that Christian doctrines must be capable of demonstration with as much clarity as a mathematical proposition. This left revelation completely under the sway of human reasoning. Unless revealed doctrines were completely demonstrable to the satisfaction of the mind, they were unworthy of belief.

Because of his views Wolff was driven from his professorship of philosophy in the University of Halle but was restored by the Prussian ruler, Frederick the Great. Liberalism and skepticism were scattered widely throughout Germany. The Enlightenment—as the movement was called—ruled almost supremely in Germany throughout this period. Revelation became almost meaningless. Rational demonstration only was acceptable in teaching Christian doctrines. The curious religious system of Emanuel Swedenborg (1688-1772) and his New Jerusalem church was a direct result of this background, as he attempted to justify the spiritual world by showing its correspondence with the natural order.

This rational movement reached its height in Immanuel Kant (1724-1804). While often called the father of German rationalism, he introduced some elements that turned away from a strict and final intellectual interpretation of all life. He demolished Wolff's idea that all truths must be demonstrable by clear ideas. While insisting that the existence of God could not be proved objectively, in his *Practical Reason* he introduced a moral imperative into life that suggested a moral governor of the universe. His entire system, however, discarded supernatural revelation and made human reason the ultimate criterion of truth. This period in Lutheran life closed with rationalism strong and religious skepticism widespread throughout the German states.

Calvinism

Calvin's system of theology was more self-consistent than that of Luther, and as a consequence, there were fewer internal controversies in the century after the death of Calvin. The controversies that did develop were in the nature of radical revolt against the entire system rather than disagreement with one facet. A brief survey of Calvinism in this period can be made in a geographical outline.

Switzerland

Calvin began his movement in Geneva about 1534. After Calvin's death in 1564 his emphasis on predestination was taught even more rigidly by his disciple, Theodorus Beza. The movement was not greatly affected by the Thirty Years War. The development of theological liberalism, along with German and French skepticism surrounding the area, greatly undermined the faith of Swiss Calvinists after 1750.

The Netherlands

The Arminian controversy of the previous period gradually diminished. The dissenters were for the most part permitted to return and propagate their views. Two outstanding theologians lived in this period. Hugo Grotius (1583-1645), often called the founder of international law, felt the persecuting hand of the extreme Calvinists. He is remembered for his theory of the atonement of Christ in terms of the vindication of the majesty of God's government. The other leader was John Cocceius (1603-69), probably the outstanding biblical scholar of his area. Cocceius popularized the idea of the covenants: the covenant of works in Adam having failed, God gave a new covenant of grace in Christ. In the middle of the eighteenth century, Dutch Calvinism was also adversely affected by deism, skepticism, and rationalism. The Dutch Reformed Church was carried to America in 1628.

The German States

The Peace of Westphalia recognized Calvinism as having equal civil and ecclesiastical rights with Roman Catholicism and Lutheranism. As suggested previously, however, the Roman Catholic Church vigorously attempted to re-Catholicize as many of the German states as they could reach and were successful in replacing Calvinism in some areas. The German Reformed Church was greatly affected by materialism and skepticism in the eighteenth century. Some of its members emigrated to the United States in 1746.

France

France had been fighting constantly (usually with Spain and the Hapsburgs) since the early days of the Reformation. The Thirty Years War brought victory almost beyond the dreams of the earlier kings. France became the principal power of the Continent. During the long reign of Louis XIV (1643-1715), his chief aim was to establish royal absolutism on the basis of divine appointment. He developed a thorough organization, a strong army, and a meticulously loyal court. His extravagances brought great burdens to the people. He had a lofty conception of his office that brooked no rivalry. He made every effort to destroy Calvinism. After the revocation of the Edict of Nantes in 1685, the Calvinists fled to the Cevennes Mountains and waged guerrilla warfare against the Catholics. For a century the persecution of the Calvinists continued intermittently. The outstanding names that are preserved from this period are those of Antoine Court, the restorer of the Reformed Church of France, and Paul Rabaut, the apostle of the desert. The closing years of this period brought some toleration through the efforts of Robert Turgot.

During this period the controversy over pietism and syncretism divided the Lutherans and encouraged rationalism. The resultant skepticism adversely affected both Lutheran and Reformed (Calvinistic) movements in every part of Europe. Roman Catholic persecution added to the misery of the period and drove many toward skepticism and revolution.

The hierarchical organization of the Roman Catholic Church fore-stalled much of the radical rationalistic influence that blighted Protes-tantism. Internal conflicts brought the suppression of the Jansenists and Jesuits, and persecution of Protestants was widespread and vicious. Politically, the Roman Church made peace with the various states, in particular with France, the strongest power on the Conti-nent.

Other small groups, such as the Mennonites, carried on in this period, but that story will not be told here.

25

British Christianity

The story of British Christianity in this period is closely related to the political history because of the union of church and state. At the close of the previous period Charles I (1625-49) had been beheaded by Cromwell to institute what has been called the Commonwealth period (1649-60). A Presbyterian Parliament had become so intolerant that Cromwell purged its membership and sponsored his own parliamentary reorganization.

Church of England

During the Commonwealth (1649-60)

After the beheading of Charles I, Cromwell was faced with armed opposition from Scotland and Ireland, who recognized Charles II as the rightful king of England. With his well-trained armies, however, Cromwell overcame the portions of the nation favoring Charles II and in 1653, after dissolving Parliament, declared himself Lord Protector of England. The Presbyterian Parliament had disestablished the Church of England from the support of the government in 1641 and subsequently had put Presbyterianism in that favored position. Cromwell altered this situation by providing that all acceptable ministers should be supported by the state. As a means of determining which ministers were acceptable, he instituted a Board of Triers to test those ministers applying for state support. Views on doctrine and polity were never to be questioned in determining who was fit for employment. Only one's character as a godly man and his ability to communicate religious truths were considered. For the most part, religious toleration was provided for all except Roman Catholics and anti-Trinitarians.

Charles II (1660-85) and James II (1685-88)

After the death of Oliver Cromwell in 1658, there was a reaction in favor of restoring the royal house of Stuart to the throne of England. The people had forgotten the unspeakable tyranny of Charles I, but they remembered the harshness of the Presbyterians and the high-handed authority of Cromwell. Perhaps the promise by Charles II of religious liberty for tender consciences caused many to turn toward him. On his restoration to the throne Charles found that he had promised more than he could give. The Church of England party was still entrenched in a powerful position and lost no time in taking the new king in hand. In addition, almost before Charles was settled as king, Thomas Venner and a group of millennial-minded fanatics known as the Fifth Monarchy Men staged an uprising in an effort to seize the throne from Charles and set up a kingdom for the return of Christ. They were repelled without great difficulty, but they certainly influenced the king against all dissenters.

The Church of England (the episcopacy) was established again in 1660, and in that year persecution against all dissenters began. Five acts were passed.

1. The Corporation Act of 1661 excluded all dissenters from taking part in local government in England by requiring them to partake of the Supper in the established church, to repudiate the Solemn League and Covenant oath, and to swear not to take up arms against the king.

2. The Act of Uniformity of 1662 required every minister to believe and follow the Book of Common Prayer in his services. Out of approximately ten thousand pastors in the Church of England at this time, two thousand were driven from the pulpits because they were unwilling to subscribe. The same requirements were prescribed for all teachers in public and private schools.

3. The Conventicle Act of 1664, aimed especially at the Baptists, forbade all religious meetings by dissenters.

4. The Five Mile Act of 1665 prohibited dissenting ministers from coming within five miles of any city or town or of any parish in which they had ministered.

5. The Test Act of 1673 was aimed particularly at the Roman Catholics. Charles had issued a Declaration of Indulgence in 1672 in an effort to spare the Catholics from the effect of some of these acts, but in direct defiance of the crown, Parliament passed the Test Act, which excluded Catholics from all civil and military positions by requiring as a prerequisite for such offices the condemnation of the doctrine of transubstantiation and the partaking of the Supper in the established church.

Although some of these acts were aimed at specific groups, all of them brought great trial to Presbyterians, Congregationalists, Baptists, Quakers, and Roman Catholics.

On his deathbed Charles II was received into the Roman Catholic Church and his brother James II (1685-88), an active Roman Catholic, succeeded him on the throne despite an Exclusion Bill that Parliament had earlier passed in an effort to prevent a Roman Catholic from assuming the crown. Without delay James attempted to aid the Roman Catholics. In 1687, without parliamentary approval, he published a Declaration of Indulgence, granting liberty of conscience and freedom of worship to all his subjects. James also released Catholics from the obligations of the Test Act of 1673. Early in 1688 James again published his Declaration of Indulgence, ordering it to be read in all the churches of England. Seven bishops refused to do so and were tried for sedition. They were acquitted amidst general rejoicing.

The birth of a male child in the home of James brought universal fear that Catholicism would be firmly planted on the English throne. On the day that the seven bishops were acquitted (June 29, 1688) seven leading members of Parliament invited William of Orange, ruler in the Netherlands and a Protestant, son-in-law of James II, to take the throne of England. Partly because William felt that his wife was properly the sovereign of England and partly as a means of circumventing Roman Catholic continental power, William agreed to accept the throne and in November 1688, with little resistance, invaded England and secured the crown. Parliament recognized his equality on the throne with his wife Mary. Coincident with this, Parliament declared Roman Catholics and those married to Roman Catholics to be forever incapable of wearing the English crown. All Catholics were deprived of whatever ecclesiastical holding they had and no Catholic was allowed to come within ten miles of London.

William and Mary (1688-1702)

One of the first moves of the new sovereigns was to pass the Act of Toleration (1689). This relieved dissenters from most of the persecuting acts of Charles II, although it still left many disabilities to pass away through the influence of public feeling. Dissenters had few political rights and still were forced to support the Anglican clergy.

Some of the bishops were unwilling to take the oath of allegiance to William and Mary, protesting that the Stuart line (James II) was divinely instituted on the English throne. Nine bishops and some other clergy refused to sign the oath and were called the Nonjuring clergy. They fled to Scotland and kept up an independent succession until 1805.

Queen Anne (1702-14)

Anne succeeded to the throne at a time when Parliament was dealing tolerantly with dissenters, but an event in the fifth year of her reign aroused her ire against dissent. In 1707 Scotland was united with England officially by the admission of fifteen Scots (Presbyterians) into the House of Lords and forty-five into the House of Commons. This, with other acts designed by a tolerant Parliament to conciliate dissenters, led to a violent reaction among the leaders of the established church. In 1709 Henry Sacheverell preached a fiery sermon against toleration. Parliament promptly tried him and punished him for libel. Anglicans were furious, and through their influence a reactionary Parliament was elected in 1710. Queen Anne favored the repression of dissent, and by 1714 several laws were prepared against dissenters. Queen Anne's death ended this movement.

The Hanover Line (1714 to end of period)

Through legislation by Parliament, George I (1714-27) was brought from one of the German states as the nearest Protestant relative of Queen Anne. He and his successors, George II (1727-60) and George III (1760-1820), followed the general policy of toleration set out by William and Mary. The English colony in America protested against taxation without representation and won independence. The Church of England was greatly influenced by the Wesleyan revival during this period, a movement that will be discussed in succeeding pages.

The Roman Catholic Church in England

Charles I (1625-49) favored Romanism and married a Roman Catholic. His overthrow and execution ushered in a period of stringent persecution for Roman Catholics. Cromwell was tolerant toward most groups but specifically excepted the Roman Catholics from this favor. Charles II (1680-85) was personally favorable to the Roman Catholics, but he was unable to aid them because of the universal feeling against them in England. He may have joined the Roman Church on his deathbed. James II (1685-88) vigorously pursued a pro-Roman Catholic policy, which was the cause of his expulsion from the English throne and the declaration that no Roman Catholic should ever wear the English crown. Roman Catholics were excepted from the Act of Toleration of 1689, and their movement was rigorously persecuted. Throughout the period Catholicism was also vigorously repressed in Ireland. The rule of the Hanovers brought no relief to the Catholics in England, although prejudice against them had died by the time of the French Revolution.

Lutheranisn in England

Lutheranism did not gain a foothold in England.

Calvinism in England

Calvinism, appearing in England under the various forms of Presbyterianism, Congregationalism, Independency, or simply Puritanism within the established church, was in control in England at the close of the previous period. A church assembly from Scotland and England, made up principally of Calvinists, was preparing the Westminster Confession of Faith. This Confession is one of the most influential of modern Christian confessions, not only in its relationship to Presbyterians, but in its modification into the basic formulations of Congregationalist and some Baptist confessions of faith as well.

Presbyterian intolerance, however, became insufferable. Their severe laws, developed in the comparatively brief period of parliamentary control, provided the death penalty for errors in doctrine. In 1648 Cromwell purged the Parliament, wresting it from Presbyterian control. Many Presbyterians became pastors of state churches under Cromwell's regime. Like all dissenters from the episcopal establishment, they suffered considerably from the persecuting legislation under Charles II and rejoiced in the coming of toleration in 1689. Unitarianism, however, made large inroads into English Presbyterianism in the eighteenth century.

Presbyterians in Scotland were forced to disestablish their church under the restoration policy of Charles II in 1661. The episcopal type of church government used by the Church of England was reestablished. Scottish Presbyterians chafed under the whip of persecution. A small group gathered and signed a covenant to continue the fight against episcopacy. From a leader, Richard Cameron, they secured one of their names, the Cameronians. They are also known as the Covenanters and the Reformed Presbyterians. Although comparatively few in number, they survived the vicious persecution that followed. Under William and Mary's Act of Toleration (1689), Presbyterianism was restored to state support.

In the first half of the eighteenth century two struggles took place in Scotland. One was against the inroads of Socinianism and deism, both of which made great gains from Scottish Presbyterianism. The other was against lay patronage. In 1711 Queen Anne restored the principle of lay patronage for Scotland, which permitted influential parishioners to control the appointment of ministers. Opposing both theological laxity and lay patronage, Ebenezer Erskine (1680-1754) was expelled from the Church of Scotland in 1733 and organized the Secession Church. In 1752 Thomas Gillespie was expelled from the state church because of lay patronage and in 1761 formed the Relief Presbytery. These two groups united in the next period.

A very significant movement occurred in Ireland. Even before the stirring events by which William and Mary seized the throne, some Scottish Presbyterians had settled in northern Ireland. After the defeat of the Irish in 1691 in the struggle over the accession of William and Mary to the English throne, the English government appropriated a large tract of land in the province of Ulster and invited Scottish Presbyterians to settle there. Thousands came and began a vigorous Presbyterian movement in Ireland. In the first part of the eighteenth century many of these Scotch-Irish Presbyterians were driven to America because of the failure of the potato crop and the raising of rents by English landlords. Those Ulster Presbyterians were never an established church and for that reason were much more democratic in spirit than English Presbyterians. From them came some of the outstanding leaders of American Presbyterianism in the early years, principally Francis Makemie.

The Congregational movement in England was greatly helped by Cromwell, who encouraged the calling of a Congregational assembly for the adoption of a confession of faith. The assembly was not convened until after Cromwell's death in 1658. A declaration of faith was adopted, which followed the Westminster Confession of faith of 1648 by the Presbyterians. The Congregationalists suffered with other dissenters during the reigns of Charles II and James II and welcomed toleration under William and Mary.

Other Denominations in English Christianity

Baptists

English Baptists became vocal during the parliamentary struggles taking place in the 1640s. Their convictions regarding religious liberty had been expressed a generation before in England, and they took the opportunity to urge their point of view. While in England in 1644 Roger Williams published his *Bloody Tenet of Persecution,* detailing the melancholy story of persecution in New England and pleading for liberty of conscience. English Baptists were prominent in the army of Cromwell. At the same time they were probably the strongest deterrent to Cromwell's ambition to lead a new line of kings in England. Perhaps beguiled by the promise of Charles II that he would allow liberty of conscience, Baptists joined in laboring for the restoration of the Stuart line. With other dissenters they suffered severely between 1662 and 1688.

Strangely enough, after toleration was legislated in 1689, Baptists did not grow rapidly, as would be expected. They seem to have exhausted their strength during the harsh days of persecution. Particular Baptists framed a confession of faith in 1677 on the pattern of the Westminster Confession. A larger assembly adopted this confession in 1689, and it has become the principal English Baptist confession. The confession was the model for the Philadelphia Confession of Faith adopted in America in the next century. General Baptists were overwhelmed by the Socinian currents in the opening years of the eighteenth century, and many of their churches became Unitarian. Particular Baptists fell under the blight of hyper-Calvinism, hemmed in on every side by what they believed was God's elective limitation.

Quakers

The Quakers were a product of the mystical experience of George Fox (1624-91). He became opposed to organized Christianity when as a young man he could not find help from the churchmen for a personal problem. Mystical in nature, although trained in Presbyterian background, he had what he felt was an inner revelation of God in 1646. His emphasis on the inner light and his defiance of organized Christianity brought much persecution. The Quaker movement grew rapidly. The size of Fox's group is illustrated by the fact that in 1661, under the persecuting acts of the Restoration, there were more than 4,200 Quakers in prison. Quaker missionaries went everywhere. In 1681 William Penn founded his colony in America as a haven for the persecuted of his group and others. The central doctrine of the Quakers was the "inner light" from God. Formal worship, singing, the ordinances of baptism and the Supper, ministers and special theological training were rejected—perhaps a reflection of Fox's intense opposition to all that constituted organized Christianity in his day. Pacifism and philanthropy have characterized the Quakers from the beginning, although the movement has lost the radical and condemnatory spirit it first knew.

The Evangelical Revival

One of the most influential movements in the modern period was the evangelical revival of the first half of the eighteenth century. In England it was known as the Wesleyan Revival; in America, the Great Awakening. The Continent, with its Pietistic movement and with historical connections between Augustus G. Spangenberg and John Wesley, deserves some share for the background of the Awakening. The unwillingness of the Pietists to organize for the perpetuation of their ideals prevented them from spreading extensively like the Methodists.

The strong rationalism that brought skepticism to Germany and France, along with the widespread destruction of property and ideals by the Thirty Years War and its projection, many on the Continent away from things of God. In England this rationalism took the form of deism or naturalism. Its influence on continental Christianity, particularly in France, was probably more hurtful than a philosophical skepticism. Deism was an effort to minimize special revelation. There is no need for a supernatural revelation, the deists argued; religion is not mysterious and mystical, but the natural expression of human need for God and virtue. In this sense, all religions of the world have equal worth insofar as they are rational. These ideas were slowly developed from the early skepticism of Lord Herbert of Cherbury (1583-1648) to their more complete description in John Toland (1670-1722) and Matthew Tindal (1653-1733). Along with deism, various other types of philosophical skepticism grew out of English rationalism in the eighteenth century. William Law (1686-1761) and Joseph Butler (1692-1752) were the most noteworthy opponents of English deism.

Other elements in English life brought Christianity into general disrepute in the opening years of the eighteenth century. The low state of morals and indifference to religion by earlier sovereigns (especially the later Stuarts), who were supposed to exemplify some Christian ideals as supreme governors of the Church of England, gradually filtered down to the common people. Social unrest and economic stringency were everywhere. The rapid industrialization of England, accelerated by continental events, crammed new and old cities with submerged masses of bewildered and frustrated people. Wealth began to concentrate, abject poverty to spread. Reacting equally against Roman rituals and mystical enthusiasm, the Church of England became less than lukewarm. Most of the dissenting groups, racked with rationalism or hyperorthodoxy, had little to say to needy people. Morals and religion alike were at their lowest ebb.

Into this arid country flowed the refreshing streams of the Wesleyan revival. Wesleyan leaders were John and Charles Wesley, bred in the parsonage of a High Church rector, and George Whitefield, son of a saloonkeeper. Both Wesleys spent a brief but important period in missionary service for the Church of England in Georgia. They came into contact with the Moravian leader Spangenberg, from whom they learned the need for a personal experience of faith in Jesus Christ. Both returned to England, and in 1738 they professed conversion and regeneration. Whitefield, too, had experienced a rebirth, and the three formed the triumvirate of the new Methodist movement.

Of the three, doubtless Whitefield was the ablest preacher. Charles Wesley was the great hymn writer, while John Wesley was a methodical organizer who gave structure and endurance to the movement. Whitefield was a Calvinist, while the two Wesleys were Arminian. As a result, two types of Methodists were developed, although the great majority followed the Wesleyan type. These three Methodist leaders preached and sang throughout Britain, Wales, and Scotland, while Whitefield made extensive preaching tours in the American colonies.

In some instances these leaders built on the foundation others had laid. In Wales a layman, Howel Harris, had begun a Welsh revival two years before the Methodist leaders arrived to kindle fresh fire. In America Whitefield built on the efforts of Frelinghuysen, the Tennents, and Jonathan Edwards.

The Wesleys did not desire to break with the Church of England. Between 1738 and 1784 they organized Methodist "societies" like those of the Moravians. The rapid growth of these societies and the acquisition of property required additional organization and supervision. In 1744 the first annual conference of preachers was held in London, and two years later England was divided into circuits for preaching. Finally, in 1784, because of the need for preachers in America, Wesley made a radical departure from his former plan. For the first time Methodist preachers were ordained and given the authority to baptize and celebrate the Supper. In addition, Wesley gave form to the annual conference of preachers and transferred to it much of the authority that he had personally exercised over the movement through the years. In 1784, because of the separation of the American colonies from England, the Methodist Episcopal Church in America was organized.

Results of this evangelical movement both in England and in America were phenomenal. Within the Church of England a whole generation of evangelical-minded leaders (James Harvey, William Romaine, Isaac Milner, Charles Simeon, and William Wilberforce) breathed new life into the old Anglican forms. In addition, came missionary, Bible, and tract societies and other aids to the spread of the gospel. Many historians believe that the Wesleyan revival so thoroughly regenerated English life that it warded off a catastrophe similar to the French Revolution. A permanent evangelical party arose within the Anglican Church. Later on a new and significant phase of Methodism was the Salvation Army.

Among other English groups the revival had profound effects. Its emphasis on personal experience validated religion for many in the face of skepticism and rationalism. It renewed the zeal of English Baptists, resulting indirectly in the beginning of the modern mission movement. Other denominations were similarly blessed. In America the movement heightened the revival already begun, and the whole is known as the First Great Awakening. Practically every religious movement in American felt the surge of the revival fires. A new church—the

(Document 41)
John Wesley: On His Mother, Susannah Wesley

Susannah Wesley is famous as the mother of John and Charles Wesley, leaders of the Evangelical Revival (about 1738) and founders of Methodism. John Wesley recorded this tribute to her in his Journal.

I cannot but farther observe that even she (as well as her father and grandfather, her husband, and her three sons) had been, in her measure and degree, a preacher of righteousness. This I learned from a letter, wrote long since to my father, part of which I have here subjoined:

Feb. 6, 1711/12

As I am a woman, so am I also mistress of a large family. And though the superior charge of the souls contained in it lies upon you,...yet in your absence I cannot but look upon every soul you leave under my care as a talent committed to me under a trust by the great Lord of all the families, both of heaven and earth. And if I am unfaithful to him or you, in neglecting to improve these talents, how shall I answer unto him when he shall command me to render an account of my stewardship?

As these and other such like thoughts made me at first take a more than ordinary care of the souls of my children and servants, so knowing our religion requires a strict observance of the Lord's day, and not thinking that we fully answered the end of the institution by going to church, unless we filled up the intermediate spaces of time by other acts of piety and devotion, I thought it my duty to spend some part of the day in reading to and instructing my family....And such time I esteemed spent in a way more acceptable to God than if I had retired to my own private devotions.

This was the beginning of my present practice. Other people's coming in and joining with us was merely accidental. Our lad told his parents; they first desired to be admitted; then others that heard of it begged leave also. So our company increased to about thirty, and it seldom exceeded forty last winter....

Since this our company increased every night, for I dare deny none that ask admittance. Last Sunday I believe we had above two hundred. And yet many went away for want of room to stand....

I cannot conceive why any should reflect upon you, because your wife endeavours to draw people to church, and to restrain them from profaning the Lord's day by reading to them, and other persuasions. For my part, I value no censure upon this account. I have long since shook hands with the world. And I heartily wish I had never given them more reason to speak against me.

As to its looking particular, I grant it does. And so does almost anything that is serious, or that may any way advance the glory of God, or the salvation of souls.... As for your proposal of letting some other person read—Alas! you don't consider what a people these are. I don't think one man among them could read a sermon, without spelling a good part of it. Nor has any of our family a voice strong enough to be heard by such a number of people....

Methodist—was founded, and other groups that emphasized a crisis experience in conversion, such as the Baptists, benefited greatly.

England was ruled as a commonwealth from the death of Charles in 1649 until the restoration of the monarchy in 1660. Oliver Cromwell served as protector from 1653 to 1658. This was a period of comparative religious toleration. After the restoration of Charles II in 1660, however, persecution began against all but the established Church of England (the episcopacy). The "bloodless revolution" of 1688 brought the Protestants William and Mary to the throne, and in the next year an Act of Toleration was enacted. Strangely enough, the end of active persecution in 1689 seemed to bring lethargy to all Christian groups in England. The Wesleyan revival, which began about 1738, profoundly affected all England and other parts of the world.

26

American Christianity

During the period from 1648 to 1789, Roman Catholic Christianity continued to develop in Latin America along lines established during the previous period. Western North America was still a wilderness, and Canada was being colonized slowly. This chapter will focus on the eastern area of the present United States.

Population along the Atlantic seaboard grew rapidly during this period. From less than fifty thousand colonists in the opening years, population increased to almost four million when the first United States census was taken in 1790. Able now to provide for their own needs, the colonies began a brisk trade. New England exported grain, livestock, cloth, fish, rum, and lumber products. The Middle Atlantic states shipped rice, tobacco, and lumber products; the South provided rice, indigo, tobacco, lumber products, and cotton.

Independence of the United States

English settlements in America were simply colonies until they gained their independence. Each colony was more directly related to the crown than to corporate life with other colonies. That the colonies would unite as an independent nation was a thought that was comparatively late in finding popular support. France and England were strong rivals for control of the North American continent. For a long time it appeared that the French might be victorious. The English won the last battle, this time in Europe. England and France had ranged themselves on opposite sides in a series of conflicts in Europe during the eighteenth century. Particularly in the War of the Austrian Succession (1740-48), known as King George's War in America (1744-48), the English colonies in the New World played a significant role. After a valiant expedition from New England captured Louisburg, the strong French fortress on Cape Breton Island, the European treaty between England and France in 1748 returned the fortress to France. Americans resented this move after they had risked so much to capture it.

The Seven Years War on the Continent, known in the American phase as the French and Indian War (1756-63), prepared the way for American independence. France was forced to surrender claims in America. This eliminated a possible rival in America for a new nation and provided an important ally against England when war for independence came. In addition, the important part played by the colonials in this war brought them a feeling of self-confidence and unity. The unwise policies of King George III brought rebellion in America. The European nations defeated by Britain in the Seven Years War (France, Spain, and others) combined against Britain to help bring about victory for the Americans by 1783.

New Religious Movements

During this period several additional Christian groups emigrated to the new land. The Society of Friends or Quakers that began in England in 1647 soon had adherents in the American colonies. They were handled roughly. Massachusetts executed four Quakers in 1659, while Virginia and New York enacted rigorous laws against them. Quaker zeal and courage, despite erratic behavior at times, carried the day, however, and they continued as a part of the wonderfully rich and complex religious heritage of America. The haven of the American Quakers became Pennsylvania, founded in 1681 by William Penn, although already in New Jersey the Quakers had developed their characteristic organizational forms. Penn had been granted a large tract of land by Charles II of England, and he specifically appealed to those suffering from religious persecution, both in England and on the Continent, to flee to "Penn's woods" in the New World. Large numbers of dissenters responded, particularly the Quakers, with whom Penn had identified himself.

Mennonites from Germany also sought Penn's colony and settled at Germantown in 1683. This was the first organized congregation of the group, although a few Mennonite emigrants from Holland, Switzerland, and Germany had appeared in America almost fifty years before. A substantial number of Mennonites from various parts of Europe came to Pennsylvania during this period.

The Moravians found Pennsylvania a welcome haven. They had first entered Georgia in 1735, but in five years most of them had moved to Pennsylvania. Nikolaus Ludwig von Zinzendorf, the founder of the group, spent about a year in the colonies in 1741 when exiled from Saxony and visited Moravian settlements in Pennsylvania and in North Carolina.

American Methodism began about 1766 because of the work of Philip Embury, Barbara Heck, and Captain Thomas Webb in New York, and Robert Strawbridge in Maryland. Growth was slow at first. The first American conference of 1773 reported a few over a thousand members. By 1775 there were about three thousand; by 1783, there were about fourteen thousand. Because John Wesley wanted to keep Methodism within the framework of the Church of England, Methodist societies were at first under orders not to assume the functions of the Anglican Church. Consequently, in both England and America during the first half century Methodism had no ordained preachers. All baptizing, marrying, communion, and other acts requiring ordination were administered by Church of England priests. American Methodists followed the English pattern for forming local classes of about a dozen members who met to pray and worship under the supervision of a class leader. Several of these classes constituted a "society." After American independence these societies were organized as local Methodist churches. Each of the early American preachers regularly visited a circuit of societies for preaching. This simple type of organization was thorough and productive of great zeal and personal enlistment.

Since the Methodist movement was a part of the Church of England before the Revolutionary war, it was looked on by American patriots with considerable suspicion. The situation had not improved when Wesley urged his followers to be faithful to the crown. Practically all of his preachers returned to England during the Revolution, the notable exception being Francis Asbury. After the war Wesley was convinced that Methodist preachers must be ordained. He first approached the Church of England with a request that they ordain Methodist preachers for America. When they declined, Wesley, a presbyter in the Church of England, ordained Richard Whatcoat and Thomas Vasey as presbyters on September 2, 1784, while Thomas Coke was ordained as superintendent for America. Francis Asbury, already in America, was to be ordained as joint superintendent with Coke. On their arrival, Asbury insisted that he would take office only if elected by the Conference of American Methodist preachers. He was elected and ordained. In December 1784 at Baltimore the Methodist Episcopal Church was organized and continued to grow rapidly until the end of the period.

Other less numerous groups such as the German River Brethren and the Shakers settled in America during this period. At the close of the period the first Protestant Episcopal church in New England became the first Unitarian church in America.

The First Great Awakening
(About 1726-1740)

One of the formative factors in American Christianity was the great revival of the early eighteenth century that swept across the colonies. With European roots, this warmhearted evangelistic movement prepared the hearts of many of those emigrating to America. Several groups of Germans in Pennsylvania who had come under its influence were among the first to experience revival. By 1726 the preaching of Theodore J. Frelinghuysen, a deeply spiritual minister of the Dutch Reformed Church in New York, became peculiarly effective in winning persons to Christ and moving his hearers toward God. He inspired others during the next several years, one of the most important of whom was the Presbyterian minister Gilbert Tennent, who became a zealous (though not always wise) promoter of the revival.

By 1734, in what seems to have been a separate movement, Jonathan Edwards, Congregationalist pastor of Northampton, Massachusetts, found a deepened spiritual sensitiveness in his congregation and in the whole community. He wrote that the town seemed to have been full of the presence of God. A great revival followed. The entire revival movement was characterized by the conversion experience of those seeking God for themselves. The revival spread rapidly to every part of the colonies. Even John Wesley in England learned about it in 1738 and marveled.

Another great name associated with this awakening was that of George Whitefield, collaborator of Wesley in England, who had a conversion experience in 1735. In 1738 Whitefield arrived in Georgia to take up the work the Wesleys had left. He returned to England to raise

---

(Document 42)
Benjamin Franklin: George Whitefield Comes to Philadelphia

In his classic Autobiography, *Benjamin Franklin described the evangelistic ministry of George Whitefield in Philadelphia.*

He had a loud and clear voice, and articulated his words and sentences so perfectly, that he might be heard and understood at a great distance, especially as his auditories, however numerous, observ'd the most exact silence. He preach'd one evening from the top of the Court-House steps, which are in the middle of Market-street, and on the west side of Second-street, which crosses it at right angles. Both streets were fill'd with his hearers to a considerable distance. Being among the hindmost in Market-street, I had the curiosity to learn how far he could be heard, by retiring backwards down the street towards the river; and I found his voice distinct till I came near Front-street, when some noise in that street obscur'd it. Imagining then a semi-circle, of which my distance should be the radius, and that it were fill'd with auditors, to each of whom I allow'd two square feet, I computed that he might well be heard by more than thirty thousand. This reconcil'd me to the newspaper accounts of his having preach'd to twenty-five thousand people in the fields, and to the ancient histories of generals haranguing whole armies, or which I had sometimes doubted. By hearing him often, I came to distinguish easily between sermons newly compos'd, and those which he had often preach'd in the course of his travels. His delivery of the latter was so improv'd by frequent repetitions that every accent, every emphasis, every modulation of voice, was so perfectly well turn'd and well plac'd, that, without being interested in the subject, one could not help being pleased with the discourse; a pleasure of much the same kind with that receiv'd from an excellent piece of musick. This is an advantage itinerant preachers have over those who are stationary, as the latter can not well improve their delivery of a sermon by so many rehearsals.

money for his orphanage in Georgia and for ordination in the Church of England. Whitefield was delayed because of military operations and spent his time in evangelistic preaching throughout Britain. After the ship embargo was lifted, Whitefield sailed for Philadelphia in route to Georgia. His fame had spread and multitudes flocked to his ministry. In all of the American colonies he trumpeted the gospel message. Using the fires of religious revival already evident in the work of Frelinghuysen, Tennent, and Edwards, Whitefield led the revival movement to its highest point.

The results of the revival were many. They will be seen more particularly in the survey of the important American denominations in
this period. The results normally to be expected for a widespread spiritual awakening were present (conversions, strengthening of
churches, ethical gains in the personal lives of the people, and moral
and benevolent institutions founded or strengthened). Christian education was advanced. Two rather unexpected results also were important.

- Great strengthening of the smaller denominations and the
  interdenominational character of the spiritual visitation combined to lay the groundwork for religious liberty in the New
  World.
- A sense of spiritual unity was engendered among the American
  colonists at the time political relations with England were being
  strained to the utmost. The tours of Whitefield from Maine to
  Georgia tied the colonies together. Whitefield's converts were
  found in every colony; his preaching was a common bond
  uniting diverse groups.

In some parts of the South the Great Awakening continued almost
unabated until the close of this period. The Revolutionary War marked
the beginning of a rapid religious decline. In addition to the loss of
church property and the difficulties confronting the holding of religious
services, the war brought the customary callusing of spiritual sensibil-
ities and encouraged moral looseness. Along with these factors, the
intellectual and theological atmosphere was discolored by deistic
speculations from England, atheistic assertions from France, and the
rationalistic systems of the German thinkers. Many outstanding elders
and patriots during the Revolutionary War were infected by such currents. Skeptical and atheistic literature circulated extensively. Even the
church-fostered schools became hotbeds for infidelity. Less than 10
percent of the population were professing Christians just before the
close of this period in 1789. A new revival was greatly needed, and it
came shortly after the opening of the next period.

The Older Denominations (1648-1789)

The Church of England

The Church of England had accompanied the English settlements
in Virginia (1607) and the Carolinas (after 1665). The Church of

England was also established in Maryland in 1692, after that colony, founded by Roman Catholics, was assumed by the English crown following the accession of William and Mary in England. New York was captured by the English from the Dutch in 1664, and in 1693 the Church of England was at least partially established there. The Society for Propagating the Gospel in Foreign Parts (established by the Church of England in 1701) was instrumental in planting missions and churches in New England after 1702.

Progress of the established church in the colonies was slow; it faced many foes. The quality of ministers sent from England was generally low, with notable exceptions. Lack of an American bishop made discipline next to impossible. The increasing number of dissenters and the aversion to ecclesiastical authoritarianism had driven many to America militated against the popularity of the leaders. In Virginia in 1619—when the Church of England was established—there were only five clergymen, two of whom were deacons. A century later the number had increased only to about two dozen, although there were forty-four parishes in the colony. Constant political and religious turmoil in England during the seventeenth century was bound to bring confusion to the American colonies and neglect of the churches established there.

Although George Whitefield was a member of the Church of England when he came preaching with power in 1739, he was not welcomed by the colonial establishments of the Church of England. For one thing, he was preaching a strongly evangelical gospel, emphasizing personal conversion and denouncing many in the ministry as "unconverted." Furthermore, he had been denied the use of churches in England and had begun to preach in fields. In addition, the enthusiasm and emotionalism of the Great Awakening were not to the liking of the orderly and staid episcopal adherents. In fact, Whitefield was called for trial before an episcopal ecclesiastical court in Charleston, South Carolina, and was convicted and suspended from the ministry by Commissary Alexander Garden for irregularities. Whitefield paid scant attention to the proceedings.

The Revolutionary War brought crisis to the Church of England in the colonies. As a part of the English system, the church was distrusted by many and hated by some. Two thirds of the clergy were loyal to England during the war. In Virginia in particular there was much loss. Only fifteen of ninety-one clergy could remain at their posts in that state, and much of their property was destroyed. Losses were not so great in Maryland, where out of forty-four parishes, each with a minister before the Revolution, almost two dozen of the clergy remained and the property loss was comparatively small. There was great opposition to the Anglican Church in New England, New York, New Jersey, and Pennsylvania, where organized efforts had been made before the Revolution to prevent the appointment of a bishop in America. At the very close of this period, steps were taken to organize the Protestant Episcopal Church, a new body holding to doctrines of the Church of England but disentangling itself from English control.

Congregationalism

By 1648 the Congregational churches in Massachusetts and Connecticut had developed a theocratic government. Right of franchise was limited to members of Congregational churches, and no new Congregational churches could be formed without permission from the old. Harvard College was flourishing at Cambridge, Massachusetts, and the clergy was supported from tax funds. Dissenters like Baptists and Quakers were rigorously persecuted.

The work of the Westminster Assembly in England inspired New England Congregationalists to prepare a doctrinal statement, which was adopted at Cambridge, Massachusetts, in 1648. One of the important provisions was the requirement that any person admitted to the Lord's Supper must have made a public profession of faith (even though he or she had been baptized as a baby) and have given evidence of a Christian experience. Unless the parents of a child fulfilled these conditions, their child could not be baptized. Controversy began immediately. Only those who could relate a conversion experience and pursue an orderly walk could partake of the Supper. Without this evidence they could not have their children baptized. Such persons were disfranchised and disqualified for civil office, and they soon knew the odium of religious ostracism. Yet they still had to give money to support the Congregational ministry and churches. Finally, in 1662 the Half-Way Covenant was enacted, providing that children of moral and baptized persons might also be baptized, even though the parents could not qualify for admission to the Supper. This action increased controversy and practically eliminated any requirements for church membership.

In an effort to regularize and stabilize the practices of the various Congregational churches, a strengthening of external authority in the associations was attempted in Massachusetts, but the movement failed. A similar program in Connecticut, the Saybrook Platform in 1708, was successfully introduced.

It can be recognized that a movement like the Great Awakening would agitate again the divisive question about a conversion experience. Jonathan Edwards was one of the outstanding figures of the revival. His deep piety, mingled with profound philosophical thought, made him one of the foremost American religious thinkers. His church at Northampton, Massachusetts, was the center of revival in 1734. Not all Congregationalists followed Edwards, however. In churches that did not favor the revival, some withdrew and formed "New Light" churches or "Separate" churches. Some later adopted immersion and became Baptist churches.

The Congregationalists were strong patriots during the Revolutionary War period. They emerged from the war with considerable prestige because of their noble service for the new nation. Skepticism and infidelity played havoc with many of their churches. In addition, the lack of organization beyond the local level hindered larger denominational development and that was soon to rob New England Congregationalism of much of its church property. Despite these factors, as well as controversy and schism, the number of Congregationalist churches in New England—to which this denomination was generally confined—increased greatly during this period.

Calvinism

Those following the teachings of Calvin came to America in various national groups during this period. The Dutch Reformed Church had begun about 1628 in what became New York, and even after the colony fell to the English in 1664, the small Reformed group of Holland carried on their worship.

Scottish and Scotch-Irish Presbyterians had emigrated early to the New World. At the opening of this period, small Presbyterian churches were found in many of the colonies along the coast. The important name in this early period of Presbyterian life was that of Francis Makemie, who came from Ireland in 1683. By his work American Presbyterianism organized the first presbytery in 1705 at Philadelphia with seven ministers. Eleven years later the first synod was formed, consisting of seventeen churches, three presbyteries, and nineteen ministers. Some French Reformed refugees (Huguenots) fled to America and settled principally in the South during the critical days after the Edict of Nantes was revoked in 1685.

The first German Reformed church was formed in 1719 at Germantown, Pennsylvania. Through the efforts of Michael Schlatter and the Dutch Reformed group, a synod was formed for the German Reformed Church in 1747, consisting of forty-seven congregations and only five ministers.

The Great Awakening brought dissension and schism among Presbyterians. Gilbert Tennent, a young minister at New Brunswick, New Jersey, influenced by the pietistic spirit of Theodore Frelinghuysen, his neighboring preacher, delivered fiery evangelistic sermons. After 1728 revival occurred among the Presbyterians and many were converted. In 1741 Tennent and his followers were ejected from the synod for unauthorized and censorious activities, causing an extensive schism that continued until 1758. Meanwhile, in 1745 the New York Synod established a college, which was to become Princeton University.

After internal peace was restored, Presbyterian growth, principally from immigration, was rapid until the Revolution. Almost without exception the Presbyterians supported American independence. They aided greatly in the successful struggle in Virginia for separation of church and state and religious liberty.

Lutheranism

Lutheranism was first planted in what became New York. While this colony was under Dutch rule (1623-64), persecution of Lutheranism was carried on, but after 1664 the English permitted relative liberty. The Swedish Lutherans who settled in Delaware faced difficulties as their colony was seized by the Dutch in 1655 and ceded to England in 1664, but a measure of religious liberty was permitted under the rule of each. Lutheran growth was accelerated with the coming of the Germans in the opening years of the eighteenth century. William Penn had visited the war-torn and suffering Germanic areas in 1681 and invited them to emigrate to his colony in America. The response came principally after 1708, and large numbers of German Lutherans settled in New York, Pennsylvania, and the Carolinas. In 1734 many Lutherans from the province of Salzburg in Austria, driven out by rigorous Roman Catholic persecution, settled near Savannah, Georgia. The first Lutheran synod was formed in 1735 in New Jersey, representing sixteen congregations.

The patriarch of Lutheranism in America was Henry Melchior Mühlenberg, who was sent from Germany in 1742 to aid the struggling American Lutheran churches. His wise and capable leadership united and organized the early American Lutheran movement.

The Great Awakening did not greatly affect American Lutherans. Germans were somewhat responsive; their rallying around Mühlenberg and their active zeal probably stemmed in part from the revival. Swedish Lutherans, on the other hand, did not enter into the movement. Almost all Lutherans in the colonies supported the American Revolution, furnishing outstanding leadership and support. The two sons of H. M. Mühlenberg, Peter G. and Frederick A. C., became eminent military and political leaders. Like all other denominations, the Lutherans suffered from the loss of leadership and interest during the Revolutionary War, but they rapidly recovered after the war.

The Roman Catholic Church

By 1648 the Roman Catholic Church had moved into North America through the work of English, French, and Spanish immigrants. French missionaries and explorers continued the work of Jacques Cartier (1534) and Samuel de Champlain (1613). LaSalle (1676), Marquette and Joliet (1673), and many lesser-known figures established missions and forts in what is today the northern and central United States. The vast mission program of French Catholics, begun and continued under severe difficulties, was abandoned when defeat in the Seven Years War (1756-63) brought cession of French claims in America. Spanish missionaries and monks were very active also in this period.

The Spanish missionary work in Florida in its early history was accompanied by coercion and the sword. By 1634 there were forty-four missions with thirty-five priests under the Bishop of Havana. In 1701, during the War of Spanish Succession, the English in the Carolinas and Georgia attacked Spanish Florida and burned St. Augustine in 1702. At the close of the war Florida was given to England, ending Spanish missions there.

Spain dominated the southwestern part of what is today the United States until the 1840s. This region was considered a thinly populated frontier of the Spanish Viceregency of New Spain, with its capital in Mexico City. Spanish priests striking northward from Mexico about 1598 planted missions in what is today New Mexico. By the opening of this period about sixty Franciscan monks were serving in this area. Mission work continued throughout the colonial period. There were rivalries between the religious orders (especially Franciscans and

Jesuits). The missionaries struggled with the military and Spanish settlers over treatment of the Native Americans.

Three centuries of missionary endeavor yielded limited results.
Many Native Americans clung to their indigenous religious practices
despite a claim of being Christian. In 1680 the Pueblo groups revolted
and drove the Spanish from New Mexico for twelve years. Between
1692 and 1700 the area was reconquered, and missionaries were
restored by force of arms, although the two principal tribes (the
Moqui and the Zuni) refused to allow missionaries among them.

A Spanish Jesuit monk toured Arizona about 1687, and in 1732
others arrived to begin missions in what is now Arizona. Jealousy
between Jesuits and Franciscans brought rivalry and strife, hindering
effective results.

A Spanish missionary expedition was sent into Texas in 1689, and
in 1716 work was begun. The indigenous peoples were nomadic,
divided into diverse groups, each with its own language. They resisted
settlement in mission villages and generally were hostile to the missionaries.

Lower California had been explored and mission stations established in the late sixteenth century. Upper California had no mission
work until 1769 when, doubtless to forestall the Russian advances
down the coast, a Mexican military and missionary expedition
entered that area. Junípero Serra led the hard and perilous work of
establishing Roman Catholic missions there. At the close of the period
there were perhaps a dozen missions operating, although friction
between the missionaries and the Spanish military leaders in Mexico
hindered the effectiveness of the work.

The Catholic colony in Maryland suffered from the political revolution in England in 1688. The overthrow of James II was the signal for
the Protestants in Maryland to seize the government, and the Church
of England was established under a new charter with Maryland as a
royal colony (not proprietary) until 1692.

As might be expected, the Roman Catholic Church felt none of the
impulses toward revival during the Great Awakening beginning about
1739. American Catholics played an honorable part in the Revolutionary War, although they were still comparatively few in number. At the
close of this period it is estimated that there were approximately
twenty thousand Catholics in the former English colonies of America.

Spain and Portugal had for a century been sending military forces
and missionaries to almost every part of South America. Missions

were established in the West Indies and Mexico, as well as Brazil, Peru, Chile, and Argentina. In this period the Roman Catholic missionaries touched almost all of Central and South America.

Baptists

The handful of Baptists that organized Providence Plantations as a colony in 1638 increased slowly in this period. Congregations were formed throughout New England, the middle states, and the South before 1700. In 1707 Baptists around Philadelphia formed the first Baptist association in America, the Philadelphia Association. A second association was organized in South Carolina in 1751. Thereafter the growth of associations of Baptist churches was rapid.

Before the Great Awakening, Baptist progress was slow. There were fewer than fifty Baptist churches in all America after one hundred years (by 1739). With the Great Awakening, Baptists began to grow in number. At first New England Baptists were reluctant to have any part in the revival, partly because those engaged in it were their persecutors and partly because of the Arminian reaction against a movement among the Calvinists. The conversion to Baptist views of Isaac Backus, a Congregationalist New Light, began a movement that brought many New Lights into Baptist life. Between the revival and the Revolution, Baptist churches in New England increased from twenty-one to seventy-eight.

The middle and southern colonies also felt the impact of the Great Awakening. Shubael Stearns and Daniel Marshall, converted under the preaching of George Whitefield, became Baptists. Assisted by Colonel Samuel Harris, Elijah and Lewis Craig, and others, they established new Baptist churches throughout Virginia, the Carolinas, and Georgia. Whereas there were only seven Baptist churches in the South before the Great Awakening, by the close of the Revolution, Virginia alone had 151 churches. Kentucky had forty Baptist churches; North Carolina had forty-two; South Carolina had twenty-seven; and Georgia, where Baptist work had begun in 1772, had six churches.

In addition, Baptists played an important part in the struggle for religious liberty in Virginia and established Brown University in Rhode Island in 1765 for the education of the ministry.

Baptists took a prominent part in the Revolution, several rising to important places in the chaplaincy and in the army. Hezekiah Smith, John Gano, and others were outstanding in New England and the middle colonies. In the South Richard Furman had a price put on his head by the British as one of the outstanding patriots. At the close of the period Baptists were active and growing.

During most of this period France and England vied for control of the vast North American continent. England emerged victorious in 1763, but the American colonies won their independence twenty years later. A steady flow of immigrants came from England and the Continent. Their religious background had an important bearing on Christianity in the new nation. The First Great Awakening, beginning after 1726, profoundly influenced both religious and political life in the American colonies. The Revolution brought a rapid religious decline, accelerated by skeptical and rationalistic currents from England and the Continent. At the close of the period, Christianity in the United States was at a low ebb, and its prospects were dark.

Bibliography

Boornstin, Daniel. *The Discoverers: A History of Man's Search to Know His World and Himself.* New York: Random House, 1983.

Cairns, E. Earle. *An Endless Line of Splendor: Revivals and Their Leaders from the Great Awakening to the Present.* Wheaton, Ill.: Tyndale House, 1986.

Cragg, Gerald R. *The Church and the Age of Reason, 1648-1789.* Grand Rapids: Eerdmans, 1962.

Manschreck, Clude L. ed. *A History of Christianity.* Englewood Cliffs, N. J.: Prentice-Hall, 1964.

Marty, Martin E. *Pilgrims in Their Own Land: 500 Years of Religion in America.* New York: Penguin, 1984.

Noll, Mark A. *A History of Christianity in the United States and Canada.* Grand Rapids: Eerdmans, 1992.

VI. Period of General Secularization (A.D. 1789 to present)

Introduction to the Period

This was a period of revolution. The American nation was organized under a constitution in the opening year of this period, after throwing off the political yoke of England. France entered the revolution at the beginning of this period. The Congress of Vienna (1815) endeavored to restore traditional boundaries, but revolution had not ceased. New nations developed in Europe and in the Americas.

There were revolutions in other areas also. Mechanical and industrial developments created a new sort of economic and social life. Scientific advance in the twentieth century has made almost every decade a startling and challenging era.

The modern mission movement helped to inaugurate this period. Its impact in the widespread enrichment of life and general humanitarianism can never be fully computed. Many extensive humanitarian movements in England and America sprang directly from missions and the revivals of religion of this period.

This was also a period of extensive secularization of culture. One writer expressed it as the development of the "religiously neutral civilization." This situation is not altogether good or completely bad, but is essentially true. To some extent this accounts for the extensive spread of denominational Christianity. Divorcing of church and state (one aspect of this secularization) has resulted in religion by conviction rather than by coercion. The second reformation in England during the first half of the seventeenth century developed numerous types of polity and doctrine. These were transplanted to America by immigration. The older movements on the Continent also moved toward America, but the tendency has been toward diversity in organization, even in those groups following a single system of theological thought. Calvinism, for example, was organized in America piecemeal by different groups. Scottish Calvinists not only did not join Calvinists from other nations but reproduced in America many other schisms that had taken place in Scotland. English, French, Dutch, Swiss, German, and Scandinavian Calvinists retained their own separate types of organization, reflecting ethnic and language distinctions when they moved to America. As a result, the Christianity in colonial America was amazingly complex and has continued to develop new forms in the centuries that have followed. Doubtless a reaction against undue proliferation gave impetus toward the ecumenical and church union movements that came into considerable strength in the first half of the twentieth century.

In religious thought, this period has witnessed the high mark of rationalism, followed by a reaction in an attempt to retain elements of the older supernaturalism. There have been vigorous and numerous attacks on traditional supernaturalism during the first half of the twentieth century.

Points of Special Interest

Students should notice the recurring cycles in religious thought. Generally the pendulum swings to one extreme, depending a great deal on historical conditioning, and then away from it. Extreme views are basically self-destructive. This fact brings some comfort in periods of uninhibited speculation and corruption.

A related observation concerns human nature. As a self-conscious and spiritual being, people will never be satisfied with any religious system that appeals only to intellect. Sterile scholasticism has no more vitality in the twentieth century than it had in the second. Often it will bring spiritual reaction and revival.

The secularization of culture and politics is not an unmixed evil. A "neutral" state and culture will remove elements of harmful influence on Christianity, eliminate Christianity as a tool of low motivations, and minimize religious coercion; it should emphasize the spiritual nature and independent worth of true Christianity.

27

Continental
European Christianity

Technological progress has brought sweeping change to modern life. Iron, steel, aluminum, and plastics successively have brought great thrusts in the manufacture of basic commodities. Coal, steam, electricity, petroleum, and atomic fission have provided power for transportation, communication, illumination, warfare, and many other uses. The industrial revolution has mobilized and exploited these resources. Astounding research has been made in sciences from anthropology to zoology. The body, mind, and soul have been subjected to intense study. Every aspect of the world and humankind have come under observation.

Charles Darwin (1809-82), after first making basic assumptions in an effort to explain change and progress in human history, developed a theory of evolution based on the survival of the fittest. The projection of this theory into the areas of religion and philosophy brought controversy that has not yet ended. Karl Marx (1818-83) propounded belief in the necessity of the ultimate victory of a "scientific social-ism"—the elimination of all economic classes and the final millennium of an equalitarian society. Marx's communistic ideas have been tested on a large scale. Hegel (1770-1831) idealized the state and Nietzsche (1844-1900) the "super race," laying the foundations for the twentieth-century totalitarian movements. Meanwhile Siegmund Freud (1856-1939) pointed out the nebulous distance between conscious and unconscious thought and went on to develop what he believed were scientific theories of consciousness and human thought. The theories of Darwin, Marx, and Freud profoundly influenced religious thought.

The political atmosphere of the world is reflected in the history of Christianity in Europe during this period. National states fought for autonomy and demanded self-expression. Latin American colonies became independent republics. Italy was unified, and France became a republic in the same year. China, Japan, and the Orient were opened to Western culture. Across southeastern Europe new independent states sprang up. Popular government has almost universally dethroned hereditary sovereigns. Almost all the world has been explored, and improved communication and transportation have made it much smaller.

The principal Christian groups on the Continent in this period were the Roman Catholics, the Lutherans, and the Calvinists. These will be viewed briefly during the three chronological sections into which this period falls.

The French Revolution (1789-1815)

The history of Europe is bound up with the French Revolution during the first portion of this period. During the eighteenth century the common people across Europe increasingly recognized that absolutism and oppression in state and church were largely responsible for their depressed economic and social condition. Corruption and luxury in high places in church and state contrasted greatly with the want and suffering of lower classes.

This was particularly true in France. The Roman Church owned half the land of France and was as reprehensible as the secular state in its dealings with the people. There was widespread resentment against the various tithes imposed by the church, against the rigorous repression of religious dissenters, and against the nonproductive orders of monks. The arbitrary national policies, costly wars, and lavish personal habits of Kings Louis XIV, XV, and XVI (from 1643 to 1793) brought France to the verge of bankruptcy. In order to levy additional taxes, the king was forced to call a meeting of the Estates General, a congress made up of the clergy, the nobility, and the commons. The Representatives of the common people (drawn from the middle class) were known as the Third Estate. This Third Estate seized control and by their audacity and accurate representation of the temper of the times were successful in beginning a radical reform. On

September 21, 1792, France was made a Republic, and four months later the king was executed.

In a reaction against the intense opposition of the Roman Church, the new republic at first was erected on atheistic lines but gradually relaxed to permit religious worship. Napoleon Bonaparte, a French general, was victorious in defeating a coalition of other powers attempting to put down the French Revolution. In 1798 Napoleon invaded Italy and dissolved the papal state, imprisoning Pope Pius VI in Paris, where he soon died. Napoleon was crowned emperor in 1804. His victories and diplomacy changed the map of Europe. Finally he was defeated by a coalition of powers and exiled to St. Helena Island in 1815. The Congress of Vienna (1815) endeavored to restore the world that Napoleon had disarranged. A reactionary period followed characterized by conservatism in politics and romanticism in literature and religion.

The Roman Catholic Church

The French Revolution disestablished the Roman Church, outlawing monasticism and stripping the church of property, tithes, and papal assessments. The reorganization of religious life in France in 1790 by the National Assembly in effect ignored religious differences. During the Reign of Terror (1793-94) hundreds, perhaps thousands, of faithful Roman Catholic priests were slaughtered. In the reaction after 1795, however, Catholics and others were allowed privileges of worship. In 1795 Pope Pius VI joined with European leaders to put an army in the field against France. Napoleon Bonaparte defeated the coalition, captured Rome in 1798, and imprisoned the pope in France, where he died in 1799.

In 1801 the new pope, Pius VII (1800-20), secured an agreement with Napoleon to restore the Roman Church in France under radical limitations, but Napoleon abrogated most of this by his arbitrary interpretation. In 1809 he annexed the papal state to France. When the pope protested, imprisonment followed. In 1813 Napoleon coerced the pope into signing an agreement allowing annexation, but with his Russian debacle Napoleon lost his power to coerce. The pope repudiated his signature and in 1814 restored the Jesuit order. Although the suppression of this order in 1773 had theoretically meant total abolishment, it was found to be completely organized and at almost full strength to take up the battle. Cardinal Consalvi represented the

(Document 43)

Estates General: Declaration of Rights

In 1790 the French Estates General published a declaration of human rights. This document had extensive implications for religious liberty.

Article 1

Men are born and remain free and equal in rights. Social distinctions may be founded only upon the general good.

Article 2

The aim of all political association is the preservation of the natural and imprescriptible rights of man. These rights are liberty, property, security, and resistance to oppression.

Article 3

The principle of all sovereignty resides essentially in the nation. No body nor individual may exercise any authority which does not proceed directly from the nation.

Article 4

Liberty consists in the freedom to do everything which injures no one else; hence the exercise of the natural rights of each man has no limits except those which assure to the other members of society the enjoyment of the same rights. These limits can only be determined by law.

Article 5

Law can only prohibit such actions as are hurtful to society. Nothing may be prevented which is not forbidden by law, and no one may be forced to do anything not provided for by law.

Article 6

Law is the expression of the general will. Every citizen has a right to participate personally, or through his representative, in its formation. It must be the same for all, whether it protects or punishes. All citizens, being equal in the eyes of the law, are equally eligible to all dignities and to all public positions and occupations, according to their abilities, and without distinction except that of their virtues and talent.

Article 7

No person shall be accused, arrested, or imprisoned except in the cases and according to the forms prescribed by law. Any one soliciting, transmitting, executing, or causing to be executed, any arbitrary order, shall be punished. But any citizen summoned or arrested in virtue of the law shall submit without delay, as resistance constitutes an offense.

Article 8

The law shall provide for such punishments only as are strictly and obviously necessary, and no one shall suffer punishment except it be legally inflicted in virtue of a law passed and promulgated before the commission of the offense.

Article 9

As all persons are held innocent until they shall have been declared guilty, if arrest shall be deemed indispensable, all harshness not essential to the securing of the prisoner's person shall be severely repressed by law.

Article 10

No one shall be disquieted on account of his opinions, including his religious views, provided their manifestation does not disturb the public order established by law.

Article 11

The free communication of ideas and opinions is one of the most precious of the rights of man. Every citizen may, accordingly, speak, write, and print with freedom, but shall be responsible for such abuses of this freedom as shall be defined by law.

papacy at the Congress of Vienna in 1815 and was able to secure the return of all that Napoleon had taken from the Roman Church.

Lutheranism

The French Revolution greatly affected Lutherans in the German states. War and suffering revealed that skepticism and infidelity were not sufficient to meet the needs of the human spirit. Multitudes returned to religious faith. After Napoleon dissolved the Holy Roman Empire in 1806, independent states like Austria, Prussia, and Bavaria became stronger. Later in the nineteenth century this contributed to the unification of the German people under Prussian leadership.

Calvinism

Calvinism in Europe also felt the shock of the French Revolution. Already skepticism had weakened this group in France, Switzerland, the German states, and the Low Counties. The unsettled political conditions that continued through the Congress of Vienna in 1815 brought disorganization and uncertainty to continental Calvinism.

Reaction and Continued Conflict (1815-70)

For a decade after the Congress of Vienna the reaction against revolution and democratic movements was apparent in the diplomacy and activity of the great powers. National feelings could not long be suppressed. In search for a responsive and stable government, France set off explosive nationalistic movements in 1830 and again in 1848. Holland (1815), Belgium (1830), and Greece (1832) established autonomous governments, and nationalistic sentiment grew in other regions.

The German states provided the key to the momentous events in the latter part of this period. The Congress of Vienna had aided in the formation of a German union (*Bund*) composed of thirty-five states, and later a North German union headed by Prussia was organized. In 1870 Prussia declared war on France, and victory brought the organization of the modern German nation. Curiously enough, during the Franco-Prussian War, the French government took the step that led to the founding of a papal court to protect the papal state. When Paris was being threatened in 1870, France ordered these troops home, and the Italian nationalists were able to overcome Rome and unify the several sections of the peninsula.

The Roman Catholic Church

The reaction against the excesses of the French Revolution brought great prestige to the Roman Catholic Church as a conservative and stabilizing factor. Leo XII (1821-29) negotiated favorable concordats, or agreements, with most of the important nations, including Protestant states. Catholics were given complete freedom in England in the year of Leo's death and during the entire period accessions to the Roman Church from the Church of England took place.

The papacy continued to make anti-Protestant outbursts. In 1816 Pius VII denounced Bible societies as fiendish instruments to undermine religion. In May 1824, Leo XII published similar views and called their translations the "devil's gospel." In 1826 he announced that "everyone separated from the Roman Catholic Church, however unblamable in other respects his life may be, because of this sole offense, that he is sundered from the unity of Christ, has no part in eternal life; God's wrath hangs over him." Pius VIII (1829-30) also denounced liberty of conscience and Bible societies among other evils. Gregory XVI (1831-46) termed religious liberty as craziness or insanity. These utterances formed the background for the sweeping "Syllabus of Errors" of Pius IX, which will be discussed soon.

Ultramontanism reached its height during the pontificate of Pius IX (1846-78). Singularly enough, his doctrinal victories within the Roman Church and his political defeats from the outside paired up to exalt him and the papacy to heights before unattainable. His strategy in his doctrinal victory was carefully planned and well executed. Pius became pope in 1846 during a stormy political period. In 1849, taking advantage of the widespread Catholic veneration (and in some cases actual worship) of Mary, the mother of Jesus, Pius sent communications to all Roman Catholic bishops asking if they wanted him to send out an authoritative pronouncement with reference to Mary. He showed his own opinions by saying, "Ye know full well, venerable brethren, that the whole ground of our confidence is placed in the most holy Virgin . . . God has vested in her the plenitude of all good, so that henceforth, if there be in us any hope, if there be any grace, if there be any salvation, we must receive it solely from her, according to the will of him who would have us possess all things through Mary."

After receiving the approval of the vast majority of the bishops, Pius proclaimed the official dogma on December 8, 1854. A canon is a church law that may be changed subsequently if circumstances warrant, but a dogma is an official declaration of truth that cannot be changed or altered and that must be believed by all the faithful as a condition of salvation. This was the first time a dogma had been promulgated by a pope without the authority of a general council. Pius claimed that this dogma was revealed by God and must be believed firmly and constantly by all the faithful. His proclamation asserted "that the most blessed Virgin Mary, in the first instance of her conception, by a singular grace and privilege of Almighty God, by the intuitive perception of the human race, was kept immune from any contamination of original sin." Mariolatry was officially brought one step further. The Roman tradition had successively declared Mary a perpetual virgin, freed her from sin after Christ's conception, extended that freedom from sin to her own birth, and this dogma declared her without hereditary sin. It remained for the twentieth century to proclaim her bodily assumption to heaven at death.

In 1864 Pius IX issued his "Syllabus of Errors," summing up encyclicals of immediately previous popes and bringing the list up-to-date. In addition to condemning Bible societies, public schools, and freedom of conscience, he specifically denounced separation of church and state, insisted that the Roman pontiffs and ecumenical councils never erred in defining faith and morals, and claimed the right to use force in carrying out papal policies. Leo XIII (1878-1903) declared that the "Syllabus of Errors" had been issued under the conditions of infallibility.

The First Vatican Council (1869-70) was the first ecumenical council in over three centuries, and many believed it would be the last. Practically every detail was arranged by Pius IX before the council convened. Despite vigorous protests by a sizable minority of bishops who refused to be coerced, the council passed four decrees. The first asserted that Simon Peter was made by Christ to be the visible head of the church, both in honor and jurisdiction. The second identified the Roman bishop as perpetual successor of Peter, endowed with all Peter's privileges. The third claimed that the Roman pontiff has immediate and full power over all the church throughout the world. The last decree asserted that when the pope speaks ex-cathedra (from the throne) in defining a doctrine concerning faith and morals to be held by the universal church, he is infallible. The statement closed with the assertion that any such definition of the pope (without a council) is irreformable.

(Document 44)

First Vatican Council: Papal Infallibility

Pope Pius IX and the First Vatican Council established the doctrine of papal infallibility in 1870. The exact meaning of ex cathedra is still a topic of debate in Roman Catholic circles.

We, adhering faithfully to the tradition received from the beginning of the Christian faith—with a view to the glory of our Divine Saviour, the exaltation of the Catholic religion, and the safety of the Christian peoples (the sacred Council approving), teach and define as a dogma divinely revealed: That the Roman Pontiff, when he speaks ex cathedra (that is, when—fulfilling the office of Pas- tor and Teacher of all Christians— on his supreme Apostolic authority, he defines a doctrine concerning faith or morals to be held by the Universal Church), through the divine assistance promised him in blessed Peter, is endowed with that infallibility, with which the Divine Redeemer has willed that His Church—in defining doctrine concerning faith or morals— should be equipped: And therefore, that such definitions of the Roman Pontiff of themselves— and not by virtue of the consent of the Church—are irreformable. If any one shall presume (which God forbid!) to contradict this our definition; let him be anathema.

The strategy that had occupied the thinking of Pius IX for many years had been accomplished. By careful diplomacy he had declared a popular teaching to have dogmatic force, without the occurrence of an ecumenical council. This prepared the way for continuing papal domination. The statement of infallibility is quite ambiguous, which exactly suited the purpose of the proponents of the action.

These doctrinal developments occurred during a political revolution. The papal state had separated the northern and southern sections of the Italian peninsula for over a thousand years. Italian nationalists like Victor Emmanuel and Garibaldi fervently desired to unify the entire peninsula and make Rome the secular capital of the unified nation. The papacy vigorously resisted. Popular revolution in the peninsula had already broken out when Pius IX came to the papal throne. In an effort to placate the Italian people, Pius granted some reforms in the papal government, but nothing less than full surrender would satisfy the nationalists in the South. Between 1859 and 1866, through diplomacy and war, Victor Emmanuel was able to secure four-fifths of the papal lands, leaving only Rome and its environs in papal hands. When France withdrew from Rome to defend Paris, Emmanuel overcame the remaining resistance and captured Rome, making it the national capital of a united Italy.

Italian nationalists tried to placate Pius, but he was never reconciled to the loss of temporal administration and refused to leave the Vatican, which he was permitted to retain. Pius IX plotted for the return of the papal state until his death in 1878. Succeeding popes considered themselves prisoners in the Vatican until 1929.

In spite of the personal humiliation in this temporal loss, the papacy was greatly forwarded by it. Many had urged the papacy for five hundred years to get out of temporal competition with other nations in the interest of spiritual influence and well-being. Gifts began to pour into the coffers of the pontiff. All the machinery of the Curia was turned toward ecclesiastical advancement rather than secular administration, and relations with the various national states eventually improved in view of the diminishing secular power of an ambitious and coercive papacy.

Some Roman Catholics, including some able scholars, rejected the papal declaration of infallibility. One group broke with the Roman Church and formed a schismatic group known as the Old Catholic Church. This movement reached a membership of perhaps a hundred thousand, but it has gradually declined and never gained the popular following that many supposed it would.

Lutheranism

The history of European Lutheranism during the heart of the nineteenth century concerns principally the movement toward church union and philosophical development.

King Frederick William III of Prussia's desire for unity after the desolation caused by the French Revolution led him to listen sympathetically to suggestions by Friedrich Schleiermacher and other leading clergy that some sort of church union be attempted. Union of Lutherans and Calvinists in Prussia was decreed in 1817 and met with approval of most Prussians. By 1827 many of the German states had followed this example. The University of Wittenberg and Halle united in one institution at Halle. A vocal minority protested against the general drift, particularly among the Lutherans. Klaus Harms led what was known as the Confessional School in opposition to union with the Reformed Church. In 1841 a number of Lutherans seceded from the state church and organized the Evangelical Lutheran Church of Prussia. Lutheranism in other parts of Europe, particularly in the Scandinavian countries, continued to be infected with rationalism.

Rationalism had brought skepticism and atheism to the forefront during the past period in European Christianity (from 1648 to 1789). Immanuel Kant (1724-1804), although a product of the Enlightment, modified the crass intellectualism of Wolff by limiting the area of philosophical data to phenomena and by conceiving of the human person as more than a mind. Hegel (1770-1831) turned to other directions but, essentially, by his philosophical optimism and theory of development, gave great impetus to a mediating position. F. E. D. Schleiermacher (1768-1834), early profoundly affected by German pietism, took a large step toward healing antagonism between rationalism and supernaturalism by making religion an inner experience—the consciousness of absolute dependence on God. His system left much to be desired for those who believed in the objective reality of a personal, loving God but gave a certain respectability to the general tenets of Christianity. Soren Kierkegaard (1813-55), the "melancholy Dane," laid the foundations for a new theological formulation during this period, but he was not widely known until the twentieth century.

Calvinism

The effects of rationalism are seen in the struggles of this period by the churches following the teachings of Calvin. In Geneva, the birthplace of Calvinism, the "venerable company" of the clergy refused to ordain candidates in 1817 if they believed the very things that Calvin emphasized—the deity of Christ, original sin, and predestination. The result was a schism, the conservatives organizing free and independent congregations. This movement spread throughout Switzerland and beyond during the rest of this period. The leaders of this conservative movement in the Swiss cantons were Alexander Vinet (1797-1847) and Frederick Godet (1812-1900).

French Calvinists had the same experience. Theological liberalism so prevailed in the French Reformed Church that the French Reformed Free Church was organized in 1849 by Frederic Monrod and Count Gasparin.

In the Netherlands a similar story may be told. Before 1834 nearly all the Reformed churches were included in the established church. Liberalism and religious skepticism reigned. Izaak de Costa (1798-1860), a convert from Judaism, became an evangel of orthodox Calvinism. After 1834, large numbers of churches left the established Reformed Church and joined with the conservative congregations, which were finally recognized in 1869 as the Christian Reformed

Church. Many conservative Calvinists remained within the older establishment with the hope of leading it back. These also separated from the established church and later united with the Christian Reformed group. Another party growing out of the rationalism of this period was known as the Groningen school, which placed emphasis on love as central to religion. They were indifferent to orthodox Calvinistic doctrines.

Struggles with Secularism and Nationalism (1870 to 1989)

Germany and Russia rose to the forefront as world powers in the late nineteenth century. World War I (1914-18) grew directly from closely woven military alliances designed to maintain the balance of power. Hotheaded nationalism, ancient hatreds and rivalries, armament races, and irresponsible impulses completed the explosive picture in 1914. The spark came in a Balkan incident, and war began in the summer of 1914. Germany and allied forces were finally defeated. After the war Germany became a republic for a decade. The manifest inequities of the peace treaty and the hard economic depression of the early 1930s encouraged the victory in 1933 of Adolf Hitler and the Nazi party in Germany. World War II began in September 1939. The German coalition was defeated in 1945. Use of atomic bombs late in the war marked the beginning of a new era. After the war the United States, Canada, and the liberal democracies of western Europe engaged in a Cold War with the Soviet Union and its affiliated states in eastern Europe. This ended with the internal collapse of the communist governments in the late 1980s.

The Roman Catholic Church

Although World War I seriously crippled the strongest Roman Catholic continental powers, the Catholic Church fared amazingly well in the conflict and appeared to be stronger in some respects after the war. The beginning of Nazi party rule under Hitler in 1933 brought repression of Catholics in Germany, which continued until the end of this period. At the same time, the threat of Russian communism came clearly into focus. At the close of this period Russia enveloped many of the small Slavic border nations into her sphere of influence, in each case repressing the Roman Church in favor of the Eastern Orthodox Church.

Internally, the activity of the Roman Church may be summarized under three heads—struggle with modernism, strictures against Protestantism, and relations with secular states.

The Antimodernist movement. While the largest Protestant churches of Europe were being overtaken by rationalism and liberalism, the Roman Catholic Church went to great lengths to resist modernism. Leo XIII succeeded Pius IX and was one of the ablest popes in this period. Although he is sometimes termed the "modern pope" because he displayed an interest in classical and scientific studies and permitted the clergy to lead in social reform, in other respects he continued the policies of his predecessors. In 1897 he set forth an encyclical censoring all books condemned before 1600, even though they might not have been included in later lists of prohibited books. Leo permitted only biblical and scientific studies that did not impugn the dogma of the Catholic Church.

Pius X (1903-14) was probably elected as a reaction to Leo. He had little appreciation of scholarship and higher education. Much of the work of Leo was virtually destroyed because of the syllabus condemning modernism. His encyclical in the same year vigorously attacked modernism in the Roman Church. Pius advocated a return to scholastic philosophy and demanded rejection of all who desired to study canon law except those with scholastic background. Any taint of modernism was sufficient for the rejection of a teacher in Catholic seminaries or universities and the expulsion of those already in these institutions. Bishops were to prevent the publication of modernistic books and to eliminate them from the schools. All meetings of priests were to be checked to see that modernism had no place. Benedict XV (1914-22) continued the fight against modernism, as did Pius XI (1922-39) and Pius XII (1939-1958).

Strictures against Protestantism. Attacks continued against Protestantism. Leo XIII went out of his way to approve the Spanish Inquisition of the Medieval age, calling the flames "blessed." He praised the infamous Torquemada, leader of the Spanish Inquisition, for his "most prudent zeal and invincible virtue." In 1896 Leo denounced Anglican ordination and succession, condemning both the form and the intention. He set forth the typical Roman point of view relative to religious toleration, asserting that when Protestants are in the control of a nation, Catholics are to be tolerated according to the Protestants general policy of religious toleration. On the other hand, when Catholics are in control, the Catholic policy of no toleration is to be followed.

Pius X disapproved vigorously all Bible reading and study. His attack in 1910 on the Reformers and their followers as "enemies of the cause of Christ" aroused considerable antagonism. Benedict XV continued the papal fight against Protestantism.

Relations with secular states. Pope Leo XIII was successful in establishing friendly relations with some of the states. Through tactful diplomacy and laborious efforts by the Jesuits, the papacy made friends of Belgium, Spain, France, England, Russia, and the United States. His successors were not so fortunate. Under Pius X and Benedict XV severe blows were struck at Rome. In 1905 France enacted legislation separating church and state. Church property was confiscated, and all financial aid to religion was withdrawn. Revolutions in Portugal and Mexico further reduced the prestige of the pope. The blow was particularly radical in the Republic of Mexico. The Mexican Constitution of 1917 separated church and state and confiscated church property. All foreign Roman Catholic officials and priests were driven into exile.

People hoped that the Concordat of 1929 between Pius XI and the Italian government would bring peaceful relations between the parties. In 1870 the Italian nationalists seized Rome, the last of the papal territories outside of a few acres constituting the Vatican. Thereafter the popes refused to leave this area, calling themselves prisoners. In 1929 Mussolini agreed to pay the papacy an indemnity added, a few acres to Vatican grounds, and recognized Vatican City as a free state. The bitterest controversy, however, was carried on subsequently because each side was unwilling to keep the agreement. In 1946 the monarchy was overturned and a republican government was adopted. Theoretically, the Roman Church was no more favored than any other religious group, but in practice the Catholic background of the people gave the Roman Church a favorite place.

In Spain in 1931 a republic also replaced the monarchy, and the constitution provided for separation of church and state, giving hope that religious equality for all groups would be practiced. Civil war began in 1936, and in 1939 pro-Catholic General Franco became dictator. The Roman Catholic Church again became dominant as the established religion. A constitutional monarchy was established in Spain after Franco's death in 1975. Religious freedom had been granted, and democratic institutions were planted.

With the increase of international communication after the Second World War, popes became international travelers and influential world figures. European colonies vanished, and Europe was divided between East and West. The Second Vatican Council was an international event of major proportions. The Roman Catholic Church, once dominated by Italy, became more international than before. This Council and its aftermath will be discussed in the global context in chapter 30.

Lutheranism

Lutheranism in Europe had undergone severe trials during this period. Luther's reform was planted in an environment of farmers and peasants and had looked to the benevolent prince of a comparatively small state to maintain the purity and well-being of the Lutheran Church in his area. After 1870 radical changes came. The late unification of Germany into a single nation required considerable readjustment at the point of Lutheran organization and control. The rapid industrialization of Germany and the mechanical revolution also thrust on European Lutheranism new social and economic patterns that demanded rapid, radical response. At the time of this challenge, the First World War paralyzed or drafted Lutheran leadership. The Weimar Constitution, adopted by the German Republic after World War I, provided for separation of church and state, and further added to the woes of traditional Lutheranism. The vitality of Luther's movement slowly diminished in the first decades of the new century. It has been estimated that 75 percent of the nominal Christians in Germany in the early twenties were indifferent to religion.

The rise of the Nazis in 1933 brought additional problems. Hitler's efforts to control Lutheran and Reformed churches for the benefit of the state brought schism and conflict. Attempts were made to paganize Christianity in order to magnify racial and national factors. Hitler was willing to see a national church organized by the Faith Movement of German Christians, but the opposition of leaders like Berlin pastor Martin Niemöller offered stiff resistance. A Confessional Synod opposing this Faith Movement was organized and included both Lutherans and Calvinists. World War II drastically curtailed all Christian work. In the Scandinavian countries Lutheranism has maintained itself as the religion of the majority.

Calvinism

The turbulent years of two wars and an almost continuous ideological tussle in Europe added to the bitter modernist-confessional struggle within European Calvinism and sapped the vitality of the Reformed Churches on the Continent. Calvinism was better prepared by its general outlook to meet the industrial and mechanical revolutions of the new day than was Lutheranism. The disestablishment of the Roman Church in France in 1905 also aided Calvinism in its struggle. The same blows that shocked Lutheranism fell on Calvinism. General disestablishment occurred in the cantons of Switzerland, partly because of Roman Catholic influx, mainly because of indifference.

From Switzerland, however, at the close of World War I came a strong protest against theological liberalism. Karl Barth (1886-1968), pastor of a small Reformed church in Switzerland, deeply moved by the violence of a world at war, formulated a theological system known as the theology of crisis and as neo-orthodoxy. Barth interpreted contemporary problems and world convulsions as stemming from man's confidence in himself and consequent neglect of God's will. This is sometimes called dialectical theology, which refers to human inability to search out God and the necessity of allowing God through His sovereign grace to speak to man. Sometimes it is called neo-orthodoxy, which relates the movement to earlier Christian orthodoxy. Barth magnified divine sovereignty as transcendent and human sin as overwhelming. Although Barth's system had elements unacceptable to many traditional supernaturalists, it was in marked contrast with the arrogant rationalism of a previous generation and influenced contemporary theology.

Many received Barth's message as a fitting critique of the easy optimism that prevailed before World War I. That war, followed by a major economic depression, World War II, and the continuing Cold War, left Europeans less optimistic than their grandparents had been. Secularism and rationalism, however, continued to make inroads into the churches of Europe, and Barth's theology may well have been little more than a corrective interlude.

❑ ❑ ❑ ❑ ❑

The last period had been one of almost constant war and political revolution on the Continent. The Roman Catholic Church had been hit hard in what had been traditionally the area of its greatest strength. Indifference and secularism were greater enemies of Rome than was modernism.

The tumultuous events of the period rained heavy blows on continental Protestantism. Internal decay because of widespread rationalism had more to do with the loss of vitality than did the frequent wars. Neo-orthodoxy, a reaction against humanistic optimism and aggressive theological rationalism, provided the starting point for new theological formulations of various sorts.

28

British Christianity

During the nineteenth and early twentieth centuries, Britain became the greatest military, colonial, and industrial power on earth. Britain never experienced a violent revolution such as the French Revolution. Instead, Britain continued the move away from absolute monarchy toward progressive democratization that began in the seventeenth century and continued into the twentieth.

In 1832 a sweeping Reform Bill was passed, greatly increasing the number who could vote. The Second Reform Act of 1867 doubled the number of voters, while legislation in 1918 and 1928 brought almost total suffrage to the people. The policy of home rule for colonial possessions was established. In 1867 Canada received practically independent status.

The twentieth century brought serious problems to the British Empire. The areas not granted a measure of independence took matters into their own hands. India and adjacent colonies took large strides toward complete independence. Most of Ireland withdrew from the empire and by 1949 became completely separated. An imperial mercantile policy providing abundant and lush fruits was no longer feasible. Two expensive world wars brought heavy and varied burdens to the people and the nation. The British Empire gave way to the British Commonwealth in 1931. The African colonies had received independence and Commonwealth status by 1966. England struggled to find its own identity between the Commonwealth and the European Common Market.

Principal Religious Trends

Five extensive religious movements affected England during this period.

Modern Foreign Mission Movement

The momentous victory of England over France in 1763 sent explorers scurrying to find new shores touched by the ocean now controlled by England—men like Commodore Bryon, Captain Wallis, and Captain Cook between 1764 and 1768. The field preaching of Wesley and Whitefield had to some extent divorced the gospel from buildings and had stirred the hearts of Christian people to compassion for those without salvation. Some, like David Brainerd in America, were seeking out the Native Americans for Christ. William Carey, a young Baptist cobbler, inaugurated and exemplified the modern foreign mission movement. A Baptist society for foreign missions was formed in 1792. Carey and others were sent to India. Inspired by Carey, English independents and the Church of England organized foreign missionary societies. During the next two centuries missionaries from the English-speaking world went to every global region.

Religious revival and humanitarian movements

The fires of revival, diminished during the wars with the American colonies and with France, burned brightly for a brief time after the defeat of Napoleon in 1814. The ending of several exhausting wars with the peril of imminent invasion was marked by a genuine recognition of divine blessings. As was true a century before, a revival in the United States preceded the spiritual emphasis in Britain. In fact, the extent and effects of the revival in America in the opening years of the nineteenth century were far greater than were evident in England. Again after 1859 revival took place in all of Britain, receiving impetus with the preaching of Dwight L. Moody more than a decade later and the influential ministry of Charles Haddon Spurgeon in London. Another major revival in Britain swept Wales about 1904. Today pietistic movements such as Keswick and Pentecostalism are active in Britain.

Moral and Humanitarian Movements

Along with this religious sensitiveness, perhaps occasioned by it, were a number of moral and humanitarian reforms. The large increase in the number of those in denominations other than the

(Document 45)

C. H. Spurgeon: On Preaching

Charles Haddon Spurgeon enjoyed worldwide influence as a London preacher. The following quotation is from Lectures to His Students *delivered at Spurgeon's College, a school he founded to train evangelical preachers.*

If I were forbidden to enter heaven, but were permitted to select my state for all eternity, I should choose to be as I sometimes feel in preaching the Gospel. Heaven is fore-shadowed in such a state: the mind shut out from all disturbing influences, adoring the majestic and consciously present God, every faculty aroused and joyously excited to its utmost capability, all the thoughts and powers of the soul joyously occupied in contemplating the glory of the Lord, and extolling to the listening crowds the Beloved of our soul; and all the while the purest conceivable benevolence toward one's fellow creatures urging the heart to plead with them on God's behalf—what state of mind can rival this?

established Church of England, along with the general democratization of legislative processes in England and the enlargement of franchise, guaranteed that existing religious disabilities on dissenters could not continue. By the 1860s the battle was almost won; one by one most of the radical discriminations were either eliminated or minimized. Unjust penal laws were slowly replaced, and the treatment and housing of prisoners were greatly improved. Slavery was abolished in 1833 and British influence helped abolish slavery elsewhere, including the United States. Legislations curbed abuses in the factory system limiting the working hours of women and children. Britain accepted additional responsibility for the education of its children and youth. A new sensitiveness to the public good brought legislation for various types of aid to the common welfare—police, cheap postage, public health, commerce and navigation. The twentieth century brought the increasing consciousness of governmental responsibility for the citizens in the problems beyond the local level.

Skepticism and Materialism

The Wesleyan revival in the previous period turned the hearts of the masses from unbelief and skepticism, but a strong core of antisupernaturalism was never touched in this or later revivals. Several factors promoted skepticism in the nineteenth century. One was the development of an organized and articulate Socinian movement that appealed mainly to the intellectual classes in Britain and America. Christian ethics was identified as the principal contribution of the

Scriptures. In this period continental philosophers made radical attacks on the Scriptures. The tendency to expurgate, negate, or modify Christian revelation undercut the faith of many.

Darwinism. Another factor inducing skepticism was the evolutionary hypothesis proposed by Charles Darwin (1809-82) in 1859. His ideas, often misinterpreted and misapplied, were enlarged from a theory based on observation of biological phenomena to encompass social, ethical, and metaphysical pronouncements. Such projections of his theory were thought to undermine the possibility of a divine revelation (particularly one handed down from a less advanced state of society) and to minimize the need for divine creative activity and providential supervision.

Faith in Science. Technological developments buttressed the older materialism. Especially before World War I, many professed a blind sort of faith in human nature and inevitable progress. The trying days of adjustment between wars, severe economic depression, the great human loss and physical destruction of war itself, the immediate social problems involved in wartime morality and displaced persons, and a thousand other stresses turned the thoughts of Britain away from spiritual things. There were unmistakable evidences of religious decline. Financial support of churches had decreased, church attendance had been quite poor, and it was difficult for the various religious denominations to find candidates for the ministry.

Ecumenism

English Christianity as a whole entered heartily into the ecumenical movement. To some extent, ecumenism was born in the burst of enthusiasm for world missions that followed the inception of the modern mission movement. The London Missionary Society, organized in 1795, was made up of Anglicans, Scottish Presbyterians, Methodists, and independents. The British and Foreign Bible Society, founded in 1804, was interdenominational; so were many other cooperative efforts in Britain, America, and on mission fields during that century. Another antecedent of the ecumenical movement was the formation of the World's Evangelical Alliance in London in 1846 after a preliminary meeting in 1845. This body sought to promote unity rather than to carry on some immediate joint task. Subsequent conferences were held in Britain, on the Continent, and in the United States. In addition, interdenominational movements among young

Christians increased the influence of the movement, including the Young Men's Christian Association, begun in London in 1844.

The immediate antecedents of the modern movement were found in the interdenominational missionary conferences. Foreign missionaries, wrestling with mutual problems, met together in conference, sometimes official, sometimes unofficial. Well-known conferences were held in London in 1854, in Liverpool in 1860, and in various parts of England intermittently until the turn of the century. Almost all denominations, except the Roman Catholics, took some part in this movement.

A large forward step in the ecumenical movement was the meeting in 1910 at Edinburgh, in which for the first time a conference composed of officially delegated representatives from mission boards and societies was held. The general motif was a united Christendom, and the Continuation Committee ensured further conferences. These conferences led to the founding of the World Council of Churches, which will be discussed in chapter 30.

The Establishment

Anglican leaders, especially those who favored sacramentalism looked with disfavor on the sweeping evangelical revivals of the eighteenth century and the increasing strength of evangelicals within the established church. The progressive growth of the dissenters and the removal of religious disabilities against them, together with the developing cooperation between evangelicals within the Anglican Church and the dissenters, was of grave concern to the older party. This general background, along with the skeptical intellectual currents sweeping across England in the nineteenth century, led to the development of three distinct parties within the Church of England.

The High Church. One group of leaders within the Church of England favored the doctrines of the Roman Catholic Church but allowed the English sovereign to be head of the church instead of the pope at Rome. They were strict sacramentalists, wanting to retain monks and nuns, emphasizing the vital nature of apostolic succession, and insisting on the establishment of the Church of England within the English state. The success and increase of dissenters aroused them to feverish activity. They began in 1833 the publication of a series of *Tracts for the Times* covering church history and doctrine. The most important tract was the last one, written in 1841 by John Henry Newman (1801-90). The writer attempted to show that the thirty-nine Articles of the Church of England, once considered as the most Protestant portion of the Anglican system, could actually be interpreted in a Roman Catholic sense.

Newman also favored other elements of the Roman Catholic system. In 1845 he was received into the Roman Catholic Church. Many others of the High Church party followed him. After his departure the leadership of the High Church party was assumed by E. B. Pusey (1800-82). In general, the High Church movement Romanized many aspects of Anglican liturgical and devotional life. Monastic life for men and women was encouraged. Auricular confession was introduced. The High Church party received a blow in 1896 when Pope Leo XIII declared that all Anglican episcopal succession was invalid, but Rome had been vague at these points since Vatican II.

The Low Church. Evangelicals in the Church of England have been termed the Low Church group. Many evangelicals left the Church of England with the Methodist movement. In 1847 a High Church bishop refused to install G. C. Gorham, an evangelical in doctrine, because of Gorham's views. The case was taken to court, where the final decision favored Gorham, determining that evangelicals had legal standing within the Anglican communion.

The Broad Church. A third party favored the widest possible flexibility in the doctrinal and ecclesiastical standards of Anglicanism. This Broad Church party had also secured legal standing in Anglicanism. In 1860 a collection of somewhat radical essays by liberal Anglican clergymen aroused the orthodox, and two of the authors were tried for heresy in ecclesiastical courts. They were finally acquitted. The case set a precedent for allowing the utmost freedom in theological thinking and writing within the Anglican Church, outward conformity to the Thirty-nine Articles and the prayer book being the principal requirement.

The Church of England was quite active in the ecumenical movement. It looked on itself as being the halfway station between Roman Catholicism and Protestantism and felt that in such a position it would be the ideal place and pattern for reunion for all Christendom. The Lambeth Conferences—a world meeting of all bishops of the Anglican communion that has met in London about every ten years since 1867—explored the possibilities of union with others. In 1888 it approved four items that it considered minimal for union: (1) the Old and New Testaments as the rule and standard of faith; (2) the Apostles Creed and the Nicene Creed as the doctrinal statements of faith;

(3) the observance of baptism and the Lord's Supper as sacraments; and (4) the historic episcopate to preserve the continuing unity of the church. The Anglican Church has looked toward closer union with all Christian groups—Protestants, the Eastern Orthodox Church, and the Roman Catholic Church. The four items set out in 1888, known as the Lambeth Quadrilateral, were the minimum. When local groups attempted to establish union in South Africa in 1913, in Canada in 1925, and in South India in 1947, the Church of England stood aloof because the proper episcopal ordination was not uniformly secured.

The Church of England was greatly hurt by the two world wars that occurred in the first half of the twentieth century, accompanied as they were by a period of secularism and economic depression. There was a marked decrease in vitality and influence, the number of candidates for the ministry declined radically, church attendance and religious interest were curtailed sharply by war activities and weariness, and there was a continuation of skeptical literature and secular thinking.

This decline, along with the depleted resources of the nation and parliamentary disapproval of the revised prayer book in 1927 and 1928, brought demands from within and without the Church of England that the church be disestablished. Those within felt that the vast endowments of the church, accumulated over four centuries, could probably provide the financial needs of a disestablished church. Others argued that disestablishment would soon be followed by disendowment. The High Church party, in particular, opposed any plan for disestablishment.

In Wales the Church of England was established at the opening of this period, although most of the Welsh were dissenters. A series of revivals, particularly among the dissenting group but also entered into by the established churches of Wales, helped dissipate the lethargic and disinterested situation at the opening of the period. The Anglican establishment ended in Wales in 1920.

Until 1949 Ireland was part of England. The parliament of Ireland had been dissolved in 1800, and representatives were given seats in the English body. The Church of England was established as the state church in Ireland for a small minority despite protests by a Roman Catholic majority and a vigorous Presbyterian minority in Ulster County. The Roman Catholic Emancipation Act of 1829, however, removed many disabilities from the majority, and in 1868 the Anglican church of Ireland was disestablished.

The worldwide Anglican community. Australia was first colonized when Great Britain made it a penal colony in 1787. The outstanding religious leader in the formative years was Samuel Marsden, chaplain of the Church of England from 1793 until his death in 1838. Through his efforts Christianity was forwarded not only in Australia but in New Zealand and other Pacific islands. Significant British immigration began during the first quarter of the nineteenth century. Most of them were Anglicans, but there were also Irish Catholics, Scotch-Irish Presbyterians, and English Methodists.

New Zealand was about a decade behind Australia in colonization. Samuel Marsden took the lead there in calling for an active missionary program. The English immigration came about 1840 and was principally Anglican.

Canada's history, predominantly French until 1763, then English, is reflected in Canadian Christianity. That story will be briefly sketched in chapter 29.

India and other colonies of England during this period received the labor of many missionary societies of Britain.

The Church of Scotland

Presbyterianism was the established church in Scotland at the beginning of the period. Scottish Presbyterians were not greatly influenced by the evangelical revival of the eighteenth century, perhaps a reaction against the Arminian doctrines of Wesley. A genuine spiritual awakening occurred, however, in the opening years of the nineteenth century, spearheaded by the Haldane brothers. This new spiritual life agitated an old problem, the question of secular control as seen in lay patronage. Do noble and wealthy patrons in the community have the right to name the minister of the church there? Doughty Scots had twice opposed this, bringing schisms in 1733 and 1760.

The nineteenth century movement was led by Thomas Chalmers (1780-1847). The General Assembly of the Church of Scotland took the side of the churches, declaring in 1834 that no pastor should be forced on an unwilling congregation. In 1842 the matter reached the English House of Lords, who decided that a church must take a minister appointed by a patron. In the following year, in an act of drama and sacrifice, nearly half the Presbyterians of Scotland left the salaries and buildings of the Church of Scotland in protest against lay patronage and formed the Free Church of Scotland. Most of these groups seceding over lay patronage came together by 1900 under the name

United Free Church of Scotland. In 1929 this body united with the established church again, the principle of lay patronage being eliminated.

Presbyterianism was carried to Australia and New Zealand in the wave of English immigration in the 1820s. Although fewer in number than the Anglicans and the Roman Catholics, they had considerable influence. The Canadian story will be told in connection with American Christianity.

English Congregationalism in this period was closely related to Presbyterianism, receiving many of its members and influencing the thinking of those who did not make the change. The Congregational movement was greatly blessed by the Wesleyan awakening in the eighteenth century, as well as by the modern missionary movement and the brief revival after the Napoleonic wars. One evidence of the increased vitality in the early nineteenth century, in addition to growth in constituency and churches, was the development of a vigorous interchurch fellowship. First came the county unions, principally inspired by the challenge of home missions. In 1832 the Congregational Union of England and Wales was formed. By the present century English, Welsh, and Scottish Congregationalism, numbering perhaps half a million in 1928, carried on a vigorous program of education and other benevolences, although two wars and depression had taken their toll.

The Dissenters

The Roman Catholics

At the opening of this period there were severe disabilities against the Roman Catholics in England. Catholics were unorganized on the higher level and not numerous. In 1829, however, the Roman Catholic Emancipation Act removed many of the civil disabilities. In 1850 the pope restored the hierarchy in England with the appointment of an archbishop of Westminster. This created a furor among those who feared the Roman Catholic movements.

Failure of the potato crop in Ireland in 1846 caused many Roman Catholic peasants of Ireland to emigrate to England, greatly swelling the number of that group there. Some Anglicans joined the Roman Church from the tractarian movement, while other Catholics emigrated from the Continent. As a result, the familiar institutions of Romanism soon appeared throughout England, Scotland, and

Wales—churches, schools, monastic orders for both men and women. The large Irish Roman Catholic immigration provided an increasing number of that faith in England during the first half of the twentieth century, increasing the Roman Catholic population to about two and a half million. This group grew rapidly and maintained vitality better than any other English denomination. Most of the Emerald Isle left the British Commonwealth in 1949 to form the new nation of Eire, a strongly Roman Catholic republic.

The Calvinists

Presbyterianism, so active in England during the Cromwellian period and shortly after, practically disappeared after the Restoration, some falling into Unitarianism and others joining the Congregational movement. In the next century the only Presbyterians in England were the small congregations of Scottish Presbyterians who retained ties with their home base. These slowly increased during the nineteenth century and in 1876 organized the Presbyterian Church of England. By the first quarter of the twentieth century this group numbered almost 85,000.

Irish Presbyterians settled in northern Ireland in the opening years of the seventeenth century. When the Protestants William and Mary came to the English throne in 1688, the hard lot of the Presbyterian minority in Ireland was improved. By 1691, through subsidies provided by the English government, large numbers settled in Ulster County. Immigrants from these Scotch-Irish Presbyterians played a very important part in the rise of American Presbyterianism. In the opening years of this period, Irish Presbyterians were successfully resisting the Unitarian views then current in England. In 1860 the General Assembly of the Presbyterian Church in Ireland was formed. The disestablishment of the Anglican Church in 1868 gave impetus to the Presbyterians in Ireland, along with the fresh spiritual awakening. Missions and education advanced, and the twentieth century found them numbering over one hundred thousand, although they suffered from two wars and religious skepticism. In the twentieth century efforts have been made to unite English Presbyterians with English Congregationalists.

The Methodists

English Methodism grew more rapidly than any other of the dissenting groups during this period, at the same time having considerable difficulty because of the great number of schisms. After the death of John Wesley in 1791, Methodism quickly separated from the Anglican Church. The rigid ecclesiastical organization and discipline of English Methodism brought a number of protests. The great leaders after Wesley were Thomas Coke (1747-1814), Jabez Bunting (1779-1858), and their contemporary John Scott Lidgett. The movement had an original divergence, one group becoming Calvinistic and the other Arminian. The latter became the dominant group. Among this group came schisms in 1797 over lay representation (the Methodist New Connection), in 1810 over camp meeting methods (Primitive Methodist Connection), in 1815 over zealous evangelism (the Bible Christians), and in 1828 over music (Wesleyan Protestant Methodists). By 1907, however, the organization of the United Methodist Church brought several of these together, and in 1932 most of England's Methodists, totaling over a million, united into one body. Methodists in New Zealand in the third decade of this century numbered near 30,000 and in Australia about 166,000. English Methodists also were dealt hard blows by two wars and the accompanying spiritual decline.

The Baptists

The Wesleyan revival brought new life into English Baptists. General Baptists benefited greatly by the work of Dan Taylor, founder of the New Connection of General Baptists. Particular Baptists were inspired to begin the modern mission movement. William Carey, a journeyman cobbler, became a Baptist in 1783. Unschooled, he became educated through private application, mastering Hebrew, Greek, Latin, and Dutch in his spare hours. With the help of Andrew Fuller, John Sutcliffe, Samuel Pearce, and John Ryland, Jr., Carey organized a Baptist missionary society in London in 1792. In the following year Carey went to India as a missionary and with his companions translated the Bible into eighteen languages and published tracts in twenty translations in nineteen years. They baptized more than seven hundred converts, and a dozen nationals surrendered for the Christian ministry.

English Baptist work, both home and foreign, grew rapidly. Schools were founded, and various social reforms were entered into in cooperation with other Christians. Preachers like Robert Hall (1764-1831), Charles Haddon Spurgeon (1834-92), Alexander Maclaren (1825-1910), John Clifford (1836-1923), and John H. Shakespeare (1857-1928) gave new respectability to the Baptist cause. In 1891 the division between General and Particular Baptists that had existed from the beginning of English Baptist life was healed, principally through the work of John Clifford.

In 1992 there were 191,000 Baptists in Great Britain, 64,000 in Australia, and 24,000 in New Zealand.

❏ ❏ ❏ ❏ ❏

In the opening years of this period, English Baptists inaugurated what had been termed the modern mission movement. During the nineteenth century practically all denominations in England carried on foreign mission programs in almost every part of the world. Skepticism and secularism have made large gains in England in the last two centuries, however, and the general picture is one of religious decline and lowered vitality. During the last century the ecumenical movement gained favor with a large majority of English denominations. The Church of England defined the four minimal points for church union, and it is apparent from developments in various parts of the world that each of these points is counted significant.

The churches and the Christian faith in England, along with the remainder of the nation, have suffered greatly from the two world wars in which England has been a principal combatant.

29

American Christianity

In 1789 the United States held the territory east of the Mississippi and north of Florida except for a strip of land across the Gulf coast to the Mississippi River. The remainder of the present nation was added, either by purchase, annexation, or war. Seven new territorial acquisitions were added: the vast area west of the Mississippi known as Louisiana in 1803; Florida in 1819; Texas in 1847; the Oregon-Washington area in 1848; California, Arizona, and New Mexico by the Mexican Cession of 1848; Alaska in 1867; and Hawaii as well as other islands in 1898. The American population in 1790 was about four million, in 1830 about fifty million, in 1915 about 100 million, in 1994 over 250 million.

The principal occupation of the nation changed since 1789 from agriculture to commerce and industry. Large cities and a highly industrialized society have altered the complexion of daily life. Advances in technology and mass production have brought wealth with its accompanying social and economic problems. The organization of labor and extensive governmental supervision have brought checks and balances to unlimited industrial empire. After World War II, the United States was leader of the Western powers, and has since become the world leader in many areas.

A number of important factors mark the religious history from 1789 to the present. They are listed and discussed in approximately the chronological order in which they occurred.

Factors in American Religious History

Church and State

Several American colonies had established churches. New Hampshire, Massachusetts, and Connecticut legally established Congregationalism by the time of the American Revolution, while Maryland and Virginia had the Church of England so established. The national pattern in relation to religion, however, followed none of these states but rather the system of Rhode Island—separation of church and state. Separation was much despised when it was first set up, but it has been winning adherents ever since. The American Revolution undercut the establishments of the Anglican Church on patriotic grounds, for it was not then known that the American followers of this system would set up an independent and national episcopal body. Furthermore, in the very region where Anglicanism was established, the strength of dissent was considerable, especially among Baptists, Presbyterians, and Methodists. The Great Awakening had deeply impressed the population, and these revivals were still occurring in Virginia and nearby states. Many had sought the New World as a haven from religious persecution, and the democratic spirit of the frontier and religious revivals resisted a national establishment.

In addition, the educated class was drinking deeply from cups of French philosophical and political liberalism. Liberty and equality were important concepts. Dignity of the common person demanded respect and recognition. Unquestioned corruption of the Roman Catholic religion in France, which had fastened itself to the state, was slowly sapping its life. This brought to skeptical American intellectuals in key political places additional reasons why there should be no religious establishment.

The victory of religious liberty began in Virginia. Amidst stringent disabilities imposed by the established Church of England, the Baptists, Presbyterians, and Methodists began an active program to throw off the establishment. This was accomplished by 1787 through the political aid of James Madison. In addition, the new Constitution was approved by Virginians, with the understanding that there would be added immediately a bill of rights guaranteeing religious liberty. This promise was carried out, and the First Amendment prohibited the national government from establishing any religion. It was, of course, a matter for the states to reflect this same spirit by eliminating establishments. New Hampshire, Connecticut, and Massachusetts, the last

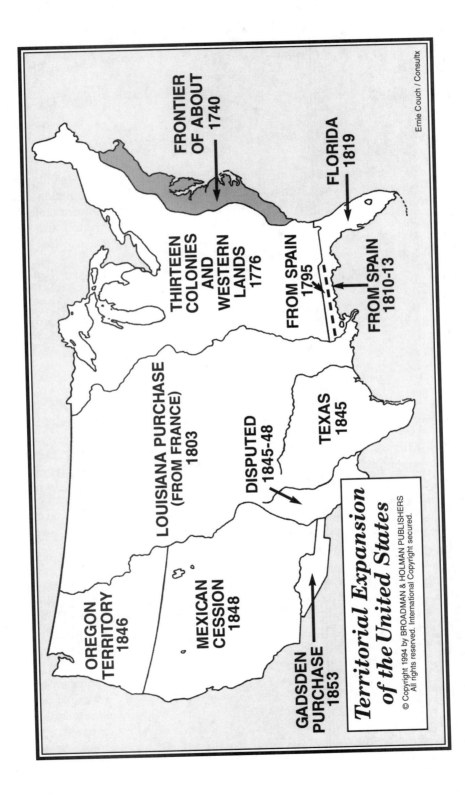

Territorial Expansion of the United States

FRONTIER OF ABOUT 1740

FLORIDA 1819

THIRTEEN COLONIES AND WESTERN LANDS 1776

FROM SPAIN 1795

FROM SPAIN 1810-13

LOUISIANA PURCHASE (FROM FRANCE) 1803

DISPUTED 1845-48

TEXAS 1845

OREGON TERRITORY 1846

MEXICAN CESSION 1848

GADSDEN PURCHASE 1853

Ernie Couch / Consultx

of these, eliminated support of Congregationalism in 1817, 1818, and 1833 respectively, principally through the efforts of John Leland, a Baptist. There are still problems involved in the separation of church and state, but the continued stability of the American nation is wrapped up with the preservation of this principle.

Early Unbelief and Skepticism

During the American Revolution and immediately after, most of the colonies experienced a wave of unbelief. Part of the reason was the bitterness and cynicism that war always brings. Both the French and Indian War (1756-63) and the Revolutionary War (1775-83) had brought widespread suffering and moral decline. Close contact with English intellectual currents before the Revolutionary War and with France during that war had brought their skepticism and infidelity to America. The anti-Christian writings of Voltaire (1694-1778) in France and Thomas Paine (1737-1809) in America were widely read and approved.

At the close of the Revolution it was estimated that less than 10 percent of the American population were professing Christians. The various church-related schools were filled with unbelievers and atheists. Only two of Princeton's student body professed to be Christian in 1782, and other schools were similar. Rationalistic and atheistic societies flourished. This was not so completely true in the lower South, where revivals of religion had continued from the days of the First Great Awakening (ca. 1739). The Second Great Awakening (about 1804) turned America again toward faith. Church membership began to multiply much more rapidly than the population. In 1790 only about 250,000 of a population of about four million were church members—about 8 percent. In 1990 about 144 million of 250 million Americans claimed church membership—about 58 percent.

The Second Great Awakening

In New England, probably the area of greatest spiritual need, a Second Great Awakening began about 1804. There was less emotional excitement and less immediate controversy over methods of revival than the first Awakening of half a century before. Single outstanding leaders were fewer, and the power of the revival was channeled into benevolent pursuits. Practically all denominations were aroused to the importance of spreading the gospel, both at home and abroad. Increased efforts were made to convert the Indians to Christianity, and plans were made to send the gospel to the ever-receding western frontier. Congregationalists organized the American Board of Commissioners in 1810 to carry on foreign mission work. Baptists developed the General Missionary Convention of the Baptist Denomination in the United States of America for Foreign Missions in 1814.

The American Bible Society was formed in 1816 on an interdenominational basis, as were also the American Sunday School Union in 1824 and the American Home Mission Society in 1826. Baptists formed their Tract Society in 1824, one year before the interdenominational American Tract Society. Baptists also formed their home mission society in 1832. The Second Great Awakening doubtless inspired these benevolent societies. The growing sentiment both in the North and the South in favor of the abolition of slavery was accelerated by these revivals, especially those of Charles G. Finney (1792-1875).

(Document 46)

Charles G. Finney: Slavery Hinders Revival

The American Revivalist Charles G. Finney (1792-1875) argued that God would send revival when Christian people paid the price. In his Lectures on Revivals *(1835), Finney identified slavery as one of the evils that hindered revival in the United States. Not all Christians opposed slavery, but Christianity was an important factor that led to the overthrow of slavery.*

Revivals are hindered when ministers and churches take wrong ground in regard to any question involving human rights. Take the question of slavery for instance. The time was when this subject was not before the public mind. John Newton continued in the slave trade after his conversion. And so had his mind been perverted, and so completely was his conscience seared, in regard to this most nefarious traffic, that the sinfulness of it never occurred to his thoughts until sometime after he became a child of God. Had light been poured upon his mind previous to his conversion, he never could have been converted without previously abandoning this sin. And after his conversion, when convinced of its iniquity, he could no longer enjoy the presence of God, without abandoning the sin for ever. So, doubtless, many slave dealers and slave holders in our own country have been converted, notwithstanding their participation in this abomination, because the sinfulness of it was not apparent to their minds. So ministers and churches, to a great extent throughout the land, have held their peace, and borne no testimony against this abomination, existing in the church and in the nation.

Meanwhile, a different kind of revival began west of the Alleghenies in Tennessee and Kentucky about the same time. Most denominations engaged in it, but one early leader was a Presbyterian from Kentucky, James McGready (1758-1817). Settlers drove from miles around to make camp in a central area. Ministers of different denominations preached at the same time at various parts of the camp-grounds to crowds as large as their voices could reach. Great emotional and physical excitement were evident in the meetings. Shouting and weeping alternated with barking, shaking, running, crawling on all fours, and in some cases, the appearance of complete loss of consciousness. As a direct result of this revival, Presbyterians refused to approve the action of one of their presbyteries in ordaining new candidates for evangelistic work without the proper prerequisites. This controversy led to a schism that resulted in the organization of the Cumberland Presbyterian Church. In general, the revival added great numbers to the churches in Kentucky and Tennessee, and practically all of the frontier denominations profited from renewed spiritual interest.

Immigration

One of the important factors in the religious history of the United States was the gigantic tide of immigration that flowed into the country. These immigrants posed a challenge to the religious denominations to which they belonged. Large communities from a single nation greatly influenced others in the immediate area. The large accessions to those denominations in America to which the immigrants belonged brought them not only immediate problems but also a rapid increase in wealth and prestige. When large numbers of immigrants landed and settled near the coast, many settlers in communities along the seaboard moved westward in search of new land.

The number of immigrants was accelerated by many factions. The westward migration after the Louisiana Purchase in 1803 and the return of peace in 1815 brought immediate demands for laborers along the coast, especially for the extensive programs of building railroads, canals, and roads. Unrest, famine, and economic crises drove many Europeans to America. The American Revolution and the War of 1812 discouraged immigration for a time, but by 1820 the immigrants began arriving at the rate of over 9,000 a year. Between 1825 and 1835 they averaged over 30,000 a year; in the following ten years they averaged 70,000 a year; while between 1845 and 1885 almost 12,000,000 immigrants flooded the country, about 25,000 a month for forty years.

In the first half of the century the largest number of immigrants came from Ireland, where the failure of the potato crop in the 1840s brought virtual famine to millions. Nearly two million Irish emigrated to America, almost all Roman Catholics. Not quite so many Germans made the journey, while a few came from practically all the countries of southern Europe, also strongly Roman Catholic. These immigrants greatly influenced the history of the several denominations in America.

Rationalism

The older European rationalism of thinkers like Christian Wolff in the seventeenth century was confounded by Immanuel Kant, Schleiermacher, Ritschl, and others, who showed that humans are not simply thinking creatures but also moral, feeling, and choosing persons. The last half of the nineteenth century, however, brought a new kind of rationalism. Physical science was added to philosophy, sociology, and psychology to raise doubts about the being of God or to oppose steadfastly the idea of a special revelation involving supernaturalism. All interest shifted to the material world. Even philosophy began to classify values according to whether they could successfully operate in a workaday world. Religion and spiritual matters were viewed in humanitarian terms and channeled into social betterment.

In this milieu it is possible to identify several attitudes in relation to traditional Christianity.

- *Skepticism or agnosticism.* Despite the phenomenal advances of Christianity in America since the Revolution, a hard-core skepticism and unbelief have never been touched. It denies the existence of God and scoffs at any idea of revelation.

- *Theism that is not distinctively Christian.* This group is in the succession of English deism, which affirms that there is a God but He has no special revelation. Hinduism is as valid a revelation as Christianity; every prophet in every religion has been inspired and adds something to the total revelation of God. More recently this has taken the form of New Age syncretistic mysticism.

- *Nonsupernaturalistic Christianity.* This group claims to follow the Christian tradition but denies many of the older beliefs. Revelation becomes meaningful only as it is reasonable. The

Christian Scriptures in the main are historically unreliable and must be sifted carefully by human reason in order to find truth and significance. Anything that cannot pass the test of reason in the human frame of reference must be discarded. A substitutionary atonement is impossible because Christ was simply a good man. The immediate confrontation of God may be sensed by the human spirit and constitutes the only valid religious authority. For this group the principle value of religion comes in broad humanitarian channels. A leading popularizer of this party in America was Harry Emerson Fosdick (1878-1969).

- *American neo-orthodoxy*. This group, differing in some aspects from the thinking of Karl Barth, but agreeing generally with his basic approach, emphasizes the essential sinfulness of humans. Like Barth, its followers reject many teachings of traditional supernaturalism but cling to older orthodoxy at the point of human sin and divine transcendent sovereignty. An outstanding figure in this school was Reinhold Niebuhr (1892-1971).

- *Traditional supernaturalism*. This group endeavors to make the traditional Christian message relevant in a materialistic and scientific age, holding to the basic tenets of New Testament revelation and accepting the "unreasonable" supernaturalism of Christianity as exemplified in spiritual regeneration of the individual by the work of the divine Spirit.

Beginning in 1912 some leading conservative Protestant scholars published a series of articles entitled *The Fundamentals*. Soon the terms *fundamentalism* and *fundamentalist* entered the language to describe defenders of fundamental doctrines of the faith. With the passage of time, however, this term was increasingly applied to religious anti-intellectualism that completely eliminates the rational element in Christianity. In the 1950s most conservative Protestants began using the term *Evangelical*. The news media often uses the word *fundamentalist* as a pejorative term, even applying it to non-Christian religious terrorists.

Western Expansion and War

The virgin land of America was slowly becoming settled. The frontier was a significant factor in American religious life; it shaped the economy to one of plenty rather than of scarcity in the ownership of land. European land space had been exhausted or pre-empted for centuries, and land meant stability and wealth. In the virgin country the presence of a constantly expanding frontier gave every American a sense of financial independence and of worth. The frontier provided a fluid society, for a person could move for any reason or for no reason; it stimulated new immigration by attracting unskilled workers to the opportunities of the virgin country. A democratic spirit was encouraged inasmuch as every person stood on his or her own worth in the harsh and rigorous areas of frontier life. Christian denominations that magnified democracy in church life were encouraged—the Baptists, Methodists, and similar bodies. The rough, and at times immoral, frontier life challenged the Christian denominations in the older communities of the east to send missionaries to the frontier to encourage Christians and to win the lost. Settlers in the sparsely populated west gathered for camp meeting revivals to hear the gospel preached to large numbers.

As civilization moved westward, new states began appearing. This threatened the political balance of power, especially in relation to slavery. This "peculiar institution" was introduced to the Virginia colony in 1619, rather it was impressed on them by England against their protest. Later it spread through the South by Northern importation and financing, and gradually embraced the South through the devastating choice of a one-crop economic system. Climatic and geographic factors limited slavery almost wholly to the South in a feudal and anachronistic system. Since those states denominated as "slave states" usually formed a united coalition, it became a political issue. Had the older states remained as the sole members of the national union, the slavery question would not have become politically explosive. Instead questions of state's rights and constitutional interpretation combined with sectional jealousies to spark a conflict about the spread of slavery.

Some of the denominations divided because of the slavery issue. War broke out in 1861 and brought sorrow and loss to every part of the nation. Union victory in 1865 assured the political unity of the nation and ended American Negro slavery. Troops were stationed throughout the South until 1878, adding to the bitterness engendered by the war.

Free Churches

The free churches have greater strength in the United States than in any other country. This strength dates back to colonial times. The Plymouth colony began with religious dissenters. The first New England Puritans were English Independents transplanted to the New World. A religious establishment based on Congregationalism was always, at best, a strange mixture. Of the European state churches, only the Anglicans ever maintained an establishment among the English colonies. Catholics, Lutherans, Presbyterians, and Reformed came to America in great numbers. These churches, however, were never established in the New World, and they gradually assumed some characteristics of free churches after becoming firmly rooted in American soil.

As civilization moved westward, the more popular churches proliferated on the frontier. Anglicans never spread so easily as the Methodists. Congregationalists never spread so rapidly as the Presbyterians, the Baptists, and later the Pentecostals. Everywhere free churches grew from conversions rather than from immigration.

With this spread of the free churches came "the proliferation of sects." Almost inevitably, the atmosphere of freedom encouraged religious individualism. Through the decades, many new religious groups sprang up in America, and some have spread around the world. The Restorationists, Adventists, Mormons, and Pentecostals eventually became major factors in the religious life of the United States and other countries.

The United States is the home of hundreds of Christian groups. Most are small and confined to one region. Some groups differ radically from others, but most differ only in details of doctrine or practice. Yet many people in these churches experience an intense Christianity, though it is impossible to describe the history of each group.

Ecumenism

Religious peace has characterized American history, though churches have often dissipated their energies fighting one another. Many factors have contributed to an increased ecumenical spirit in the twentieth century:

- Interdenominational movements have strengthened the underlying desire for unity by coordinating missionary, social, and humanitarian efforts.

- "Family denominations" have increasingly worked together in joint missionary enterprises.

- Liberal theology has undercut the doctrinal basis for denominationalism. On the other hand, Christians have united across denominational lines to oppose liberal theology.

Specific antecedents of the modern ecumenical movement in America may be seen in the interdenominational missionary and Bible societies organized shortly after the turn of the nineteenth century. The American branch of the World's Evangelical Alliance, an interdenominational organization for the promotion of Christian unity, was organized in 1867. For almost half a century it promoted the cause of church union and ecumenism in the context of conservative evangelicalism. Other important organizations looking to the minimizing or eliminating of denominational lines were the Student Volunteer Movement (1886) and the World's Student Christian Federation (1895). The interdenominational missionary conferences, beginning in 1854 in New York, produced the Foreign Missions Conference of North America. The Federal Council of Churches of Christ in America was organized in 1908; now the National Council of Churches. Denominations affiliated with the NCC also participate in the World Council of Churches, organized in 1948. Most of the older Protestant denominations belong to the NCC. These groups have been in decline for the past two decades, and the media has been filled with descriptions of "the decline of mainline Protestantism." Nonetheless these churches still report a total membership of 46,900,000.

Since 1960 the Consultation on Church Union (COCU) has attempted to integrate nine participating denominations through a series of mergers. Institutional union has proven more difficult than expected. Nevertheless three Lutheran bodies united to form the Evangelical Lutheran Church of America, and two Presbyterian bodies merged to form the United Presbyterian Church in the U.S.A. After intensive discussions of theology and polity, participants drew up a plan of church union in an attempt to bring about an institutional merger, but this has not been accepted. Since about 1980 COCU has encouraged "covenanting," whereby participating churches recognize a common ministry and common sacramental practice, looking forward to the eventual establishment of a Church of Christ Uniting. Although institutional unity has been postponed indefinitely, mergers will probably continue among similar denominations.

More conservative Protestant denominations were not comfortable with the prevailing liberalism of the National Council of Churches. In 1942 some leading Evangelicals formed the National Association of Evangelicals (NAE). Today over forty denominations cooperate through this organization. Most are small and growing, but total NAE membership is still less than five million. The NAE has provided a forum for discussion and cooperation in many fields and has fostered goodwill among Evangelicals.

Several of American's largest denominations participate in neither the NCC nor the NAE. These include the Southern Baptist Convention, the Church of God in Christ, and the Lutheran Church, Missouri Synod. Yet these denominations have also developed increased appreciation for other Christians and cooperate with other groups in many ways.

The Struggle for Equality

American Christianity has been involved in numerous social issues throughout its history. Christians worked together to oppose slavery, and their involvement hastened the demise of "the peculiar institution." Other reform movements have swept American Christianity, including prohibitionism. Under the impact of Liberal Protestantism, Walter Rauschenbusch (1861-1918) led the Social Gospel movement. Since then the Ecumenical Protestant churches have had a long social agenda, though this has not necessarily been internalized by the membership.

The end of slavery was only one of many steps in the struggle for racial equality in America. The civil rights movement has passed through several stages, and in most of these leadership has come from black pastors. The best known of these was Martin Luther King, Jr. (1929-68), who died because of his leadership in the struggle against racial discrimination. Although American Christians must be uncomfortable that their churches are more segregated than society as a whole, the black church continues to play a vital role in and is the center of African-American community life.

The churches, especially black churches, have at times led in the struggle for human rights and racial equality. Yet it is more than obvious that, in a nation composed primarily of church members, Christians have been the causes of injustice as often as they have been the solution.

(Document 47)
Booker T. Washington: Against Racial Prejudice

Booker T. Washington (1856-1915) was born a slave and went on to establish Tuskegee Institute, a school for African Americans. His Up from Slavery *(1901) is an engaging memoir that includes the following reflection on his acquaintance with President Grover Cleveland.*

Mr. Cleveland has not only shown his friendship for me in many personal ways, but has always consented to do anything I have asked of him for our school. This he has done, whether it was to make a personal donation or to use his influence in securing the donations of others. Judging from my personal acquaintance with Mr. Cleveland, I do not believe that he is conscious of possessing any colour prejudice. He is too great for that. In my contact with people I find that, as a rule, it is only the little, narrow people who live for themselves, who never read good books, who do not travel, who never open up their souls in a way to permit them to come into contact with other souls—with the great outside world. No man whose vision is bounded by colour can come into contact with what is highest and best in the world. In meeting men, in many places, I have found that the happiest people are those who do the most for others; the most miserable are those who do the least. I have also found that few things, if any, are capable of making one so blind and narrow as race prejudice. I often say to our students, in the course of my talks to them on Sunday evenings in the chapel, that the longer I live and the more experience I have of the world, the more I am convinced that, after all, the one thing that is most worth living for—and dying for, if need be—is the opportunity of making some one else more happy and more useful.

The Larger Denominations

This section reviews the largest Christian denominations in the order of their appearance. Unfortunately many smaller groups necessarily have been omitted, even though some practice an intense and vibrant Christianity.

The Episcopalians

The American political revolution was also a religious revolution for the Church of England in America. There was no bishop in America for this church, and the political break with England left its status uncertain. After a period of indecision, a general convention was held in 1789 by representatives from all of the former colonies, and the

Protestant Episcopal Church in the United States of America was formed. The church was based on doctrine, discipline, and worship formerly observed in the Church of England. Episcopal ordination for American bishops was received from Scotland and England between 1782 and 1790. The General Convention, consisting of a House of Bishops and a House of Clergy and Lay Deputies, was constituted as the governing body for the church.

Many factors combined to make the first four decades disheartening for the new church. Its historical and doctrinal ties with England (again in a war with the United States in 1812) brought it unpopularity. Its formal worship was not effective on the American frontier, so it was confined generally to settled areas. Shock of disestablishment, along with the lack of effective discipline and national leadership, brought many problems. General skepticism and infidelity that followed the Revolution greatly crippled this church.

This lassitude was gradually overcome. Members of the Episcopal church were educated and from the upper economic group. Revival movements involving emotionalism and physical excitement were of no interest to them. Seminaries and missionary societies were organized in the second and third decades of the nineteenth century. After 1835 there was an increased zeal for converts, and growth began under leaders like William A. Mühlenberg. New members immigrated from England. In fact, the American Episcopal Church has been greatly influenced by trends in the Church of England. High Church, Low Church, and Broad Church parties of England were reproduced in America. The effect of the Tractarian movement in England was also felt in America, when Bishop Ives of the Episcopal Church in North Carolina submitted to the Roman Catholic Church. There was no schism in this church during the Civil War. Southern bishops were simply marked absent at the meeting of the General Convention in 1862, and after the war they were seated again.

The awakened rationalism that emerged in the last half of the nineteenth century affected the Protestant Episcopal Church. The first American Unitarian church came from their ranks. There was a rapid growth in the Broad Church party, which emphasized the social implications of the gospel and accepted liberal theology.

This church has been active in the ecumenical movement. Negotiations for church union have been carried on with the Russian and other Orthodox churches of the East, as well as the Old Catholics who left Rome after the promulgation of the fallibility decree, and others. In

1886 the General Convention suggested the plan for Christian reunion, which later became the Lambeth Quadrilateral. The Episcopal Church in the U.S.A. is related to the worldwide Anglican community and has actively participated from the beginning in both the National and World councils. Reported Episcopal membership currently stands at 2,448,000.

The Congregationalists

Congregationalist leaders supported the American Revolution. State support of Congregationalist clergy in Massachusetts, Connecticut, and New Hampshire was a sensitive area for those in other churches. Through the efforts of Baptists (Isaac Backus and John Leland), by 1833 Massachusetts eliminated the last of American establishments.

Early skepticism probably affected Congregationalism more than any other denomination in America. Unitarianism, which denies the essential deity of Christ, took large numbers from their churches. In some cases entire churches became Unitarian, including the first Congregational church in America—the Old Pilgrim Church of Plymouth. Through a legal technicality a minority of Unitarians were able to secure the church property in many cases from a Congregational majority. Harvard University became Unitarian in 1805. Within twenty years the Unitarian group organized and became vocal. In 1992 the Unitarian Universalist Association reported 141,000 members.

Congregationalism was greatly blessed by the Second Great Awakening at the opening of the nineteenth century. Many new churches were founded; schools and seminaries were begun. Societies for home and foreign missions, publication of tracts, and the advancements of education were formed.

The westward movement challenged Congregationalists. Some thought that all of New England was moving to the West in the first half of the nineteenth century. Congregationalism lost many constituents as people moved westward. Congregationalists made agreement with the Presbyterians in 1801 to plan cooperative efforts in founding new churches. The majority was to decide whether the church should be Presbyterian or Congregationalist. Almost all of the union churches were probably lost to the Presbyterians before the plan was abandoned.

Congregationalism strongly opposed slavery and aided the abolitionist movement, particularly in its early years. The Civil War did not affect the fellowship of the churches because this group did not have churches in the South. Renewed rationalism after the war profoundly affected Congregational leadership. Many accepted liberal theology and gave almost exclusive emphasis to the social aspect of the gospel. Ecumenism and church union attracted Congregationalists. Congregationalism united with the Evangelical Protestant Church of North America in 1925 and with the Christian Church in 1931, forming the Congregational Christian Churches. In 1959 Congregational Christian Churches merged with the Evangelical and Reformed Church to form the United Church of Christ (UCC). Despite this rich history and succession of mergers, UCC reports a current membership of only 1,599,212.

The Calvinists

Calvin's religious system, altered in some ways by the various national groups of Europe who adopted it, is represented in America by Presbyterians and Reformed churches. In a sense, the Congregationalists belong to this family, but their independent background and type of church government differentiate them enough to discuss them under separate heading. Evangelicals as a whole owe a great deal to Calvinism.

Most Presbyterians had favored the American Revolution. The physical damage and general disruption of war were more than offset by the heightened prestige after the founding of the new nation. In 1790 there were about eighteen thousand members, but several factors contributed to a rapid increase in constituency. They gained considerably from the sweeping revivals in Pennsylvania, Kentucky, and Tennessee in the opening years of the nineteenth century. Immigration added some. Completing the organizational structure doubtless gave impetus to growth also. At the close of the previous period, the organization of the General Assembly was the capstone of the local and territorial organizations. After that Presbyterian growth accelerated.

Several schisms have divided American Presbyterians. In 1810 a small group in Kentucky withdrew over the question of prerequisites for ministerial ordination and organized the Cumberland Presbyterian Church. The schism lasted about a hundred years, although at the reunion in 1906 a minority refused to return. Doctrine and organizational forms brought separation in 1838 between the old and new school groups, while slavery also caused a schism between North and South.

The twentieth century has brought theological controversy to Presbyterian churches. Princeton Theological Seminary was the bastion of American Protestant orthodoxy until the 1920s. Shifts at Princeton occasioned the defection of a few conservative congregations. During the 1980s the United Presbyterian Church (Northern Presbyterian) went through a progressive merger with the Presbyterian Church in the U.S.A. (Southern Presbyterian). The resultant denomination is known as the Presbyterian Church (U.S.A.) with a reported membership of 3,788,000 in 1992. Some of the more conservative congregations left to form the Presbyterian Church in America, which has affiliated with the National Association of Evangelicals and reports 224,000 members.

Dutch Calvinists have a long history in the United States, especially in New York and in the upper midwest. The largest groups are the more ecumenical Reformed Church in America (reporting 327,000) and the more evangelical Christian Reformed Church in the North America (reporting 226,000).

The Lutherans

Lutherans were loyal to the colonies and active participants in the American Revolution. Although there were fewer than eighty Lutheran ministers in America at the close of the Revolution, the next several decades brought rapid growth, mostly by immigration. Both the growth and the type of growth brought problems of languages, organization, and doctrine. The strength of continental Lutheranism was in Germany and the Scandinavian areas. The modified congregational system made it difficult to secure uniformity, and immigration from the Continent transplanted to America many of the divisive problems found in Europe. In the nineteenth century, controversies arose over confessional and liberal points of view, as well as over differences of language, racial distinctions, and organizational forms.

American Lutheranism has stressed the authority of each congregation, although some autonomy has been surrendered to developing general organizations. The local church is governed by the pastor and a church council. The larger organizational forms are the conference and the synod. Before 1820 American Lutheranism had no general body. In that year the General Synod was organized, although it did not receive widespread support for many years.

Because of immigration and the development of general organization, American Lutherans by 1833 could count more than three hundred ministers serving 680 congregations with almost sixty thousand communicants.

The nineteenth-century controversies have been succeeded in the present century by a spirit of increasing unity among Lutherans. The Synodical Conference was organized in 1872 for conservative or "strict" Lutherans, and two distinct conservative groups remain from this: the Missouri Synod (2,603,000) and the Wisconsin Synod (420,000). The more ecumenically oriented Lutherans have passed through a series of mergers resulting in 1989 in the formation of the Evangelical Lutheran Church of American. This is now the largest Lutheran body in America, reporting 5,241,000 members in 1992.

The Roman Catholics

American Catholics numbered only about 20,000 in 1789. Some played valiant roles in the Revolution. The disorganized state of the new nation offered great opportunity for growth. The Great Awakening of 1800 influenced Catholics very little, but immigration from Catholic countries of Europe brought remarkable growth. In 1820 Roman Catholics in America were estimated at almost 250,000; in 1830, over 350,000; in 1840, 1,000,000; in 1860, 3,000,000; in 1890, over 10,000,000; and in 1992, 58,568,000. Much of this growth has come from immigration and birth.

The Roman Catholic Church was quick to complete its organization in America, mainly because of the sagacity of John Carroll of Maryland, who became the first American bishop in 1790 and the first archbishop in 1808. For a brief period this church was plagued by a movement called "trusteeism," which in effect was the application of congregational authority. Language and ethnic divisions also transplanted tension from the Old World. During the nineteenth century Catholicism was harassed by accusations of anti-Americanism. This century has been comparatively free from such problems.

Two distinctive organizations have been developed on American soil. Elizabeth Ann Seton (1774-1821) began the parochial school system in the United States, which has become an outstanding institution for the Roman Church. The second influential organization has been the Knights of Columbus, a fraternal society for Catholic men begun in 1882. This has become an aggressive and militant propagator of the Catholic faith.

During many decades most American Catholics were European immigrants or children of immigrants. More recent Catholic immigrants have come from Latin America, especially Cuba and Mexico. The Catholic Church has often been linked with ethnic identity. After several generations in America, this identification with Catholicism began to wane. Secularism is no doubt making inroads into the Catholic constituency. Despite its well-known problems, however, the Roman Catholic Church is the largest religious organization in American and is among the most vigorous.

The Baptists

Baptists wholeheartedly supported the American Revolution, many of their ministers serving as army chaplains. Baptists in Virginia and New England took the lead in movements that ended state religious establishment, and Baptists also helped secure constitutional guarantees of religious liberty.

Baptist organization and doctrine were peculiarly fitted for the extensive American frontier, and much of the Baptist story deals with intrepid ministers who pioneered during the day and preached at night and on the weekend. The great revival along the frontier in the opening years of the nineteenth century added many to Baptist ranks. Baptists were successful in communicating their faith to the slave population, and many Afro-Americans are Baptists. Numerical growth of Baptists reveals their vitality and activity. They numbered less than 100,000 in 1789; at present they report numbers of over 30,000,000. Almost none of this has resulted from immigration.

Several factors help explain this increase:

- Baptists preached a simple gospel, minimizing theological formulations and emphasizing a life-changing experience.

- Baptist preachers came from among the common people. Problems of ordination, organization, and ecclesiastical authority were overshadowed by the necessity of proclaiming the story at the command of God. There was fire in the bones of the simple farmers and pioneers that transformed them into preachers. The fire spread.

- The economic aspect of the ministry offered no difficulty. Most of these early preachers labored during the week and preached without remuneration at the end of the week.

Whether by making tents or tilling the soil, the gospel was preached.

- Each Baptist church was completely independent. This principle appealed to frontier democracy. It gave opportunity for free expression of dissent as well as assent and stripped away the possibility of ministerial immunity when it came to consistent living and morality.

- Baptists were missionary minded. Mission efforts to Canada and within the United States began even before the organization in 1814 of the first national foreign mission society and of the first national home mission society in 1832. A tract or publication society was organized in 1824 as a missionary aid.

Many Baptist denominational groups are in America. There have been controversies and divisions over organization, over the mission enterprise, over slavery and abolitionism, and over modernism. Modernism has caused much controversy in the twentieth century.

The Southern Baptist Convention (SBC) (reporting 15,038,409 members) was formed as a regional organization in 1845 because of tensions over slavery and abolition. Today the SBC is a nationwide movement (despite its name) and is the largest non-Catholic denomination in America. The National Baptist Convention, U.S.A., Inc. (7,800,000 members) and the National Baptist Convention of America (2,269,000 members) are primarily black denominations, as are the Progressive National Baptist Convention (2,500,000) and the National Primitive Baptist Convention, Inc. (250,000 members). The American Baptist Church in the U.S.A. (1,536,000 members) is a more ecumenically oriented group of older churches, whereas the Baptist Bible Fellowship (1,405,000 members) is oriented toward fundamentalism. The American Baptist Association (250,000) and the Baptist Missionary Association (230,000) are active in the South and Southeast. Baptist denominational statistics (as reported in this paragraph, for example) are difficult to evaluate because some churches belong to two or even three bodies; other churches are completely nonaffiliated.

The Methodists

The close relationship of Methodism with English life, particularly during the lifetime of John Wesley (who died in 1791), and the fact that many Methodist ministers in the colonies were loyal to England during the American Revolution made the task of American Methodists difficult in the opening years of this period. Several factors soon altered this picture, however. The organization of the Methodist Episcopal Church in America in 1784 brought a new unity. The great leader of these early years was Francis Asbury (1745-1816), who introduced the office of bishop into Methodism. By his example as a tireless itinerant minister and his stern demand that his preachers follow this pattern, Asbury helped assure the phenomenal growth of American Methodism. The simple organization, the emphasis on experiential salvation, and the singing were ready-made for the extensive American frontier. The sweeping revivals in the West in the opening years of the nineteenth century brought Methodism a large gathering. Methodists actively evangelized the black populations, and many blacks today are Methodists.

Because it was a people's church, Methodism was among the first to feel the impact of the slavery-abolitionist controversy in the fourth decade of the nineteenth century, and schism came in 1844-45. Other important excisions from organizational unity came because of disagreement over church government and the doctrine of holiness. The new rationalism prevalent in the second half of the nineteenth century greatly affected Methodism and brought considerable controversy over the modernist issue.

The schism over slavery ended in 1939 with the reuniting of the northern and southern divisions to form the Methodist Church. This was followed in 1968 by another merger with the Evangelical United Brethren to form the United Methodist Church. Methodism was once America's largest Protestant denomination, numbering almost 11,000,000. United Methodism has suffered with the general decline of Ecumenical Protestantism; by 1992 membership had fallen to 8,905,000. The African Methodist Episcopal Church reports 2,210,000 members, and the African Methodist Episcopal Zion Church reports 1,200,000. The decline of Methodism has been more than compensated by the rise of Holiness and Pentecostal movements, which carry the imprint of their Wesleyan and Methodist origins.

The Restorationists

A widespread movement arose after 1800 seeking to restore primitive Christianity by eliminating all creeds and denominational organization. Thomas Campbell and his son Alexander were the most important American leaders, but they were influenced by their contacts with Scottish Christianity, especially with Greville Ewing, John Glas, and Robert Sandeman. Practically every distinctive doctrine of the restoration movement was patterned after the Scottish practices. In America both of the Campbells left Presbyterian ranks and in 1812 joined the Baptist fellowship. About 1830 Alexander Campbell and his group separated from the Baptists and took the name "Disciples of Christ." Campbell taught that baptism completes salvation, observed the Supper each week, and frowned on any distinction between ministers and people, as seen in such titles as "clergy" and "laity." Walter Scott of Ohio and Barton W. Stone of Kentucky joined with Campbell in promoting the movement.

Although Campbell wanted to eliminate denominationalism, his movement increasingly assumed denominational characteristics. Division occurred within this movement because of disagreements over denominational structure and liberal theology. Instead of eliminating denominational Christianity, Campbell began a new movement that slowly developed the characteristics of other denominations.

Ecclesiological and theological tension has produced three Restorationist groups, each with certain links to Campbell. The non-instrumental Churches of Christ maintain staunchly independent congregations. They are believed to include about 1,600,000 members, mostly in the South and Southwest. Another conservative group is the North American Christian Convention, a loosely aligned fellowship also known as Churches of Christ-Christian (Independent). In 1992 they reported 1,075,000 members. The Christian Church (Disciples of Christ) is the oldest of these groups; it has adhered to the ecumenical movement and has suffered greater erosion than other ecumenical churches. From a reported membership of 1,793,000 in 1952, the Christian Church (Disciples of Christ) has declined to 1,027,000 members in 1992. The Disciples are currently discussing a possible merger with the United Church of Christ.

The Adventists

In 1831 William Miller (1782-1849), by carefully counting the symbolical numbers in the Book of Daniel, concluded that Christ would return within the next few years and gathered a group known as the Adventists. This group has undergone a number of changes and has made some doctrinal shifts in the direction of Evangelicalism. Adventists have taken a keen interest in foreign missions and in developing family values. In 1992 the Seventh Day Adventist Church reported 717,000 members.

The Eastern Orthodox

The national churches of the East that broke fellowship with Rome in 1054 were slow in developing in the United States, but by immigration and birth these churches have grown steadily. Various national groups formed their own churches—Greek Orthodox, Rumanian Orthodox, Serbian Orthodox, and others. Accurate statistics on these groups are unavailable, but they are believed to have about two or three million constituents in America.

The Holiness

John Wesley taught that Christians should systematically eliminate sins from their lives with the goal of reaching perfection. Perfection for Wesley was something any Christian could hope to achieve. The first Methodists were so called because of their methodical efforts to eradicate sins from their lives. Yet Wesley's doctrine of perfection has been a point of disagreement among subsequent Methodists. Some Methodists, especially in the south, were strongly influenced by the frontier revivals and taught that Christians should seek a sanctification experience. Other Methodists feared the emotionalism of the sanctification movement. In 1894 the Southern Methodist Episcopal Church took a firm stand against certain forms of this sanctification movement. Many pastors and entire congregations left Methodism and formed various denominations, some of which have prospered. Holiness churches are found today in all parts of the United States. These include the Church of the Nazarene (573,000 members in 1992) and the Church of God with headquarters in Anderson, Indiana (206,000 members in 1992). In addition the Salvation Army, numbering about 446,000 members, is in some ways associated with the Holiness movement.

The Pentecostals

After 1894 many Holiness Christians searched intensely for a new identity, but they shared no common explanation of the sanctification experience. In 1899 Charles Fox Parham (1873-1929) of Topeka, Kansas, concluded that the evidence of sanctification was the "baptism of the Holy Spirit" evidenced by speaking with other languages.

This experience would result in an "enduement of power" such as the first Christians received at Pentecost. In 1900 students in his Bible school received this experience; afterwards Parham spoke in tongues.

At first Parham's new Pentecostal movement spread slowly and without receiving attention. In 1906 the revival at Azusa Street in Los Angeles received coverage by the international media. Participants in the revival were from the poorest classes of persons. One almost unique feature for that time was that both black and white Christians participated in the Azusa Street revival.

Holiness leaders came to Azusa Street from all directions, and Pentecostalism spread almost immediately across America and into other countries. Today the largest Pentecostal body is the Church of God in Christ (reporting 5,500,000 members). This predominantly black denomination was founded by Charles H. Mason (1866-1961), a participant in the Azusa Street revival. The Church of God in Christ combines both Holiness and Pentecostal teachings. The Church of God with headquarters in Cleveland, Tennessee (membership 620,000), is a predominately white denomination that combines both Holiness and Pentecostal doctrine.

Many other Pentecostal groups, however, have distinguished themselves from the Holiness movement. The Holiness have generally been more cautious than the Pentecostals in emphasizing "signs and wonders" and have not accepted the Pentecostal interpretation of Pentecost. Pentecostals, on the other hand, have moved away from emphasizing the doctrine of "entire sanctification," choosing rather to emphasize "the enduement of power." Among these groups are the Assemblies of God (membership 2,200,000), the United Pentecostal Church (membership 500,000), and the International Church of the Foursquare Gospel (membership 199,000).

Canada

In the opening years of this period Canadian Christianity was principally Roman Catholic of the French type. After the Seven Years War (1756-63) Canada was ceded to Great Britain by France, accompanied by an unusual religious settlement. By the Quebec Act of 1774 the Roman Catholic religion was guaranteed free exercise, and the Constitutional Act of 1791 practically gave Catholicism control of what became Lower Canada. As a result, Roman Catholicism is in a dominant position in Canadian religious life. Canada is regarded as 46 percent Catholic and 41 percent Protestant.

The considerable Protestant immigration to Canada from the United States and England during and after the Revolutionary War gave the Church of England a foothold in Canada. After a period of trial and error with respect to state support and ecclesiastical organization, the Church of England in Canada was organized in 1861, although it was not supported or controlled by the government. In 1893, a general synod was formed to govern the Church of England.

In the twentieth century this denomination has not kept pace numerically with other groups. A dwindling immigration from England was one reason for this. Although favoring the establishment of an interdenominational church union in Canada, the Church of England refused to enter the United Church of Canada when that body was organized in 1925 because the other parties refused to continue the historic episcopate.

The United Church of Canada is the largest Protestant church in Canada and resulted from a merger of Congregationalists, Disciples, Methodists, and some Presbyterians.

Congregationalism was one of the earliest groups to begin work in Canada, but Congregationalism never really became a prominent part of Canadian Christianity. Baptists and Presbyterians profited by excisions from this denomination. Despite valiant work by a joint home missionary society organized by Congregationalists, Baptists, and Presbyterians in 1827, and the work of the Colonial Missionary Society formed in England in 1836, Canadian Congregationalists numbered only 12,586 when the United Church of Canada absorbed them in 1925.

Canadian Presbyterian life before 1875 was complex, representing a melting pot of Calvinistic thought from various radical and doctrinal groups. Foreign quarrels and problems were transplanted from every part of the world. Formation of the Presbyterian Church in Canada in 1875, representing a merger of several bodies, brought increased vitality in all benevolences and education. In 1925 Canadian Presbyterian churches reported over 400,000 constituents. Most of these entered the United Church of Canada, but about 180,000 refused to participate in the union, continuing as the Presbyterian Church of Canada. In 1992 this group reported 246,000 members.

Canadian Methodists also had an almost infinite variety in organization and thought before 1884. In spite of gathering all of the organizational, political, and doctrinal tensions of American and English Methodists and adding some problems distinctly their own, Canadian

Methodists made good progress. When the Methodist Church of Canada was formed in 1884, its constituency numbered over 157,000. This denomination took the lead in working toward church union, and in 1925, when it became a part of the United Church of Canada, its membership numbered over 415,000.

Not long after the issuance of the Lambeth Quadrilateral (1888), interest was aroused in Canada over the possibility of church union. First efforts were not encouraging because only the Church of England desired to perpetuate the historic episcopate. At the turn of the century, however, Methodists, Congregationalists, and Presbyterians laid the groundwork for union. Baptists declined an invitation to become a part of the movement. After two decades of negotiations, Methodist, Presbyterian, Disciples, and Congregational churches formed the United Church of Canada in 1925, bringing together 609,729 constituents. A few other small groups have entered since. This denomination in 1992 reported an inclusive membership of 2,050,000, of which 808,000 were considered full members.

Other Protestant denominations in Canada, listed with their reported inclusive membership, include the following groups.

- The Anglican Churches of Canada—848,000

- Presbyterian Church of Canada—246,000

- Greek Orthodox Church—230,000

- Evangelical Lutheran Church—206,000

- Pentecostal Assemblies of Canada—195,000

Canadian Baptists number about 200,000 in six denominational groups. Mennonites also have churches in Canada.

The Roman Catholic Church is the largest denomination in Canada. From constituting about 40 percent of the population in 1922 and about the same in 1931, the Roman Church outstripped the population in the next decade and rose to about 44 percent of the population in 1941. Because of the high birth rate among the predominantly French and rural members, the ratio has risen even higher in the last decade. Today the Roman Catholic Church of Canada reports 11,376,000 members.

Latin America

Beginning in 1808 a series of independence movements began in Latin America, and Spanish power came to an end on the American Continent in 1826. Two colonial institutions survived independence—the church and the army. At first almost all Latin Americans were Roman Catholics. The church defended traditional values and operated all educational and philanthropic services. The various national armies were often anticlerical and sometimes defended separation of church and state, secularization of cemeteries, schools, and hospitals, and many other anticlerical measures.

Authoritarian military regimes have come and gone since independence, and participative democracy has been the exception rather than the rule. During the era of the Cold War (1945-89), authoritarian military regimes often justified themselves as necessary alternatives to communism. Since about 1972 the Roman Catholic Church has in many countries become a strong advocate of social programs, and some theologians and clerics have become active in leftist political movements. This "popular church," as it is sometimes called, has met papal opposition. The distance between the left and right may have lessened after the fall of Marxist regimes in eastern Europe. Liberal democracy may at last be coming into its own in Latin America.

Protestant missionaries began working throughout Latin America in the nineteenth century. Today the largest Latin American Protestant churches are Pentecostal. They have grown significantly, especially among the poor and dispossessed on the fringes of the principal cities. The media in North America has reported that Protestantism is taking over Latin America. Although these reports are probably exaggerated, Evangelical Christianity will certainly be a significant force in the future of Latin America. Catholic power there is waning, but the Catholic Church in Latin America is still vigorous.

❑ ❑ ❑ ❑ ❑

Christianity in the United States was separated from secular authority by the Constitution. The last state establishment was abolished in 1833. The revival in the opening years of the nineteenth century, known as the Second Great Awakening, greatly strengthened the Christian movement in the young nation. It established the dynamics for the extensive development of benevolent work. Societies for missions, publications, and Bible distribution sprang up quickly.

To a considerable extent a large immigration from abroad and the westward thrust of the frontier in the homeland shaped the characteristics of Christianity in the United States. Missionary zeal was advanced, new denominations were founded, older denominations grew and in some cases divided. A distinctive type of Christianity in general took shape. The "grass roots" denominations grew rapidly.

30

Global Christianity

Modern times have brought new challenges and new opportunities to Christianity. During its first thousand years, Christianity nearly disappeared from the land of its birth but spread across Europe. Many believe that Western Europe has entered a post-Christian era, though some countries still maintain established churches. Two centuries ago Christians in Europe, Britain, and North America began sending missionaries into other parts of the world. Today churches in some of the "receiving countries" are more vigorous than those in the "sending countries." Christianity is becoming a worldwide, multicultural, multiracial movement, not only in theory but also in practice.

The Retreat of Colonialism

European colonialism took place in two waves. In the first wave, Spain and Portugal established empires in Asia, Africa, and the Americas. France, England, and Holland soon joined these two colonizing powers. European claims to the Americas were shaken off between 1776 and 1826, but the American republics still bear the imprint, in varying degrees, of European civilization.

The second wave of European colonial expansion took place during the nineteenth century. Britain, France, and Belgium divided Africa among themselves. There were also French and British zones of influence in the Near East and the Far East. The Hapsburg Empire of Vienna divided the spoils of the Turkish Empire in Eastern Europe

with the Russian Empire while Russia continued to spread its dominion across the ethnically diverse peoples of northern and central Asia.

Colonial powers had claimed practically all unoccupied territory on
earth when World War I broke out in 1914. Many Europeans expected
colonies to bring them great wealth. Germany and Italy, however, had
arrived too late to become major players in the colonial game. European military, political, and intellectual leaders feared that their own
lands would be dominated by the European empire that held the
most colonies. For this reason, colonial rivalries contributed to the
outbreak of World War I (1914-1918) and World War II (1939-45). In
fact the second war was in many ways an extension of the first. These
wars became known as "world wars" because fighting took place not
only in Europe but also in Africa, the Near East, and Asia.

These two wars hastened the collapse of European colonialism. The
Russian Empire fell from within during World War I. By the end of
World War II even France and Britain were too severely weakened to
think of imposing their power on the world. Rising nationalism forced
Britain to grant self-rule to India in 1947. In quick succession the European powers withdrew from southeast Asia and northern Africa. By
1965 the European powers had withdrawn from almost all of Africa.

European authority in these colonies had always been weak. Britain did not colonize India in the nineteenth century as it had colonized
the eastern seaboard of North America in the seventeenth. Relatively
few Europeans moved their families to these newer colonies. Many
colonies were little more than commercial hegemonies. The colonized
peoples increasingly resented colonialists. There were not enough
Europeans to rule the whole world, and by 1950 imperialism was not
proving particularly profitable to Europeans anyway.

Three Worlds

At the end of World War II the victorious Allies established the
United Nations, an international organization to promote world peace
and international cooperation. With the world apparently in collapse
and threatened with nuclear holocaust, many despaired for the future
of humanity. Although the United Nations was composed of about
180 nations, it was common to lump them into three groups.

The First World

Western Europe, the United States, Canada, Australia, and New
Zealand were often referred to as the First World.

The United States emerged from World War II with the world's strongest economy and quickly imposed its own economic model on Japan and western Germany. Western Europe gradually recovered from the war. Governments functioned increasingly as democracies, even where formal monarchies continued. Nations began setting aside ancient rivalries in order to cooperate with one another. In 1949 ten European countries joined with Canada and the United States to form NATO, the North Atlantic Treaty Organization, a mutual-defense pact. The European Economic Community, or Common Market, was established in 1958 and has been successful in unifying the economies of western Europe and bringing prosperity to all classes.

Amidst this unprecedented economic prosperity, Christianity continued as the predominant European religion, though its influence was diminishing. The "main churches" (state churches or former state churches) were nearly empty in many countries. The free churches were also struggling. Most Europeans quit going to church as a generalized secularization increasingly prevailed.

The Second World

The Soviet Union and the Communist states of Eastern Europe were referred to loosely as the Second World.

Already in 1917, during the First World War, the Russian Empire collapsed before an internal Communist revolution. After the war the former Russian and German empires were divided into various national states. Russia was eventually able to incorporate its Asiatic holdings into the Union of Soviet Socialist Republics. During World War II, the Soviet Union defended itself from Nazi attacks by successfully invading Germany. In this march westward the Soviets occupied the lands of Eastern Europe—Bulgaria, Romania, Hungary, Czechoslovakia, Poland, and into Germany. After the war, the Soviets imposed their economic model in these six countries and exercised hegemony over them. In 1954 these Communist governments formed the Warsaw Pact, a military alliance linking the communist governments of Eastern Europe.

The Marxist theory behind the communist states of eastern Europe opposed not only Christianity but all religion. The new governments disestablished the church in each country. Unable to eradicate religion immediately, Marxist governments sought to control or manipulate the churches while awaiting an eventual withering away of religion. Schools taught communist theory and discouraged youth from identifying themselves as Christians. In reality communist practice varied greatly from country to country and from time to time, and the communists were more successful in some places than others in diminishing religious influence.

During four decades after World War II, Europe appeared deadlocked in a struggle between the liberal democracies of NATO to the West and the Soviet bloc of the Warsaw Pact to the East. After the war there were strong communist parties in many countries of Western Europe, and during the 1950s there were demonstrations and even short-lived anticommunist revolts in the East, but basically the situation appeared fixed. The two sides were locked in a "cold war," each heavily armed and awaiting what seemed the inevitable outbreak of thermonuclear war. Many believed the resolution of this conflict depended on the choice of the rest of the world between democracy and communism.

The Third World

Since the end of World War II the unaligned countries of Asia, Africa, and Latin America have often been called the Third World. These countries have five common characteristics.

1. Third World countries are former colonies or zones of influence of First World countries. Some bear deep imprints of colonialism.

2. Third World countries have been regarded as poor and underdeveloped (or nonindustrialized). Of course the First World is not uniformly prosperous or industrialized, and the Second World has always been poorer than was generally recognized. Some Third World countries are more prosperous and more industrialized than others, yet most persons in the Third World live in poverty, some near starvation.

3. Third World countries have received the impact of modern science more rapidly than they have been able to absorb it. For instance, modern medicines have swelled populations, but most of the people have resisted birth control techniques.

4. Third World countries have been bombarded by the mass media from the First World, creating a "crisis of rising expectations." The masses in these countries have been left with a feeling of deprivation that governments have been unable to fulfill.

5. Third World countries have had difficulty developing participatory democracy.

The term *Third World* is at best a generalization. Two-thirds of the earth's people live in the Third World. Some of these countries are more prosperous than others, a few may be more prosperous than parts of Eastern Europe. A Communist government took over China in 1949, but China always maintained a distance from the Soviet Union. From time to time Third World countries have adopted Marxist policies, but it has been difficult to determine what they have in common with the peoples of the Second World.

The Collapse of the Second World

Democracy has often been perceived as being weak in the twentieth century. Authoritarian regimes, on both the left and right, appeared strong. Marxists have been convinced that someday the whole world would come under the "dictatorship of the proletariat." The most vocal anticommunists have feared this would happen, and they have argued that no country could shake off a Marxist government once it was installed. Conservatives often excused right-wing dictatorships in the Third World, and many left-leaning thinkers often thought Marxist authoritarian regimes were the best solution for Eastern Europe, perhaps even for the Third World. On both the left and right, many feared that democracy was weak and that most of the world was not yet "prepared for democracy."

The Second World collapsed in the late 1980s, surprising everyone. The fall of communism has not been adequately explained, but several factors were clearly involved. Although many Second World countries tried to isolate their peoples from communication with the West, these peoples suffered from a "crisis of rising expectations." They eventually tired of shortages, poverty, and authoritarianism. Some resented governmental opposition to their religion. Perhaps most important of all, ethnic rivalries still divided the peoples of Eastern Europe. The Soviet Union had replaced the former multinational empires (Turkish, Russian, or Austrian) in imposing order in ethnically diverse regions. The day came when the Soviet Union was no longer able to bear this load.

Despite four decades of state atheism, Christianity continued in Eastern Europe. In Poland the Roman Catholic Church became the center of opposition to the regime, and the church emerged as a major shaper of public opinion. In some other countries, Christianity declined. In any case Christianity has apparently emerged as strong or stronger after four decades of communist opposition in Eastern Europe than after four decades of secularism in Western Europe.

Three Faces of Christianity

As Christianity approaches its third millennium, Christians are divided into many groups, and these groups are often divided. Increasingly, however, Christians are discussed in three categories: Catholics, Ecumenical Protestants, and Evangelicals.

Catholic Christianity

Most of the world's Christians belong to churches of the Catholic tradition. During many centuries the states of Europe maintained these as established churches, and some still do. These churches value the historic episcopate; they confess the Nicene Creed and maintain certain traditions of the ancient ecumenical councils. The Roman and Orthodox churches separated in 1054, and the Anglican Church separated from Rome in 1534.

Orthodoxy. Almost 200 million persons today are related to the Orthodox churches, most of these in Eastern Europe. For centuries the Orthodox churches survived under Moslem repression in the Turkish Empire. More recently the Orthodox people have lived under communism, and these churches have been subject to a good deal of government manipulation. Ethnic strife in Eastern Europe has been related to religion. Most Greeks, Russians, Bulgarians, and Romanians are Orthodox. Most Poles and Hungarians are Roman Catholics. Many western Evangelicals hope to see strong Evangelical churches established in these lands, yet Orthodoxy and Roman Catholicism are closely associated with nationalism in many of these countries. There is danger that in some countries Orthodox churches will use government force to suppress the spread of other forms of Christianity. Ethnic violence will probably increase with the proliferation of national states. These ethnic rivalries will probably complicate relations between Orthodoxy and Roman Catholicism.

Roman Catholicism. Over one billion people are Roman Catholics. This has for centuries been a strong religious movement, characterized by firm doctrine and centralized control. As the forces of modernity were sweeping Protestantism, the Roman Catholic Church took extraordinary measures to resist change.

The Roman Catholic Church has changed considerably since the Second Vatican Council (1962-65). The First Vatican Council (1869-70) gave the pope such sweeping powers that many believed there would never be another council. To the surprise of many, Pope John XXIII called another council, the twenty-first by Roman Catholic reckoning. The pope said the church needed *aggiornamento*, an Italian word meaning "updating." This council met each year from 1962 through 1965. Pope John XXIII died after the first session, but Pope Paul VI led the council to its conclusion. The council did not revoke any previous dogma, but it unleashed many new forces in Catholic life.

The council authorized changes in the liturgy, including the end of the Latin mass and the use of vernacular. Cultivation of new and indigenous forms of music and art have also strengthened Roman Catholicism in emerging countries and among youth.

The council also brought a change of tone in relation to modern culture and freedom of thought. It encouraged popular distribution of the Bible and published a "Declaration on Religious Liberty." Changes have brought new openness toward Orthodox, Anglicans, and other "separated brethren." Protestants were no longer dismissed as "sects" or "heretics," and the council demonstrated new cordiality toward Jews, Moslems, and unbelievers.

The years after Vatican II brought sweeping changes to the Roman Catholic Church. Catholic theologians rapidly appeared with ideas similar to those of Liberal Protestants. How far the Roman Church will move in this direction is unknown.

Vatican II did not satisfy all Catholics. Popes Paul VI and John Paul II have become international travelers. Wherever the pope travels, he meets dissatisfied Catholics, but protesters are unhappy about different things. Many European and American Catholics dislike their church's teaching on sexuality, especially on birth control. Many Latin American clergy favor leftist Liberation theology. Pope John Paul II lived under Marxism in Poland and has a different perspective. In Europe the church has been losing influence, especially in France and Italy. Still Catholicism continues to play a vital role in the lives of millions and it continues to grow in many new parts of the world.

Anglicanism. Earlier in this century Pope Leo XIII declined to recognize the validity of Anglican claims to the historic episcopate. Documents of the Second Vatican Council are vague about the status of Anglicanism. Apparently there is a crack in the door toward reunion between Roman Catholics and Anglicans. This has been made more difficult, however, by divisions within Anglicanism.

British leadership of Anglicanism has declined because of world events. Since 1867 the Anglican and Episcopal bishops have met once each decade at Lambeth, the residence of the bishop of London. With the passage of time differences among Anglicans have become more pronounced. Most recently women's ordination has divided Anglicans. Some of the national churches, including those in Canada and the United States, had already ordained female clergy. The Church of England long resisted this, and the High Church wing of Anglicanism particularly opposed it, fearing it would erect another barrier to reunion with Rome. Nonetheless, the Lambeth Conference voted to favor women's ordination and the Anglican church followed that lead. Many active Anglicans have defected to Roman Catholicism, further weakening the High Church party and pushing the remaining Anglicans toward Ecumenical Protestantism.

The worldwide Anglican community may be losing its identity. The churches in many countries are small, but in some former British colonies these churches are vigorous. Bishop Desmond Tutu in South Africa has become a world personality, receiving the Nobel Peace Prize in 1986. There and in some other countries, the Anglican church has thrived as the mouthpiece of popular aspirations.

Ecumenical Christianity

In 1948 representatives of ecumenically oriented Protestant and Orthodox churches from around the world met in Amsterdam to establish the World Council of Churches. Since that time, the ecumenical movement has been more or less coterminous with the World Council of Churches. Ecumenism had been gathering momentum for decades, and the postwar situation offered an excellent occasion. The world had tired of war, and many hoped that unity among the churches would help prevent another war. As the United Nations provided a forum for international discussion, the World Council of Churches would be a forum for religious dialogue. More important, however, many participants yearned for the eventual establishment of a united church that would break down the barriers of denominationalism. The Orthodox churches participated from the first, though never so enthusiastically as the churches of the Liberal Protestant tradition. The Roman Catholic Church refused to participate, and there seemed little likelihood that union would be achieved with Orthodoxy, but the Liberal Protestants might well achieve organic union among themselves.

The largest of these groups were the main churches of Europe. These were established or formerly established churches of northern Europe, and they were heirs of the Reformation of the sixteenth century. Most had undergone the influence of pietism during the eighteenth century, and some had suffered defections as a result. Each had undergone the influence of the Liberal theology during the nineteenth century, and some suffered conservative defections. Each participated in the missionary movement during the nineteenth and early twentieth centuries and entered the ecumenical movement during the twentieth.

In addition to these European main churches, Ecumenical Protestantism includes churches established elsewhere by emigration. In the United States these prefer to be called "mainline" churches. Like the main churches of Europe, these churches have felt the influence of the Catholic tradition, the Reformation, pietism, Liberalism, and the missionary movement.

In addition to the main and mainline churches, the World Council of Churches included most of the churches established in the colonies or former colonies by missionary activities of these main and mainline churches.

The World Council of Churches has from the beginning included the Orthodox church and some Evangelical Protestants. More recently a few Third World Pentecostal churches have joined. The main, mainline, and similar Third World churches have always been the center of the movement.

From the first the Council agenda related to issues of church union and social justice. The Council was organized amidst euphoria about the possibility of achieving organic union of the churches. Some hoped to achieve this goal within five years. This initial zeal began to cool after the New Delhi conference in 1961. Since then, issues of social and international justice have increasingly dominated the World Council of Churches. In reality the church union issue was always of primary interest to the First World churches, whereas the justice issues were more related to Third World churches.

Evangelical Christianity

In addition to the Catholic and Ecumenical churches, a "third wave" has increasingly emerged during the twentieth century. Evangelical-

(Document 48)
Second Vatican Council: On Religious Liberty

*The Second Vatican Council
(1962-65) brought significant
change for the Roman Catholic
Church in its approach to other
religions and to religious liberty.
The following excerpt from the second section of the Council's* Declaration on Religious Liberty *reflects
this new approach.*

This Vatican Synod declares that
the human person has a right to
religious freedom. This freedom
means that all men are to be
immune from coercion on the part
of individuals or of social groups
and of any human power, in such
wise that in matters religious no
one is to be forced to act in a manner contrary to his own beliefs. Nor
is anyone to be restrained from
acting in accordance with his own
beliefs, whether privately or publicly, whether alone or in association with others, within due limits.

The Synod further declares that
the right to religious freedom has
its foundation in the very dignity of
the human person, as this dignity
is known through the revealed
Word of God and by reason itself.
This right of the human person to
religious freedom is to be recognized in the constitutional law
whereby society is governed. Thus
it is to become a civil right.

It is in accordance with their dignity as persons—that is, beings
endowed with reason and free will
and therefore privileged to bear
personal responsibility—that all
men should be at once impelled by
nature and also bound by a moral
obligation to seek the truth, especially religious truth. They are also
bound to adhere to the truth, once
it is known, and to order their

whole lives in accord with the
demands of truth.

However, men cannot discharge
these obligations in a manner in
keeping with their own nature
unless they enjoy immunity from
external coercion as well as psy-
chological freedom. Therefore, the
right to religious freedom has its
foundation, not in the subjective
disposition of the person, but in his
very nature. In consequence, the
right to this immunity continues to
exist even in those who do not live
up to their obligation of seeking the
truth and adhering to it. Nor is the
exercise of this right to be
impeded, provided that the just
requirements of public order are
observed.

Further light is shed on the subject if one considers that the highest norm of human life is the divine
law—eternal, objective, and universal—whereby God orders,
directs, and governs the entire universe and all the ways of the
human community, by a plan conceived in wisdom and love. Man
has been made by God to participate in this law, with the result that,
under the gentle disposition of
divine Providence, he can come to
perceive ever increasingly the
unchanging truth. Hence every
man has the duty, and therefore
the right, to seek the truth in matters religious, in order that he may
with prudence form for himself the
right and true judgements of conscience, with the use of all suitable
means.

Truth, however, is to be sought
after in a manner proper to the dignity of the human person and his
social nature. The inquiry is to be
free, carried on with the aid of

teaching or instruction, communication, and dialogue. In the course of these, men explain to one another the truth they have discovered, or think they have discovered, in order thus to assist one another in the quest for truth. Moreover, as the truth is discovered, it is by a personal assent that men are to adhere to it.

On his part, man perceives and acknowledges the imperatives of the divine law through the mediation of his conscience. In all his activity a man is bound to follow his conscience faithfully, in order that he may come to God, for whom he was created. It follows that he is not to be forced to act in a manner contrary to his conscience. Nor, on the other hand, is he to be restrained from acting in accordance with his conscience, especially in matters religious.

For, of its very nature, the exercise of religion consists before all else in those internal, voluntary, and free acts whereby a man sets the course of his life directly toward God. No merely human power can either command or prohibit acts of this kind.

However, the social nature of man itself requires that he should give external expression to his internal acts of religion; that he should participate with others in matters religious; that he should profess his religion in community. Injury, therefore, is done to the human person and to the very order established by God for human life, if the free exercise of religion is denied in society when the just requirements of public order do not so require.

There is a further consideration. The religious acts whereby men, in private and in public and out of a sense of personal conviction, direct their lives to God transcend by their very nature the order of terrestrial and temporal affairs. Government, therefore, ought indeed to take account of the religious life of the people and show it favor, since the function of government is to make provision for the common welfare. However, it would clearly transgress the limits set to its power were it to presume to direct or inhibit acts that are religious.

ism has its roots in several earlier movements: the Reformation, pietism and the evangelical revivals, the missionary movement, the fundamentalist movement, and the para-church movements. Since World War II these churches have grown rapidly and have begun to have a common identity. The word *evangelical* does not universally have this accepted meaning, but the same could be said for the words *catholic* and *ecumenical*. This third wing of Christianity has increasingly adopted this title since World War II.

Several factors have contributed to the emergence of the Evangelical consensus. One was the formulation of the National Association of Evangelicals (1942) and the World Evangelical Fellowship (1951).

Another factor has been the ministry of Billy Graham, a highly publicized international evangelist who has been an effective leader of the

Evangelical movement. Graham has been a catalyst of many Evangelical enterprises including *Christianity Today,* an influential publication, and the International Congress on World Evangelization, held in Lausanne, Switzerland, in 1972.

Evangelical Protestants have been more concerned than Ecumenical Protestants to speak out on issues of personal morality, but they have been more reluctant to address social issues. In 1947, however, the Evangelical leader Carl F. H. Henry published *The Uneasy Conscience of Modern Fundamentalism.* Since that time many Evangelicals have shared some of the same social concerns that Ecumenical Protestants share, but their primary emphasis is on the gospel of salvation.

Pentecostalism has grown phenomenally during the twentieth century, especially in the Third World. Almost all Pentecostals are squarely in the Evangelical camp.

The Contemporary Scene

World population has doubled since 1950; it now stands at about 5.5 billion and is still rising. About 1.8 billion can be classified as Christians. Over one billion of these are Roman Catholics, a little less than 200 million are Orthodox. The rest are either Anglicans, Protestants, or are at least identified as Christians.

Islam, the second largest world religion, claims almost one billion followers, mostly in the Near East and Africa. Hinduism claims over 700 million in India. There are also over 300 million Buddhists, most of whom live in Asia.

Challenges Facing Christianity

The statistics presented above are misleading. If one third of the world's people are Christians, it might appear that the Great Commission could be easily fulfilled. If every Christian won two of his or her neighbors to Christ, would the whole world be Christian? In fact, the situation is more difficult than this question suggests, for numerous challenges currently face Christianity including lack of commitment, rival systems of thought, the unequal distribution of Christian resources, and world population trends.

Lack of commitment. Studies of world population estimate that there are 1.8 billion Christians in the world, but nobody argues that these are all practicing Christians. Most of these rarely attend church, and many of them claim no particular church affiliation. The free churches, standing in the tradition of the Radical Reformation, require conscious commitment for membership, but even the membership statistics of the free churches include millions who never appear in services. Among the established churches of Europe, the level of commitment is even lower. Although 1.8 billion persons might be culturally identified as Christians, most of these never participate in a church. They certainly would never participate in world evangelization.

Furthermore, many churches are no longer committed to spreading the faith to others. Many believe that Christianity is in some sense true and relevant to their own culture and to their personal lives, yet they see no need to take the gospel to others and ask them to commit themselves to Jesus Christ. Many professed Christians, together with their churches, believe that all religions are true and that there is no particular reason to spread Christianity to other lands. Many associate Christian missions with the Crusades, colonialism, and even with international terrorism and religious violence.

Rival systems of thought. Three historic world religions are appealing to the world's masses: Christianity, Islam, and Buddhism. Islam is spreading more rapidly than Christianity, especially in Africa. Buddhism has taken many forms and is even penetrating the West. Other traditional religions also exist, though many are in decline.

Christianity's greatest rivals today are not traditional religions but rather irreligions or new semi-religions that appeal to the nonreligious. Communism spread rapidly during most of the twentieth century, and a Marxist government still dominates over a billion people in China. Wherever it has gone, communism has attempted to spread atheism, not always with great success. The future of communism is uncertain, though it appears to be in full retreat. Secularism is spreading across much of the Christian world. Many persons live in a spiritual and religious vacuum, and some are turning to new semi-religious quests for a sort of nature mysticism and/or ecological spirituality. Some of these new movements include astrology and other forms of pre-Christian religious thought.

Unequal distribution of Christian resources. Christians are unequally distributed across the world. Most live in Europe and the Americas. The following chart shows estimates of the world's population by region and how many millions of persons in each can at least vaguely be called Christians:

Some nations have almost no Christians. In much of the Moslem world, Christianity is strictly forbidden. Billions of people today have never heard the gospel. They have little if any contact with committed Christians. In fact, most people have not heard the Christian story and been asked to make decision about it.

Region	Population	Christians
Asia	3,120	260
Africa	820	320
Europe	600	510
Americas	740	670
Australasia	270	20

This situation will probably not change as long as Christian churches and ministries continue to focus their human and financial resources almost entirely on those who are already committed Christians. Much of the world's wealth is concentrated in Europe and North America. Many professed Christians are wealthy, but their churches minister almost exclusively to those who are already participating church members. Some minister to those who evidence little commitment but invest nothing to spread the gospel among the unevangelized masses of the world.

World population trends. The non-Christian world is growing more rapidly than the Christian world. Asia and Africa are exploding while Europe and North America are growing little if at all. The Christian share of world population is declining year by year.

Spreading the Gospel

Christianity spread during its first three centuries because believers shared their faith with others. Then Christianity became associated with the Roman Empire, and the government tried to spread the faith (or at least a reduced form of it) for imperial ends. This situation did not change much with the Reformation. The nineteenth-century missionary movement extended the faith through evangelism, but even this movement was too often associated with colonialism. More

(Document 49)

The Lausanne Covenant

Evangelical leaders from throughout the world assembled at the International Congress for World Evangelization in Lausanne, Switzerland, in 1974. The following selections from The Lausanne Covenant reflect some concerns of the Congress.

2. The Authority and Power of the Bible

We affirm the divine inspiration, truthfulness, and authority of both the Old and New Testament Scriptures in their entirety as the only written Word of God, without error in all that it affirms, and the only infallible rule of faith and practice. We also affirm the power of God's Word to accomplish his purpose of salvation. The message of the Bible is addressed to all mankind. For God's revelation in Christ and in Scripture is unchangeable. Through it the Holy Spirit still speaks today. He illumines the minds of God's people in every culture to perceive its truth freshly through their own eyes and thus discloses to the whole church ever more of the many-colored wisdom of God. (2 Tim. 3:16; 2 Pet. 1:21; John 10:35; Isa. 55:11; 1 Cor. 1:21; Rom.1:16; Matt. 5:17,18; Jude 3; Eph. 1:17,18; 3:10,18)

3. The Uniqueness and Universality of Christ

We affirm that there is only one Savior and only one Gospel, although there is a wide diversity of evangelistic approaches. We recognize that all men have some knowledge of God through his general revelation in nature. But we deny that this can save, for men suppress the truth by their unrighteousness. We also reject as derogatory to Christ and the Gospel every kind of syncretism and dialogue which implies that Christ speaks equally through all religions and ideologies. Jesus Christ, being himself the only God-man, who gave himself as the only ransom for sinners, is the only mediator between God and man. There is no other name by which we must be saved. All men are perishing because of sin, but God loves all men, not wishing that any should perish but that all should repent. Yet those who reject Christ repudiate the joy of salvation and condemn themselves to eternal separation from God. To proclaim Jesus as "the Savior of the world" is not to affirm that all men are either automatically or ultimately saved, still less to affirm that all religions offer salvation in Christ. Rather it is to proclaim God's love for a world of sinners and to invite all men to respond to him as Savior and Lord in the wholehearted personal commitment of repentance and faith. Jesus Christ has been exalted above every other name; we long for the day when every knee shall bow to him and every tongue shall confess him Lord. (Gal.1:6-9; Rom.1:18-32; 1 Tim. 2:5,6; Acts 4:12; John 3:16-19; 2 Pet. 3:9; 2 Thess. 1:7-9; John 4:42; Matt. 11:28; Eph. 1:20,21; Phil. 2:9-11)

4. The Nature of Evangelism

To evangelize is to spread the good news that Jesus Christ died for our sins and was raised from the dead according to the Scriptures, and that as the reigning Lord he now offers the forgiveness of sins and the liberating gift of the Spirit to all who repent and believe. Our Christian presence in the world is indispensable to evangelism, and so is that kind of dialogue whose purpose is to listen sensitively in order to understand. But evangelism itself is the proclamation of the historical, biblical Christ as Savior and Lord, with a view to persuading people to come to him personally and so be reconciled to God. In issuing the Gospel invitation we have no liberty to conceal the cost of discipleship. Jesus still calls all who would follow him to deny themselves, take up their cross, and identify themselves with his new community. The results of evangelism include obedience to Christ, incorporation into his church and responsible service in the world. (1 Cor. 15:3,4; Acts 2:32-39; John 20:21; 1 Cor. 1:23; 2 Cor. 4:5; 5:11,20; Luke 14:25-33; Mark 8:34; Acts 2:40,47; Mark 10:43-45)

5. Christian Social Responsibility

We affirm that God is both Creator and the Judge of all men. We therefore should share his concern for justice and reconciliation throughout human society and for the liberation of men from every kind of oppression. Because mankind is made in the image of God, every person, regardless of race, religion, color, culture, class, sex or age, has an intrinsic dignity because of which he should be respected and served, not exploited. Here too we express penitence both for our neglect and for having sometimes regarded evangelism and social concern as mutually exclusive. Although reconciliation with man is not reconciliation with God, nor is social action evangelism, nor is political liberation salvation, nevertheless we affirm that evangelism and sociopolitical involvement are both part of our Christian duty. For both are necessary expressions of our doctrines of God and man, our love for our neighbor and our obedience to Jesus Christ. The message of salvation implies also a message of judgement upon every form of alienation, oppression, and discrimination, and we should not be afraid to denounce evil and injustice wherever they exist. When people receive Christ they are born again into his kingdom and must seek not only to exhibit but also to spread its righteousness in the midst of an unrighteous world. The salvation we claim should be transforming us in the totality of our personal and social responsibilities. Faith without works is dead. (Acts 17:26,31; Gen. 18:25; Isa, 1:17; Psa. 45:7; Gen. 1:26,27; Jas. 3:9; Lev. 19:18; Luke 6:27,35; Jas. 2:14-26; John 3:3,5; Matt. 5:20; 6:33; 2 Cor. 3:18; Jas.2:20)

recently some have supported Christian missions out of concern to spread Western culture, to ensure humane treatment for others, to increase literacy and world prosperity, and to halt the spread of communism. Some have supported world missions more for these reasons than to spread the gospel. World Christianity today rests on this legacy.

Christianity now faces a twofold task: (1) spreading the faith to most of the world's peoples and (2) pressing the claims of the gospel to the millions of nominal but uncommitted Christians.

Missionaries and others concerned for world evangelism are increasingly concerned to distinguish between Christianity and Western culture, they are giving special attention to the *contextualization* of the gospel. They are concerned to present the gospel on its own terms so that persons can hear it within their own cultural setting. In this manner the Christian faith can spread because of its own vitality. Those who accept it will express the faith through forms relevant to their own culture.

Today the Christian faith is spreading in forms that little resemble the cathedrals of Europe. Many in the so-called Third World have accepted Christ and are spreading the gospel with a zeal more intense than most First World Christians find imaginable. Although many professed Christians in traditional Christian lands have little interest in spreading the faith, many Third World Christians are accepting Christ's command to be a light to the world and salt of the earth.

Bibliography

Abbot, Walter M. ed. *The Documents of Vatican II.* New York: Association Press, 1966.

Almanac of the Christian World. Wheaton, Ill.: Tyndale House. Published annually.

Burgess, S. M., G. B. McGee, and P. H. Alexander. *Dictionary of Pentecostal and Charismatic Movements.* Grand Rapids: Zondervan, 1988.

Chadwick, Owen. *The Christian Church in the Cold War.* London: Penguin, 1992.

George, Timothy. *Faithful Witness: The Life and Mission of William Carey.* Birmingham, Ala.: New Hope, 1991.

Manschreck, Clyde L, ed. *A History of Christianity.* Englewood Cliffs, N. J.: Prentice-Hall, 1964.

Marty, Martin E. *Pilgrims in Their Own Land: 500 Years of Religion in America.* New York: Penguin, 1984.

Matthews, Arthur H. *Standing Up, Standing Together: The Emergence of the National Association of Evangelicals*. Carol Stream, Ill.: National Association of Evangelicals, 1992.

Noll, Mark A. *A History of Christianity in the United States and Canada*. Grand Rapids: Eerdmans, 1992.

Reid, Daniel G. *Dictionary of Christianity in America*. Downers Grove, Ill.: Inter Varsity Press, 1990.

VanElderen, Marlin. *Introducing the World Council of Churches*. Revised Edition. Geneva, Switzerland: WCC Publications, 1990.

Vidler, Alec R. *The Church in an Age of Revolution: 1789 to the Present*. Grand Rapids: Eerdmans, 1961.

Yearbook of American and Canadian Churches. Nashville: Abingdon Press. Published annually.

Sources of Documents

1. From the Holy Bible, *New International Version*, Copyright 1973, 1978, 1984 by International Bible Society.

2. Alexander Roberts and James Donaldson, ed., *The Ante-Nicene Fathers* (Buffalo, N.Y.: Christian Publishing Company, 1885–96), 1:185–86.

3. F. C. T. Besanquet, ed., *The Letters of Caius Plinius* (London: G. Bell and Sons, 1910), 392–96.

4. Roberts and Donaldson, *Ante-Nicene Fathers*, 1:330–31.

5. Ibid., 5:423.

6. Anne Freemantle, ed., *A Treasure of Early Christianity* (New York: Viking Press, 1953), 441–42.

7. Ibid., 484–85.

8. *The Constitution of the United Presbyterian Church* (Philadelphia: Office of the General Assembly of the United Presbyterian Church in the U.S.A., 1970), 1.

9. Philip Schaff, ed., *The Creeds of Christendom* (Grand Rapids: Baker Book House, 1985), 2:62–63.

10. Ernest F. Henderson, ed., *Select Historical Documents of the Middle Ages* (London: George Bell and Sons, 1905), 289.

11. James Harvey Robinson, ed., abridged volume *Readings in European History* (Boston: Ginn and Co., 1906) 50–51.

12. Henry Bettenson, ed., *Documents of the Christian Church* (London: Oxford University Press, 1963), 133–34.

13. Augustine, *The City of God*, chapters 19:20.

14. Anselm. *Proslogium*, chapters 2 and 3.

15. Henderson, *Select Historical Documents*, 372, 385–86.

16. Fiona Bowie and Oliver Davies, eds., *Hildegard of Bingen* (New York: Crossroads, 1992), 76–77.

17. *The Little Flowers of St. Francis*, many editions, chapter 1 .

18. Robinson, *Readings in European History*, 226.

19. Julian of Norwich, *Revelations of Divine Love* (London: Milhuen and Co., 1901), 193–94.

20. Thomas à Kempis, *Imitation of Christ*, 47–48. Granted with permission by Mercer University Press, Macon GA 31207.

21. Bettenson, *Documents*, 189.

22. Matthew Spinka, ed., *Advocates of Reform* (Philadelphia: Westminster Press, 1953), 14:201.

23. Ibid., 61–62.

24. Robinson, *Readings in European History*, 253–55.

25. Ibid., 271–72.

26. Theodore G. Tappert, ed., *The Book of Concord* (Philadelphia: Fortress, 1959), 32–35.

27. Robinson, *Readings in European History*, 2:128–29.

28. *The Complete Work of Menno Simon[s]*(Elkhart, Ind.: John F. Funk and Brother, 1871), 94.

29. Schaff, *The Creeds of Cristendom*, 3:487–516.

30. *Book of Common Prayer* (London: William Clowes and Sons, 1968), 43–44.

31. William L. Lumpkin, *Baptist Confessions of Faith* (Philadelphia: Judson Press, 1959), 168–69. Spelling modernized.

32. John Bunyan, *Pilgrim's Progress*, many editions.

33. *The Spiritual Exercises of Ignatius Loyola* , first week.

34. F. C. Happold, ed., *Mysticism* (Middlesex, England: Penguin Books, 1976) 352–53.

35. Schaff, *The Creeds of Christendom*, 3:545–49.

36. Frank E. Robbins, ed., *Epistola de Insulis Nuper Inventis* (Ann Arbor: University Microfilms, 1966), 17–18.

37. Antônio Vieira, *Sermões* (Lisbon: Lello e Irmão, 1951), 12:334. English translation by Sharon Bamberry Landers.

38. Germàn Arciniegas, ed., *The Green Continent* (New York: Alfred A. Knopf, 1959), 187–88.

39. William Bradford, *Of Plymouth Plantation* (New York: Alfred A. Knopf, 1952), 47–48.

40. G. Thomas Halbrooks, ed., *Pietism* (Nashville: Broadman, 1981), 200–201.

41. John Wesley, *Journal*, entry for August 1, 1742, many editions.

42. *The Autobiography of Benjamin Franklin*, many editions.

43. Robinson, *Readings in European History,* 440–41.

44. Bettenson, *Documents,* 384–85.

45. Charles H. Spurgeon, *Lectures to His Students* (Grand Rapids: Zondervan Publishing House, 1950), 179.

46. *Lectures on Revivals of Religion,* 1835, many editions.

47. *Up from Slavery,* 1901, chapter 14, many editions.

48. *Dignitatis Humanae Personae,* 1965, many editions.

49. Joseph Sindorph, ed., *The Manila Manifesto* (Pasadena, Calif.: Lausanne Committee for World Evangelization, 1989), 47.

General Bibliography

Bettenson, Henry, ed. *Documents of the Christian Church*. New York & London: Oxford University Press, 1947.

Cunliffe-Jones, Hubert, ed. *A History of Christian Doctrine*. Philadelphia: Fortress Press, 1978.

González, Justo L. *The Story of Christianity*. 2 vols. New York: Harper Collins, 1985.

Neill, Stephen. *A History of Christian Missions*. Revised edition. Harmondsworth, England: Penguin, 1986.

Walker, Williston, Richard A. Norris, David W. Lotz, and Robert T. Handy. *A History of the Christian Church*. 4th ed. New York: Charles Scribner's Sons, 1985.

Westin, Gunnar. *The Free Church Through the Ages*. Translated by Virgil A. Olson. Nashville: Broadman, 1958.

Index